Sport and Leisure Operations Management

Tourism, Hospitality and Leisure Titles Available from Thomson Learning

Andersen & Robinson: *Literature & Tourism*

Arnold: *Festival Tourism* (forthcoming)

Aronsson: *The Development of Sustainable Tourism*

Baker, Huyton & Bradley: *Principles of Hotel Front Office Operations 2/e*

Ball, Jones, Kirk & Lockwood: *Hospitality Operations*

Baum: *Managing Human Resources in the European Tourism & Hospitality Industry*

Bray & Raitz: *Flight to the Sun*

Brown: *Tourism & the Olympics* (forthcoming)

Buhalis & Laws: *Tourism Distribution Channels*

Bull & Church: *Tourism in World Cities*

Carmouche & Kelly: *Behavioural Studies in Hospitality Management*

Clark, Riley, Wilkie & Wood: *Researching & Writing Dissertations in Hospitality & Tourism*

Clark: *Interpersonal Skills for Hospitality Management*

Clift & Carter: *Tourism & Sex*

Clift & Grabowski: *Tourism & Health*

Clift & Page: *Health and the International Tourist*

Clift, Luongo & Callister: *Gay Tourism*

Collins: *Becoming a Tour Guide*

Cooke: *The Economics of Leisure & Sport*

Cullen: *Economics for Hospitality Management*

D'Annunzio-Green: *HRM in Tourism & Hospitality*

Deegan & Dineen: *Tourism Policy & Performance*

Diamantis: *Ecotourism*

Doolan: *Applying Numbers: IT for Tourism & Leisure*

European Tourism University Partnership: *Resort Management in Europe*

Fattorini: *Managing Wine & Wine Sales*

Foley & Lennon: *Dark Tourism*

Foley, Lennon & Maxwell: *Hospitality, Tourism & Leisure Management*

Forsyth: *Maximizing Hospitality Sales*

Go & Jenkins: *Tourism & Development in Asia*

Godfrey: *The Tourism Development Handbook: A Practical Approach To Planning & Marketing*

Goldsmith, Nickson, Sloan & Wood: *HRM for Hospitality Services*

Hall & Jenkins: *Tourism & Public Policy*

Hall & Page: *Tourism in the Pacific*

Horner & Swarbrooke: *Marketing Tourism, Hospitality & Leisure in Europe*

Howie: *Managing the Tourist Destination*

Hudson: *Cities on the Shore*

Hudson: *Snow Business*

Huyton & Baker: *Principles of Hotel Front Office Operations 2/e*

Ingold, McMahon-Beattie & Yeoman: *Yield Management*

Ioannides: *Mediterranean Islands & Sustainable Tourism*

Johns & Lee-Ross: *Research Methods in Services Industry Management*

Jones & Lockwood: *The Management of Hotel Operations*

Jones & Merricks: *The Management of Food Services Operations*

Jones & Newton: *Hospitality & Catering: A Closer Look*

Jones: *An Introduction to Hospitality Operations*

Julyan: *Sales & Service for the Wine Professional*

Knowles, Diamantis & El-Mourhabi: *The Globalization of Tourism & Hospitality 2/e*

Kotas: *Hospitality Accounting*

Kotas: *Management Accounting for Hospitality & Tourism*

Law: *Urban Tourism*

Laws & Prideaux: *Managing Tourism & Hospitality Services*

Laws & Prideaux: *Researching Tourism & Hospitality Services*

Laws et al.: *Tourism in the 21st Century 2/e*

Laws: *Improving Tourism & Hospitality Services*

Laws: *Tourism Marketing*

Laws: *Tourist Destination Management*

Leask & Yeoman: *Heritage Visitor Attractions: An Operations Management Perspective*

Lee-Ross: *HRM in Tourism & Hospitaltiy*

Lennon: *Tourism Statistics*

Lockwood & Jones: *People & the Hotel & Catering Industry*

Lockwood: *The Management of Hotel Operations*

Lumsdon: *Tourism Marketing*

MacLellan & Smith: *Tourism in Scotland*

Mawson: *The Fundamentals of Hospitality Marketing*

Morgan: *Resort Management in Europe*

O'Connor: *Using Computers in Hospitality & Tourism 3/e*

Page, Brunt, Busby & Connell: *Tourism: A Modern Synthesis*

Pender: *Travel Trade & Transport*

Raitz & Bray: *Flight to the Sun*

Robinson et al.: *Sports Tourism* (forthcoming)

Ryan: *The Tourist Experience 2/e*

Seaton & Bennett: *Marketing Tourism Products*

Shackley: *Managing Sacred Sites*

Shackley: *Wildlife Tourism*

Shone & Parry: *Successful Event Management 2/e*

Stokowski: *Leisure in Society*

Thomas: *Management of Small Tourism Firms*

Tribe: *Corporate Strategy for Tourism*

Van Der Wagen & Davies: *Supervision & Leadership in Tourism & Hospitality*

Verginis & Wood: *Accommodation Management*

Webster: *Environmental Management in the Hospitality Industry*

Wood: *Working in Hotels & Catering*

World Tourism Organization: *National & Regional Tourism Planning*

Yeoman & McMahon-Beattie: *Revenue Management & Pricing*

Yeoman & McMahon-Beattie: *Sport & Leisure Operations Management*

Sport and Leisure Operations Management

Edited by
Una McMahon-Beattie and Ian Yeoman

THOMSON

Australia • Canada • Mexico • Singapore • Spain • United Kingdom • United States

THOMSON ™

Sport and Leisure Operations Management

For more information, contact Thomson Learning, High Holborn House;
50–51 Bedford Row, London WC1R 4LR or visit us on the World Wide Web at
http://www.thomsonlearning.co.uk

British Library Cataloguing-in-Publication Data
A catalogue record for this book is available from the British Library

ISBN 1–84480–063–6

Published by Thomson Learning 2004

Typeset by YHT Ltd, London
Printed and bound in Great Britain by TJ International, Padstow, Cornwall

CONTENTS

EDITORS AND CONTRIBUTORS

Una McMahon-Beattie is a lecturer, researcher and consultant at the University of Ulster. She graduated with a MSc in International Hotel Management from the University of Surrey. Her research interests focus on the areas of revenue management, variable pricing and consumer trust. She has published widely in the UK and internationally in these areas. Una is Practice Editor for the *Journal of Revenue and Pricing Management*.

Ian Yeoman is a champion of revenue management and pricing within the service industries, having published over 50 journal articles, book chapters and conference presentations and Editor of the *Journal of Revenue and Pricing Management*. Ian is a graduate of Sheffield Polytechnic and Napier University, with degrees in Hotel Management and Operational Research. Ian is the Scenario Planning Manager for VisitScotland, Scotland National Tourism Agency.

Gerald Barlow is Lecturer in Operations Management and Management Science at Canterbury Business School, University of Kent at Canterbury. His current research area involve work with the NHS into problems around capacity management and queuing psychology.

John Buswell is Principal Lecturer in the School of Sport and Leisure at the University of Gloucestershire where his teaching and subject-based research interests are focused in particular on service quality and service operations management in leisure, sport and tourism services. He is also a liaison officer and member of the Management Team of the Learning and Teaching Support Network (LTSN) UK Subject Centre for Hospitality, Leisure, Sport and Tourism based at Oxford Brookes University and Chair of the Professional Development Board of the Institute of Leisure and Amenity Management.

Stephen Doyle is a Lecturer in Marketing within the School of Marketing and Tourism at Napier University, Edinburgh. Doyle's research and teaching is primarily focused on retail marketing and in particular the contextual role of design.

David Edgar is the Head of Division of Business Information Management at Caledonian Business School, Glasgow Caledonian University, Scotland. He is an active researcher in strategic management and knowledge management. A recent triumph has been the award of funding to set up a Knowledge Management Studio in the Division and to support further research into the application of knowledge management in business.

John Harris is a Senior Lecturer in the School of Sport, PE and Recreation at University of Wales Institute, Cardiff. He has published work in the trade and academic press on a variety of subjects and is currently developing research in the areas of sport and national identity and relationship marketing in the health and fitness industry.

Clay E. Harshaw is a Visiting Instructor and the Chairperson in the Department of

Sport Studies at Guilford College in Greensboro, North Carolina. He received his Bachelor's degree from Newberry College and his Master's degree from Appalachian State University. His primary interests are sport finance, legal aspects and sport marketing.

Li-Jen Jessica Hwang is a Lecturer in Service Operations Management in the School of Management at the University of Surrey. Her research interests are quality management and benchmarking in service industries especially healthcare, food and beverage production and tourism. She is currently involved in a research project concerning inflight catering operations as well as the Hospitality Industry Forum Adoption Programme project, which looks at best practice in small and medium enterprises in the UK.

Peter Jones is the IFCA Professor of Production and Operations Management, and Director of the Travel Catering Research Centre at the University of Surrey. He is the author/editor of nine textbooks and over 30 refereed journal articles. He is currently leading a DTI-funded Industry Forum Adaptation Programme research team investigating UK best practice in hospitality and leisure. He has a doctorate from the University of Surrey and an MBA from London Business School.

Mike Jordan is a Senior lecturer in Business Information Management at Glasgow Caledonian University. He is a former systems analyst with British Steel and software engineer with ICL. He has extensive IT consultancy experience. He now lectures in telecommunications and electronic commerce with particular research into mobile commerce. He is currently, programme leader for a masters programme in electronic business.

Eddie T. C. Lam is an Assistant Professor of Sport Management at Cleveland State University, Ohio. He has produced a number of scholarly publications in such journals as *SMQ*, *IJSM*, *MPEES*, *ISJ* and *AJHS* and has completed over 60 regional, national and international presentations. His Service Quality Assessment Scale (SQAS) is being used by numerous health fitness clubs (over 10,000 members).

Julian Leybourne MSc is Director of Insight Leisure Management and Icon Training. He is a chartered marketer and has had considerable service sector experience, in senior management strategic roles, working for a number of blue-chip companies specialising in business development and marketing.

Javier Martínez del Río is Lecturer in Operations Management at the University of Almería (Spain). He has professional experience in research centre management and internet marketing. He specialises in tourism and leisure marketing, consumer behaviour of environmentally friendly products and internet marketing.

Guy Masterman is an Assistant Professor of Sport Management at New York University and formerly a Senior Lecturer and MSc Course Leader at the UK Centre for Events Management, Leeds Metropolitan University. Guy has 20 years' experience in the event industry, initially working with Fulham FC and World Championship Tennis and then with clients such as Seb Coe, Lennox Lewis, Steve

Backley, Team Scotland and Chelsea FC. He has managed events at the Royal Albert Hall, Royal Festival Hall, The Oval and Earls Court and served as a Director of the World Games and the Coca-Cola Music Festival.

Manuel Recio Menéndez has been a Professor at the University of Almería (Spain) since 1997. He has also held positions at the Universidad Complutense and Universidad Pontificia Comillas, Madrid. He has published more than 30 books and research papers in different areas of marketing. His main research interests currently are tourism and leisure marketing, international marketing and internet marketing.

Robert Oberwetter is a Senior Officer with the United Nations in New York where he is Chief of the Research in New Technology section. He has more than 18 years' experience in application development and information technology systems with international experience living and working in Europe and Asia.

Adrian Palmer is Professor of Services Marketing at the University of Gloucestershire Business School, Cheltenham, UK. After holding marketing management positions within the travel industry, he joined academia where he has researched buyer-seller relationships within the services sector. Recent research has been published in the *European Journal of Marketing*, *Journal of Marketing Management*, *Journal of Strategic Marketing* and *Journal of Services Marketing*.

Bryn Parry is a Senior Lecturer in the Southampton Business School, at the Southampton Institute, specialising in strategy. Graduating from Surrey University, in Hotel and Catering Administration and completing postgraduate study in Facilities Management at Strathclyde University, his management experience encompasses hospitality management and international consultancy. He is co-author of *Successful Event Management*.

James Reese is an Assistant Professor in the undergraduate Sport Industry Programme and the graduate Sport Administration and Facility Management Programme at Ohio University in Athens, Ohio (USA) and a former Ticket Assistant with the Denver Broncos of the National Football League.

James J. Riordan is a 20+ year veteran of the sport and entertainment industry, specialising in event and public assembly facility management. He has served in management positions for what is now known as the First Union Spectrum in Philadelphia, New York's Nassau Coliseum, the New York Mets and Shea Stadium, the Atlanta Olympic Games and the US Open Tennis Championships. He is currently the Director of Florida Atlantic University's MBA in Sport Management in Fort Lauderdale, Florida.

Martin Robertson is a Lecturer in the School of Marketing and Tourism, Napier University, Edinburgh. His first degree was in Politics and Modern History and he has a Master's degree in Leisure, Policy and Practice. His specialist research areas include event management and destination marketing, the socio-economics of urban tourism and the social science of leisure management.

Liz Sharples is a Senior Lecturer in the School of Leisure and Food Management at Sheffield Hallam University. She has worked as a duty manager with a major hotel chain and as a catering manager in charge of a multi-site operation. Her research interests include environmental policy within catering operations and catering for visitors at tourist destinations.

Tracy Taylor is an Associate Professor in Leisure and Sport Management at the University of Technology, Sydney, with over 20 years' experience with sport and recreation industries in both Canada and Australia. She is actively involved in research, consultancy and community project work that encompasses dimensions of inclusivity and diversity in sport, recreation and leisure.

Jetske van Westering is a Lecturer in Hospitality Management in the School of Management at the University of Surrey. Her research interests include productivity in small and medium enterprises as well as the interrelationship between food, wine, culture and tourism. She is currently involved in the Hospitality Industry Forum Adoption Programme project, which looks at best practice in small and medium enterprises in the UK.

Lesley-Ann Wilson lectures in Cultural Management at the University of Ulster. She formerly worked for the Arts Council of Northern Ireland, served for three years on the Board of National Museums and Galleries of Northern Ireland and, prior to returning to Northern Ireland, worked in heritage management consultancy on projects throughout the UK and Ireland.

John T. Wolohan is an Associate Professor of Sports Law in the Department of Sport Management and Media at Ithaca College, Ithaca, New York, where he teaches courses in Sports Law and Labour Relations in Sports.

INTRODUCTION

The sport and leisure industries have seen substantial and diverse growth over the last ten years, with the subject now accepted as an area in its own right. Definitions and concepts of sport and leisure are blurred and misunderstood, as confusion arises where one begins and the other finishes. The concept of leisure and sport within this book is associated with leisure pursuits or words such as 'sports', 'games', 'play', 'events', 'hobbies' and 'recreation'. Many of these words are associated with 'activities', specifically 'time-based activities' or 'physical duration'. Therefore, a blurred contextualisation of this book focuses on the operational management of games, events, experiences and activities.

The operations function of sport and leisure is the arrangement of resources, which is devoted to the production of the sport and leisure transformation process. All operations produce goods and services by devising processes, which transform or change the state or condition of something to produce output. Operation processes take in a set of input resources, which are then used to transform something into outputs, which vaguely satisfy customer needs. This transformation process in sport and leisure is the processing of 'customers', 'visitors', 'leisure users' or 'supporters'. It can be seen as a transformation process of location and movement of visitors at festivals and events or a psychological transformation state at a sporting occasion. The operations manager is responsible for the activities, decision making and duties associated with managing the transformation process. This book therefore sets out to explain and explore the process of operations management within the context of sport and leisure, thus enabling readers and students to learn about sport and leisure operations.

This book is devoted to operations as activities, where the reader explores the component parts of the transformation process. The book is split into six parts:

- sport and leisure in context
- design of sport and leisure facilities
- inventory management
- operations strategy
- merchandising and marketing
- cases and opinions.

Sport and leisure in context introduces the reader to the concepts of the sport and leisure experience by exploring the nature and management of such an encounter. The *design of sport and leisure facilities* enables the reader to understand how the transformation process is designed and operated. Design in sport and leisure management is concerned with the functional processes of transformation, in which supporters or leisure users are transformed through a process. This means balancing the sport and leisure experience with process design. This process usually involves the leisure user as part of the service encounter, in which production and consumption cannot be separated. It includes a range of activities such as the physical planning of venues and events, visitor flows and queues, service quality, productivity and the management of people. *Inventory management* views the sport and leisure activity or event as an intangible, time-based experience that cannot be put into storage if is not sold. Fundamentally, the unit of inventory is 'a piece of time'. This may be the FA Cup Final or the Boston Marathon. Many sport and leisure experiences are also capacity constrained. Constrained capacity means that there are a fixed or relatively fixed number of seats in a sports stadium or the number of tee-off times in golf. As such, many sport and leisure experiences are subject to the combination of 'unique timing' or 'constrained capacity'. Therefore, the task of the operations manager is concerned with the process of marrying the supply and demand that is unique to sport and leisure experiences. This covers the components of economics, understanding the dimensions of demand and supply, revenue management and ticketing operations.

Every sport and leisure organisation needs some sort of *operations strategy*. The operation needs to understand the environment in which it operates, as the transformation process has to be designed to reflect organisational policy and strategy. Operations strategy is concerned with the long-term direction of the organisation and sets of decisions that will deliver the purpose of the sport and leisure transformation. Operations strategy is concerned with the questions, processes and models of delivering strategy to a front line. For the operations manager to do this he/she needs an understanding of the key areas of risk management, planning, ethics and legal issues. *Merchandising and marketing* cannot be considered a separate function, but rather a close and integrated function of operations management. In operations management, the visitor or supporter is the centre of the sport and leisure organisation's activity. The role of marketing to understand the leisure goers or visitors needs and to communicate a brand image of a organisation such as Manchester United that results not only in sell-out games but also in massive retail sales of pens, replica football strips, fashion wear and financial products. A marketing manager at Manchester United may seek to segment supporters and markets, but it is the operations manager who sells and organises the football match or the merchandise to the supporter. Marketing and operations requires a seamless process of transformation that is customer oriented, which sees no divide between the component parts. Finally, the book highlights a number of *cases and opinions* that allows the reader to understand the application of theory into practice. Case studies include Guilford College and the YMCA, Almería 2005, football revenue management and retailing in the museums and galleries of Northern Ireland.

We hope the book will provide readers and those interested in the operations function with a unique body of knowledge, applications and understandings that will assist them in learning how operations are managed and practised in sport and leisure.

Una McMahon-Beattie and Ian Yeoman

PART 1

SPORT AND LEISURE IN CONTEXT

CHAPTER 1

Sport and Leisure Service Encounter

John Buswell

INTRODUCTION

At the core of both service quality and service operations management in the sport and leisure industry is the service encounter and how it is managed. The chapter examines the different views of the service encounter ranging from those based more on the social encounter (Bettencourt and Gwinner 1996; Johnston and Clark 2001) to others who suggest that it embraces wider elements of service operations including systems, procedures, information or even the organisational culture (Bitner 1990; Walker 1995). The service encounter can involve outcomes and therefore satisfaction and dissatisfaction with service performance of the organisation but a central thrust of the chapter is that the level of satisfaction with the service or transaction is affected by the experiential properties of the product or service and how they are understood and managed by the organisation. Waterhouse (2000) suggests that, 'increasingly, we are buying experiences rather than goods' and the Henley Centre points out, 'increasingly, who you are matters less than how you feel at the point of consumption' (1996: 1).

The chapter argues that there is a need for a greater understanding of the sport and leisure experience and how it relates to the management of the contexts in which it takes place. It develops a model of the sport and leisure experience in which consumer motives are translated into outcomes or benefits through a consumer process involving interaction between three key factors of time, flow and expression.

AIMS AND OBJECTIVES

By the end of the chapter you should be able to:

1. appreciate the experiential properties of the sport and leisure product
2. understand the nature of the service encounter in sport and leisure management and how it is managed
3. examine the relationship between the sport and leisure and experience and management of the service encounter

4. consider how certain approaches to managing the service encounter can enhance the sport and leisure experience.

PLANNING THE SERVICE ENCOUNTER: WHY?

Before we begin to synthesise an understanding of the sport and leisure experience with the management of the service encounter, it is worth considering the etymology of the term in order to establish the implications for service management. It might be exercising a little licence to question the use of the term 'service encounter' as part of planned and managed service delivery, but the word encounter suggests a spontaneous or unplanned meeting, even conflict; in some contexts or in some customers' eyes a contrived approach ('have a nice day'!) can be counterproductive. A premise of the chapter is that many service encounters cannot be left to chance and are planned and managed most effectively when the characteristics of the service process and the psychology of the consumer process are fully understood and accounted for. Furthermore, such understanding is beneficial to organisations for the following reasons:

- Sport and leisure is a service whose core is based on an experience and whose success is determined by the enhancement of the experience and the emotional responses of the individual to the attributes of the service offering.
- The service offering is complex mix of attributes and quality dimensions including contextual, human, social environmental and physical factors with the interaction between customers and staff and the frequent role of the customer in the service encounter providing distinctive characteristics.
- The service encounter, and how it is managed and perceived, are at the core of the management of service quality and provide the potential in this industry for achieving a competitive edge through management of the process and the customer experience.
- Service operations management embraces particular challenges facing sport and leisure managers, such as the peaks and troughs in customer attendances and the problems of managing queues, and is particularly concerned with management of the service encounters and the enhancement of the overall experience. These factors all have an impact on the service offering but it would be pertinent at this point briefly to examine the distinctiveness of the sport and leisure product.

CHARACTERISTICS OF THE SPORT AND LEISURE PRODUCT

The features of intangibility, heterogeneity and inseparability of production and consumption exemplify the distinctiveness, if not the difficulties, of managing sport and leisure services and highlight the lack of complete control over the activity by the provider (because of the nature of sport and leisure activity, timing, the unpredictability of consumer behaviour or conditions such as the weather). When mistakes are made by the operator, in many instances it is impossible to rectify them because the customer consumes the product or service package as it is offered. Much of the typical sport and leisure product, as we have seen, is a process with few tangible reference points and is potentially subject to considerable variation in the way it is delivered because of this factor as well as the difficulty of standardising approaches by staff or volunteers. The interaction between customers and the organisation, and particularly staff, has been highlighted as a key factor in the delivery of service quality and the distinction between technical and functional quality is more blurred as result. The way an aerobics session is delivered, and the charisma and style of the instructor, may be almost as much of the core product and its technical quality as the activity itself. In other cases like attending professional sport, there is more concern with tangibles such as seating and access; but in all contexts there is more than simply the product and the service.

This chapter adopts the premise that there is an additional dimension to the sport and leisure product, that is, the consumer experience, and that this has implications for the management of the service encounter. Much leisure theory has been constructed on the socio-psychological constraints of perceived freedom and intrinsic motivation. Manfredo *et al.* (1996) suggest that there are three interrelated approaches to the study of the psychological nature of leisure. One is definitional (leisure or non-leisure). The second is the immediate conscious experience approach; Manfredo *et al.* (1996) describe it as a phenomenological topography of the leisure experience – its meaning, quality, duration, intensity and memorability. The third is post-hoc satisfaction, related to the notion of expectations although much service quality literature has emerged from the conceptual framework of 'disconfirmation theory'.

This chapter focuses on the second of Manfredo's approaches and postulates that the product, seen as an activity and/or a setting, together with the way in which they are managed or delivered, create and shape the distinctive feature of sport and leisure – the customer experience.

THE EXPERIENTIAL PROPERTIES OF THE SPORT AND LEISURE PRODUCT

The challenge, therefore, for sport and leisure professionals in the management of the service encounter would appear to lie in their understanding of its experiential properties and features. The overwhelming evidence from studies of the sport and leisure experience is that its meaning in many managed contexts is shaped by myriad complex perceptual constructs and this explains why it is regarded as a multidimensional phenomenon (Gunter 1987; Howe and Rancourt 1990; Hull *et al.* 1996; Lee, Dattilo and Howard 1994; Russell and Hultsman 1987; Tinsley and Tinsley 1986). The manager's skill lies in the ability to analyse and interpret the meaning attached by people to the events and phenomena taking place, for the study of sport and leisure management involves complex perceptual constructs and relationships in many contexts.

Thus, the essence of managing service quality in most sport and leisure organisations would seem to lie in the relationship between the consumer and the managed contexts or environments in which the consumer experience occurs and the patterns or themes of this relationship. All of these contexts, of course, contain myriad individual experiences, whether rich and fulfilling or superficial and mere entertainment and raise many questions about the managed processes and the interaction between consumer and the leisure environment and leisure provider. The pivotal component is the product or experience and the way in which it is managed and delivered and the recent developments in generic service management literature provide an underpinning for this. Increasingly, the customer is viewed as both consumer and co-producer or prosumer (Normann 1991) and often plays an interactive role in shaping the experience; the sport and leisure experience can be perceived as a service process containing a service encounter or a series of sequential encounters, symbolised by the term 'moments of truth' (Carlzon 1987).

THE SERVICE ENCOUNTER

So what exactly *is* the service encounter and why is its management so important? Some observers regard the service encounter as the contact between staff and customers; it is interesting that many of the dimensions of the SERVQUAL model are concerned with human attributes. Yet others perceive it to be a wider concept which reflects any contact the customer has with the organisation within the process of consumption.

The service encounter, therefore, can be defined as the stage of the service process when the consumer engages or interacts with staff (the psychological service encounter) but also systems, procedures, information or even the organisational culture. The service encounter, as Figure 1.1 demonstrates, can involve outcomes and therefore satisfaction or dissatisfaction supported by a post-transaction evaluation by the customer of the service performance. A central thrust of the chapter is that the level of satisfaction with a transaction represents more than the organisation getting things right. As we shall examine, the encounter, and its evaluation, are also affected by the experiential properties of the product or service.

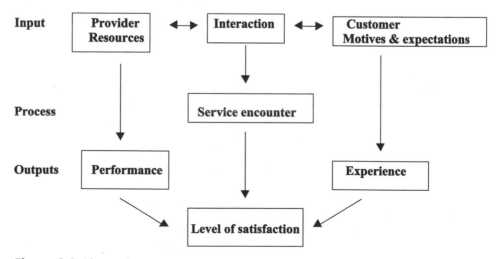

Figure 1.1 *The service encounter*

The level of psychological encounter between staff and customers varies greatly across the sport and leisure industry but its importance in achieving customer satisfaction is well documented (Bitner 1990; Lee-Ross 2001; Normann 2000, Valker 1995). Indeed, Johnston and Clark (2001) recognise the complexity of such encounters because of the variability and possible intensity of the human dimension. Some operations (for example Alton Towers or Disney) build in customer contact to their service concept and package and train and prepare key personnel for engaging in conversation with guests. The use of script theory provides further evidence for the opportunity in the design process to manage and manipulate the exchange and rapport between staff and customers.

It could be argued that at a micro level the system of sport and leisure becomes a system of service delivery and focuses on the human dimensions of individual consumption and participation. This chapter is concerned with the relationship between the system of delivery of the product and service and its experiential properties perceived by the customer. This approach embraces the contextual aspects of the setting, environment and activity and the social dimensions of the experience and interface. Sport and leisure activities may be viewed as not merely self-centred acts but as experiences which have a particular meaning.

The human dimension of such interactions provides the rationale for the approaches to managing service quality in sport and leisure management examined in the chapter and underline the need for much research into the meaning of sport and leisure and their features such as participation patterns, consumer behaviour and demand. As Glancy and Little (1995) suggest:

> The fact that we know little about the interactive experience in which leisure meaning forms limit our capacity to understand leisure on a personal and empirical level. (1995: 308)

Furthermore, if we argue that sport and leisure is a process governed by human interactions (Henderson 1991; Titz 2001) and that the basis of meaningful sport and leisure is the human experience (Glancy 1993; Glasford 1987), then the study of the sport and leisure service encounter, perhaps, needs to focus on the process and the way in which the different elements of the process interact. As Bitner et al. (1997) argue:

> Service experiences are the outcomes of interactions between organisation related systems/processes, service employees and customers. (1997: 193)

Service encounters, therefore, involve motives and outcomes as well as processes and experiences. It might be useful to integrate these dimensions into one model to develop our understanding of the linkages.

MODEL OF SPORT AND LEISURE AND SERVICE ENCOUNTER MANAGEMENT

Johnston and Clark (2001) suggest that service operations managers must understand the need of customers, but must also work to integrate value-adding activities to enhance both outcomes and experience. They and others (Bitner et al. 1997; Chandon 1996) argue that there is a blurring between the outcomes of a service and the experience of the service and encounters. The following model attempts to conceptualise this integration and to represent the dynamics of the service encounter and how it is managed.

The model comprises several components.

Sport and leisure service concept

The first component is the leisure service concept. This represents customer needs and the features of the product or transaction and the nature of the service encounter. The customer utility and benefit – both the description of the customer needs to be satisfied and how they are to be satisfied through the design of service package – are important elements in the sport and leisure experience.

The sport and leisure service concept contains the bundle of attributes or benefits the consumer is seeking and relates to the core product or activity and the augmented product or additional services like hospitality. It also defines what business the organisation is in and how it should promote and organise itself.

An example is provided by the David Lloyd Group where there is a feeling that it is their approach to service quality that is the distinctive feature of their service concept. They believe that their core product – the activities provided by their sports and leisure facilities – are important but are underpinned by highly trained staff, high standards of cleanliness and maintenance, friendly, attentive service and a pleasant and relaxing environment. It is the company's aim to exceed members' expectations by providing an enhanced service and delighting members and increasing their perceived value of their membership. The aim is also to give all members individual attention and to try and meet every service encounter with care and compassion. The David Lloyd core values are 'caring, passion and trust' and their philosophy on service quality is to offer every member the best combination of quality product, standard of service and value for money in the leisure industry.

Sport and leisure service system

The production management model of adding value and converting inputs into outputs, adapted to apply to service industries, is further modified here to embrace sport and leisure management. As Figure 1.2 demonstrates, the sport and leisure service system establishes what is needed in order to meet the customer requirements and the product features described by the service concept. It refers to the resources and inputs to the service process and how they are deployed and helps to identify the service standards in all aspects of the operation. The service system has several elements which interrelate as they shape service encounters.

Customers and their motives
The relationship between the goals and motives of the customer and the attributes of the product or service package also helps to shape the outcomes of the transaction and the quality of the sport and leisure experience. Much evidence suggests that the prerequisites for achieving leisure are a sense of freedom of choice, freedom from evaluation and intrinsic motivation or the expectations of preferred experiences. It could be argued that all positive experiences will contain enjoyment and then will range from a level of relaxation to fun, entertainment, excitement and adventure or escapism apart from the specific motives of, for example, health and

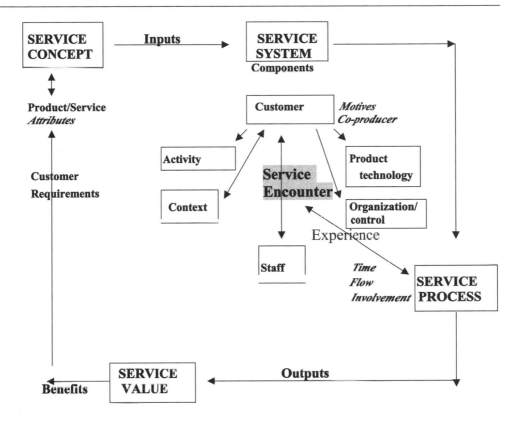

Figure 1.2 *Model of service design and delivery in sport and leisure*

fitness, education or personal development. Whichever applies to particular activities, the model points to the need for balance in the key factors of time, flow and involvement and emphasises the dialectical nature of the sport and leisure experience. The role of the customer is often more significant in services than in the manufacturing industry, and within services the involvement of the customer can also be more distinctive in the sport and leisure industry (see question 3 at the end of this chapter).

The activity

The interaction between the customer and the leisure opportunities provided by the activity embraces many aspects of sport and leisure management. It more naturally represents the core element of the product such as the game of squash or the airline seat or the theme park ride and in some cases places more emphasis on the nature and quality of the facility or environment.

The setting

This environment can be referred to as the setting and embraces not only the physical and technical environments for the activity but also intangible features such as atmosphere and ambience and the social context. It can range from pur-pose-built settings such as facilities and pitches (servicescape) to the natural resource of a national park (landscape). All require managing in some way, whether direct or indirect, with implications for service encounters and, indeed, the consumer experience.

Product technology

Product technology is concerned with tangibles such as facilities, equipment and technology in the activity itself. It includes buildings such as cinemas and leisure centres, the equipment within them and their use of technology as a feature of the product such as screen and sound systems in cinemas or white-knuckle rides or simulators in visitor attractions.

Staff

Staff are also a key factor because of the service encounter in many sport and leisure contexts and the interaction in such social settings defines the critical moments of truth. Receptionists, instructors, guides, attendants and waiters and waitresses are particular frontline staff whose role is to animate, motivate and engage with customers and methods like service blueprinting can be useful in defining such roles, how they interact with customers and each other and how they are to be supported.

Organisation and control

This is the final element and although regarded as bureaucratic, work procedures and other documentation and communication with customers are important aspects of service quality and also help with customer flow and circulation as well as shaping attitudes. They can include ticket purchase, automatic entry, signage and sight lines and booking systems and the technology concerned with underpinning the delivery of the product.

Sport and leisure service process

The system is more concerned with the 'what' of service delivery whereas the service process is more related to the 'how'. The service process in sport and leisure is the chain of activities and stages the customer goes through and involves much interaction between the customer and the other inputs which make up the service system. It refers to functional quality (the how) as opposed to technical quality (the what) and, in many contexts, is more important in determining the overall quality of the consumer experience. The service process defines the interaction between customers and the organisation as in the three interfaces described by Kingman-Brundage, George and Bowen (1995). Customers and the organisation are linked through:

- the *encounter interface* involving direct contact with front-line employees
- the *technical interface* based on technology, systems and procedures
- the *support interface* containing work tasks and the relationships between frontline and backstage staff.

These interfaces represent the systemic aspects of the process but it is also necessary to consider the softer aspects of the process such as individuals' state of mind and their perceptions of time.

Time

The notion of time as a social construct in addition to a chronological sequence is relevant to our analysis of the service encounter and highlights the pivotal role of some professionals in enhancing the quality of the experience. As an example, the author was involved in some research in the 1980s with a leisure centre that was experiencing some dissatisfaction with its bowls users, most of whom were senior citizens with their time-rich, cash-poor lifestyles. The centre was in the middle of the town and was built over a car park that was also used by many shoppers. Everybody paid the normal rates which were in timebands and became quite expensive over a certain period of time. Unfortunately, at that time the centre users did not get their parking fee back; it meant that the bowls players, in an activity and at a stage of life when time should not matter, were constantly looking at the clock. The sense of timelessness, which occurs with the best sport leisure activities, was not present and the overall experience was impaired. Happily, the recommendation to refund the parking fee to users was accepted and that usage, income and customer satisfaction with their service encounters were all improved.

Flow or state of mind

Time is always a factor in any analysis of leisure, but more significant in determining many experiences is how customers actually feel and react at any stage. State of mind is a factor in the next element of the model which considers the relationship between the participant and the activity. There is a need to examine the distinction between serious, committed leisure and everyday activities although we should think, perhaps, less in terms of a dichotomy and more of a continuum. There is a spectrum ranging from Maslow's peak experience theory and Csikszentmihalyi's concept of flow (Csikszentmihalyi 1991) which describe more sporadic but intense moments of fulfilment and self-actualisation particularly in physical, outdoor activities to activities of a more mundane and less memorable nature. We should note that the latter represents much managed sport leisure but, perhaps, poses as much of a challenge for the management of the service encounter as do the less common but distinctive and special moments in a range of contexts.

The characteristics of flow or peak experience illustrate the attraction and, indeed, function of many activities in sport and leisure yet we must not forget that the more regular activities like the visit to the health club or the cinema or urban park also involve feelings and sensations as well as the benefits beyond the visit. They can also involve the customer to varying degrees.

Involvement of the customer

We have seen how some contexts in sport and leisure require or allow considerable participation in the service and its creation. Many instructional classes in a range of activities are highly participative; interactive experiences in museums and heritage centres, audiences in sports and entertainment venues or education as leisure all provide opportunities for active and creative participation. Not only can customers be regarded as partial employees but their contribution to the features of the product and service can be an additional dimension and, in some cases, integral part of the overall experience. The interaction between customers provides much satisfaction for many people and much participation in a range of activities incorporates the motive of socialisation. Thousands of spectators in sports such as football, rugby and ice hockey are attracted by the noise, singing and social bonding of which they are part. Furthermore, we can also recognise that providers are also affected by the actions and behaviours of customers.

Service value

The final component of the model takes us back to the needs and motives of the customer as identified or disseminated by the service concept. The model described provides a picture of the elements in the design of both the service and its system of production and delivery in sport and leisure. It demonstrates the traditional view of production in which inputs are converted through a process into outputs or outcomes but also emphasises the link, in the loop, between the organisation's service concept and, eventually, the benefits customers take away with them and their satisfaction with how the benefits have been created. Service value not only relates to the concept of value for money but also accounts for other variables such as cost, time, including travelling, and the general effort required for the activity (a problem faced by the Millennium Dome).

Benefits and outcomes

Having examined the motives for consumption and the process and context involved we, finally, also need to consider the benefits and psychological outcomes of the sport or leisure experience. The psychological benefits of the leisure experience, perhaps, can be seen in a number of ways, which incorporate the dichotomies described earlier but which also represent a hierarchy of needs and motives for sport and leisure:

- *passive*: relaxation, peace, tranquillity, solitude, space
- *stimulating*: escape, fantasy, adventure, novelty
- *lively*: fun, excitement, entertainment
- *competent*: health, fitness, sport, crafts and hobbies (DIY!)
- *social*: family, friendship and esteem, social networks/groups
- *personal development*: cultural awareness, self-expression, personal identity.

Furthermore, the relationship between the goals and motives of the customer and the attributes of the product or service package also helps to shape the outcomes of the transaction and the quality of the leisure or sport experience. Gummesson (1994: 78) refers to the 'interactive productivity of services' which recognises the value or benefits of the experience for the customer. Rosman (1994) demonstrates how activities experience outcomes such as fun or enjoyment and long-term personal benefits are important dimensions for the professional to consider in designing programmes and services.

Synthesis

Such a view provides a much more holistic theory of leisure satisfactions, motives and benefits, personal relations and social networks and poses the following key questions for the sport and leisure operator to answer in determining the approach to planning and managing the service encounter in any particular context:

- What are the service concept and service package?
- What are our customers' expectations and their motives?

- What is the level of psychological encounter?
- How standardised or customised is the product and service?
- How much customer participation is required?
- How much interaction with staff is encouraged?
- How is the interaction between customers/participants planned for?
- What levels of customer competency are required?

To answer the questions, the interaction between the customer and the leisure opportunities provided by the activity must be acknowledged and, indeed, understood. The model provides a backcloth against which the service encounter and service delivery can be analysed and broken down to enhance its understanding by both staff and customers and the way it is designed and managed. However, the model does not necessarily highlight the interaction between the various components of the service system or some of the options open to management in their planning process. In order for managers to evaluate and to plan new developments, an understanding of the whole process is required.

A more coherent approach to the study of the service encounter, and a greater understanding of how it can be managed, may be achieved through the synthesis of the perspectives of the consumer experience and the management of it. We have established that sport and leisure is a complex and multifaceted phenomenon, which can also be multi-phasic and transitory. The experience of the activity or its context, as an emotional response, is part of the motivation for the individual consumer and requires careful and sensitive management. Consumers will experience the activity or context in different ways and a conundrum for operators is to decide how much the market can be differentiated and the degree to which the service encounter is to be customised. The greater the differentiation, the more difficult it is to achieve consistency of delivery.

Next, the nature of the sport and leisure industry also involves considerable interaction between customer and staff. This draws on aspects of human resource management and service quality and, in particular, focuses on the psychological or service encounter which takes place between staff and customers.

CONCLUSIONS

The roles of the sport and leisure professional require an understanding of how people define the world around them. Furthermore, they need to understand this reality in order to provide the most appropriate settings, activities and experiences. The approach of the chapter accepts that the sport and leisure industry is, at one level, engaged in providing recreational activities and does this through managing facilities, amenities and programmes. There is a product and a process and they contain particular features or attributes that are important to the customer. However, a premise of the chapter is that the leisure provider and the customer are engaged in more than a product transaction; there is the potential for the achievement of a leisure experience. Recreational participation, and experience of the sport and leisure product in the managed contexts this book is addressing, are affected by the individual consumer's self-awareness and personal motives, the system of service delivery and its understanding by the leisure or sport provider. The move towards the use of systems models will help with the conceptualisation of the study of sport and leisure management and the understanding of the various interactions which provide the scope for conceptualising and understanding the service encounter.

Questions

1. Why can many sport and leisure experiences involve a dialectical process?
2. How can the relationship between the customer and staff be regarded as 'bi-directional'?
3. Why can the customer be viewed as a productive resource?

References and further reading

Bettencourt, L. and Gwinner, K. (1996) 'Customization of the service experience: the role of the frontline employee', *International Journal of Service Industry Management*, 7, 2, 3–20.

Bitner, M. J. (1990) 'Evaluating service encounters: the effects of physical surroundings and employee responses', *Journal of Marketing*, 54, 2, 69–82.

Bitner, M. J., Faranda, W. T., Hubbert, A. R. and Zeithaml, V. A. (1997) 'Customer contributions and roles in service delivery', *International Journal of Service Industry Management*, 8, 3.

Canziani, B. F. (1997) 'Leveraging customer competency and roles in service firms', *International Journal of Service Industry Management*, 7, 1.

Carlzon, J. (1987) *Moments of Truth*. Cambridge, Massachusetts: Ballinger Publications.

Chandon, J.-L. and Philippe, J. (1996) 'Service encounter dimensions – a dyadic perspective: measuring the dimensions of encounters as perceived by customers and personnel, *International Journal of Service Industries Management*, 7, 1, 65–86.

Csikszentmihayli, M. (1991) *Flow – The Psychology of Optimal Experience*. New York: HarperCollins.

Glancy, M. (1993) 'Achieving intersubjectivity: the process of becoming the subject in leisure research', *Leisure Studies*, 12, 45–59.

Glancy, M. and Little, S. L. (1995) 'Studying the social aspects of leisure: development of multiple-method field investigation model (MMFI)', *Journal of Leisure Research*, 20, 4, 305–23.

Glasford, R. G. (1987) 'Methodological reconsiderations: the shifting paradigms', *Quest*, 39, 295–312.

Gummesson, E. (1994) 'Service management: an evaluation and the future', *International Journal of Service Industry Management*, 5, 1, 77–96.

Gunter, B. G. (1987) 'The leisure experience: selected properties', *Journal of Leisure Research*, 19, 2, 115–30.

Henderson, K. (1991) *Dimensions of Choice – A Qualitative Approach to Recreation, Parks and Leisure Research*. State College, Pennsylvania: Venture Publishing, Inc.

The Henley Centre (1996) *Hospitality into the 21st Century – a Vision for the Future*. Henley: The Henley Centre.

Howe, C. Z. and Rancourt, M. (1990) 'The importance of definitions of selected concepts for leisure enquiry', *Leisure Sciences*, 12, 395–406.

Hull, R. B., Michael, S. B., Walker, G. J. and Roggerbuck, J. W. (1996) 'Ebb and flow of brief leisure experience', *Leisure Sciences*, 18, 299–314.

Johnston, R. and Clark, G. (2001) *Service Operations Management*. Harlow: Financial Times/Prentice Hall.

Kingman-Brundage, J., George, W. R. and Bowen D. E. (1995) 'Service logic: achieving service system integration', *International Journal of Service Industry Management*, 6, 4, 20–39.

Lee, Y., Dattilo, J. and Howard, D. (1994) 'The complex and dynamic nature of leisure experience', *Journal of Leisure Research*, 26, 3, 195–211.

Lee-Ross, D. (2001) 'Understanding the role of the service encounter in tourism, hospitality and leisure services' in Kandampully, J., Mok, C. and Sparks, B. (eds) *Service Quality, Management in Hospitality, Tourism and Leisure*, New York: Haworth Hospitality Press.

Manfredo, M. J., Driver, B. L. and Tarrant, M. A. (1996) 'Measuring leisure motivation: a meta-analysis of the recreation experience preference scales', *Journal of Leisure Research*, 28, 3, 188–213.

Normann, R. (1991) *Service Management*. Chichester: John Wiley & Sons.

Normann, R. (2000) *Service Management* (3rd edn). Chichester: John Wiley & Sons.

Rosman, R. (1994) *Recreation Programming: Designing Leisure Experiences* (2nd edn). Champaign, IL: Sagamore.

Russell, R. V. and Hultsman, J. T. (1987) 'An empirical basis for determining the multidimensional structure of leisure', *Leisure Sciences*, 10, 69–76.

Svensson, G. (2001) 'The quality of bi-directional service quality in dyadic service encounters', *Journal of Services Marketing*, 15, 5, 357–78.

Tinsley, H. E. A. and Tinsley, D. J. (1986) 'A theory of the attributes, benefits and causes of leisure experience', *Leisure Sciences*, 8, 1, 1–44.

Titz, K. (2001) 'The impact of people, processes and physical evidence on tourism, hospitality and leisure service quality' in Kandampully, J., Mok, C. and Sparks, B. (eds) *Service Quality, Management in Hospitality, Tourism and Leisure*, New York: Haworth Hospitality Press.

Wakefield, K. L. and Blodgett, J. G. (1996) 'The effect of the servicescape on customers' behavioural intentions in leisure service settings', *Journal of Services Marketing*, 10, 6, 45–61.

Walker, J. L. (1995) 'Service encounter satisfaction conceptualized', *Journal of Services Marketing*, 62, 1, 5–15.

Waterhouse, R. (2000) 'Are you experienced?', *Sunday Times*, 3 December.

Wathen, S. and Anderson, J. C. (1996) 'Designing services: an information-processing approach', *International Journal of Service Industry Management*, 6, 1, 64–76.

CHAPTER 2

Sport and Leisure Narrative

Martin Robertson

BACKGROUND AND INTRODUCTION

Satisfying people's needs is good for business (Torkildsen 1999). In order to satisfy the needs of people it is necessary to understand what it is that motivates them. By understanding these needs it should be possible to establish a way of pre-empting people's wants and providing something which retains their attention – whether for company, money or some other socio-economic prupose. Similarly, if leisure or sports activities in a rural 'natural' environment are to be managed – whether for money or for some other social profit such as environmental and economic sustainability – the pursuit of success must be based on satisfying the needs of visitors whilst also ensuring regulation of the possible negative effects on the environment in which these activities are set.

This chapter frames an operational management view by summarising core definitions of the following four elements:

1. values of nature and its resources as a product
2. leisure choice
3. image creation
4. narrative.

It then goes on to suggest the cognitive function of these elements in the management of nature-based leisure, sports and activity tourism.

WHY LOOK AT NATURE-BASED SPORTS, LEISURE AND TOURISM?

The World Tourism Organisation states that, globally, nature-based tourism generated 7% of international tourism expenditure (cited in Deng, King and Bauer 2002: 423). While the dynamic changing nature of demand means the actual forms of this consumption are not so precise and despite nature-based activities or activity tourism taking a downturn in 2001 and early 2002 in the UK due largely to the foot and mouth epidemic, the growth of leisure in the natural environment throughout the world is set to grow. In 1999 the English Tourism Council found that 20% of people had taken part in sports and leisure while visiting the countryside. Moreover, in 2001, Mintel estimated that domestic (UK) activity holiday market was worth £2.1 billion and the overseas market about £1.8 billion (Mintel 2001). In addition, it is suggested that the worldwide travel for the purpose of adventure tourism has grown over three times as much as that for tourism in general (Smith and Jenner 1999: 47).

However, there is a danger that the rapid growth of nature- and activity-based tourism has become its own worst enemy, creating a prolific entertainment and recreation-based phenomenon dependent on the attributes of protected and real nature while at the same time risking that the numbers it attracts destroy the very resources that it depends on for attracting visitors and their expenditure.

Many documents offering management strategies to counter this potentially doomed relationship, while very important, have repeatedly offered one of two directional avenues: one which offers an abstracted address of the need to draw together the various stakeholders of any rural domain in the production of a codefied strategy, referred to as limits of acceptable change (LAC) in which 'use levels are agreed by all parties' (Johnson and Clark 2000: 97); and others which offer a more regimented model based on the *area zoning*, in which areas are zoned in an attempt to manage impacts on any given area or areas – such as that offered in the national parks of Canada and America (Johnson and Clark 2000). However, it is the conjecture of this chapter that nature-based tourism, predominantly located in the rural environment, has to include an operational view of management based on the belief that marketing and understanding the consumer's role in the environment is a pivotal operational component. Moreover, in this management perspective, it is important to see nature both as a resource and as a commodity and the countryside in which it is located as a place of consumption, with special identities, images and themes (Roberts and Hall 2001: 148). Furthermore, effective management is about ensuring that the commodity is a desirable experience and that desirability is a complete management action in which the ensuring of appropriate image form, presentation and management are as an integral management function as that of providing a good product with appropriate services.

This article attempts to synthesise the views of social scientists and the school of market- and marketing-oriented models of the competitive destination (Buhalis 2000; Godfrey and Clark 2000), towards a model appropriate to operational objectives in those rural, natural settings which have the opportunity (and often the need) to create a leisure- and sports-oriented experience for visitors.

PLANNING FOR PEOPLE MEANS UNDERSTANDING PEOPLE

George Torkildsen (1999) clearly highlights the fundamental significance of understanding people's leisure needs before planning the provision of sports or leisure facilities for them. In what Torkildsen (1999: 256) refers to as 'an awakening to recreation' in the UK, the Local Government Act of 1972 and the Local Government (Miscellaneous Provisions) Act were clear frameworks in which provision and administration of facilities for sport, recreation and outdoor physical recreation became an established obligation of local authorities (Torkildsen: 259). However, the reaction then, in the 1970s, to the provision of leisure facilities or services was mixed: veering from success to mild derision to failure. While the provision of sports and swimming leisure centres, both in the urban and suburban setting, were largely successful at least in the early years, local council provision of free sports or leisure facilities, for example football pitches and football posts, leisure facilities, leisure parks, and children's play areas, were often the recipients of either abuse and vandalism or, at best, degrees of despondency. While a great many voices may have called this wanton ingratitude, Torkildsen argues, as do most modern-day planners, that the failure was not that of the users, but that of the *providers*. Consequent development by national government recognised the need for recreational policy areas, with special funding to counter particular socio-economic needs (Department of the Environment 1975). This was followed by the central government's cooperation with the Sport Council to start more sophisti-cated sports and recreation projects, from which sprang the notion of 'community recreation' (Tomlinson 1987).

Concomitantly, then, it can surmised that without first finding out the needs of the people who are most likely to use the leisure experience (such as swings on the edge of a multi-storey housing project in an economically deprived area) the likelihood of successful provision is severely restricted. Understanding needs is not a simple financial equation. Our needs are as much about how we think as they are about how much can be afforded. Later in this chapter an address will be made as to how people consume leisure, sports and tourism activities in the natural envir-onment in general, and in relation to extreme sports in the natural environment in particular. The chapter will then explain why this understanding helps evaluate people's leisure needs and is a fundamental operational management dynamic. Initially, it is constructive to think of the predominant influences on our leisure needs.

LEISURE PERCEPTIONS AND NEEDS

Torkildsen provides one model that clearly illustrates the influences of individual or grouping of people's perceptions as well as determinants of physical participation in leisure. This is to say it illustrates the influences on our leisure needs. The model is entitled *influences on leisure experiences*, and is based on the premise that a person's decision, choice and motivation relate to all the principal variables in his or her life – which Torkildsen refers to systematically as, first, the *personal influ-ences*; then second, the *social and circumstantial influences*; and third, the *opportunity influences*. In this, the *personal influences* relate to our prime indivi-dual, personal and family influences, i.e. our age, family history and social back-ground. This is to say, all the things which have formed us. In analysing *social and circumstantial influences* a study is made of the factors in the current stage of a person's life, inclusive of job type, income, the people we socialise with and the cultural values with which a person lives. All these affect how we perceive leisure and sport forms and activities. The third influence, *opportunity influences*, runs concurrently with the other two factors but is, in many senses, the most tangible as it addresses the physical environmental aspects which allow participation to occur. This third set of influences can thus be seen as the attributes of *access*, inferring that it is not just what has made us and our social status that affects what we do but also those factors which ensure that we have the physical potential to enter leisure. This

Table 2.1 *Influence on personal participation (adapted from Torkildsen 1999: 114)*

Personal	Social and circumstantial	Opportunity factors
Age	Occupation	Resources available
Stage in lifecycle	Income	Facilities – type and quality
Gender	Disposable income	Awareness
Marital status	Material wealth and goods	Perception of opportunities
Dependants and age	Car ownership and	Recreation services
Will and purpose of life	mobility	(available)
Personal obligation	Time available	Distribution of facilities
Leisure perception	Duties and obligations	Choice of activity
Attitudes and motivation	Home and social	Transport
Interests and preoccupation	environment	Costs: before, during, after
Skills and ability (physical,	Friends and peer groups	Management: policy and
social and intellectual)	Social roles and contacts	support
Personality and confidence	Environment factors	Marketing
Culture born into	Mass leisure factors	Programming
Upbringing and social	Education and attainment	Organisation and
background	Population factors	leadership
	Cultural factors	Political policies

third set of influences is the response to availability of resources (e.g. leisure facilities); whether there are appropriate sources of information (often in the form of marketing and promotion) to ensure people are aware of the leisure opportunity and whether there is the political or social will of national or local government authorities and/or private organisations supporting the provision of leisure opportunities to give potential for participation. In Table 2.1 Torkildsen shows in each column a great many of the core affecting elements in each of these three influence areas.

This model has borne many others and is indicative of the importance now ascribed to finding and understanding why people do or don't participate in sports and leisure activities. As the experiences sought in the natural environment are part of our leisure time, the same factors can be attributed to the way in which visitors to it either do (or simply don't) experience the environment, i.e. in the way in which people consume the nature experience. Thus, as Meethan (2001: 72) states, people's values of what is appropriate and the ways in which they actually consume 'can be predicted through the presence or absence of factors such as socio-economic position, gender, age, housing tenure and other "lifestyle indicators"'. Moreover these predictions can – and should – be seen as formative market segments: potential groupings to target by offering the products that most readily fulfil the needs particular to the traits of that segment. In order to do so, any mixture of the variables documented earlier can be linked and analysed to form 'cluster segments' (Meethan 2001: 72), i.e. defined groupings of similar variables with similar consumer needs. This is the foundation for defining market segmentation and niche marketing, both of which will be documented more fully later on in this chapter.

UNDERSTANDING NEEDS AND RISK

For the company or provider of outdoor leisure activities, sports or adventure pursuits it is further suggested here that in order to make certain that the product (the experience) offered matches the needs of the adventure- or nature-oriented visitor/consumer they must understand what their perception of nature and/or adventure is. Weber (2001) opines that by engaging in the pursuit of consumer understanding, one is able to determine what it is that motivates a visitor to visit a place and involve him or her in an activity in (or at) that place.

One long-standing model of defining how people choose one product or experience over another is the *theory of perceived risk* (Cheron and Brent Richie 1982) in which the choice of any purchase involves a consumer equating the risk of that decision in, for example, buying one product instead of another. Cheron and Brent Richie (1982) took this consumer behaviour analytical framework further and applied it to people's leisure activity choice. By measuring people's perception of risk in 20 leisure activities (snowmobiling, shopping, bowling, golfing, playing cards, alpine skiing, handicrafts, gardening, TV viewing, doing odd jobs, swimming (pool), swimming (lake, etc.), skating, movies, visiting friends, tennis, walking, reading, bicycling, cross-country skiing), they sought to interpret people's overall perception of risk as well as more systematically their perception of risks in terms of the following senses: *financial risk* (possibility that activity will not provide value for money); *functional risk* (possibility activity will have problems, mechanical or otherwise); *psychological risk* (individual's personality/self-image); *physical risk* (possibility of physical danger or injury); *social risk* (possibility participation will affect others' opinions of individual); *satisfaction risk* (possibility that activity will not provide personal satisfaction/self-actualisation); *time risk* (possibility that activity will either take too long or be a waste of time) (Cheron and Richie: 145).

What they found was that the two most profound and overarching perceived risk areas associated with leisure activity choice were *functional risk* and *psychological risk*. In the first, functional risk, prime reference was made to the possibility that the person may not be able to perform the activity or that it involves some physical risk. In the second, psychological risk, prime reference was made to the perceived risk of not attaining personal or socially ascribed values, or that time would be wasted (Cheron and Richie: 153). The essence derived from these findings was that different people have different perceptions of what risk is and different people have difference perceptions of whether danger made the experience more or less attractive or valuable.

Risk and knowledge

While the notion of risk is certainly a core factor in determining the way in which people (subconsciously or consciously) evaluate their experience choice and the key factors suggested by Cheron and Brent Richie do offer a strong basis from which to analyse the choice made by sports, leisure or tourist users, it can also be argued that this does not fully explain the reasons for involvement in adventure and outdoor activities. Thus it is likely that the term 'risk' does not suitably define the factors that enable and animate the actual involvement in the activity. Rather, as Weber

(2001) goes on to say, the motivation and enabling factor can indeed encompass degrees of risk evaluation, but is more probably the prospective participant's need to find insight or knowledge. The suggestion therefore that it is quite possible that participants of these (and other) leisure experiences are unaware of – or only partially contemplating – risks and are instead searching for what marketers would normatively evaluate as *added value*.

Weber comments that those aligning the chosen activities of adventure tourism and outdoor sportspeople to degree of risk are guilty of harping back to a time when adventure was defined in terms of the pursuit of unknown areas – of expeditions into the unknown as encapsulated in the image of a sweat-drenched figure hacking his or her way through the jungles of, say, Borneo. However, modern-day acceptance of the visiting of foreign destinations as an ordinary not extraordinary activity, the accompanying ease of travel and the packaging of holiday experiences in lands, nations and countries previously seen as intangible, unattractive or frighteningly alien, have all played a part in normalising the experience of adventure. Thus, the conjecture of this chapter is that the activity – whether backpacking, bicycling, hang-gliding, rock-climbing, abseiling, canoeing, kayaking, bungee-jumping, snowboarding, mountain biking, sky-diving or taking part in any of the activities suggested as being those of 'adventure pursuits' or 'extreme sports' – is less an experience of risk taking, but more an exercise in stretching skills or an attempt to reach a new level of ability or, as Weber calls it, *knowledge and insight*. Some are more prosaic about this search and refer to the way 'outdoor leisure offers the opportunity to develop different ways of expression and a tolerance of for the non identical' (Suerdem 1993, cited in Varley and Crowther 1998: 311) and an 'exploration of new places, a new renewed (or new) relationship with nature' (Lyotard 1988, cited in Varley and Crowther: 311) or a 'journey of the mind' (Grant, cited in Roberts and Hall 2001: 166). However, all indicate that the motivation or choice decision is based or clearly influenced by the user's creation of leisure characters, i.e. a desire to develop through the experience.

The importance of accommodating the pursuit of knowledge and insight can thus be seen as a market need. As when considering the future for any product, the market cannot be seen as homogeneous. There are many categories of people requiring different levels of knowledge and insight. Thus while the experienced rockclimber may feel the need to stretch their knowledge to the very edge of physical and tactical ability, the leisure canoeist may be seeking to expand his or her knowledge of the area rather than stretch the ability of his/her canoeing performance.

This understanding is as important for the owner or manager of a sports or leisure product as it is for those local authorities with responsibilities for the provision of leisure in any given area and whose remit is to oversee it and ensure its economic and social strength. The chapter will now look at how this knowledge should both influence and be incumbent on the managerial operation for all these stakeholders first, by reviewing the function of image in motivation and second, by forming conclusions as to how the use of images should be applied and managed.

IMAGE AND CHOICE

In all areas of service experience consumers have become increasingly more demanding and their product loyalty ever more dynamic. People's expectations are influenced every day, not least by myriad images received through the media and popular culture – local, national and international – at home, in work and, of course, in the leisure experiences which link both. In attracting both tourism and business, countries, regions, cities and towns have sought to differentiate themselves as distinct destinations so as to establish, maintain or reach new markets. As Echtner and Ritchie orate (1993: 3), 'creating and managing an appropriate destination image are critical to effective positioning and marketing strategy'. While the observation that 'image creation is not incidental to overall development, it is a catalyst for other changes' (Robertson 1998: 221) was said in relation to competition between cities to attract visitors, the same is nonetheless true of the rural, natural destination. This has been recognised and 'rural areas have sought to differentiate themselves (and their products and services) in an increasingly competitive market place, through the use of quality and regional imagery' (William 2001, cited in Roberts and Hall 2001: 214). As Leisen (2001: 49) points out, 'the images held by individuals in the marketplace are crucial to a destination's marketing success' and 'marketers must identify the images held by travellers and select those segments that represent the most receptive target markets'. Thus success is dependent on product image creation and manipulation appropriate to each market segment whereby the images can form a relationship – a narrative – with the targeted markets (Deng, King and Bauer 2002).

Image and narrative management

In looking at the outdoor leisure market, Varley and Crowther (1998) refer to the 'managerial implications for service providers in this specialised market' and the importance of understanding the value of forming a relationship narrative. More specifically, they highlight the importance of forming a narrative between the participant and the provider, i.e. suggesting a development role for images which can, as the term 'narrative' suggests, relate to the user beyond the initial stage of the user's knowledge, indicating that this can stem from 'organic' non-tourist, official sources or from 'projected' designated and designed promotion. Thus they talk of the interactive role that should be played in the user's search for knowledge or insight in the experience. Utilised, it is concluded, this will improve the likelihood of customer satisfaction based on continued knowledge and/or skills development and thus be more liable to evoke repeat visit success. Correspondingly, by managerial understanding of the way in which, for example, a climber enjoys the climb as an almost Zen-like mixture of ritual experience, e.g in the preparation for the climb, and the attainment of a new experience, a new knowledge, the manager can more confidently attempt to match the needs of the market with what is on offer. Likewise, extreme sports, the pursuit of activity commonly perceived as testing its participants' abilities in the form of risk, is heavily reliant on a salient and attractive narrative. The build-up, enjoyment and market success of extreme sports may, in some of its forms, be transitory, with some extreme sports in fashion for a short time while others likely to remain for a long time. However, it is nonetheless reliant on various level of narrative, some based on the sharing of insight dependent on skills, some – particularly for those between the ages of 12 and 19 (Mintel 2001) – based on the sharing of a knowledge of consumer product recognition alone (Mintel estimate that consumers spent £78.7 million on extreme sports goods in 2001). The interest and participation in extreme sports, often dependent on the natural environment for their consumption, is volatile. Correspondingly the need to gauge and provide for the needs of the market, i.e. facilitate the reach for the adrenaline high or the search for mastering technique, means managing is dependent on the marketing dynamic. It is only with the strategic application of marketing that the expectations of the market are enhanced by the image of the product and that these, in turn, are responsive to the changing attractions of those very same images.

Both in the pre-experience imagery formulated through promotion campaigns, through brochures, posters, reports and guides, and in the user's direct experience with staff, management can ensure that product is consumed in a way which ensures that a level of knowledge and insight is attained. Furthermore, it is suggested that it would be possible to offer additional experiences as a composite part of the user's search for knowledge and insight – offering a sense of value addition to the user and offering a sense of product loyalty to the provider (Varley and Crowther: 315). Consequently, the perception by outsiders and visitors alike that nature and adventure experiences are for solitary, independent or introverted characters is a failure to realise that those who participate actually share many of the traits of popular culture in that the people who pursue such activities, whether alone or as group, circulate and share values with others who do the same (Fiske 1989: Chapter 2). So, to summarise, it can be concluded that new management ideas must encapsulate the needs of the nature or adventure pursuit market by ensuring that a narrative is formed between those offering the service and those participating in it. There are a number of tools which can sanction this. A summary of the essential elements of these follows.

Brand as narrative

While at a very different point on the nature experience spectrum, the consumption of nature through nature parks, camping or, as is the focus here, enclave or nature theme holiday resorts, success is still the consequence of narrative formation. Here, however, the narrative often springs from the taxonomy of the brand name. Examples of these are Eurocamp, Eurosites, CenterParcs and Oasis, each with its own form of narrative with the customer.

In the case of CenterParcs (consisting of three sites in England, occupying over 400 acres of woodland) (Tribe *et al.* 2000: 40) and Oasis Holiday Villages (a very large holiday resort set in forest land and acquired by the CenterParcs group in 2002), the narratives are at once both formulaic and yet open to change. Currently, CenterParcs' promotion (May 2002) claims that: 'In the heart of the forest and in harmony with nature' you will 'unwind in a 400 acre forest setting that surrounds you with nature and makes you feel good again.' 'Do as much or as little as you please' provides a clear narrative with its users, i.e. consumption of a self-enclosed holiday destination set in a forest with a provision for a mixture of family-related attractions, activities and services attached which allows the participant's desire to search for knowledge in the lower scales of required insight be as telescopic as required. It would be a misguided soul who went to one of these expecting to participate in extreme sports. Appropriate brand messages, in this example for CenterParcs and Oasis, serve to ensure the recipient – in this case the holiday maker – has created a mental construct of what they will receive, which matches what they perceive to be their needs. This should ensure that no such mismatch will happen.

Interpretation as narrative

When applied to natural resources such as parks and forests, interpretation may be thought of as restrictive or lecturing monologue with no facility for integration. It may be that they are thought of as signs denoting messages of 'no access', 'do not disturb' or 'do not litter'. However, more profoundly defined, interpretation is 'an educational activity that aims to reveal meanings and relationships through the use of original objects, by first hand experience and by illustrative media, rather than simply to communicate factual information' (Tilden 1957, cited in Roberts and Hall 2001: 93). Thus interpretation should have an enabling and full role in the management function of creating a narrative between the provider and the user. As Roberts and Rognasvaldsson put it (cited in Roberts and Hall 2001: 94): 'Interpretative materials must contain communication strategies that create links between visitors and theme, and enable people to establish personally meaningful connection within the interpretative experience.' While this area of management is a particularly complex communication function it does, nonetheless, have a fundamental educational and marketing role and is an integral part in the narrative relationship. For the function of this chapter this is an area in which the reader is encouraged to pursue further reading.

OTHER ISSUES RELEVANT TO NATURE-BASED SPORTS AND LEISURE OPERATIONAL MANAGEMENT

Access, conflict and legislation

'The countryside is one situation where the needs of the tourist and the sports participant are virtually indistinguishable. Both groups are facing problems over access to land' (Weed and Bull 1998: 282). Both the sports lobby and those of the tourism industry are campaigning for improved access but are having little success. This is, in part, due to the fact that the reading each has of the natural environment experience is such that they would not think of campaigning together, even for similar ends. The banning of mountain bikes in national parks in England may be seen as an attack by one group on the rights of another to enjoy the pursuit of insight through extreme sports, while another group will see it was an infringement on their enjoyment of an activity holiday and yet another group may seen it as a spoil (or godsend) to a leisurely or family break or holiday. Thus, it would appear that none wishes to support another for fear of undermining their own position.

An additional factor that will influence both the product entrepreneur or owner in the product that can be offered, and the narrative that needs to be afforded to its preferred target markets in the natural environment, is the legislative requirement of provision. Two very pertinent ones for the UK are the Activity Centres (Young Persons) Act 1995 and the Adventure Activities Licensing Regulations 1996 which followed the Act of 1995 (Grainger-Jones 1999: 206–208).

CONCLUSIONS

'Management is as much about the nature of the leisure experience and the needs of the people in leisure as it is about the process and practice of management' (Tor-kildsen 1999: 549). Managers may perceive leisure as a framework of opportunity for people to be attracted, to choose and to experience satisfactions, which lead to interests and life-enhancing pursuits. 'Satisfying people's needs is also a very powerful way of making good business'. (Torkildsen 1999: 550). Image creation and utility is a vital part of the success of that business. It has been indicated in this text that there is a body of thought that suggests the creation of a narrative between the areas or product and the potential user is extremely important. In fact, it is further advised that only through researching for and activation of this process that the needs of the user will be appropriately met. Moreover, it is opined that the dynamic nature of the many experiences on offer in the natural or rural environment, particularly those offered to the predominantly younger groups involved, or desiring to be involved in, extreme sports, depends on ongoing research and eva-luation of the image being utilised and the ones which may be used in the future. This is an operational must. Beyond this, it should be recognised that initial – often organic – perceptions of a product or service will differ from those of secondary perceptions and that the management of an ongoing narrative between the provider and the user is paramount for market success as well as the achievement of other social or economic goals.

A narrative relationship can be sought both through images carefully selected to reach target markets and interpretative materials utilised as a facilitating tool, enabling linkages and narrative development to be interpreted by the users as a value-added ongoing experience. Staff can also be trained in the purveyance of a sense of comradeship, in the sharing of insights and knowledge (Varley and Crowther 1998)

This chapter has drawn an inclusive but necessarily abstract view of the issues and solutions linked to a managerial operational shortfall suffered by many nature-based sports and leisure providers. It has not attempted to address all the pursuits possible within the natural or rural environment. There are many pursuits and each has its own requirements. However, it is the conjecture of this author that the operational management of each of these would be enhanced by a strategic and inclusive notion of customer needs and the formation of a narrative towards – and in guidance of – these.

Questions:

1. What is the dynamic associated with perception and how can this be used to enhance the experience of these three types of leisure user:

(i) a mountaineer improving his climbing skills on a climbing wall (the man is in his thirties, single and is employed as a financial analyst)

(ii) a family with teenage children cycling alongside designated areas of outstanding beauty

(iii) new participants (aged 17–24) in 'extreme sports' trying snowboarding in a designated area in a ski resort.

2. Consider ways in which staff at an outdoor adventure centre could aid the participant customer's sense of knowledge and skills attainment. How might these vary for different types of customer?

3. What are the forms of narrative that could successfully be applied to holiday resorts in natural environments if they wished to target sports activists for the quieter parts of the holiday season?

References

Buhalis, D. (2000) 'Marketing the competitive destination of the future', *Tourism Management*, 21, 97–116.

Cheron, E. J. and Brent Richie, J. R. (1982) 'Leisure activities and perceived risk', *Journal of Leisure Research*, 2nd quarter, 139–54.

Collins, M. F. and Cooper, I. S. (eds) (1998) *Leisure Management Issues and Applications*. Oxford: Cabi Publishing.

Deng, J., King, B. and Bauer, T. (2002) 'Evaluating natural attractions for tourism', *Annals of Tourism Research*, 29, 2, 422–38.

Department of the Environment (1975) *Sports and Recreation*, Cmnd 6200. London: HMSO.

Echtner, C. M. and Brent Richie, J. R. (1993) 'The measurement of destination image: an empirical assessment', *Journal of Travel Research*, 3, 4, 3–13.

Fiske, J. (1989) *Understanding Popular Culture*. Boston, USA: Unwin Hyman.

Gautner, W. C. and Lime, D. W (eds). (2000) *Trends in Outdoor Recreation, Leisure and Tourism*. Oxford: Cabi Publishing.

Godfrey, K. and Clark, J. (2000) *The Tourism Development Handbook: A Practical Approach to Planning and Marketing*. London: Cassell.

Grainger-Jones, B. (1999) *Managing Leisure*. Oxford: Butterworth-Heinemann.

Font, X. and Tribe, J. (eds) (2000) *Forest Tourism and Recreation – Case Studies in Environmental Management*. Oxford: Cabi Publishing.

Johnson, D. and Clark, A. (2000) 'A review of ecology and camping' in Font, X. and Tribe, J. *Forest Tourism and Recreation – Case Studies in Environmental Management*. Oxford: Cabi Publishing, 93–102.

Kraus, R. G. and Curtis, J. E. (2000) *Creative management in recreation, parks, and leisure services* (6th edn). New York: McGraw-Hill Higher Education.

Leisen, B. (2001) 'Image segmentation: the case of a tourism destination', *Journal of Services Marketing*, 15, 1, 49–66.

Meethan, K. (2001) *Tourism in Global Society – Place, Culture, Consumption*. Basingstoke, UK: Palgrave.

Mintel International Group Limited (2001) *Extreme Sports*, November.

Roberts, L. and Hall, D. (2001) *Rural Tourism and Recreation: Principles to Practice*. Oxford: Cabi Publishing.

Smith, C. and Jenner, P. (1999) 'Adventure travel market in Europe', *Travel and Tourism Analyst in Europe*, 4, 47.

Tomlinson, M. (1987) 'State intervention in voluntary sport: the inner city policy context', *Leisure Studies*, 6, 329–45.

Torkildsen, G. (1999) *Leisure and Recreation Management* (4th edn). London and New York: E & FN Spon.

Tribe, J., Font, X., Griffiths, N., Vickery, R. and Yale, K. (2000) *Environmental Management for Rural Tourism and Recreation*. London: Cassell.

Tyler, D., Guerrier, Y. and Robertson, M. (eds) (1998) *Managing Tourism in Cities – Policy, Process and Practice*. Chichester: John Wiley & Sons.

Varley, P. and Crowther, G. (1998) 'Performance and the service encounter: an exploration of narrative expectations and relationship management in the outdoor leisure market', *Marketing Intelligence and Planning*, 16, 5, 311–7.

Weber, K. (2001) 'Outdoor adventure tourism – a review of research approaches', *Annals of Tourism Research*, 28, 2, 360–77.

Weed, M. and Bull, C. (1998) 'The search for a sport-tourism policy network' in Collins, M. F. and Cooper, I. S. (eds) *Leisure Management Issues and Applications*. Oxford: Cabi Publishing, 282.

CHAPTER 3

Leisure Venue Management

Ian Yeoman, Una McMahon-Beattie and Liz Sharples

This chapter introduces the reader to the concepts of operations management in leisure venues. The chapter overviews:

- a definition of the term 'operations management'
- an examination of the nature of service operations management
- a discussion about the distinction between a 'product' and a 'service'
- an identification of the operations functions within leisure venues with reference to the Schmenner model of management, to include:
  - service features
  - process features
  - customer-oriented features
  - labour-related features
  - management features
- a debate about the current and future challenges to management within the different sectors of leisure venues.

WHAT IS OPERATIONS MANAGEMENT?

Operations management is defined as the management of resources within an organisation with an aim to provide a product or service in the most efficient and effective way possible. Ray Wild adopts a systems approach to the discipline defining operations management in the following way:

> Operations Management is concerned with the design and operation of systems for manufacture, transport, supply, or service. (Wild 1995)

This is a useful if broad definition, as it introduces the concept of a business as an 'operating system' (sometimes called a productive system) and it also recognises that different systems have individual aims and objectives. Any organisation such as a leisure venue exists as an operating system with definite goals and objectives that it strives to achieve. The debate concerning the aim of leisure venues is a controversial one with some sites focused totally towards preservation of leisure in its original state while others are geared towards maximum access by the public as a profit-making venture. No doubt the discussion will continue for many years to come but by adopting the view that all leisure venues are concerned with providing a quality service of some kind, it can be appreciated that the design and operation of that system requires efficient and thoughtful management. The discipline of operations management is relatively new, its roots being traced back to the Industrial Revolution within the UK, with the emergence of the so-called 'factory system'. In 1776 a Scottish economist called Adam Smith established the principles of 'division of labour' which he published in a book called *The Wealth of Nations* (Smith 1776). Smith's work provided the foundations of work simplification methods which exist in an evolved form in many industries today.

There have been two main areas of development in the field of production/operations management. One significant change has been the expansion of the field into the 'service' sector of the economy as it has been acknowledged that many of the tools and techniques used within the manufacturing field can be beneficially employed within many service industries. This move away from a purely manufacturing/production basis has initiated the use of the more general term 'operations management' to describe the discipline.

Another development in operations management in this field has been a 'systems' approach to look at the complex interrelationships both within a business and with its external environment.

What is operations management today?

It is important to remember that operations management is a very practical subject dealing with real people and real issues. Many managers and supervisors, working in organisations around the world, deal with operational issues, such as staff scheduling and visitor management as part of their day-to-day job with very little reference to theories, models or instruction manuals. Having acknowledged this, a manager cannot always rely on intuition and common sense to solve complex business problems, the most successful businesses being those that adopt a strategic approach to the planning, operation and control of their core activities.

Within the context of a leisure venue, the operations function could include:

- the concept development/design of the venue
- the management/control of leisure goers
- the organisation and training of staff
- the management of the plant – buildings, equipment etc.
- the management and monitoring of quality issues
- the matching of supply and demand (capacity management)
- the measurement of leisure user satisfaction
- crisis management
- revenue and pricing management
- risk assessment
- the management of operating systems such as stock control and ordering.

This list is by no means exhaustive, but we can already start to see that operations management is not a peripheral concern; it is a key function at the heart of every organisation. Quite simply, a business relies on efficient management of its operations in order to survive.

NATURE OF OPERATIONS MANAGEMENT

Operations as a business function

Operations management is a vital business function alongside other functions such as human resource management, purchasing, marketing and financial management (Finch and Luebbe 1995).

In some organisations these functions may exist in isolation, but in the majority of businesses there is a 'blurring around the edges' of where one function starts and another begins. Finch and Luebbe (1995) comment on the management of resources as part of this business function:

> The operations function is charged with the management of resources required to produce a product or service, including people, facilities, inventory, processes and systems.

This definition introduces the concept of resources to the discussion identifying that the careful management of resources is key to the production of a product or service. Without the correct utilisation of raw materials, the considered design of the layout and equipment and the efficient organisation of staff, the organisational goals and objectives cannot be met.

Slack *et al.* (1995) classify these resources as either:

- *transformed resources*: the resources that are treated, transformed or converted in some way
- *transforming resources*: the resources that act on the transformed resources.

Transformed resources are usually a mixture of materials, information and customers. There are two types of transforming resources that are common to most operations:

- *facilities*: site, buildings, equipment, plant, technology
- *staff*: who operate, supervise, manage, maintain the operation.

In systems terminology these resources (or 'inputs') are used in varying degrees during a 'transformation process' in order to achieve the desired output.

Organisation as an operating/productive system

Most organisations exist as operating systems of one form or another converting inputs (resources) into outputs which are required by the user/customer, primarily by *adding value*. Finch and Luebbe (1995) show this 'transformation process' with the aid of a simple systems diagram (see Figure 3.1).

Porter (1985) argues that this notion of 'adding value', while utilising a range of resources, allows a company to differentiate itself from its competitors, thus gaining a competitive edge.

Schmenner (1995) develops the idea of offering a quality experience for customers/clients, by highlighting the challenges that managers face when attempting to operate different types of service provision which have differing degrees of staff involvement and customisation. His ideas are explored in more detail later in the chapter. It is also important to recognise that an operating system is rarely static.

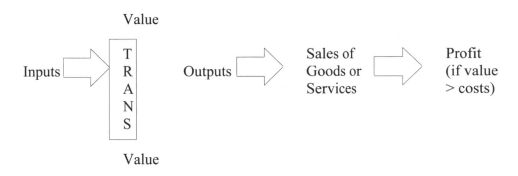

Figure 3.1 *Systems view of value-adding transformation process*

Cook and Russell (1980) describe an operating system as 'the mechanism by which goods and services are created', stressing the dynamism of a system which consists of moving parts working together to create the desired product or service. An organisation can develop standard procedures in an attempt to offer a quality service, but any business is subject at any time to external and internal influences that can affect the output.

Management of operations

The operations function in any organisation is dependent on an individual or a group of people to manage it. Slack *et al.* (1995) provide the following definition:

> Operations Managers are the staff of the organisation who have particular responsibility for managing some or all, of the resources which comprise the Operations function.

In a small business, one person may manage the whole of the operations function, but in a large enterprise, the operations function may be split into several elements managed by a team of specialist people. In many organisations, the operations managers may be called by some other name, e.g. site manager/duty manager, but nevertheless will fulfil all or part of the operations function.

Nature of services

At one time a 'service' was viewed as a supporting feature of a manufacturing industry, but it is now acknowledged that many companies exist as service operations in their own right. Some academics have suggested that it is sometimes easier to define services in a residual way, i.e. by what they are not (Schmenner 1995). We know, for example, that service companies are not involved in the core activities of mining, agriculture, or manufacturing, but they are companies that provide some type of benefit or assistance for their customers.

When the word service is used to describe the primary output of a business, it is important to realise that it refers to an activity that has value in its own right. Services can take many forms, a night out in a high-quality restaurant provides psychological benefits at the end of a busy week; a hospital or clinic provides medical care for its patients. Hotels, restaurants, theatres and cinemas are just some of the industry sectors involved in providing services of one type or another.

Leisure venues are also part of this service sector as they provide a number of benefits for their leisure users including activities, excitement, and interest.

The earliest attempts to differentiate between 'goods' and 'services' used a dichotomous approach which consisted of a continuum with pure goods at one end and pure services at the other (Lashley, Lockwood and Taylor 1997). It is now widely accepted that this simplistic approach is not sufficient as most service organisations offer a 'complex bundle' of both tangible and intangible elements and a service can only be defined as such when the bundle is intangible dominant (Sasser, Olsen and Wyckoff 1978).

To explain this in simpler terms: nearly all goods are accompanied by a 'facilitating service', e.g. the front office in a car sales room; and almost every service is accompanied by a 'facilitating good', e.g. the shampoo and conditioner used at the hairdressers. A leisure venue has primarily an intangible offering and therefore can be classified as a service delivery system. The distinction between goods and services has been explored by many researchers in this field (e.g. Zeithaml, Parasuraman and Berry 1985) with an aim to highlight the special characteristics of the two outputs.

It is generally accepted that the characteristics of a service are:

- perishability
- inseparability of production and consumption
- tangibility/intangibility
- heterogeneity.

Perishability

A service provision cannot be stored for future use or transported easily to another location. If leisure users do not turn up at the point of service delivery then that potential capacity could be lost forever. This obviously has major implications for a leisure venue with regards to income generation, as the service cannot be 'stored up' for peak days; capacity management is a key issue for leisure venue managers, so that both peak and off-peak demands can be accommodated.

Inseparability

Most tangible goods are produced, then transported to a point of distribution where they are sold and subsequently consumed. In many service industries, the services are first sold or requested, then produced and consumed simultaneously through interaction between the customer and the producer (Wright 1995).

Tangibility/intangibility

A service such as an leisure venue may be associated with something physical, but customers who are buying the service are paying for something 'intangible' – a 'feel-good' factor that has no physical attributes. For example, a visitor to the football museum may sense a strong feeling of the past, experience and excitement when taking in the moments of England's World Cup victory of 1966. If this leisure user has an excellent day out, it is probably because of the intangible nature of what has been provided rather than the associated physical feature, although this is obviously 'key' to the experience.

Heterogeneity

This term refers to the potential for variable, non-standard output in the service delivery system. Within the sport and leisure experience, a football fan is purchasing and consuming a unique experience, varying by occasion, time and customers.

Occasion

The experience provided by service providers can be significantly different on different occasions. For example, at a leisure venue the weather may have an important impact on the way users feel about their day out.

Time

The service performed by an individual may vary over time. For example, a tired employee serving ice creams at an leisure venue on a hot August bank holiday may give a less welcoming reception to the user at the end of the day than the one he/she gave at the opening, despite there being quality control procedures in place.

Customers

Interactions between users and providers may vary depending on personality, age and situation. For example, a member of staff may communicate differently with a child, his parents, and his grandparents (Zeithaml, Parasuraman and Berry 1985).

Since it is difficult to control this level of variation, particularly when there is a direct interface between customer and employee, there tends to be a greater risk attached to purchasing services than to purchasing goods.

SERVICE ENCOUNTER

Muhlemann, Oakland and Lockyer (1992) suggest that the presence of customers during the provision of a service can be a 'mixed blessing'. The customers are vital as a resource (an input) to the system, but they also introduce a certain level of unpredictability, in that it is hard to estimate how long they will stay, what their needs will be and how they will behave.

At the centre of this service exchange, is the so-called service encounter (Heskett, Sasser and Hart 1990). This is the point at which the customer comes into contact with the part of the organisation that provides the service. In a leisure venue it may be the reception desk or the member of staff who serves in the gift shop.

Several academics have coined the phrase 'the moment of truth' (Carlzon 1987; Zemke and Schaaf 1989) which is the point in the service encounter when the customer has an opportunity to assess the quality of service provided. This is also sometimes known as 'the critical incident'. The service may meet expectations, exceed expectations or completely fail to meet expectations. Unfortunately, in a service delivery situation, the organisation only gets one chance and poor quality in a particular situation cannot be fixed. It is therefore essential that the number of 'customer defections' is kept to the minimum, as repeat visits and 'word of mouth' advertising are important (Reicheld and Sasser 1990).

This management of the employee/customer interaction presents a challenge to the manager of a service operation that is absent in the field of production/

manufacturing. Service quality is the 'successful matching of the actual level of desired service with the customer's desired level of service' (Lashley, Lockwood and Taylor 1997). It is essential therefore that the operations manager works closely with the marketing/sales team and the human resources manager to ensure that the service provided meets the customer's needs and expectations.

THE SCHMENNER MODEL

In 1995 Roger W. Schmenner proposed a model which provided a way of categorising service delivery systems into four main categories: service factory, service shop, mass service and professional service. The grouping takes account of the degree of labour intensity and the degree of customisation and interaction.

The background to Schmenner's thinking is in the recognition of the primacy of the service encounter and the three aspects of service that surround it: the service task, service standards and the service delivery system itself:

- *service task*: states why the service exists and what the customer values about the service. In clearly stating what the service provides for the customer, it provides clear goals for both management and workforce
- *service standards*: the measurable standards which define what is an efficient service provision for the customer; concerned with the quality of delivery and also the cost effectiveness
- *service delivery system*: a specification of how the service is produced including controls for quality, customer satisfaction and cost.

By attempting to identify the key characteristics of different types of service delivery system with regards to the goals of the organisation, the way in which the service is delivered and the amount of personal contact that is possible between customer and staff, it is possible to identify the challenges that managers face when coordinating a particular service operation. This approach is particularly relevant for leisure venues, many of which have specific and individual organisational goals but share the need to provide a high-quality user experience.

The model suggested by Schmenner takes the form of a matrix and locates organisations dependent on the degree of *labour intensity* of the process on one hand, with the degree of *interaction and customisation* of the service for the consumer on the other (See Figure 3.2).

The majority of leisure venues fit quite easily into the category of 'service factory' in that labour intensity is fairly low and they rarely offer the 'one-to-one' professional service that would be offered by, say, a hospital consultant or a solicitor.

For example, Old Trafford being used for a European football match will be managed by an appropriate number of stewards and venue staff operating the ticket booth, marshalling spectators around the venue and serving refreshments. Personal contact will very much be about directions, safety or catering. Of course, this categorisation is not quite so simple as it first appears. In many leisure venues the user is expected to gather his/her own information from signage, programmes or electronic sources and may have little contact with the venue staff.

Schmenner's matrix therefore provides a simple way of categorising different

		DEGREE OF INTERACTION and CUSTOMISATION	
		LOW	HIGH
DEGREE OF LABOUR INTENSITY	LOW	Service factory e.g. hotels, restaurants, resorts, recreation	Service shop e.g. hospitals, car repair
	HIGH	Mass service e.g. retailing, schools	Professional service e.g. doctors, lawyers

Figure 3.2 *The Schmenner (1995) service process matrix*

types of service organisation, but it is important to recognise that within each quadrant there is the considerable capacity for variation.

Challenges to management

Schmenner (1995) also outlines the challenges that managers face when operating different categories of service provision. A service industry that is highly labour intensive or highly customised, will provide a different set of challenges to one with low involvement (see Figure 3.3).

A leisure venue, as a service factory, has to look carefully at decisions regarding capital investment such as effective use of land, facilities and equipment and an understanding of the technological advances that could be beneficial. The capacity of the venue is relatively inflexible, so it is vital to manage the demand in order to smooth peaks and to promote the off-peak times.

The low degree of interaction and customisation also implies an important marketing challenge for the venue manager. As the user has limited contact with the staff it is essential that in some way the service offered is made to feel 'warm and exciting' (Schmenner 1995) and this will involve detailed consideration of the layout and physical surroundings which can influence atmosphere. Schmenner (1995) also suggests that in a service factory situation the hierarchy tends to be fairly rigid and standard operating procedures can often apply. This is certainly the case in some leisure venues where users are dealt with in a highly organised way with little personal attention.

Operational features of leisure venues

Schmenner (1995) advocates a systematic way of looking at the features involved in a service delivery system as a method of applying process-related tools, with an aim of improving the service operation.

He examines the service operation under five sets of attributes namely:

- service features
- process features
- customer-oriented features
- labour-related features
- management features.

Challenges for managers
(low labour intensity)
- capital decisions
- technological
- managing demand to avoid peaks and to promote off-peaks
- scheduling service delivery

Challenges for managers
(low interaction/ low customisation)
- marketing
- making service warm
- attention to physical surroundings
- managing fairly rigid hierarchy with need for standard operating procedures

Service factory
Low labour intensity/low interaction and customisation

Mass service
High labour intensity/low interaction and customisation

Service shop
Low labour intensity/high interaction and customisation

Professional service
High labour intensity/high interaction and customisation

Challenges for managers
(high interaction/ low customisation)
- fighting cost increases
- maintaining quality
- reacting to consumer intervention in process
- managing advancement of people delivering service
- managing flat hierarchy with loose subordinate relationship
- gaining employee loyalty

Challenges for managers
(high labour intensity)
- hiring
- training
- methods development and control
- employee welfare
- scheduling workforces
- control of far-flung geographical locations
- start-up of new units
- managing growth

Figure 3.3 *Schmenner's view of challenges for service managers*

An examination of these sets of attributes allows us to take a more in-depth look at the operational challenges of managing a leisure venue. Table 3.1 outlines these challenges.

Table 3.1 *Venue process features*

Leisure venues: service factory features	
Service features	**Implications for a leisure venue (LV)**
● A limited mix of services are provided with new services being introduced or performed infrequently ● Price, speed and perceived warmth/excitement are the primary basis of competition	The range of services on offer at a leisure venue are limited and to a large extent are dependent on the 'experience' that is being presented. There is a need to understand the leisure experience and what each customer sees in the experience, i.e. fun, educational, accessibility etc. There is also a need to examine the accessibility of the venue and the role of supporting services such as catering services and retail outlets. An integrated approach is required to create a strategic plan for leisure venues as such users need to be segmented by pricing behaviour
Process features	**Implications for a leisure venue**
● High capital intensity with equipment often being used as an integral part of the system. The use of equipment and the performance of tasks need to be carefully balanced in order to ensure smooth process functioning. A line flow-like layout is often simplest to operate ● The pattern of process is rigid with changes to the nature of the processing sometimes being routine and occasionally radical ● Excess capacity is not easy to manage with additions to capacity requiring injections of capital and labour ● Scheduling can sometimes be difficult, especially at peak times but bottlenecks are usually predictable ● The service provision is dependent on a good flow of materials	The location of the venue is geographically fixed and can rarely be moved (e.g. Old Trafford). This has major implications in terms of capital funding, accessibility and customer demand A high volume throughput is generally required to provide return on investment especially those with high initial capital requirements e.g. The Granada Studio Tours costing £8 m. (Stevens 1997) The use of technology as a means of streamlining the process and providing customer interest requires consideration e.g. football supporters being kept informed of other matches and replaying highlights Seasonality is a key issue within the management of leisure venues The careful utilisation of staff, equipment and other resources is crucial to avoid under-utilisation or the inability to cope. Many football stadiums have multiple use i.e. football matches and pop concert venues

Customer-oriented features	Implications for a leisure venue
• The attractiveness of the physical surroundings is crucial to the marketing of the service	The design and layout of new attractions and the upkeep of existing ones is crucial to the marketing of the site
• The interaction between staff/customer is brief and therefore the opportunity for customising the service is minimal	The 'service encounter' is key to ensuring that the customer is made to feel that his/her wishes are being met
• Demand of peaks/non-peaks can sometimes be managed through pricing policy	The use of innovative pricing policies such as the introduction of season tickets and targeting specific sectors of the community needs further development
• Formal quality control systems can be adopted	The introduction of formal methods to assess the quality of the leisure exercise e.g. SERQUAL (Parasuraman *et al.* 1986)

Labour-related features	Implications for a leisure venue
• Pay at a 'service factory' is typically hourly	The development of comprehensive training programmes is essential if the quality of the leisure experience is to be guaranteed and job satisfaction achieved
• Skills levels of staff are not necessarily high	
• Additional skills/seniority can lead to advancement	

Management features	Implications for a leisure venue
• Effective line supervision and trouble shooting are critical	There is a need to establish clear lines of communication between managers, supervisors and staff members to ensure that the goals of that particular attraction are being met
• The means of control can sometimes be profit centred but this is not always the case	There is a need to establish clear goals and objectives for each venue in order to avoid conflicting messages to users and staff e.g. profit, education, pleasure etc.

Managers of leisure venues need a practical tool to assist in the design, maintenance and improvement of the leisure experience. Schmenner's process features matrix can be used as a decision-making tool to move around the matrix, for example, from service factory to professional service. Once the service style is changed, management can address the features element of the matrix. What needs changing? What needs improving? What needs substituting? These questions imposed through the matrix provide the operations manager with a powerful decision-support tool.

CONCLUSIONS

The careful management of the operational aspects of a leisure venue are crucial if the venue is to meet its organisational objectives successfully. A holistic, integrated approach is required, using the expertise of concept developers, retailers and resource managers in the definition of clearly designed plans and policies that are understood by both staff and management. The adoption of specific operational tools can be a key part of this process.

Operations management in leisure venues needs a new recipe built around the characteristics of service and the ingredients that make up the operations management dimensions within Schmenner's matrix need discussion and development. Therefore subsequent chapters develop some of these ideas through an in-depth examination of the operational aspects of a leisure venue from initial concept stage to design, process and quality experience.

Questions

1. Select four leisure and sport experiences and classify them as a service factory, service shop, mass service or professional service. Justify your classification.

2. Building on question 1, what are the challenges for management in the following scenarios:

   low labour intensity

   high labour intensity

   low interaction/low customisation

   high interaction/high customisation.

3. Design a service comparison matrix for those sport and leisure experiences using:

   service features

   process features

   customer-oriented features

   labour-related features

   management features.

References

Carlzon, J. (1987) *Moments of Truth*. New York: Ballinger.

Cook, T. M., and Russell, R. A. (1980) *Contemporary Operations Management*. London: Prentice Hall.

Finch, B. and Luebbe, R. (1995) *Operations Management – Competing in a Changing Environment*. Boston: Dryden Press.

Heskett, J. L., Sasser, W. E. and Hart, C. W. L. (1990) *Service Breakthrough*. New York: Free Press.

Lashley, C., Lockwood, A. and Taylor, S. (1997) *Aligning Operating Strategies for*

Service Quality in Hospitality Operations. Paper presented at Sixth CHME Hospitality Research Conference.

Muhlemann, A., Oakland, J. and Lockyer, K. (1992) *Production and Operations Management.* London: Pitman.

Parasuraman, A., Zeithaml, V. A. and Berry, L. L. (1986) *SERVQUAL: A Multiple-item Scale for Measuring Visitor Implications for Future Research.* Marketing Science Institute, Working Paper Report No. 86–108, August.

Porter, M. E. (1985) *Competitive Advantage.* New York: Free Press.

Reicheld, F. and Sasser, W. E. (1990) 'Zero defections: quality comes to services, *Harvard Business Review*, September/October, 105–11.

Sasser, W. E. Olsen, R. P. and Wyckoff, D. D. (1978) *Management of Service Operations, Text, Cases and Readings.* Boston: Allyn & Bacon.

Schmenner, R. W. (1995) *Service Operations Management.* London: Prentice Hall.

Schorten, F. (1995) 'Improving Visitor Care in Leisure Venues', *Tourism Management*, 16, 4.

Slack, N., and Johnson, R. Chamber, S. (1995) *Operations Management*, London: Pitman.

Smith, A. (1776) *An Inquiry into the Nature and Causes of the Wealth of Nations.* London: Strahan and Cadell.

Stevens, T. (1997) 'Heritage as design: a practitioner's perspective' in Herbert, D. (ed.) *Heritage, Tourism and Society.* London: Pinter Press.

Wild, R. (1995) *Essentials of Production and Operations Management.* London: Cassell.

Wright, L. K. (1995) 'Avoiding services myopia' in Glynn, W. and Barnes, J. (eds) *Understanding Services Management.* Chichester: John Wiley & Sons.

Zeithaml, V. A. Parasuraman, A. and Berry, L. L. (1985) 'Problems and strategies in services marketing', *Journal of Marketing*, 49, 33–46.

Zemke, R. and Schaaf, D. (1989) *The Service Edge: 101 Companies that Profit from Customer Care.* New York: New American Library.

PART 2

DESIGN OF SPORT AND LEISURE FACILITIES

CHAPTER 4

Facilities Planning

Bryn Parry

INTRODUCTION

In recent years, there has been a reassessment of sport and leisure venues. Stadia are now seen as income generators, instead of cost centres and many leisure facilities can be found within mixed-use developments.

Despite this, the sport and leisure sector is not perceived as having dramatically improved facility performance. As in other sectors, there is a mismatch between the performance indicators preferred by the facilities management (FM) industry and those looked for by the core businesses (Hinks 1999). Hence, this chapter will not revisit the research findings of previous operational FM studies (Then 1999: 465) but ask you to rethink how you will make the best use of your sport and leisure facilities.

Sport and leisure-related books tend to range from the generic (Grainger-Jones 1999) to the specialist (Inglis 1996) and to focus on the purely operational. We will be taking more of a systems approach (Forrester 1995; Johns and Jones 1999a and b) that emphasises performance throughout the asset's lifecycle (Langston 1999; Parry 1999).

Seiler (1984) offers an observation that demonstrates why facilities planning is central to effective sport and leisure operations management (SLOM):

> Influencing behaviour is almost all of what management is about, and buildings influence behaviour.

Doggart (2000), who was researching non-sports workplaces, is more strident in how FM can support core productivity:

> A 1 per cent gain in productivity is typically worth more than saving the entire fuel bill, while a 5–10 per cent loss in productivity can wipe out a company's profit and send it to the wall.

HISTORICAL PERSPECTIVE

There is a tendency to focus on the present day as somehow unique and to denigrate the achievements of preceding decades and eras. This gives a false perspective that does not help in the search for new insights. In fact, Hero of Alexander had developed coin-operated vending machines, self-opening doors and lifts before the time of Christ. The ancient world also boasted perhaps the best designed sports facility ever built – the Colosseum in Rome.

The Colosseum delivered a level of integration and efficiency that modern stadia have failed to match. The 45,000 spectators moved quickly to their allotted seats, via 76 numbered stairwells, which enabled the entire stadium to be evacuated in minutes, and would find shade under a retractable roof – something not really attempted again until the Skydome, in Ontario, Canada, in 1989. While the plans for the second Wembley Stadium struggled with how to convert the stadium merely from football to athletics in months (BBC 2002a), the Colosseum was able to be flooded and host mock sea battles. The network of rooms and corridors beneath the stadium floor enabled efficient operations of the various elements that made up the games held there, animals, men, and scenery being raised up to the arena floor via lifts. After the games ended the building was used as a fortress, bullring, hospital and source of material for use in other buildings, yet it has still lasted longer than any of our modern venues is likely to.

COMPARING FACILITIES

In order to compare different facilities, in different locations, different sectors, possibly different historical eras, mere description is not good enough. Duffy (1990) and Brand (1994: 13) recommend that you do this by breaking the facilities down into layers and imagine them moving against each other. Since this should be done against a total lifecycle, you end up with the model (Parry 1996; Parry and Norman 1996) in Figure 4.1.

Before you continue any further, use the description of the Colosseum to work through the different layers. Then, think of a modern sport or leisure venue – such as the Wembley Stadium project (BBC 2002b) or the Twickenham project (Hewett 2000) – and explore which 'layers' you think create synergies and which you think cause conflict.

The key to the overall success of the lifecycle of each layer is the conception phase. The design and operation of the Colosseum was exceptionally well thought out and it underpinned the venue's success. The concept of the recent Wembley Stadium project, meanwhile, was poorly developed and so even the best architect's plans (the definition) were unlikely to make it work well. As late as 2002, the plans for athletics relied on a prefabricated platform and an expensive temporary warm-up track – despite aspirations of providing a venue capable of hosting world-class athletics events (Sport England, 2002).

The differing lengths of each lifecycle tend to catch the unwary out. After all we build a venue whose structure is capable of lasting over 50 years but only really focus on the first 5–10 years of its life when financing it; we know that changes in fashion (market/cultural environment) and operation will require us to adapt the initial space plan and skin (at least once) during these five decades – but do not build this into the overall design, even less rarely is it built into the budgets.

This may not be an approach with which you are familiar but it will enable us to navigate an increasingly complex sport and leisure sector. When Manchester United paid a record transfer fee for Rio Ferdinand in 2002, a large proportion of that fee was expected to be recouped through the sale of replica shirts (stuff), through the stadium shop (space plan), via the internet (support services – organisation) and from partner firms (staff – external). Old Trafford's mix of stadium,

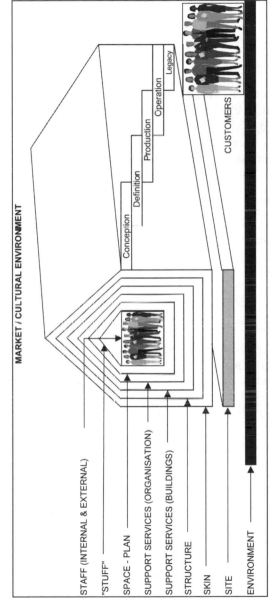

FACILITIES PLANNING IS THE MANAGEMENT OF CHANGE

FACILITIES PLANNING INTEGRATES OVERLAPPING LIFE-CYCLES

STAFF - Internal: e.g. grounds staff or serving staff
STAFF - External: e.g. contract caterers
"STUFF" : e.g. goalposts and benches, seats and tables, etc.
SPACE - PLAN: e.g. pitch markings, seat sizes, room layouts, etc.
SUPPORT SERVICES (Organisation): e.g. booking system
SUPPORT SERVICES (Building): e.g. Electricity, Water & Gas
STRUCTURE: e.g. Shell; Framed or Cantilevered
SKIN: e.g. Brick or Glass; Loadbearing or Facade
SITE: e.g. Parkland or Roadside; Flat or Sloping
ENVIRONMENT: e.g. Rural or Urban; Prosperous or Deprived
MARKET / CULTURAL ENVIRONMENT: e.g. commercial / cultural environment within which the sport or leisure complex operates

Figure 4.1 *SLOM model*

shop, restaurant, conference centre, hotel, museum etc., is by no means untypical of the type of venue that you will be asked to consider or work in.

To demonstrate the importance of facilities planning and how the techniques of SLOM can help you to outperform your competitors, we will focus on the space plan layer – looking at its linkages with other layers and following it through the lifecycle.

SLOM TECHNIQUES

The key operations management techniques of SLOM are explained in detail, in leading texts such as Hope and Muhlemann (1997: 293) and Slack *et al.* (2001). It is not intended to repeat such evaluations here, but to focus on their application. So, if you have any concerns over the central tools and techniques of operations management, you should refer back to these sources before continuing. You will find the following particularly useful:

- process flow charts/diagrams
- Pareto analysis
- Ishikawa diagrams ('cause-effect' or 'fishbone' diagrams)
- statistical process control charts (SPCC)
- network analysis.

Concept

Becker and Steele (1995) address the different approaches that you can take to a multistage lifecycle, through the metaphors of the 'relay race' and 'rugby'. In the former, each team does its work and then passes it on to the next team. In the latter, everyone is involved from the inception and acts as an integrated whole, although individuals' input varies throughout the 'game'. We will be advocating the holistic approach of the latter.

Lipton (1994) believes that, 'the costliest mistakes occur on the drawing board – not on the construction site' and points out that, 'Rectifying mistakes can cost 15 per cent of total budgets'.

The (1966) Downey Report recommended that up to 15% of the total development cost should be incurred by project definition. The (1971) Rayner Report recommended 15–25% of total costs, yet British projects averaged only 8% (Morris 1994: 259).

Hence, while your project may appear to be progressing quickly, trying to fasttrack the conception stage will affect your quality and cost you more throughout the full lifecycle of the facility (Figure 4.2), Drivers Jonas (2002:23).

Famously, Walt Disney got one of his artists to produce a conceptual drawing of his planned Disneyland theme park (Dunlop 1996: 28) and, although the park built differs markedly from the detail of that drawing, it is remarkably true to the original concept. Indeed Disney Corporation makes a point of calling its designers 'imagineers' (Marling 1997), thus putting the emphasis on developing concepts that engineers have to put into effect – rather than the conservative buildings, with

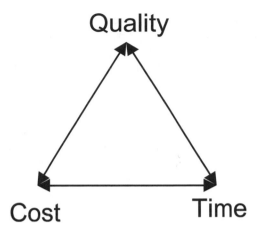

Figure 4.2 *Dynamic tension in projects (adapted from Slack et al. 2001: 523)*

a thin veneer of concept or theming, that typify many sport and leisure-related buildings.

So, how do we use SLOM to improve our *space plan*, throughout its full life-cycle? Taking a standard input–transformation–output approach (Slack *et al.* 2001: 10), you ensure that you really think through what you are trying to deliver and how this will change over the life of the venue; feeding back any new information and insights into a revolving planning process (see Figure 4.3).

Importantly, you will emphasise how the specific layer (we're looking at the space plan) interacts with each of the other layers and feed this back to amend your

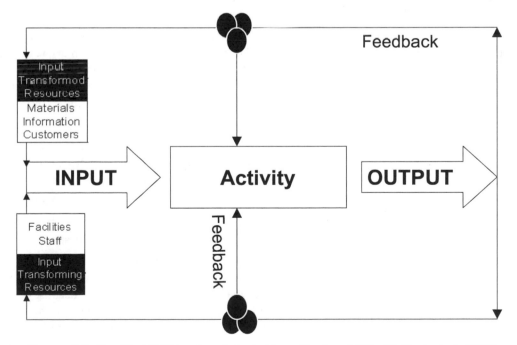

Figure 4.3 *Simplified SLOM system (adapted from Harrison 1996: 48; Slack et al. 2001)*

original inputs and preferred outcomes. For instance, the space plan of a multiuse sports hall will generate a need for adequate storage space for equipment (stuff); while the height that various types of player (customers) can raise a basketball or shuttlecock (stuff) will dictate the lowest point of anything suspended from the hall's roof (structure/skin).

Critically evaluating such decisions, you would make full use of a strong blend of SLOM techniques (Slack *et al.* 2001). There are some excellent technical books (Adler 1999) to help you, but these should only ever be a starting point from which to *begin* considering the optimum range of alternative solutions. At the conception stage, you should not restrict your thinking – that will come later – or you will never come up with the more innovative or elegant solutions that will give you a competitive edge.

Definition

It is when we come to defining the specifications of the space plan that we begin to see the benefit of spending time on conception paying off.

Statutory regulations define the required number and sizings of fire escapes, but research (Hinks 1993) has indicated that a rough-textured wall covering (skin) will cause your customers to avoid getting close to the wall – reducing the throughput of the escape corridor by some 7%. We also know that in an emergency customers tend not to follow escape route signs but seem to prefer retracing their route into the building. This helps to explain the recommendation of one fire enquiry, observing that:

> Some architects tend to rely on regulations and available guides, rather than on their own understanding of the principles, to design against fire risk.' (Toft and Reynolds 1997: 18)

Hence, our building's performance during a disaster will be improved if our definition of the layout of the space plan is based on a conception that has already taken into account how sighted, blind, deaf, disabled etc. customers are likely to interact with the layout. In a fire we are all blind and deaf. Using the bottom six inches of a smoke-filled room you'll soon find out how well the designer considered the needs of a crawling toddler.

Brand (1994) is a convincing advocate of keeping definitions fluid and enabling buildings to 'learn' during their lifecycles, reminding us that we tend to prefer low-tech buildings that can be cheaply adapted to highly specified high-tech buildings that quickly fall from fashion and require expensive retro-fitting. So, don't define the building too tightly around the current space plan, accept that this will change markedly over the years and ensure that, for example:

- there are enough plug sockets to enable flexibility in the use of space
- your cabling can carry power, voice and data and has spare capacity
- that, in a project with a lengthy design and build phase (e.g. Wembley Stadium) you don't find that you are using outmoded equipment, because it took five years to get the project off the ground and several years to build but specified and defined every last detail at the very start (Burke 1993).

Barrett (1998) addresses this last point, while discussing a phased method of briefing, developed by Stichting Bouwresearch (Building Research Board) in Rotterdam:

> The basic principle of the system is that the brief contains, prior to each new planning phase, only the minimum amount of information necessary to be able to direct the next phase ... A series of phases allows clients and users to become familiar with problems and to become aware of new possibilities ... users and clients can introduce their requirements at strategic moments, rather than having to consider all their options from the outset.

Where technical books can be very helpful at this stage is with the proportion of different types of space, such as useable, non-useable, primary, circulation, etc. For this, you will find the approaches outlined in Brand (1994) and Duffy (1997) extremely helpful with the finer detail, but remember that many sport and leisure venues benefit from an atmosphere and an intangible sense of majesty that transcends minimum space allocations (Eley and Marmot 1995; Geraint and Sheard 2000).

Production

This involves actually building the venue and fitting it out, which can take anything from several days to many decades.

Effective use of such SLOM techniques as Gantt and Network diagrams (Slack *et al.* 2001: 535–46) should get the optimum blend of cost–time–quality during this phase. Once again, how we manage the space plan impacts the rest of the project. If our venue includes a hotel component, we might choose to pre-build room pods in a covered factory, achieving economies of scale because the contractor (staff – external) is using a standard pod size (space plan) and is not restricted by the weather on the building site (environment) or the speed of other contractors. The space plan of such pods enables them to be shipped on trucks, already fitted out (skin), containing furniture (stuff), plumbed in and cabled up (support services – buildings), requiring only that they be dropped into place and final connections made.

Egan (1998) confirmed that the construction industry had failed to make the same efficiency gains that other sectors had and contractors seemed almost opposed to seeing other firms involved in a project as their partners. Yet:

> Where partnering is used over a series of construction projects 30% savings are common ... a 50% reduction in cost and an 80% reduction in time are possible in some cases.

Such potential efficiencies would allow sport and leisure venues far more flexibility in terms of when various components of a facility are built; while the cost savings might enable a more generous space plan or higher quality fittings (skin, stuff) to be delivered.

For larger scale facilities, the production phase can take many years and require you to be building while you are trying to deliver a high-quality service elsewhere on the site. Sometimes, you need to shut down completely, as the City of Manchester Stadium did when it opened for a very successful Commonwealth Games and then closed while it was rebuilt as the new home of Manchester City Football Club.

Venues such as the Gleneagles Hotel that have planned for lengthy development periods have been able to gradually develop their available land (site, space plan) as necessary. Those with more constrained sites and/or shorter planning horizons, such as Twickenham Rugby Stadium, Lords Cricket Ground or a third division football club, tend to be forced into constraining production into what can be fitted into the off season or periods of surplus funding. Some venues find that they must move their site during each production phase, Arsenal's many relocations being a prime example.

The huge complexity and cost of modern sport and leisure venues (Drivers Jonas 2002) is making the production of a virtual reality model (Slack *et al.* 2001: 534), so that all stakeholders can provide detailed input and comments before building commences, more and more cost effective. An early form of this application, at the Winter Olympics in Lillehammer, is credited with revealing that – as designed – the tower housing the ski-jump judges would not enable them to see the competitors actually landing (*Sunday Times*, 13 February 1994).

Operation

Although conception of your space plan has the greatest impact on facility performance and definition tends to impose the most constraints, the key to a successful facility is its operation. Although it is widely recognised that it costs more to run a building than it does to build it (Brand 1994: 13), sport and leisure is just one of the sectors where false economies tend to be made during the early stages of the lifecycle. These benefit the financiers, designers, managers and builders, who are often long gone by the time your facility goes into operation – leaving the operators and customers to pay for these shortcomings over the coming decades.

You should already be ahead of the game due to the approaches previously discussed; we'll now look at how you can stretch your advantage even further.

To show one of the ways in which we can utilise SLOM techniques critically to evaluate the operation phase while we are still planning, let's consider flow charts and flow diagrams, which you'll find explained in detail in Slack *et al.* (2001: 130–4) and (Hope and Muhlemann 1997: 230–3). While these excellent descriptions may be useful for operations management specialists, they do not tend to communicate the benefit that even an SLOM generalist can gain. For this we need to superimpose the flow chart on our space plan (see Figure 4.4).

We can now start to see how the various users of our reception area interact with the space plan and where amendments might improve overall efficiency and effectiveness.

Underhill (2000: 46) found that we tend to enter a facility at some speed and take a while to slow down. So, left unchanged, the travelling activity at the entrance would take our customers past all the information signs and leave them stranded in the heart of the area. Rethinking the approach to the entrance and providing the right blend of space plan, skin and stuff, we can ensure that customers are encouraged into the space, welcomed, and slowed down. We might use the colour contrast of the harder-wearing floor covering at the high-traffic entrance with the more aesthetic floor covering in the rest of the space, to signal the extent of the 'transition zone'. Knowing which way customers are most likely instinctively to turn helps us to position seats, brochure racks and other stuff more appropriately.

Figure 4.4 highlights that the brochures in the corner are likely to cause con-

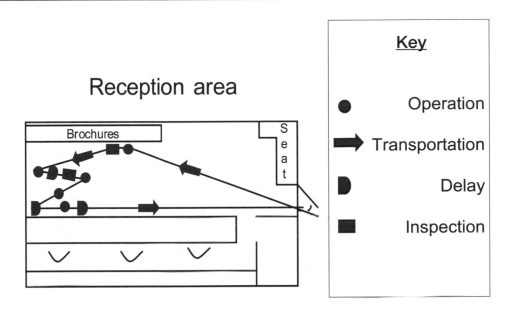

Figure 4.4 *Flow diagram (adapted from Hope and Muhlemann 1997: 232; (key) Slack et al. 2001)*

gestion; thinking of a supermarket layout and how its shelves are stacked can help us here. Sometimes supermarkets position items in easily reached places, for speed, and sometimes they put high demand items out of the way, to make us browse through other items – use the flow diagram to plan the optimum layout for your brochures. Underhill (2000: 17–8) points out that we will look at racks of items for quite a while but the second we fear someone brushing behind us, our instinctive defensive reflex is to abandon even an important task and leave. So the space plan must leave enough distance for the brochure rack to be viewed comfortably and for typical customers (with associated bags, etc.) to reach down to the lowest shelf; leaving enough circulation space behind this to avoid what Underhill called the 'butt-brush effect'.

There is such an expanding literature on dealing with queues (Matthews 2000) that we will merely observe that if theme park designers can persuade their customers to queue over an hour for a ride that lasts just a few minutes, it must be possible for you to ensure that queues of a few minutes are managed effectively.

Figure 4.4 has thrown up several issues for feeding back into our conception and definition, but not all the solutions will come through our redesign of the space plan itself. For instance, if we position information terminals (stuff, support services – organisation) throughout the venue, we are likely to reduce pressure on reception and to prompt impulse purchases; we might even extend this idea and offer an extranet, so that many activities traditionally undertaken at reception are relocated to our customers' homes and offices.

Underhill (2000: 17) advocated distributing baskets throughout a store; because, while only 8% of customers picked up a shopping basket, of those that did some 75% bought something. The sport and leisure facility equivalent is ensuring that the information terminals (stuff, support services – organisation) distributed throughout the complex can be used for marketing and purchasing, possibly, through personal credit cards or via smart cards that double as membership cards.

We can now expand on the critical evaluation of our space plan to see where our space plan might heighten risks. The Portman Group (1998) estimated that some 20% of all pub violence is linked to use of the pool table, so we should be using a blend of SLOM techniques to highlight similar hotspots in our venue and ensuring that these don't detract from its operation. This might involve a blend of alert staff, effective CCTV (support services – buildings) and investing in beer glasses (stuff) that break into beads rather than lethal shards. Kivlehan (2000) demonstrates how the space plan of pubs can raise customer enjoyment and reduce risks. While it is hoped that your facility will not require ultra-violet lights in its toilets (to deter intravenous drug use), it is your duty to ensure that the planning of your facilities has considered all the critical issues and developed the optimum response.

It is widely recognised (Duffy 1997: 108; Thomson 1994; Underhill 2000) that our use of the space plan will vary from month to month, day to day and hour to hour, so we need to utilise the full range of SLOM techniques to ensure that we optimise this. Since you cannot store an unsold slot on a tennis court, we should ensure that our computer system (stuff, support services – organisation) uses the yield management techniques (Ingold et al., 2000) that airlines and hotels have pioneered to full advantage. We can learn from easyJet that a well-planned internet-based booking system (support services – organisation) reduces the space plan required for staff involved in order taking and storage space needed for documentation, as well as cutting the cost of each transaction processed.

If we think of the office space required at our facility, there will be times when staff need to focus on individual work and times when they need to cooperate on a group task. On some days of the week, some of your staff can work more effectively at their homes or the facilities of your stakeholders, at other times staff might benefit from a 'club' area where the social ties that bind your organisation can be renewed and reinforced (Duffy 1997: 60–7).

In the customer areas, the facility (or specific parts of it) is likely to range from periods of heavy congestion to periods of light use, throughout the day – often within minutes. The more that this variety in take-up of the space plan has been planned for, the more effective the overall facility will be; but this might require us to explore new approaches – one venue has a bar that can be moved on a cushion of air, as needed.

You may not need a permanent wall (structure) to delineate different spaces; the same effect might be achieved through folding dividers and different coloured carpets (skin) or various layouts of furniture and plants (stuff). Your food area might employ screens (stuff) or a variety of levels (structure, space plan) to ensure that it is as welcoming when ten people are dining there, as it is when 100 are seated.

Divestment/legacy

If the operation phase is the 'poor cousin' of the planning process, the divestment/ legacy phase seems to be the relative that no one talks about. Yet it can be critical to both the initial funding and to the longevity of your organisation.

You'll have seen a 'final value' considered in your finance texts, while looking at project finance, but when did you last see it addressed in your general management or sport and leisure management texts? Once again, you have an opportunity, through effective planning, to exploit an advantage over your competitors. If our facilities have an increased final value, we can then increase our initial budgets, release value (e.g. through sale and leaseback) and ensure that should we need to relocate (site) that we can sell this facility quickly and profitably.

The leisure industry often adopts a funding model pioneered by the influential developments of Regent's Park (Summerson 1991: 177–9) and Birkenhead Park (Thornton n.d.), whereby the site chosen enables a space plan that includes more land than needed for the core project – plots of now desirable land, on the perimeter of the parks, were sold for development and the profits used to pay for the park's site and production. Dunlop (1996: 45–6) demonstrates how Disney used this approach, extremely successfully, at Walt DisneyWorld; yet many venues still pass on this opportunity.

An approach to value analysis that is particularly useful for evaluating divestment options is shown in Figure 4.5.

Using this during our planning, we can determine the optimum approach. Hence, one venue might adopt a very unique and high-profile bespoke design to support the strategic objectives of its host organisation while another might choose a design precisely because it can be easily sold, franchised, outsourced or leased to the widest range of potential occupiers. As always, this critical decision needs to be fed back into each stage of our planning.

Legal and environmental considerations are increasingly important (Slack *et al.*, 2001: 713–9) and many an organisation has fallen foul of an overlooked covenant or the discovery of ground pollution. Do not let the little space that we have time to devote to it here belie the impact that it could have on your organisation.

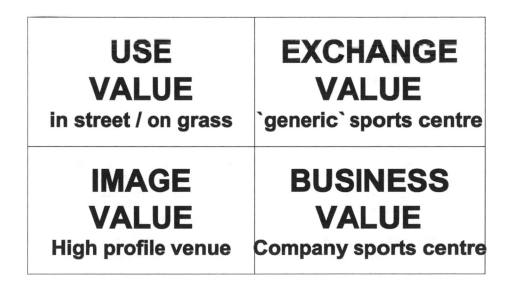

Figure 4.5 *Value analysis and divestment options (amended from Parry and Norman 1996: 421–2)*

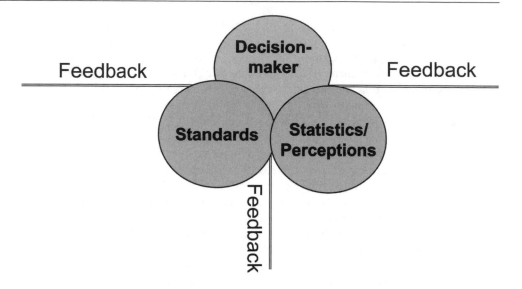

Figure 4.6 *SLOM system (detail) (adapted from Harrison 1996: 48; Slack et al. 2001)*

Feedback interpretation

Having explored how the use of the models, in Figures 4.1 and 4.3, help to underpin effective facilities planning, we are now able to look at one element of the input-transaction-model in more detail (Figure 4.6). The feedback that we have seen is so critical to effective planning will, inevitably, be filtered and so we must be aware of how this filtering process affects our decisions.

The feedback will result from the interplay (and inherent tensions) between the key decision makers, the corporate and governmental standards influencing the sport and leisure sector and the collected statistics and perceptions.

Woodhead (2000) subdivides the various decision makers into:

- decision approvers
- decision takers
- decision shapers
- decision influencers.

He notes that, if the end project is seen as 'capital expenditure', the emphasis will be on cost reduction. If the project is viewed as 'capital investment', the emphasis will be on optimising returns. We have already noted how this affects the divestment phase, but we must also recognise its effect on any feedback on the facility as being 'successful' or not.

A common scenario, to be guarded against, is where 'the main goal of the shapers during the pre-project stage is to win budgetary sanctioning from the decision approvers' (Woodhead 2000). Facilities planned under these conditions are constrained by unnecessary burdens. The remedy lies not in your planning skills but in influencing the perceptions of the decision makers; or trying to raise a more appropriate set of standards up the corporate agenda.

Your planning may, also, need to guard against the mixed messages that different sources (and styles of monitoring) feed back to you. Abdou and Lorsch (1994) concluded that, in many case studies, occupants (customers, staff) were very dissatisfied with their environment, even though measurements seemed to indicate that recommended standards were being met.

RECOMMENDATIONS

This chapter has focused on the broader issues of facilities planning, in order to highlight areas of opportunity for you to exploit. Other chapters in this book and texts such as Slack *et al.* (2001) will provide advice on the detail of day-to-day *SLOM* that supports the approaches outlined. Since such resources tend to focus on the definition, production and operation phases, you are likely to gain a competitive advantage from emphasising the conception and divestment phases as part of an holistic planning process.

So far, neither the sport and leisure sector nor the construction industry has demonstrated itself to be a hotbed of innovation, so look for your innovations in the facilities management and service sector literature.

Questions

1. Who should be involved in facilities planning?
2. What *SLOM* techniques should I favour?
3. How does thinking in 'layers' help me?

References

Abdou, O. A. and Lorsch, H. G. (1994) 'The impact of the building indoor environment on occupant productivity: part 3: effects of indoor air quality' in Clements-Croome, D. (ed.) (2000) *Creating the Productive Workplace*. London: E & FN Spon, 11.

Adler, D. (ed.) (1999) *Metric Handbook: Planning and Design Data* (2nd edn). Oxford: Architectural Press.

BBC (2002a) 'Wembley in pictures'. Available at http://news.bbc.co.uk/sport1/hi/photo_galleries/football/1719386.stm (accessed October 2003).

BBC (2002b) 'Search for a new Wembley'. Available at http://news.bbc.co.uk/sport1/hi/in_depth/2001/search_for_a_new_wembley/default.stm (accessed October 2003).

Barrett, P. (ed.) (1998) *Facilities Management: Towards Best Practice*. Oxford: Blackwell Science, 91.

Becker, F. and Steele, F. (1995) Workplace by Design: Mapping the High-Performance Workspace, San Francisco: Jossey-Bass, 70.

Brand, S. (1994) *How Buildings Learn*. London: Viking.

Burke, R. (1993) *Project Management: Planning and Control*. Chichester: John Wiley & Sons, 51.

Doggart, J. (2000) 'Future design – guidelines and tools' in Clements-Croome, D. (ed.) *Creating the Productive Workplace*. London: E & FN Spon, 304.

Drivers Jonas (2002) *Stadia Development Handbook*. London: Drivers Jonas. Available at: http://www.driversjonas.com (accessed September 2003).

Duffy, F. (1990) 'Measuring building performance', *Facilities*, May, 17.

Duffy, F. (1997) *The New Office*. London: Conran.

Dunlop, B. (1996) *Building a Dream*. New York: Henry N. Abrams.

Egan, J. (1998) *Rethinking Construction*. London: DTI/HMSO.

Eley, J. and Marmot, A. F. (1995) *Understanding Offices*, London: Penguin, 34.

Forrester, J. (1995) 'The beginnings of systems dynamics', *McKinsey Quarterly*, 4, 4–16. Available at http://mckinseyquarterly.com

Geraint, J. and Sheard, R. (2000) *Stadia: A Design and Development Guide*, 3rd edn. Oxford: Architectural Press.

Grainger-Jones, B. (1999) *Managing Leisure*. Oxford: Butterworth-Heinemann.

Harrison, M. (1996) *Principles of Operations Management*. Harlow: FT/Prentice Hall.

Hewett, C. (2000) 'Twickenham plans £80m roof garden', *The Independent*, 11 September, 23.

Hinks, J. (1993) 'Modelling and managing escape from fires' in Barrett, P. (ed.) *Facilities Management: Research Directions*. London: RICS Books, 90–103.

Hinks, J. (1999) *FM in the Future – A Speculation on Key Performance Issues*. Proceedings of the International conference on Futures in Property and FM: Creating the Platform for Innovation. University College, London.

Hope, C. and Muhlemann, A. (1997) *Service Operations Management*. Hemel Hempstead: Prentice Hall.

Inglis, S. (1996) *Football Grounds of Britain* (3rd edn). London: CollinsWillow.

Ingold, A., McMahon-Beattie, U. and Yeoman, I. (eds) (2000) *Yield Management* (2nd edn). London: Continuum.

Johns, N. and Jones, P. (1999a) 'Systems: mind over matter', *Hospitality Review*, 1, 3.

Johns, N. and Jones, P. (1999b) 'Systems and management: the principles of performance', *Hospitality Review*, 1, 4.

Kivlehan, N. P. (2000) 'Safe houses', *Caterer and Hotelkeeper*, 23 March, 34–5.

Langston, J. (1999) Keynote speech at the Eighth Annual CHME Hospitality Research Conference. Guildford, University of Surrey.

Lipton, S. (1994) 'Builder's charter', *Financial Times*, 26 August, 21.

Marling, K. A. (ed.) (1997) *Designing Disney's Theme Parks*. Paris: Flammarion/CCA.

Matthews, R. (2000) 'Ladies in waiting', *New Scientist*, July, 40.

Morris, P. W. G. (1994) *The Management of Projects*. London: Thomas Telford.

Parry, B. (1996) *Who Manages Your Facilities in Marketspace*? Paper presented at the CHME Research Conference. Nottingham Trent University.

Parry, B. and Norman, P. (1996) *Facility Performance in the European Hospitality Industry*. Paper presented at the Euro FM Conference, Barcelona.

Parry, B. (1999) *Understanding the Language of Recession – Interpreting Business Cycles*. Paper presented at the CHME Research Conference. University of Surrey.

Portman Group (1998) 'Keeping the peace – updated'. Available at http://www.portman-group.org.uk/uploaded-files/documents/35_49_keeping the peace.pdf (accessed September 2002).

Seiler, J. A. (1984) 'Architecture at work', *Harvard Business Review*, September–October, 120.

Slack, N., Chambers, S. and Johnston, R. (2001) *Operations Management*, (3rd edn). Harlow: FT/Prentice Hall.

Sport England (2002) 'Wembley Stadium'. Available at http://www.sport england.com/whatwedo/wembley/key_features.htm (accessed October 2003).

Summerson, J. (1991) *Georgian London*. London: Penguin.

Then, D. S. (1999) 'An integrated resource management view of facilities management', *Facilities*, 17, 12/13, 462–9.

Thomson, T. (1994) *Innovations in Use – Making Facilities Work for the Organisation*. Paper presented at the Meeting the Challenges of Change Conference BIFM, London.

Thornton, C. E. (n.d.) *The People's Garden: A History of Birkenhead Park*. Birkenhead: Williamson Art Gallery & Museum.

Toft, B. and Reynolds, S. (1997) *Learning From Disaster: A Management Approach*. (2nd edn). Leicester: Perpetuity Press, 18.

Underhill, P. (2000) *Why We Buy: The Science of Shopping*. London: Orion Business.

Woodhead, R. M. (2000) 'Investigation of the early stages of project formulation', *Facilities*, 18, 13/14, 524–34.

CHAPTER 5

Managing Human Resources in Sport and Leisure

Tracy Taylor

INTRODUCTION

Human resource management (HRM) policies and practices are key components in the implementation and reinforcement of an organisation's strategy. Therefore, effective human resource planning and management are vital functions for any sport and leisure organisation. This chapter will discuss how such organisations can strategically and effectively use HRM to position and develop their human resources.

Over the past few decades the sport and leisure industries have experienced considerable organisational change in focus, operations and structure. Historically, most sport and leisure organisations were publicly funded and government run (e.g. local council swimming pools) or community based and reliant on substantial volunteer involvement (e.g. community football clubs). Many sport and leisure organisations have retained these forms of structure and delivery, however, a significant proportion do not fit these traditional modes and have adopted more commercially driven operations to deliver their sport and leisure services. Today, government-funded and operated sport and leisure organisations competitively tender for the right to provide services; privately owned and operated sport and leisure businesses are increasing in number and scope; globally oriented organisations have emerged from locally initiated enterprises; volunteer administrators have been replaced by salaried professionals; and many sports have transformed their core business from amateur to professional.

All that notwithstanding there is still a heavy reliance on volunteer contributions, especially at grassroots levels (e.g. canteen duty for a netball club). Therefore, sport and leisure organisations must recognise and plan for both paid and volunteer workers in managing their human resources (Chelladurai 1999). It is important here to define what is meant by volunteering, that is, what it is and what it is not. Volunteering is unpaid, freely chosen, done through an organisation or agency and done for the benefit of others or the environment as well as oneself. As defined by Sheard (1995) volunteering is not low- or semi-paid work, compulsory or coerced (i.e. by government or law orders), informal assistance for friends or family, or self-help, religious or leisure activities (although it may be done in one's leisure time). While the specifics of what volunteering involves varies between countries and cultures, Davis Smith (1999) suggests that there is a shared understanding of the basic elements of volunteering across the globe.

The structural and organisational changes noted earlier require a different and more strategically focused way of thinking about and executing human resource management than previous administrative-type approaches that were suitable for older style sport and leisure organisations. This chapter will take into account the changing organisational environment and the development and implementation of appropriate and relevant HR strategies for recruitment, placement, training and development of human resources within the leisure and sport industries.

HUMAN RESOURCE MANAGEMENT PROCESS

The process of HRM encompasses activities associated with managing people within an organisation. The key components of the HRM process can be represented via a six-phase model (See Figure 5.1).

The phases can be described as follows:

1. *Human resource planning* is linking organisational strategy to people management policies and processes.

2. *Recruitment and selection* are engaged in to provide the organisation with the human resources necessary to achieve their goals.

3. *Orientation and socialisation* involve assisting new recruits to adapt to the organisation, its processes, procedures and culture.

4. *Training and development* are undertaken to improve performance, develop new skills and enhance workforce flexibility.

5. *Performance management* is the evaluation of an employee/volunteer's performance.

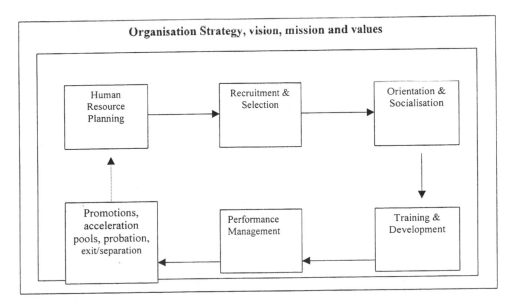

Figure 5.1 *The human resources management model*

6. *Promotions, acceleration pools, probation, exit/separation* are all aspects of the reward system.

Human resource planning and strategy

An organisation's strategy, mission and values should be the reference point for the development of HR strategy, policies and programmes. This means that HR functions are integrated with other areas within the organisation such as marketing, sales, finance, information and knowledge management. This, in turn, allows the identification of people and HR issues that need to be managed to achieve the desired strategic outcomes. The use of an integrated approach is evidenced in the following box.

Advance Sport and Fitness Centre (ASFC) has been operating for ten years as a community-focused business. ASFC has a good reputation for quality customer service and has consistently won awards for friendly and dedicated staff. Initially, hiring practices were informal and the owners made new appointments on an ad hoc basis. When the business expanded and opened two new centres they decided to develop a formal HR policy for recruiting staff for these facilities. An audit of existing employees found that they were mainly local residents who were passionate about sport, had formal training in fitness or health and demonstrated strong communication and interpersonal skills. This information was used to document the core competencies and capabilities required by ASFC staff. Initially used for recruitment purposes, the competency framework was then expanded to encompass different levels of attainment and formed the basis for performance appraisal and promotion criteria. Staff qualifications and expertise were highlighted in subsequent promotional campaigns and built into the marketing strategy.

One of the main drivers of HR planning is ensuring that the organisation has the right people in the right jobs at the right time. This means that it is necessary to identity the critical success factors that will facilitate not only organisational effectiveness, but more importantly, sustainable success. These factors are then built into recruitment strategies, performance appraisal systems, reward and promotion structures, training and development programmes, and separation/exit processes. In organisations where volunteers are integral to the mission, strategic plan and business operations, volunteer management is most often handled as part of an organisation's overall human resource management system (Kuric and Koll 2000). However, some sport and leisure organisations with a significant volunteer base may have separate HR strategies for their volunteers and specific policies that address the interaction of volunteers and the organisation.

The challenges and opportunities associated with an increasingly diverse population are a major consideration for sport and leisure organisations. Diversity management refers to 'the systematic and planned commitment by organisations to recruit, retain, reward, and promote a heterogeneous mix of employees' (Ivancevich and Gilbert 2000: 75). The benefits of effective diversity management are embedded in the premise that an inclusive and non-threatening work environment can maximise human resource potential, lower turnover rates and create a tangible competitive advantage. Using strategic human resource practices and processes to gain competitive advantage via diversity management is one way of capitalising on this challenge.

SportsCap (USA), which aims to ensure employment opportunities in sport are available to women, people of colour and people with disabilities (Lapchick and Matthews 2001), and TopLink (UK), which provides opportunities for young people to develop skills in sport officiating, coaching and leadership and administration and management while exploring the long-term value of sport and diversity (Commonwealth Institute 2001), are examples of best practice in diversity management.

Recruitment and selection

Recruitment is the definition of job requirements and the activities associated with attracting candidates to fill these positions. *Selection* is the set of activities associated with choosing the right candidate for the position. The recruitment and selection process involves defining human resources needs, attracting appropriate candidates, choosing appropriate selection methods and selecting the right candidates.

Recruitment is one part of a systemic and integrated approach to employee planning and development. Recruiting good-quality employees should be approached with the primary aim of aligning the strategic objectives of an organisation with the capability of its people to achieve these strategic objectives. Selecting the right people is arguably one of the most important components of HRM. The costs associated with poor recruitment and selection practices are enormous. These costs can include decreased productivity, increased interpersonal tensions and conflicts and increased staff turnover (Bratton and Gold 1999). Once the right people are in the organisation it is then crucial to develop, motivate and retain them – aspects that will be discussed later in this chapter.

Job analysis

Before effective recruitment can occur for a specific position, an analysis of what skills, knowledge, experience and capabilities the organisation requires for the job is undertaken. This *job needs analysis* specifies the requirements needed to perform certain organisational tasks. The competencies required for successful performance in the designated role are identified by an analysis of the organisation's vision/strategy as well as the specific requirements of the target role. These may be precise and technical, such as related to the capabilities of swimming pool attendants (life-saving certificate and bronze medallion) or capability focused, such as for senior management positions (problem-solving abilities, proven leadership skills). Voluntary positions are usually described in more general terms and often related to interests or attitudes (e.g. museum tour host – an interest in cultural pursuits, commitment to public education) as the aim is to appeal to a wide range of people.

There are a variety of techniques used in job analysis, with most approaches using two or more methods to collect all the information needed for a valid analysis. Some of the more common techniques are:

- direct observation of employees
- task diaries completed by employees
- critical incident identification

Position	Venue and events manager
Education	Degree or equivalent qualification in sport or leisure management
	Some knowledge of financial and risk management preferred
Experience	Minimum of 5 years including at least 2 years in a position with financial accountability
Essential performance dimensions	Oral and written communication, planning and organising, attention to detail, negotiation and conflict resolution, staff coordination, volunteer management, teamwork, tolerance for stress

Figure 5.2 *Job specification*

- work samples
- individual or group interviews
- focus groups or seminars
- questionnaire surveys.

The analysis provides the necessary information to produce a *job description* and *job specifications* that identify the knowledge, skills and abilities required to perform the job. The job description focuses on what the job involves. That is, what tasks are to be performed. The job description also includes reporting relationships, working conditions, authorities and responsibilities of that position. The job specification focuses on the type of person required to fill the job. That is, the skills, knowledge, personal qualities, qualifications and experience required to competently perform the job. An example of how a job specification might be written is shown in Figure 5.2.

Organisational goals and strategic frameworks are also used to inventory tasks required of volunteers. Volunteer tasks should be formulated in accordance with key priority areas e.g. membership recruitment, fund raising, event organisation. The next step is to prepare a task brief to identify all opportunities for volunteer involvement. This is then used to determine the number and skill requirements of volunteers. The benefit of this process is that there is a clear task outline, complete with any specific expectations of the task, to give to a prospective volunteer.

Sourcing candidates

Once the specifications have been articulated the next step is to recruit candidates for the position. The recruitment of personnel can be achieved from a range of sourcing options. There are several matters that should be considered before choosing the recruitment medium; these are represented in Table 5.1.

In sourcing volunteers, it has been proven that personal contact with potential volunteers through friends, family or individuals already involved in an organisation is the most common way that volunteers first became involved in sport and leisure voluntary work (Cuskelly 1996). While the most successful strategy for recruiting volunteers is the direct one-to-one approach, other methods of recruiting should not be dismissed, e.g. local radio/papers, noticeboards, newsletters, email etc. A well-thought-out combination of all methods that are relevant to the membership should be used. When recruiting volunteers it is important to emphasise the benefits for the volunteer rather than the needs of the organisation.

Table 5.1 *Sourcing considerations*

Source	Suitability for recruitment
Internal candidates	There is sufficient talent in the organisation Familiarity with the organisation is desired Less expensive option
Newspaper/professional and trade publications	Skills needed are not present in current employees Wide canvassing of candidates is required Need to achieve diversity in employee base
Internet lists, databases and e-recruiting	Can target specific internet group memberships Easy to get worldwide coverage Low-cost option Can be used to complement other methods
Outsourcing to employment agencies, search firms etc.	High levels of confidentiality and discretion are needed May fill temporary needs Short supply of talent
Graduate recruitment from educational institutions	Useful when substantial experience is not essential For entry level positions or traineeships

To this end it is useful to think about the main reasons people volunteer. Sheard (1995: 121) summarised these reasons (in order of importance) as:

- altruism
- having a personal interest in the activity
- responding to a direct request
- religious concerns
- filling in spare time
- gaining work experience.

Approaching potential volunteers with a clear picture of the intended role (position description) and with an explanation as to how the position or task will affect the overall performance of the organisation yields the most productive results (Sport and Recreation Victoria 2001). All volunteers like to feel that they will be doing something that is valuable to the effective operation of the organisation.

Selection techniques

Choosing the right techniques to select the best candidate for a position is a crucial part of any good selection process. To be effective, techniques such as written applications, interviews, psychological assessments etc. must have *validity*. Validity means that there must be a proven relationship between the technique used and its predictive ability in relation to effective performance of the job. Selection techniques should also be *reliable*, that is, they should measure the same thing each time they are used (see Table 5.2).

Interviews are a popular technique used in candidate selection. However, as the structure and quality of interviews can vary enormously, the interview is often not

Table 5.2 *Selection techniques*

Technique	Overall reliability and validity rating
Application form	Low
Behaviour-based interviews	Moderate – high
Traditional interviews	Low
Ability tests	Moderate – high
Assessment centres	High
Modern personality tests	Moderate

reliable or valid as a selection device (Cook 1998). Research consistently demonstrates that interview techniques alone, even when well structured and performed, only have 50–60% or lower chance of selecting the best person for a job or choosing a person who subsequently executes all aspects of a job to the standards sought.

To be effective an interview must be well structured and gather relevant information for decision making about the applicant's abilities to meet the job requirements. This involves collecting all relevant information and allows for direct comparision between candidates (Stone 1998). One method of interviewing that has particularly good reliability and validity is *behavioural-based interviews* (McGraw 2001). These interviews are structured to find out about the applicant's behaviour and do not focus on feelings, opinions, inferences or generalisations.

Clusters of behaviours, motivations and knowledge related to job success or failure are determined and questions are structured to elicit past experiences which demonstrate these. The underlying principle of this type of interview is that past behaviour predicts future behaviour. It provides a more objective set of facts to make employment decisions than other interviewing methods. Traditional interview questions typically ask general questions such as: 'Tell me about the strengths you would bring to the position.'

The process of behavioural interviewing is much more probing. Questions are designed to determine if the candidate possesses the skills that have been identified as necessary for the job in the job analysis stage. Questions are asked to elicit specific and detailed situations that relate to the question, what the applicant did specifically and the positive result or outcome. This is framed within a three-step process (see Figure 5.3):

1. situation
2. action
3. result/outcome.

Some typical behaviourally based questions are:

- Can you provide a specific example of a time when you used good judgment and logic in solving a problem?
- Describe a time on any job that you held in which you were faced with problems or stresses that tested your coping skills. How did you deal with these problems?

Question
Tell me about a time when you went out of your way to satisfy a customer
Situation/task
I was working in the marketing department of a professional sport organisation. We received a letter from a customer who was unhappy because the print quality of a fan memorabilia book she had purchased was sub-standard and wanted a refund. I handled the complaint
Action
I immediately requested a refund cheque from our accounting department. I also called our printer, who investigated and identified one run of the book which had been improperly printed. I obtained a properly printed copy of the book and sent it with a refund cheque and a personal letter, thanking the customer for pointing out the problem and apologising for the inconvenience
Result
The customer called to thank me for the response and ordered several more copies of the book for friends

---

Figure 5.3 *Sample behaviour-based interview questions*

- Provide an example of when you used your written communication skills in order to get an important point across.
- Outline an instance when you had to go above and beyond the call of duty in order to get a job done.

Assessment centres, by way of contrast, have high reliability and validity. Candidates participate in a wide range of simulation exercises while trained observers note and then assess behaviours. Assessment centres engage applicants in a range of selection techniques that may include:

- targeted behavioural interviews
- in-basket exercises
- peer interactions
- coaching interactions
- analysis exercises
- motivational fit inventory
- 360° instruments.

One drawback of assessment centres is the high cost of processing applicants through all the elements. As a result the centres are usually reserved for selection of senior managers and executive positions.

After the selection process has taken place a letter of offer should be sent to the preferred candidate, stating salary, conditions and associated employment details.

In the case of volunteers an information form that collects all relevant details should be completed. If the applicant meets the organisation's needs for the volunteer position then they should be contacted, notified of their acceptance and scheduled to attend a volunteer briefing or induction session.

Deciding which form of selection is best for your organisation will depend on selection policies, resources, the level of the position and the number of applications anticipated. In situations where there are a large number of applicants it may be appropriate to screen them prior to the formal application process. Screening is commonly done via telephone contact and appropriately suitable applicants are identified and invited to apply for the position.

Selection decisions should be carefully planned. The cost of a poor appointment decision is not only job underperformance, but also the negative impacts it can have on other staff and difficulties that may arise in termination. That said, a good choice can contribute to productivity and profitability and can also positively affect morale. An appropriate selection can strengthen an organisation's strategic capability by providing a pool of well-skilled and committed people from which future managers and leaders can emerge. These outcomes are equally relevant to paid and volunteer selection decisions.

Orientation and socialisation

Orientation and socialisation programmes and initiatives are designed to provide new recruits with the information they will require to feel comfortable and perform effectively within the organisation. The information provided in orientation activities should cover: general information about how the organisation runs on a daily basis; coverage of the organisation's mission, values, objectives and the new recruit's role in helping to achieve these; and precise details on organisational procedures, work conditions and employee benefits.

Orientations for volunteers will include similar information, albeit with a different focus; the detail required will depend on the volunteer's role and expected time with the organisation. It is also common for volunteers to receive induction kits. These typically include position descriptions, explanations of roles of other people within the organisation, rights and responsibilities/codes of conduct, grievance and conflict resolution policies, confidentiality arrangements and relevant technical information. An example of a rights and responsibilities policy is outlined in the following sections.

Volunteer rights
Volunteers:

- have the right to know as much about the organisation as possible
- have the right to receive training for the job
- have the right to receive sound guidance and direction
- have the right to participate across all facets of the organisation
- have the right to be heard and consulted
- have the right to work in a safe and supportive environment
- have the right to be reimbursed for approved out-of-pocket expenses
- have the right to have their contributions recognised and respected.

Volunteer responsibilities
Volunteers will be expected to:

- make realistic commitments in terms of both time and areas of involvement. The organisation will expect these commitments to be filled
- keep all details of recipients, other volunteers and members confidential and

private unless prior consent has been obtained from the individual and/or the volunteer manager

- value and support all recipients, volunteers and others in a way that is non-judgemental and non-discriminatory.

In summary, orientations should reduce the anxiety felt by newcomers when entering the organisation for the first time, clearly set out organisational expectations and answer any questions that might arise.

Training and development

A sport and leisure organisation's business strategy should be the determinant of all training and development initiatives. Typically, *training* will be based around technical, job-related skills and abilities. Programmes may comprise on-the-job or off-the-job training. *Development* is concerned with more generic interpersonal or managerial/leadership skill development.

On-the-job training typically encompasses four major initiatives. These include: *training positions* where individuals in the organisation are given specific responsibilities to perform that are outside their normal position and/or are allocated a senior person to work with and learn from; *planned work activities* where work assignments are given to develop skills, experience and contacts. These are typically used to give the trainee insights into how the organisation functions at a functional and cultural level; *job rotation*, which involves moving an individual between jobs to broaden experience and exposure in a variety of the organisation's operational areas; and *coaching* (or *mentoring*), which is an increasingly popular method used by managers to train and develop subordinates. Coaching involves setting performance objectives and holding constant discussions about these dimensions.

Off-the-job training removes the person involved in the training from the workplace and can be individual or group based. Organisations using off-the-job training should ensure that it is tied back to strategic goals (see the following box). It is also essential that mechanisms are put in place for the transfer of learning back to the workplace. Examples of programme types are on- or off-site classroom sessions, technical or professional courses that provide accreditation or upgrade skills. There is an increasing use of online training packages and programs that target the development of specific skill areas in a self-paced approach.

A community sport complex wanted to implement their business strategy through the enhancement of a service and accountability-driven culture. The employee development strategies for accomplishing this included increasing the customer service skills of all employees through off-the-job training. Due to the strong relationship between employee satisfaction and customer satisfaction, they decided to train their managers in how better to interact with employees and brought in external consultants to run a series of programmes. In addition, both managers and employees were trained in performance appraisal skills and assessed customer service skills. This ensured that the corporate strategic intents were effectively and constructively cascaded throughout the whole organisation.

Opportunities for volunteers to enhance existing technical and interpersonal skills, develop new skills and develop confidence in the role should be provided.

Gaps between the level of skill and knowledge required for the role and the abilities of the volunteer are identified and access to the appropriate level of support and/or training provided.

Career development initiatives aim to improve an employee's abilities and positioning for future opportunities and challenges in the organisation. Career planning and development is a cyclical and dynamic process. There are four core steps in creating a comprehensive development model (Watt, Bennett and Taylor 2001). These are:

1 *Identifying the competencies required for successful performance*
This begins with the analysis of the organisation's strategic plan and allied documents to determine behaviours necessary to achieve the organisation's goals. A range of methods is used to gather the information including:

- visioning
- critical incident identification
- interviews with targeted high-performing staff
- experts in each domain
- union involvement (where required).

Capabilities are not meant to be static and should be routinely reviewed, particularly if there is a change in business strategy or organisational structure. The identification and development of internal talent aims to foster a higher level of continuity of management. Having some pre-identified management capabilities and personnel assessed against these criteria can assist an organisation to meet both long-term and immediate managerial needs.

2 *Diagnosis of both the strengths and developmental needs of individual employees; systematic evaluation of skills against the success profile*
Following the establishment of the profile of capabilities, identified employees are then assessed against these capabilities. Assessment techniques can involve the use of performance appraisal data, multi-rater feedback instruments, personality and psychological testing, analysis of work samples, simulations/role plays. The choice of assessment will vary between organisations but it is essential that assessments are validated and transparent. After their assessment, participants are informed of their results including strengths and development opportunities. Development programmes that target the participant's areas for improvement are then devised. These can include in-house training, formal education, job assignments, project-based work, coaching and the like. The process should aim to foster continuous learning for all participants (Metz 1998).

The next step is to provide feedback to the individual, as development can begin only when there is a personal acceptance of development needs and a commitment to improvement.

3 *Development plan to prioritise developmental needs and pursuit of targeted activities to address these needs*
The development activities can include such tasks as workshops, special assignments, rotational assignments, mentoring relationships and other learning resources.

Figure 5.4 *Development cycle (© Development Dimensions International Inc, MMI. All rights reserved)*

4 *Process to measure and monitor the success of the development plan at individual and organisational levels*

Follow-up measurement ensures that an individual is getting periodic feedback on his or her progress. This creates accountability and motivation to show an improvement in performance results. The full implementation of the development cycle for a set of development needs could take as little as six months or as long as two years (see Figure 5.4).

The rewards or subsequent career opportunities and progress toward developmental goals should be clearly documented. Career development requires a significant investment not only in making resources available to individual employees but also in allowing time off the job to gain new development experiences or attend programmes targeted to enhance specific skills. These can include: team-building programmes, leadership sessions, time and stress management classes and even college and university courses.

Performance management

Evaluating the performance of individuals is an important component of effective management of human resources. The information gained from performance appraisals can be used to make a range of HRM decisions such as monetary rewards, promotions, transfers, termination and training and development needs (Bratton and Gold 1999).

Performance management can be quite broad and may include informal feedback, job re-design, rewards etc. Whereas the more narrowly defined *performance appraisal* deals with goal setting, evaluation and development. Performance appraisal methods include:

- *rating systems*, which involve ranking job performance on a standardised set of criteria
- *behaviour reviews*, which can be highly specified using detailed job scales or may involve observational techniques
- *instruments* such as 360° feedback surveys and psychological tests
- *assessment centres*, which employ a combination of techniques to determine current and potential performance
- *management by objectives*, which is results-focused assessment based on set objectives
- *self-assessment*, which is used in conjunction with other methods.

These techniques are most commonly used by supervisors to assess the employees who are reporting directly to them. Some can also be used in peer, customer and self-report situations. For example, the use of 360° feedback instruments involves self-assessment along with ratings from selected other individuals who work with the individual.

Volunteers should also be given regular performance feedback. A volunteer should be evaluated after he or she has been with the programme after a fixed time period (e.g. six months) and thereafter yearly. It is a good idea to develop a volunteer performance evaluation form from the position description. This can be used to rate the volunteer's performance in each area. Then proceed to the volunteer's individual goals, and determine jointly with the volunteer whether those goals were met completely and discuss any areas of concern. Finally, the performance appraisal should include a plan of action to address any training needed or desired.

If problems arise between the scheduled feedback sessions, a non-scheduled appraisal can be arranged. The purpose of the appraisal is to give feedback and offer input to help the volunteer improve on the job. Appraisal should not be a punitive process and volunteers should be encouraged to participate by offering an opportunity for self-evaluation, asking what areas they would like to improve or what they could learn more about.

Succession management and acceleration pools

Another key HRM dimension is succession management. Succession management ensures that within an organisation the 'right' leaders are available at the 'right' time. It is, 'any effort designed to ensure the continued effective performance of an organisation, division, department or work group by making provision for the development and replacement of key people over time' (Rothwell 1994: 5). Succession management practises focus on identifying and developing leadership capabilities, not specific job requirements. Succession management efforts are most likely to be successful if they are embedded in management operations and involve HR and other managers throughout the organisation and are concerned with implications for other career planning practices such as formal education training or secondments.

There are several critical elements that have been identified as keys to effective succession management. Eastman (1995) has suggested that effective succession management:

- receives visible support from the CEO and top management
- is owned by line management and supported by staff
- is simple and tailored to unique organisational needs
- is flexible and linked with the strategic business plan
- evolves from a thorough human resources review process
- is based on well-developed competencies and objective of candidates
- incorporates employee input
- is part of the broader management development effort
- includes plans for development job assignments
- is integrated with other human resource systems
- emphasises accountability and follow-up.

The establishment of an acceleration pool for nominated participants is a feature of some succession management and career development schemes. In an acceleration pool system, high-potential candidates are identified and given training, coaching and a wide range of professional experience within the organisation (Byham, Smith and Paese 2000). This identification and development of a pool of high-potential employees marks another distinct change from earlier succession planning approaches. Large organisations might have more than one acceleration pool that could include a pool for supervisory level participants, one at middle management and one feeding into senior levels. Each pool, which might encompass one or two organisational levels, would prepare people for the next major step in the organisation. The size of a pool will depend on the number of positions it is expected to supply and the selection ratio that the organisation would like to have in filling target positions. The number of acceleration pools reflects how an organisation is structured, as well as how it thinks about its high-potential and talented employees. Organisations may incorporate formal mentoring or coaching programmes for employees into acceleration pools.

Exit/separation

Termination of an employee's or volunteer's services may be required when a breach of the employment contract has occurred, if volunteer responsibilities have been abrogated, if performance is not satisfactory or if the position becomes redundant. The legal requirements associated with such terminations should be clearly understood by all parties. These conditions will vary depending on the type of employment contract, union stipulations and relevant legislation. These conditions will usually require a notice of termination, although in some cases summary termination (i.e. without notice) can be implemented, usually when there has been a serious misconduct or breach of contract.

Exit strategies can include the provision of references, assistance with job seeking or outplacements and retraining opportunities. Exit interviews are valuable to determine the person's reasons for leaving and identify workplace improvements. Many departures from an organisation are understandable and are for reasons of family, age, ill health, relocation etc. Reasons for departures should not be assumed, but rather need to be fully understood particularly if a reoccurrence of a negative situation is to be avoided. This process will act as a debriefing for the departing employee/volunteer.

SUMMARY

Human resource management comprises activities surrounding the attraction, selection, development and maintenance of an effective workforce, including volunteers, that are required to achieve the organisation's strategic goals. Effective human resource management polices and practices will facilitate the recruitment, development and maintenance of a productive, committed, motivated and fulfilled workforce.

In this chapter human resource management was presented as an integrated management strategy applicable to both paid employees and volunteers. A six-phase human resource process was presented: human resource planning, recruitment and selection, orientation and socialisation, training and development, performance management and promotions–exit strategies. The planning phase identifies the way forward for the organisation, the competencies required for each position, whether new staff or volunteers should be recruited, how new recruits can be effectively oriented into the organisation, the training and development needs for existing personnel, transparent reward and recognition structures and appropriate separation pathways.

Effective human resource management systems will create a solid motivational fit between the individual and the organisation. This means that the abilities of the staff member or volunteer will match with the capabilities required by the organisation. However, just as important is a good match between the culture and value system of the individual and the sport or leisure enterprise. The motivation and culture fit is essential for the satisfaction and well-being of all parties involved.

Human resource management strategies in sport and leisure organisations need to be based on client-centred, market-driven approaches. Human resource plans should be structured so that they support and facilitate the organisation to run effectively and meet its goals and objectives. Effective and strategic HRM is just as important for a small community leisure organisation whose main aim is to provide a diverse range of low-cost and inclusive programmes to marginalised groups in its environs, as it is to a large sport marketing agency whose vision is to increase its market share. HRM should be structured to understand and respond to these demands and contribute to an organisation's success.

Sport and leisure organisations need to attend to changes in financial, structural and social environments. Increased internationalisation, global price competitiveness, demographic shifts such as an aging workforce, changing employment legislation, advances in technology, e-business, the e-workforce and e-customers will impact human resource policies and practices of the future. Changes to the sport and leisure sector will impact stakeholder demands, consumer relationships and organisational strategy. Aspects of organisational performance and human resource management are inextricably linked. Consequently, human resource practices will need to respond accordingly to facilitate and develop employees and volunteers that meet the organisation's new directions.

Changes to the nature and scope of volunteering may also impact the human resource management procedures, practices and responsibilities of sport and leisure organisations. Recent industrial cases, imprecise boundaries on minimum wage requirements, welfare to work schemes, changes in labour force participation (particularly for women), shifts in social attitudes and behaviours, public liability issues and mandatory volunteer contracts all contribute to an obscuring of the volunteer–employment distinction. This new environment has produced varying reactions from traditional volunteers. The human resource management challenge will be to build a sound participatory base for volunteering that rewards, recognises and empowers individuals while meeting the needs and requirements of the sport and leisure organisation.

Continued societal and organisational change, the increased emphasis on moving sport and leisure operations firmly into the business world and demands for improving productivity are significant challenges for the future. These changes require HR systems that are flexible and offer cost-effective and equitable responses. Global approaches and techniques that are identified as 'best practice' will be increasingly adopted as each organisation searches for ways not only to cope with change but opportunities to develop a competitive advantage. This may mean anything from simple changes to recruitment and selection procedures to the decentralisation of HR functions to line managers to outsourcing all key aspects of HRM. It will depend on what system best meets the organisation's objectives. Innovative and creative approaches to the management of human resources are an integrative part of effective change management.

Sport and leisure organisations that develop responsive and effective and strategic human resource management approaches to these challenges can obtain long-term sustainable competitive advantage.

Questions

1. Discuss the similarities and differences involved in recruiting and selecting volunteers and paid employees for sport/leisure organisations.

2. Write a job description and specification for the position of manager of a council-controlled leisure centre.

3. Identify the types of training and development programme that staff might undertake if they worked as a sport development officer for football.

References and further reading

Bratton, J. and Gold, J. (1999) *Human Resource Management* (2nd edn). Basingstoke: Palgrave.

Byham, W., Smith, G. and Paese, M. (2001) *Grow Your Own Leaders*. Pittsburgh: Development Dimensions International.

Chelladurai, P. (1999) *Human Resource Management in Sport and Recreation*. Champaign, IL: Human Kinetics.

Commonwealth Institute (2001) 'Diversity matters'. Available at http://www.commonwealth.org.uk (accessed November 2001).

Cook, M. (1998) *Personnel Selection: Adding Value Through People*. Chichester: John Wiley and Sons.

Cuskelly, G. (1996) *The Organisational Commitment of Volunteer Administrators in Sport*. Canberra: ASC Publications.

Davis Smith, J. (1999) *Volunteering and Social Development*. Bonn: UNV.

Eastman, L. (1995) *Succession Planning: An Annotated Bibliography and Summary of Commonly Reported Organisational Practices*. Greensboro, NC: Center for Creative Leadership.

Ivancevich, J. and Gilbert, J. (2000) 'Diversity management time for a new approach', *Public Personnel Management*, 29, 1, 75–92.

Kuric, C. and Koll, S. (2000) *A Roadmap to Managing Volunteer Systems: From Grassroots to National*. Washington DC: National Health Council, Inc.

Lapchick, R. and Matthews, K. (2001) *Racial and Gender Report Card*. Boston: Northeastern University.

McGraw, P. (2001) 'Attracting, selecting and recruiting people' in CCH *Australian Master Human Resources Guide*. Sydney: CCH Australia Ltd, 119–212.

Metz, E. (1998) 'Designing succession system for new competitive realities', *Human Resource Planning*, 21, 3, 31–7.

Rothwell, W. (1994) *Effective Succession Planning: Ensuring Leadership Continuity and Building Talent from Within*. New York: Amacom.

Sheard, J. (1995) 'From lady bountiful to active citizen' in Davis Smith, J. Rochester, C. and Hedley R. (eds) *An Introduction to the Voluntary Sector*. London: Routledge.

Sport and Recreation Victoria (2001) *Volunteer Management Plan Workbook*. Melbourne: The Office of Sport and Recreation.

Stone, R. (1998) *Human Resource Management*, (3rd edn). Brisbane: John Wiley & Sons.

Tyson, S. (1997) *Human Resource Strategy*. London: Pitman.

Watt, B., Bennett, A. and Taylor, T. (2001) 'Career planning and development' in CCH *Australian Master Human Resources Guide*. Sydney: CCH Australia Ltd, 345–60.

CHAPTER 6

Managing Queues

Gerald Barlow

Today many people are basically surprised to discover a queue, especially when the service itself is not overloaded. The customer feels that they are wasting their time or even that they are being robbed of their much valued time. One of the main problems facing service organisations is that their customers generally arrive at random intervals. Even when they have a specific start point as in sporting events or appointments, and when the time arrives to perform the service, it is not specific or exact. Therefore, both arrival and service times can become overloaded causing a queue to form. However, on another day, with the same number of staff and the same hourly flow of customers the operation can have periods where the staff are idle, because the time taken to service the customers was shorter or their arrivals occurred more evenly.

Queuing has become a feature of modern life, as complaining about it has become a subject for discussion while waiting. Evidence cited in Jones and Dent (1994) suggests that nearly two-thirds of all service complaints in retail and leisure operations are time related in terms of too long to pay or too long to be served. Increasing standards of living brought about by the emergence of a single global economy has shifted values to such an extent that customers 'seek out those goods and services which will minimise the expenditure of their time' (Davis and Heineke 1994) and thus 'are willing to pay to avoid or reduce queuing delays' (Kleinrock, cited in Larson 1987). This indicates the importance of managing the queuing within any leisure service, where the customer is likely to be less inclined or prepared to waste their 'valuable' leisure time waiting. Additionally, at sporting events, the customer is now no longer prepared simply to wait patiently in line as was the case in the past, neither are they prepared to wait without an explanation for any extended period of time. If any lesson is to be learnt from the Hillsborough disaster, it is that the management of queuing must be fully considered and managed. Safety issues along with customer satisfaction must be considered when events are being planned, if organisations intend to achieve happy, satisfied customers along with continued success.

The management of queues represents an evolving process of refinement within the area of capacity management. Managers of service organisations ideally want the service to be continuous, this means that just as the service of one customer ends the next has arrived and is ready to be served. This provides for a busy worker and happy customers. However, life is not as simple as that and the result is that management has to recognise the need to manage the queues that develop, in order to create a balance between the need financially and operationally to manage the fluctuation in the customer demand for the service and their customers' acceptance of a wait during busy periods. One traditional method of measuring this 'trade-off' can be seen in Figure 6.1.

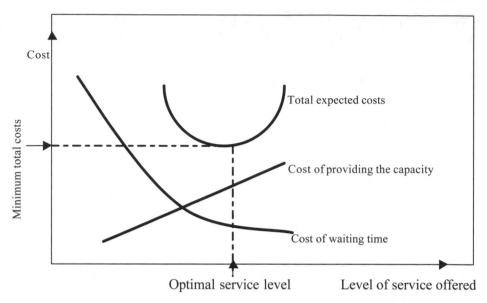

Figure 6.1 *The trade-off between the cost of waiting and the cost of capacity*

Capacity costs can be seen to increase where an organisation is seen raising its level of service. This, therefore, leads to a point where the optimum level of service can be offered. The result of offering such a financially based optimum is that where it is exceeded, a queue will be created. The waiting costs reflect the loss in productivity of the employees combined with the estimated costs of lost customers because of delays and poor service.

THE MANAGERIAL IMPLICATIONS OF WAITING OR QUEUES

Within a service operation, management has a number of reasons to worry about queues or customers waiting. These are likely to include:

- possible loss of a customer
- potential loss of goodwill
- possibility of gaining a poor reputation
- cost involved of providing waiting areas and a suitable environment
- risk of negative publicity
- risk of reducing the level of customer satisfaction
- risk of an increase in level of stress to the employees.

It is important for organisations today to realise that queues can be lines of visible or virtual customers awaiting service, as with a supermarket check-out or the queue of calls to a call centre. There are two approaches an organisation can consider to help them manage the waiting process: the first is through the use and development of queuing theory. This is the mathematical approach to managing queuing and involves recognising and measuring the characteristic of the waiting line, its population and forecasting the queue's behaviour. The second approach is by managing the process of the customers and the staff and is know as *queuing psychology*. An organisation might elect to operate one or other of these approaches, or both; or, as some service organisations have done, simply ignore the problem altogether.

CHARACTERISTICS OF QUEUING

There are numerous queuing models used to help analyse a queue. The model most appropriate to help an organisation address its queuing problem will be affected by the characteristics of the systems. The main characteristics of a queuing system are:

1. source of the population
2. number of servers (channels)
3. arrival patterns
4. service pattern
5. queuing discipline.

Source of the population

Any approach to analysing or managing a queuing problem is going to depend on the potential number of customers. Here there are two possibilities: the source of customers will be unlimited (infinite) or restricted (finite). In the infinite source, the customer arrivals are unrestricted and the potential number of customers will greatly exceed the available capacity of the organisation to deal with them. In the finite population, the number of potential customers is restricted and although they may exceed the organisation's capacity, this will only be in a minor way and occur rarely.

Number of outlets or channels

The capacity in any queuing system is the function of the capacity of each server (channel) and the number of servers available for service. Operating systems can be either single- or multi-channel, that is one or more servers serving the population. It is important to note that a group of servers working together as a team to process one facility represent one channel. Figures 6.2–6.6 outline the variety of variation of queuing systems.

Arrival patterns

The arrival characteristics of a queue has three main elements:

1. size of the arrival population
2. behaviour of arrivals
3. arrivals and service pattern.

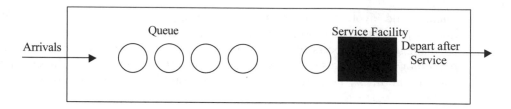

Figure 6.2 *Single-channel, single-phase system*

Figure 6.3 *Single-channel, multiphase system*

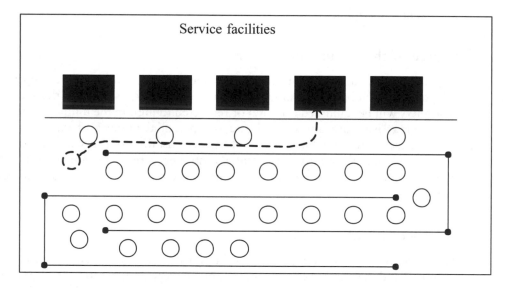

Figure 6.4 *Multichannel single queue*

Size of the arrival population

The potential population size of a queue are considered to fall into one of two areas, either unlimited (essentially infinite) or limited (finite). When the number of people arriving at any one moment is just a small portion of those capable of arriving, the population is considered unlimited. Examples of an unlimited population include the number of people arriving at a public leisure centre or major public sporting event where the tickets are not pre-sold, the London Marathon for example. An example of a limited or finite population would be the daily demand for a gym or fitness club, where entry was by membership only and there is a need for an introductory session prior to membership usage (see Figure 6.7).

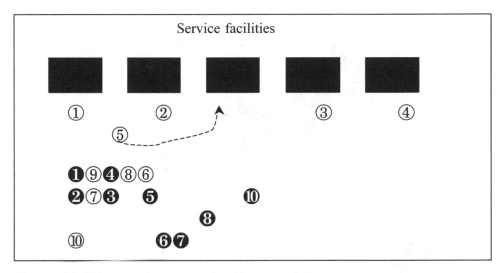

Figure 6.5 *Take a number system of multi-server queuing*

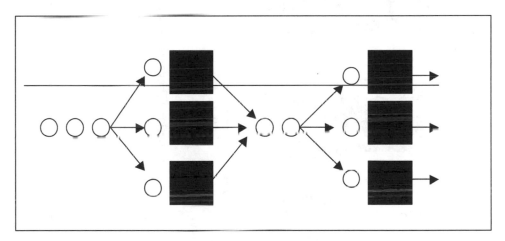

Figure 6.6 *Multi-channel, multiphase single queue*

Behaviour of arrivals

Most queuing models assume that people arriving to queue are patient. Patient customers are people who wait in the queue until it is their time to be served. They do not switch lanes or baulk (attempt to cover more than one lane at a time). Unfortunately, life is not that simple and not all people behave in a routine manner. Some will baulk while others might renege (customers who enter the system but are so impatient that they leave without completing the transaction).

It is interesting to note that the Poisson and negative exponential distributions are alternate ways of presenting the same basic data. This means that if the service time (time taken to service the customer) is exponential, then the service rate (the speed of arrivals) will be Poisson. Similarly, if the arrival time for customers is Poisson, then the interval between arrivals will be exponential.

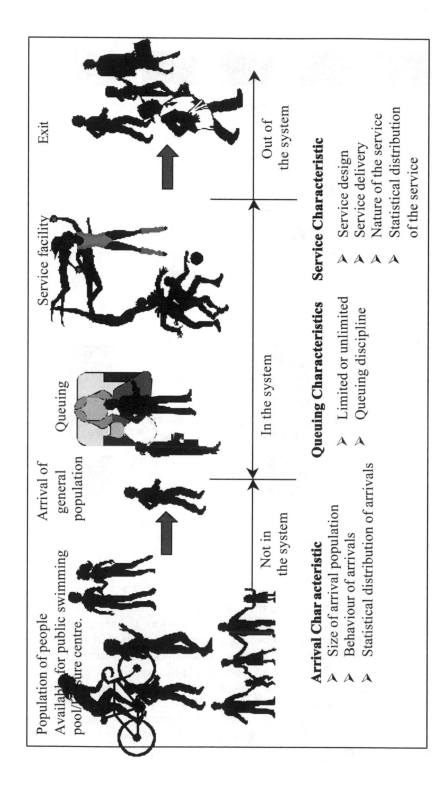

Figure 6.7 *Main stages of a queuing system at a leisure centre*

Arrivals and service pattern

A queue and the size of it are a direct result of the rate of arrivals, the speed of service and the number of servers available. This problem is often caused because of the random nature of the arrivals, which can be highly variable, with many patterns and suffering from many external factors (as simple as the weather or traffic flows). In many cases, this variability can be described by theoretical distributions. In fact, most of the common queuing models assume the customer arrival rate to be described by a Poisson distribution and the service pattern is described by a negative exponential distribution.

Queuing discipline

This simply refers to the way in which the customers are processed through the service. Most systems will use a simple first-come, first-served principle (FCFS or FIFO). There are a range of variations, from the triage system established in field hospitals during the First World War and now used in hospital accident and emergency centres today, to the 'less than ten items' approach of rapid check-out lanes at many supermarkets.

MEASURING THE PERFORMANCE OF A QUEUE

Queuing models are aimed at helping management reach decisions and to balance the service costs with the effect of queuing. The various models produce many differing measures of performance. The following are the main and more important ones:

1. average time spent in the queue
2. average number of customers waiting:
   - in the system
   - in the queue
3. average time that each customer spends in the system (waiting plus service time)
4. average number of customers in the system
5. level of utilisation of the system, the percentage occupancy
6. probability of the service being idle
7. probability of a specific number of customers in the system
8. probability that any arrival will have to wait for service.

Basic models

Queuing formulas for a simple system (M/M/1) single server, single queue
Assumptions made:

1. Every customer arriving waits to be served, no reneging.

2. First-come, first-served system.

3. All arrivals are independent of each other and the average number of arrivals does not change with time.

4. Arrivals are described as Poisson probability distribution and from a very large population.

5. Service times vary from customer to customer.

6. Service times occur in accordance with the negative exponential probability distribution.

7. The rate of service is faster than the rate of arrivals overall.

When these criteria are met, then the following series of equations can be used (see box).

The queuing formulas for a simple system (M/M/I) single server, single queue

λ = mean number of arrivals per time period
μ = mean number of people served per period of time
L_s = average number of customers in the system

$$= \frac{\lambda}{\mu - \lambda}$$

W_s = average time a customer spends in the system (waiting plus service)

$$= \frac{1}{\mu - \lambda}$$

L_q = average number of customers waiting in the queue

$$= \frac{\lambda^2}{\mu(\mu - \lambda)}$$

W_q = average time a customer spends waiting in the queue

$$= \frac{\lambda}{\mu(\mu - \lambda)}$$

p = utilisation factor of the system

$$= \frac{\lambda}{\mu}$$

P_0 = probability of no customers being in the system e.g. the server is idle

$$= 1 - \frac{\lambda}{\mu}$$

$P_{n>k}$ = probability of more than K customers in the system, where n is the number of customers in the system

$$= \left(\frac{\lambda}{\mu}\right)^{k+1}$$

Example   The New Harbour Leisure Centre is able to check in (service rate) customers at the rate of one every 30 seconds (120 an hour), according to exponential distribution. On a Monday, customers arrive at the rate of 100 an hour, following a Poisson distribution. There is technically no limit to who might use the leisure centre and they are served on the basis of FCFS.

The information that can be derived from this information is:

λ = 100 arrivals per hour
μ = 120 served per hour on a Monday

$$L_s = \frac{\lambda}{\mu - \lambda} = \frac{100}{120 - 100} = \frac{100}{20} = 5 \text{ customers in the system on average}$$

$$W_s = \frac{1}{\mu - \lambda} = \frac{1}{120 - 100} = \frac{1}{20} = 0.05 \text{ hrs or 3 minutes average wait}$$

$$L_q = \frac{\lambda^2}{\mu(\mu - \lambda)} = \frac{100^2}{120(120 - 100)} = \frac{100^2}{120(20)} = \frac{10,000}{2400} = 4.17$$

= 4.17 customers waiting in the queue

$$W_q = \frac{\lambda}{\mu(\mu - \lambda)} = \frac{100}{120(120 - 100)} = \frac{100}{120(20)} = \frac{100}{2400} = 0.04$$

= 0.04 minutes (2.5 seconds) average wait per customer

$$P = \frac{\lambda}{\mu} = \frac{100}{120} = 0.833 = 83.3\% \text{ efficient}$$

P_0 = probability of no customers being in the system i.e. the server is idle

$$P = 1 - \frac{\lambda}{\mu} = 1 - \frac{100}{120} = 1 - 0.83 = 0.17 = 17\% \text{ chance of no customers being in system}$$

$P_{n>k}$ = probability of more than K customers in the system, where n is the number of customers in the system

$$= \left(\frac{\lambda}{\mu}\right)^{k+1} = \text{If } K = P_{n>k} = \left(0.833\right)^{k+1}$$

$$0 = 1 - 0.833 = 0.1667$$

$$1 = 0.166^{0.833} = 0.13889$$

$$2 = 0.13889^{0.833} = 0.1157. \text{ This suggests an 11.5\% chance of more than two customers waiting in the system}$$

New Harbour Leisure Centre

Waiting lines M/M/1 (single server model)

Data

Arrival rate (λ)	100
Service rate (μ)	120

Results

Average server utilisation(ρ)	0.833333
Average number of customers in the queue(L_q)	4.166667
Average number of customers in the system(L_s)	5
Average waiting time in the queue(W_q)	0.041667
Average time in the system(W_s)	0.05
Probability (% of time) system is empty (P_0)	0.166667

Probabilities

Number	Probability	Cumulative probability
0	0.166667	0.166667
1	0.138889	0.305556
2	0.115741	0.421296
3	0.096451	0.517747
4	0.080376	0.598122
5	0.066980	0.665102
6	0.055816	0.720918

7	0.046514	0.767432
8	0.038761	0.806193
9	0.032301	0.838494
10	0.026918	0.865412
11	0.022431	0.887843
12	0.018693	0.906536
13	0.015577	0.922113
14	0.012981	0.935095
15	0.010818	0.945912
16	0.009015	0.954927
17	0.007512	0.962439
18	0.006260	0.968699
19	0.005217	0.973916
20	0.004347	0.978263

Using EXCEL for operations management and queuing, the example of the New Harbour Leisure Centre queuing problems show how the M/M/1 system operates with EXCEL and the basic data from the question. The operating system is a simple process to set up, although there are a number of established EXCEL-based POM's programs available which will offer a variety of queuing models.

Queuing formulas such as single channel (M/M/1), multi-channel system (M/M/S) and constant service (M/D/1) may be found in a range of operational research textbooks and operations management books (Cox and Smith 1961; Hall 1991).

More complex queuing models and the use of simulation techniques

Many examples of queuing will follow the examples available as mentioned earlier. However, there are occasions and situations where variations may occur, there may be a series of processes with differing queues for each process, where the population, service time and so on will vary. Models to handle such problems have been developed and are constantly being reviewed by operational researchers. The computations become more and more complex and far more time consuming than the simple ones, such as M/M1, M/M/S and so on. As a result the researchers turn to *simulation*.

Simulation is an attempt to replicate the features, processes and characteristics of a real-life situation. Using this technique, it is possible to use computers to help with the 'what if' situation. Random numbers are used to help develop probability distributions, for example, the arrival rates, the rates of service of a system. By using this technique many hours, days, even months of data can be created and developed to help management arrive at a suitable solution to a problem, in a matter of minutes or hours. The process allows for additional factors to be added or taken away, for example, extra service staff or changes in the pattern of service or flow.

QUEUING PSYCHOLOGY

Queuing from another perspective

All Disney's operations (Disney World, Disneyland, Paris's Euro Disney, Tokyo's Disney Japan) have a common feature: their queues, long, seemingly endless, but happy people waiting. Disney is one of the world's leading organisations in the scientific analysis of queuing theory and queuing behaviour. They are able to predict queue lengths and waiting times of each attraction or ride. They are able to manage their queues so that they never seem to stop moving. Even when you're waiting you are being entertained. Additionally, they advise you how long the wait is likely to be. In fact, they obfuscate the times, perhaps extending the expected wait, so that the customer is happy when it is shorter than they have been told. Consider the Test Track ride, at the Epcot Centre, where for up to one hour the queue is delivered through a series of (mainly) General Motors testing equipment until the customers eventually arrive at the ride, which lasts for a few minutes; but all customers leave happy and contented.

To really understand queuing and the process of queuing in a service environment, it is necessary to consider the reasons why queues form, the inevitability of them, particularly in service operations and then the implications that are created by asking the customers to wait before receiving a service, and then to pay for the pleasure of not only the service but also the wait. Therefore, to understand fully how to manage queuing problems one should consider the issue not simply from the mathematical perspective but also from the psychological perspective. David Maister (1985) was the first operations management academic to cover this area in detail. In his work he put forward two laws of service and then applied them to the problem of customer queuing. His first law of service is that if a customer expects a certain level of service and perceives that the service they receive is greater than their expectation, they will be happy. Conversely, if a customer perceives the level of service to be slower or worse than they expected they will be unhappy or dissatisfied. The reality here is that both the expectation and the perception are psychological elements and not actual reality. From this came his first law of service:

Customer satisfaction = Customer perception − Customer expectation

The second law of service is a follow-on from the first. Here, if a customer is already unhappy with their service, it will be almost impossible to retrieve the situation and have a happy satisfied customer at the end of the encounter. Indeed, the opposite is also true, that is if the customer starts the service encounter happy, in a good mood, then it is much easier to keep them happy and satisfy them. As a result the second law of service proposed by Maister was:

It is hard to play 'catch-up'. There is a halo effect created by the early stages of any service encounter

From these two laws of service it is possible to see how they can be applied to a queuing situation. There are two directions management can consider: managing what the customer *expects* and managing what the customer *perceives*. Sasser, Olsen and Wyckoff (1978) offered good examples for both approaches. In one example they quote the case of a large well-known hotel group that had received complaints from customers about long waits in the hotel lobby for lifts. After detailed analysis and engineer's reports it was decided to try to change the customers' perception of the wait by placing mirrors on either side of the lifts, near to where the guests waited. The actual lifts were in no way altered, but as a result of people's own natural tendency to inspect and observe themselves in the mirror, the level of complaints substantially reduced.

Maister went on to make eight propositions related to waiting, all of which have been observed, researched, confirmed, modified and added to by a variety of researchers over the intervening 20 years. The propositions about the psychology of queues, each of which can be considered as areas available to influence directly customer satisfaction with their waiting times are as follows:

- *Unoccupied time feels longer than occupied time.* Many service organisations have, to some extent, discovered this to be a fact and have started to address it, for example pre-match displays and programmes at sporting events, magazines in doctors' waiting rooms, newspapers and magazines in hairdressers, but today there is a need to consider this in a more appropriate way.

- *Pre-process waits feel longer than in-process waits.* Waiting seems to be shorter once the service has started, providing that the gaps between the stages are not excessive. When waiting, there is always the fear of being forgotten and this seems to diminish if the service has started (examples can be seen in areas such as hospital clinics). However, if the wait after the initial service is extended this fear intensifies, particularly if others appear to be served out of order.

- *Anxiety makes waiting seem longer.* As already mentioned the idea of being forgotten is a problem and causes anxiety, as is not knowing how long the wait is likely to be, if you have everything need for the service to be completed, if you will be on time for the start of the service and so on. This issue can lead to the next proposition.

- *Uncertain waits are longer than known, finite waits.* If you know the approximate waiting time the wait seems less. This proposition has been seen to be used extensively at Disney's resorts, where all rides and experience centres that are known to have long waits have notices advising the customers of the anticipated wait. Disney have also discovered that if the stated waiting time is shorter than the actual wait, then the dissatisfaction increases, so they have tended to extend their stated expected waiting times. So when you eventually arrive at the ride starting point earlier than expected, you are already in a happier frame of mind.

- *Unexplained waits are longer than explained waits.* Waiting in an airport departure lounge for boarding seems to be an endless process, particularly when it becomes extended with no explanation. This is an example many people will have experienced, whereas once the organisation has given an acceptable explanation the wait becomes more acceptable. This is also an example where honesty is the best option. The announcer who states, 'only a few more moments before boarding commences', without actually knowing this to be true, is simply adding an insult to an already problematic situation.

- *Unfair waits are longer than equitable waits.* Sasser, Olsen and Wyckoff (1979) noted that in a restaurant situation one of the most frequent problems related to the situation where customers felt that other customers were successfully pushing in or being served earlier than they were. This is unfortunately common in many service operations, for example when a supermarket opens another check-out aisle or a server who interrupts the service to take a telephone order prior to finishing the current one, and so on. This is an area where operations with differing levels of service need to consider how they advise people of the situation. For example, a hospital clinic with more than one clinic operating from the same point has service times which will vary according to the clinic and have specific problems, but the patient does not know that this situation exists.

- *The more valuable the service, the longer a customer will wait.* This does not necessary mean monetary value, but the value the customer places on a service. So, for example, a patient waiting in a heart clinic will put a high value on the service they are waiting for. Similarly, the use of express check-outs at the supermarket reduces the risk of customers with fewer items being unhappy or even reneging due to what they see as a less valuable wait than someone with a trolley full of shopping.

- *Solo waits feel longer than group waits.* Waiting is obviously not a solo event, however, watch most queues and there is little, if any, interaction between the customers, until there is an announcement of a problem. Consider the wait in an airport departure lounge: there is seldom much conversation between travellers until there is an announcement of a delay. Then the sharing of the extended wait encourages the waiting customers to become distracted from observing their wait. Time passes much more slowly if unoccupied. Thus a technique employed by some operations is to encourage the potential users of the service to come in groups or couples so they can usefully occupy the waiting time.

This list has been added to by Davis and Heineke (1994) with the proposition that *uncomfortable waits feel longer than comfortable waits*. In circumstances where the wait is uncomfortable, the length of wait seems extended. Conversely, if the wait is made more comfortable, the perceived wait is shorter. This can be seen to advantage in some doctors waiting rooms or fast food operators, such as McDonald's where they generally have three styles of seating, a stool and two types of chair, each with differing times of comfort ranging from eight to approximately 25 minutes, aimed at ensuring an appropriate seating turnaround, without offending customers.

Then Jones and Peppiatt (1996) with *new or infrequent users feel they wait longer than frequent users*. Frequent customers may become attuned to their anticipated wait and not fully notice the time taken, whereas new customers are likely to be more anxious about the length of the anticipated wait.

Barlow (2002) showed that in the case of long waiting periods, the value of the service overshadowed the solo versus group waiting issues, where only one of the waiting group was the actual recipient of the service. Here the original idea of encouraging the waiting customers to wait as a group or accompanied was noticed to have disadvantages. If only one of the waiting group is actually awaiting the service, then this member will have, or see, a far greater value in waiting than any of the other members of the waiting group. This has been noticed in hospital clinics, where patient problems and complaints has been observed as coming from the non-patient in the group, not the actual patient. This can lead to different advice and approaches from the organisation's management to the advice given to patients. Take, for example, the case of a patient attending a clinic where the patient has a serious heart complaint. The patient will place a far greater value on the service irrespective of the time spent waiting, whereas the friend or relative accompanying them will naturally place far less value on the service, as it has little actual value for them.

APPROACHES TO MANAGING CUSTOMER WAITING

Researchers and organisations have found the following issues to be the most important areas to concentrate their efforts on when investigating approaches for managing customer expectation and perception:

1. *Fairness.* Ensure that the approach taken is seen as being fair and equal to all customers.
2. *Environment.* Is the wait comfortable? Could it be made more comfortable? The use of furniture, colour and sound may be considered here.
3. *Entertainment.* Ensure some form of entertainment wherever possible.
4. *Communication.* Ensure that the organisation keeps communicating with the customers, particularly if there are delays, and make any communication clear, short and honest.

Develop strategies and techniques to help manage customer expectation and perception

Most service organisations today are realising the level of customer dislike for queuing and are now considering how they can manage this issue. But many seem reluctant to develop anything more than a basic approach to the problem. How often have customers waited in the departure lounge of an airport for a late departure of a plane with little or no communication from either the airline or airport management. In a waiting room, it is not the age of the seating or the magazines that matters, more the state of them, how well arranged or comfortable the seating is or how neat, tidy and readable the magazines are. After all, a current or three- or even nine-month old magazine about gardening or homes or sailing is still interesting and readable (unless you have already read it) however, if it is scruffy, with pages ripped out etc. it is less desirable or readable and so less effective.

To this end, here are two approaches currently found to help in managing these problems by a variety of service operations:

- Wherever possible, consider an appointment system and ensure that the customers know it is an appointment system to be adhered to.
- Ensure the service staff pay 100% of the service's attention to the customers and the service.

Communicate

Wherever possible, advise waiting customers of any potential wait time and or reasons for the delays:

- up-to-date information with reference to any problems, e.g. delays in airline departures with truthful explanations

- advise of any potential delay causing problems *before* they happen

- known lengths of delays, e.g. the wait from this point is one hour (as seen at Disney)

- information sent out to the customers should advise them of any potential wait. For example, a clinic sending out appointment information should also advise the patient of the possible length of their wait and to come prepared. In the case of an eye clinic offering an initial glaucoma visit, to expect a wait of say two or three hours as felt appropriate and that they won't be able to drive for four hours after the treatment, so that they know what to expect, can bring reading material etc. and arrange to be collected afterward.

It is also possible here to educate while communicating with the customers, for example, providing information about the service the person is awaiting, for example, a museum providing information boards about the exhibition they are about to visit and so on.

Entertain

Entertaining the customer will help the passing of time. Approaches available include:

- the use of magazines, newspapers

- children's play areas

- television, including the use of information and advertising as seen in UK post offices' and some banks' waiting areas. It is important to use television selectively because if programmes with short-period repeats are shown it can re-emphasise the wait, for example, early morning news-based programmes, where the news items are repeated every 20 or so minutes. The same effect can be found with programmes with well-identified lengths, e.g. soap operas, where, if the customer has been able to watch the entire episode, the length of their wait is re-emphasised

- information boards and posters, as often seen in museums etc. This gives information concerning what is about to be seen or viewed and can help speed up the throughput

- use of entertainers, as seen with busking outside theatres. One bank in New York used this in its banking halls during busy periods and discovered it not only decreased the dissatisfaction with waiting times but actually increased its number of customers

- the use of pre-match and interval entertainment at sports events.

Obfuscate

In managing perception the concept of trying to make the actual wait seem short is one of the key elements, so the following options need to be considered:

- Snaking any queues, this means that the queue will continue to move. If possible use layout and design to ensure that the queue does not appear too long, better the customer can't see the full length than it cause dissatisfaction.

- Advising the customer of the anticipated length of wait; here Disney has shown the value of overstating the expected waiting time. They say that they are not trying to deceive their customers, just that if customers know what to expect it is better and if, at the end, they have gone through the wait a little quicker than they expect, they will be happier.

- Speeding up automated programmes, e.g. museums' electronically managed programmes, where the programme time can be decreased without seriously affecting the customer appreciation, but permitting additional capacity.

Automate

The use of automation can help reduce queues and queuing problems, as seen in the banking industry with the development of ATMs. But there are opportunities in many sectors of the service industry, from the use of automated coffee machines, to self-registration computers. When the customer participates in the service process this creates some interest and involvement. It occupies the time and reduces anxiety and even if the total service time increases, it is likely that the customer will perceive the time as having been reduced.

Discriminate

This may seem to contradict many of the other issues, i.e. unfairness. But it also ensures that the service continues to be progressive. It ensures that customers who might otherwise have been lost or who might transfer their business elsewhere, particularly high-profit segments, are kept happier, for example first-class and business-class passengers of an airline having a rapid check-in, boarding and dis-embarkation. However, by separating this service it is not seen as being unequal by the majority of fliers. Similarly, the rapid check-out at the supermarket ensures that the customers with the least value in waiting are not disadvantaged and so not lost unnecessarily.

Provide complementary services

This means making the best of a wait for both parties, so that the waiting customer has their time occupied while providing the service provider with an opportunity to increase sales. For example the range of sales outlets in airports, on both sides of the departure barriers. The provision of coffee shops and newsagents in hospitals and so on. This can be seen at many sporting events, where there are associated services, from catering to outlets selling T-shirts etc. to sporting equipment. Most leisure centres today offer catering or coffee shops or at least vending machines.

The aim of all these tools is to try to reduce all the problems identified earlier;

they need to be designed to match the specific problems and issues of the particular service. Providing the customers do not feel they are being abused or treated unfairly, then these techniques can be used to help manage the queuing problems.

Finally, there are the elements not to be ignored:

1. Treat the customers as individuals.
2. Treat them as you would like to be treated yourself.
3. Treat them openly and honestly.
4. Communicate with them as soon as possible.

And don't forget: the majority of customers never complain. However, if they are *dissatisfied* they can easily become ex-customers.

Questions

1. How might an organisation determine the economic costs of keeping customers waiting in a queue?

2. Select a sports or leisure organisation and suggest diversions that could make waiting less painful for customers.

3. At the start of the new football season a first division club gets very busy during the last few days prior to the deadline for buying its season tickets. Customers are arriving at the rate of four every ten minutes with an average time for the transaction of two minutes. What suggestions can you make to prevent customer frustration about waiting? How might the experience be made actually pleasurable for the customers – and profitable for the club?

References and further reading

Barlow, G. L. (2002) 'Auditing hospital queuing'. *Managerial Auditing Journal*, 17, 7, 397–404.

Cox, D. R. and Smith, W. L. (1961) *Queues*. London: C&H Publications.

Davis, M. M. and Vollman, J. E. (1990) 'A framework for relating waiting time and customer satisfaction in a service-operation', *Journal of Service Marketing*, 4, 1, 61–69.

Davis, M. M. and Heineke, J. (1994) 'Understanding the roles of the customer and the operator for better queue management', *International Journal of Operations and Production Management*, 14, 5, 21–34.

Davis M. M. and Heineke, J. (1998) 'How disconfirmation, perception and actual waiting times impact customer satisfaction', *International Journal of Service Industry Management*, 9, 1, 64–73.

Hall, R. W. (1991) *Queuing Methods for Services and Manufacturing*. Englewood Cliffs, NJ: Prentice Hall.

Jones, P. and Dent, M. (1994) 'Improving service: management response time in hospitality operations', *International Journal of Operations and Production Management*, 14, 5, 52–8.

Jones, P. and Peppiatt, E. (1996) 'Managing perceptions of waiting times in service queues', *International Journal of Service Industry Management*, 7, 5, 47–61.

Katz, K. L., Larson, B. M. and Larson, R. (1991) 'Perception for the waiting-in-line blues: entertain, enlighten, and engage', *Sloan Management Review*, Winter, 44–53.

Larson, R. C. (1987) 'Perspectives of queues: social justice and the psychology of queuing', *Operations Research*, 35, 6, 895–905.

Maister, D. H. (1985) 'The psychology of waiting lines' in Czepiel, J. A., Soloman, M. R., Surprenant, M. R. (eds) *The Service Encounter*. Lexington, MA: Lexington Press, 113–23.

Sasser, W. E., Olsen, J. and Wycoff, D. D. (1979) *Management of Service Operations: Text, Cases and Readings*. New York: Allyn & Bacon.

Tansik, D. A. and Routhieauz, R. (1999) 'Customer stress-relaxation: the impact of music in hospital waiting rooms', *International Journal of Service Industry Management*, 10, 1, 68–81.

Taylor, S. (1994) 'Waiting for service: the relationship between delays and evaluation of services', *Journal of Marketing*, 58, 56–69.

CHAPTER 7

Service Quality

Eddie T. C. Lam

CONCEPTS OF SERVICE

Service and the management of service are currently popular themes within both the public and private sectors (Backman and Veldkamp 1995). Kotler and Armstrong (1997) referred to service as an activity or benefit offered by one party to another that is 'essentially intangible and does not result in the ownership of anything' (p. 265). In order to illustrate its nature, service is explained in the following sections based on its characteristics and classification.

Characteristics of service

There are four distinguishing characteristics of services:

- intangibility
- inseparability
- perishability
- variability (Kotler and Armstrong 1997; Sasser, Olsen and Wyckoff 1978).

Services are intangible because they are not tactile, audible or visual at the time they are purchased. Whether the service providers are persons or machines, services are produced and consumed simultaneously. This provider–consumer relationship makes services inseparable from either the server or the person being served. Services are also perishable in the sense that they cannot be stored for later usage. In addition, the nature of the services can be determined by many factors. Examples include the skill and training of the persons who provide the services, as well as how the services are provided and the circumstances of the delivery. Services are variable. Different service providers can deliver the same service in a different manner. The same person may not consistently provide the same service because of different situations and different requirements of the customers. According to Kotler and Armstrong (1997), the quality of service depends on 'who provides them, as well as when, where, and how they are provided' (p. 265). However, service can be grouped under different categories according to its nature. The most common classification is based on the extent of interaction between the customers and the personnel of the organisation.

Classification of service

Based on the degree of contact between the service provider and the consumers, Chase and Tansik (1983) identified three types of service:

- pure service
- mixed service
- quasi-manufacturing service.

In pure service, customers must be present for service production (e.g. fast food restaurant, nursing home). Mixed service includes both face-to-face as well as back-office (or non-face-to-face) contact between the organisations and the customers (e.g. commercial airline). In quasi-manufacturing service, however, face-to-face contact with the customers is not necessary (e.g. credit card, long-distance telephone company).

Similarly, Bitran and Hoech (1990) asserted that all services fall somewhere between the customer continuum of *high contact* on one end and *low contact* on the other. In fact, most services contain both high- and low-contact elements. The health fitness industry, for example, has the high-contact club operations (e.g. front-desk staff or instructors who take care of members) as well as the low-contact functions (e.g. janitors and maintenance workers). Similarly, restaurants have waiters and receptionists whose main function is to serve customers (high contact) and cooks who work in the kitchen (low contact). Since the nature of high- and low-contact services is different, there is also a difference in their quality attributes and their implementation.

MEANING OF QUALITY

Quality is difficult to define since, under different circumstances, quality can mean different things. The definition of quality was standardised in 1978 by the American National Standards Institute (ANSI) and American Society for Quality Control (ASQC). Quality is defined as 'the totality of features and characteristics of a product or service that bears on its ability to satisfy given needs' (ASQC 1978). Takeuchi and Quelch (1983) assert that consumers do not easily articulate quality and its requirements. Parasuraman, Zeithaml and Berry (1985) contend that the substance and determinants of quality may be indefinable. After reviewing the related literature, Genestre and Herbig (1996) stated that quality has traditionally been defined in one of three ways:

- Quality is conforming to specifications.
- Quality is fitness for use.
- Quality is innate excellence.

The following sections identify some of the roles of quality.

Quality as a conformance

Crosby (1979) considered quality as a conformance to requirements. This indicates that a product should be generated based on formally stated specifications and that quality is achieved only when that product is created to match its design intent. Bitran and Hoech (1990) argued that in low-contact services, quality basically means the conformance of specifications. For example, the dining fare in fast food restaurants should be carefully produced to meet specific requirements of taste, temperature, appearance etc. However, the definition of 'conformance to specification' cannot reflect the nature of the high-contact services where the human encounter is hard to depict. Therefore, higher order human needs in the high-contact services must be satisfied to a much greater extent than in low-contact services.

Quality as an assessment tool

Researchers generally agree that quality is similar to attitude in the overall assessment of a product or service (Holbrook and Corfman 1985; Olshavsky 1985; Parasuraman, Zeithaml and Berry 1988). Parasuraman, Zeithaml and Berry (1988) identified two forms of quality in the assessment process: perceived quality and objective quality. *Perceived* quality is the customer's assessment about the overall excellence of an entity. *Objective* quality, by way of contrast, is a kind of attitude that results from a comparison of the customer's expectations with the perceptions of actual performance.

Cues as determinants of quality

Researchers in product quality indicate that consumers use cues to differentiate among products and their quality (Olson and Jacoby 1972; Wheatley, Chiu and Goldman 1981). These determinants used by consumers to determine product quality are classified as either *intrinsic* or *extrinsic* cues. Olson and Jacoby (1972) asserted that intrinsic cues are those product attributes that are inherent to the product itself (i.e. the physical characteristics of the product); whereas extrinsic cues are those attributes that are not part of the physical product itself but are product-related (e.g. the product packaging). Unlike product quality, service quality is more complex and difficult to determine. Genestre and Herbig (1996) have summarised these differences (see Table 7.1). When buying any product, the consumer can employ many tangible cues to determine the quality, such as style, colour, texture, feel, package etc. However, when purchasing services, these tangible cues often do not exist. Therefore, consumers must rely on other cues to judge quality. In such circumstance, tangible cues are limited only to the physical properties of the service (e.g. facilities, equipment, personnel etc.).

DIMENSIONS OF SERVICE QUALITY

Service quality is not stand-alone, but the result of a complex network involving several dimensions (Wuest 2001). The identification of the dimensions of service

Table 7.1 *Comparison of service quality and product quality*

Characteristic describing	Service quality	Product quality
Measurable	Usually vague	Quantifiable standards usually exist
Maintenance/repairability	Difficult	Usually designed to be easily repaired
Commonality	Heterogeneous	Identical (typically mass produced)
Reliability	Variable	Usually consistent
Dependence on proximate physical facilities	Required	Not required
Dependence on proximate provider	Required	Not required
Human element (employees)	Definitely required	Not required
Customer expectations	Variable	Highly understood

(modified from Genestre and Herbig 1996)

quality is critical because it provides some points of reference for evaluating service quality. From general to specific, the following section examines how service quality is classified under different dimensions.

Grönroos (1984) classified service quality according to the way it is delivered. He postulated two components of service quality: technical quality and functional quality. *Technical* quality of service concerns *what* the customer is actually receiving from the service and it consists of such factors as employee knowledge, equipment, facilities etc. The *functional* quality of the process is the *way* the service is delivered and thus involves the interaction between the customer and service provider. Functional quality might include courtesy, employee friendliness, speed of service etc. Obviously, the functional dimension is perceived in a subjective way and cannot be evaluated as objectively as the technical dimension. Together, these two dimensions can strongly influence the corporate image as well as how favourably the organisation is publicly perceived.

Edvardsson, Gustavsson and Riddle (1989) proposed four constructs of service quality:

- technical quality
- integrative quality
- functional quality
- outcome quality.

Technical quality includes both personnel skills and the design of the service system. Integrative quality is the ease with which different portions of the service delivery system work together. Functional quality includes the aspects of style, environment, availability and the way in which the service is delivered to the customer. Outcome quality determines whether the actual service meets both the standards and the customer's needs and expectations. The technical quality aspects of Edvardsson, Gustavsson and Riddle (1989) and Grönroos (1984) are similar (i.e. they consider who provides the service and what system design is the best). The integrative quality, functional quality and outcome quality refer to how, where and when the service is provided. This is similar to what Grönroos (1984) called functional quality.

In developing their service quality measurement instrument, the SERVQUAL, Parasuraman, Zeithaml and Berry (1988) proposed the following five constructs of service quality:

- tangibles
- reliability
- responsiveness
- assurance
- empathy.

Parasuraman, Zeithaml and Berry (1988) asserted that the service quality of an organisation can be captured by these five dimensions. According to them, tangibles refer to the physical properties of the facilities and personnel. Reliability relates to the dependability and accuracy of the service. Responsiveness concerns the helpfulness of the staff to the customers and the provision of timely service. Assurance refers to the 'knowledge and courtesy of employees and their ability to inspire trust and confidence' (p. 23) and empathy is the individualised attention the organisation provides to the customers.

The SERVQUAL has been used or modified by a number of researchers to examine the service quality dimensions in the hospitality industry. Baker and Fesenmaier (1997) used the SERVQUAL model to compare service quality expectation among three groups of people (visitors, employees and managers) in a tourism service encounter. Wuest, Emenheiser and Tas (1996) used the SERVQUAL to assess travellers' perceived lodging service quality. Knutson and his colleagues (1991) modified the SERVQUAL to LODGSERV in order to examine the expectations of customers in the lodging industry. Stevens, Knutson and Patton (1995) developed the DINESERV, a modified version of the SERVQUAL, to evaluate the expectation of guests in the restaurant industry.

While many businesses have adopted the SERVQUAL as a service quality measuring instrument, researchers in the sport and leisure industries attempted to identify dimensions of service quality in their own settings. Chelladurai, Scott and Haywood-Farmer (1987) identified five fitness service dimensions as measured by their Scale of Attributes of Fitness Services:

- primary professional
- primary consumer
- primary peripheral
- primary facilitating goods
- secondary services and goods.

The first two dimensions belonged to core services, which differentiate them from the third dimension, peripheral service. Examples of core service may include instructional programmes and fitness evaluation that supplement fitness services. Contrariwise, peripheral services are those items that surround and complement the core service, such as locker rooms and parking facilities. There are also distinctions between the primary service and secondary service dimensions. According to Chelladurai, Scott and Haywood-Farmer (1987), the primary segment of a fitness club includes all those services that are related to fitness, such as equipment, trainers, courts and reservation system; whereas the secondary services are not related to fitness per se, such as food and beverage services.

Lam (2000) developed the Service Quality Assessment Scale (SQAS) specifically for evaluating service quality within health fitness clubs. Based on the results of factor analysis, the 40-item SQAS had six factors, which captured a total of 61.34% variance. Those six dimensions were labelled as:

- staff
- programme
- childcare
- locker room
- physical facility
- workout facility.

The staff dimension examines the appearance and the attitude of the employees and attributes such as neatness and dress, courtesy, patience, communication and willingness to help. In the programme dimension, justifications of service quality are based on the variety, availability, quality and convenience of the programme. Both the environment and the personnel are evaluated in the childcare dimension. The rest of the dimensions are concerned with the facility and equipment and service quality is judged according to their availability, maintenance, accessibility etc.

All the dimensions just examined consider what services are provided by the organisation and how well those services are delivered. How a service is delivered involves the interaction between the employees of the organisation and the customers. These basic dimensions are the theoretical framework of an instrument for assessing service quality.

IMPORTANCE OF SERVICE QUALITY

Service quality is one of the many components that affect the profits of an organisation (Zeithaml, Berry and Parasuraman 1996). The implications of inadequate or poor service are serious. An unhappy customer will not only be unlikely to return, but will more readily communicate the bad experience to other people. It has been suggested that a dissatisfied customer will tell 11 people about their experience while a satisfied one may tell only three people (Horowitz 1990). The provision of high service quality is critical to the profitability of an organisation because of two major reasons: it earns customer loyalty or customer retention and it enhances customer satisfaction.

Customer retention

By demonstrating the impact of customer retention on profitability, Zeithaml, Berry and Parasuraman (1996) asserted that customers who stay with the firm longer are more likely to buy additional services and refer the firm to others than customers who remain with the firm for a shorter period of time. Furthermore,

Rose (1990) found that the average profit on credit card services purchased by a ten-year customer is three times higher than that of a five-year customer. Fornell and his colleague's findings demonstrated that marketing resources are better spent on keeping existing customers than attracting new ones (Fornell 1992; Fornell and Wernerfelt 1987, 1988). Sonnenberg (1989) reported that it costs five times less for an organisation to retain a customer than for it to attract a new one.

Customer satisfaction

In terms of customer satisfaction, Reichheld and Sasser (1990) reported that satisfied customers are:

- likely to be involved more frequently and in a larger volume of other services from the organisation
- more willing to pay for the benefits they receive
- more likely to be tolerant of price increases.

In addition, high customer satisfaction means fewer resources are devoted to handling and managing complaints (Crosby 1979; Garvin 1988), a lower cost of attracting new customers (Fornell 1992) and enhancement of the organisation's overall reputation (Anderson, Fornell and Lehmann 1994).

CONCEPTS OF QUALITY ASSURANCE

Quality assurance refers to the process of assessment and evaluation of a service. The term 'quality assurance' has been used widely among healthcare providers and in the hospitality field, such as hotels and resorts. When applied in the sport and leisure environment, quality assurance can be viewed as a practice that aims at improving the service such that customers may experience a better quality of service (Edginton et al. 1998).

Quality assurance and evaluation

Quality assurance is similar to evaluation since both are aiming at programme control and accountability. However, the major difference between quality assurance and evaluation is the method of assessing services. According to Edginton et al. (1998), when using evaluation as a tool to examine the programme quality, the emphasis will be on how well performance and service in the sport or leisure programme match its goals and objectives. Attkisson et al. (1978) asserted that the basic objectives of programme evaluation are:

- to maintain high levels of effort relative to programme capacity for effort
- to assess outcome and select most effective/efficient programmes
- to assess relevance and impact of service needs in a specified community.

By the same token, the quality assurance procedure examines the programme process, such as how the participants or clients are affected by the way the persons (usually an instructor or a leader) conduct the sport or leisure programme

(Edginton *et al.* 1998). Attkisson *et al.* (1978) stated that the main purposes of quality assurance are to detect deficiencies and errors in service provider capacity and to ensure that proper care is afforded to individual clients. Furthermore, there is a marked difference between the two in the reviewing process. Programme evaluation requires an extensive administrative review, as contrasted to quality assurance programmes, which rely primarily on peer review.

Quality assurance in sport and leisure programmes

Sport and leisure programmes are customer oriented and customer driven. Since the expectations of customers may change over time, quality assurance activity is an ongoing process. The expectation and perceived service quality of the clients should be evaluated from time to time in order to maintain a high level of customer satisfaction. Deming (1986) identified the 'quality improvement cycle' as a means to continuous improvement of service quality (Figure 7.1).

The quality improvement cycle starts with a staff meeting, during which employees of the organisation will identify opportunities for service quality improvement. In the second step, focus teams are formed to work on those issues. Each focus team can be formed by soliciting volunteers. Members of the focus team then address and prioritise those issues, as well as suggest solutions. Next, the solutions to those issues are implemented and strictly monitored to ensure effec-

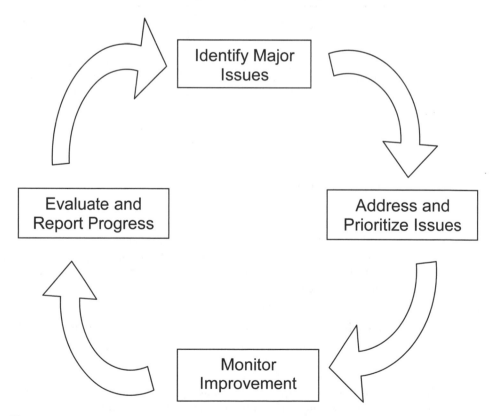

Figure 7.1 *The quality improvement cycle (modified from Deming 1986)*

tiveness. Corrective action, if any, is taken during this process. Every staff member in the organisation is encouraged to provide further improvement ideas at any time. The fourth step is to evaluate the process and to prepare a report. The progress report has to be prepared at least twice a year.

EVALUATION OF SERVICE QUALITY

The evaluation of service quality is important because it helps in planning future strategy and direction of the organisation. Based on the results of the evaluation, top management can redefine goals and objectives as well as priorities in order to meet the expectations of the customers or the requirements of the circumstance. Collier (1994) identified the following major reasons to explain why the evaluation of service quality is necessary. First, service quality evaluation can maximise revenues and customer satisfaction while minimising administration costs. Second, evaluation is important for the organisation to make future decisions and improvements. This critical element allows the organisation to make better and faster decisions than its competitors. Furthermore, evaluation can enhance the service provider's and manager's experience and intuition for decision making.

Service quality evaluation methods

Service quality can be easily examined and presented by using checklists, charts or diagrams. This may include:

- checklist
- cause-and-effect diagram
- histogram
- Pareto chart
- trend chart
- scatter diagram
- process flowchart.

These seven basic methods are referred to as the 'Seven Tools of Quality Control' and should be used at all levels of the organisation (Collier 1994).

According to Collier (1994), a checklist can be used to index all possible causes of a certain outcome. It simply lists things that should be done before, during and after performing a service encounter. A cause-and-effect diagram can be used to identify potential causes of a problem or circumstance that may have caused a certain result. It looks like a series of successive treelike branches indicating the hierarchy of the analysis. A checklist and a cause-and-effect diagram can complement one another in providing a fuller picture of the evaluation.

A histogram depicts the results of evaluation data. For example, it can be used to demonstrate the differences between the expectation and perception of service quality by customers. Pareto charts visually illustrate that a small percentage of the causes typically account for a large percentage of the problem areas. This method is another tool to illustrate cause-and-effect evaluations. Trend charts denote the measured variables over several periods of time. Scatter diagrams show graphically the relationships between two variables. They are best used to indicate the results of data analysis from a large sample size. Process flowcharts identify the steps and relationships among the process activities. They are pictorial representations that trace the logical sequence and directional flow from the beginning to the end of a process. Process flowcharting is an effective method for quality improvement (Collier 1994). For more detail and discussion about these and other methods of service quality assessment, see Chakrapani (1998), Evans and Lindsay (1989), Gitlow *et al.* (1989), Juran and Gryna (1980), Naumann and Giel (1995) and Rosander (1985).

Assessing service quality instruments

Very few instruments have been developed specifically for sport and leisure settings. The following section illustrates three service quality assessment instruments. One is used for recreation services, one for sport and leisure centres and one for professional sports. These instruments assess the expectation and/or perception service quality of the participants.

Measuring quality of recreation services

In 1990 MacKay and Crompton generated a 25-item instrument to measure the quality of recreation services. The scale was modified from the SERVQUAL and thus contained the same five dimensions of the SERVQUAL (i.e. tangibles, reliability, responsiveness, assurance and empathy). The scale includes one negative choice, one neutral and five positive choices: (1) disagree, (2) neither agree nor disagree, (3) slightly agree, (4) agree, (5) strongly agree, (6) very strongly agree and (7) extremely strongly agree.

This instrument has 25 paired desired and perceived service quality items (five paired items per dimension). Initially, respondents are asked to indicate the extent to which they think the programme should possess the features described by each statement (i.e. expectation of service quality). In the second part of the instrument, respondents are asked to indicate the extent to which they feel the programme in which they are now participating has the features described (i.e. perception of service quality). A sample of the scale (MacKay and Crompton 1990: 52) is as follows:

TANGIBLES:
    The facility should be visually aesthetically attractive
    The staff should be well dressed and appear neat
RELIABILITY:
    The facility/programme should start on time
    Information provided should be accurate
RESPONSIVENESS:
    The staff should be willing to go an extra step to help participants
    The staff should take time with participants
ASSURANCE:
    The staff should be polite
    The staff should be trustworthy

EMPATHY:
The staff should give individual attention to you
The staff should understand your needs

Since this scale is just another version of the SERVQUAL instrument, it is appropriate only for gathering general information from the participants. In order to pinpoint the areas of improvement, more specific questions should be formulated.

Assessing service quality in sport and leisure centres

Howat and his colleagues (1996) developed the Center for Environmental and Recreation Management (CERM) scale to measure customer quality in sports and leisure centres. The CERM has 15 items and measures four dimensions of service quality. These dimensions are:

- core services
- staff quality
- general facility
- secondary services.

The scale includes one negative choice, one neutral and four positive choices: (1) disagree, (2) neither agree nor disagree, (3) slightly agree, (4) agree, (5) strongly agree and (6) very strongly agree. A sample of the CERM scale (Howat *et al.* 1996: 83) is as follows:

CORE SERVICES:
Programme information
Start/finish on time
Activity range
STAFF QUALITY:
Staff responsiveness
Staff presentation
Staff knowledge
GENERAL FACILITY:
Safe parking
Facility cleanliness
SECONDARY SERVICES:
Food and drink
Child minding

Since the CERM scale has only 15 general items, some specific aspects of service quality may not be captured by the scale. As indicated by Howat *et al.* (1996), the scale 'is designed to measure customer service quality at a macro level ... the 15 attributes are reasonably broad' (p. 82). Users who adopt CERM based on their specific needs may add a few more items to the scale to make it more meaningful. However, if time is the issue, the short CERM scale can be used by top management to identify major problem areas.

Evaluating spectator satisfaction of professional sports

In order to examine spectator satisfaction of professional hockey games, Zhang *et al.* (1998) formulated the Spectator Satisfaction Inventory (SSI). The initial version of the SSI has 32 items. However, based on factor analysis, the scale was refined to 24 items under five dimensions. These dimensions are classified according to customer satisfaction with:

- ticket service
- audio-visuals
- accessibility and parking
- arena staff
- event amenities.

Item response is based on a five-point Likert scale: very satisfied, satisfied, average/no opinion, unsatisfied and very unsatisfied. The following is a sample of the SSI (Zhang *et al.* 1998: 7–8):

SATISFACTION WITH TICKET SERVICE:
    Phone order service
    Box office service
    Ticket personnel friendliness
SATISFACTION WITH AUDIO-VISUALS:
    Scoreboard
    TV broadcast
    Volume of music
SATISFACTION WITH ACCESSIBILITY AND PARKING:
    Parking
    Restroom availability
    Food/drink price
SATISFACTION WITH ARENA STAFF:
    Ticket takers
    Security officers
SATISFACTION WITH EVENT AMENITIES:
    Pre-game activities
    Intermission activities

The SSI was originally designed for assessing spectator satisfaction with regard to professional hockey games. However, it is a 'generic' scale that can be applied as easily in other professional sports such as basketball, football and baseball.

QUESTIONS

1. Name all the major characteristics of service.
2. How does service quality different from product quality in terms of human element and customer expectations?
3. Discuss the relationship between customer satisfaction and the profitability of an organisation.

4. Visit a local health and fitness facility and identify those areas that need to be improved in order to provide a better service quality.

References

Anderson, E. W., Fornell, C. and Lehmann, D. R. (1994) 'Customer satisfaction, market share, and profitability: findings from Sweden', *Journal of Marketing*, 58, 3, 53–66.

ASQC (1978) *Quality Systems Terminology*. Milwaukee, WI: American Society for Quality Control.

Attkisson, C. C., Hargreaves, W. A., Horowitz, N. J. and Sorensen, E. (eds) (1978) *Evaluation of Human Service Programs*. New York: Academic Press.

Backman, S. J. and Veldkamp, C. (1995) 'Examination of the relationship between service quality and user loyalty', *Journal of Park and Recreation Administration*, 13, 2, 29–41.

Baker, D. and Fesenmaier, D. (1997) 'Effects of service climate on managers' and employees' rating of visitors' service quality expectations', *Journal of Travel Research*, 36, 1, 15–22.

Bitran, G. R. and Hoech, J. (1990) 'The humanization of service: respect at the moment of truth', *Sloan Management Review*, 31, 2, 89–96.

Chakrapani, C. (1998) *How to Measure Service Quality and Customer Satisfaction*. Chicago, IL: American Marketing Association.

Chase, R. B. and Tansik, D. A. (1983) 'The customer contact model for organization design', *Management Science*, 29, 1037–50.

Chelladurai, P., Scott, F. L. and Haywood-Farmer, J. (1987) 'Dimensions of fitness services: development of a model', *Journal of Sport Management*, 1, 159–72.

Collier, D. A. (1994) *The Service/Quality Solution: Using Service Management to Gain Competitive Advantage*. Milwaukee, WI: ASQC Quality Press.

Crosby, P. B. (1979) *Quality is Free: The Art of Making Quality Certain*. New York: McGraw-Hill.

Deming, W. (1986) *Out of the Crisis*. Boston, MA: Massachusetts Institute of Technology, Center for Advanced Engineering Study.

Edginton, C. R., Hanson, C. J., Edginton, S. R. and Hanson, S. D. (1998) *Leisure Programming: A Service-centered and Benefits Approach* (3rd edn). Boston, MA: McGraw-Hill.

Edvardsson, B., Gustavsson, B. O. and Riddle, D. J. (1989) *An Expanded Model of the Service Encounter, with Emphasis on Cultural Context*. Sweden: University of Karlstad, Services Research Center, Research Report No. 89–4.

Evans, J. R. and Lindsay, W. M. (1989) *The Management and Control of Quality*. St Paul, MN: West Publishing.

Fornell, C. (1992) 'A national customer satisfaction barometer: the Swedish experience', *Journal of Marketing*, 56, 1, 6–21.

Fornell, C. and Wernerfelt, B. (1987) 'Defensive marketing strategy by customer complaint management: a theoretical analysis', *Journal of Marketing Research*, 24, 337–46.

Fornell, C. and Wernerfelt, B. (1988) 'A model for customer complaint management', *Marketing Science*, 7, 2, 271–86.

Garvin, D. A. (1988) *Managing Quality: The Strategic and Competitive Edge*. New York: Free Press.

Genestre, A. and Herbig, P. (1996) 'Service expectations and perceptions revisited: adding product quality to SERVQUAL', *Journal of Marketing Theory and Practice*, 4, 4, 72–82.

Gitlow, H., Gitlow, S., Oppenheim, A. and Oppenheim, R. (1989) *Tools and Methods for the Improvement of Quality*. Homewood, IL: Richard D. Irwin.

Grönroos, C. (1984) 'A service quality model and its marketing implications', *European Journal of Marketing*, 18, 4, 36–44.

Holbrook, M. B. and Corfman, K. P. (1985) 'Quality and value in the consumption experience: Phaldrus rides again' in Jacoby, J. and Olson, J. C. (eds) *Perceived Quality*. Lexington: MA: Lexington Books, 31–57.

Horowitz, L. (1990) *How to Win Customers: Using Customer Service for a Competitive Edge*. London: Pitman.

Howat, G., Absher, J., Crilley, G. and Milne, I. (1996) 'Measuring customer service quality in sports and leisure centres', *Managing Leisure*, 1, 77–89.

Juran, J. M. and Gryna, F. M. (1980) *Quality Planning and Analysis*. New York: McGraw-Hill.

Knutson, B., Stevens, P., Wullaert, C., Patton, M. and Yokoyama, F. (1991) 'LODGSERV: a service quality index for the lodging industry', *Hospitality Research Journal*, 14, 2, 277–84.

Kotler, P. and Armstrong, G. (1997) *Marketing* (4th edn). Englewood Cliffs, NJ: Prentice-Hall.

Lam, E. T. C. (2000) *Service Quality Assessment Scale: An Instrument for Assessing Service Quality of Health-Fitness Clubs*. Unpublished doctoral dissertation, University of Houston, Houston, TX.

MacKay, K. J. and Crompton, J. L. (1990) 'Measuring the quality of recreation services', *Journal of Park and Recreation Administration*, 8, 3, 47–56.

Naumann, E. and Giel, K. (1995) *Customer Satisfaction Measurement*. Cincinnati, OH: Thomson Executive Press.

Olshavsky, R. W. (1985) 'Perceived quality in consumer decision making: an integrated theoretical perspective' in Jacoby, J. and Olson, J. C. (eds) *Perceived Quality*. Lexington: MA: Lexington Books, 3–29.

Olson, J. C. and Jacoby, J. (1972) *Cue Utilization in the Quality Perception Process*. Proceedings of the Third Association for Consumer Research Annual Conference. Ann Arbor, MI, 167–79.

Parasuraman, A., Zeithaml, V. A. and Berry, L. L. (1985) 'A conceptual model of service quality and its implications for future research', *Journal of Marketing*, 49, 4, 41–50.

Parasuraman, A., Zeithaml, V. A. and Berry, L. L. (1988) 'SERVQUAL: A multiple-item scale for measuring consumer perceptions of service quality', *Journal of Retailing*, 64, 1, 12–36.

Reichheld, F. F. and Sasser, E. W. (1990) 'Zero defections: quality comes to services', *Harvard Business Review*, 68, 105–11.

Rosander, A. C. (1985) *Applications of Quality Control in the Service Industries*. Milwaukee, WI: ASQC Quality Press.

Rose, S. (1990) 'The coming revolution in credit cards', *Journal of Retail Banking*, 12, 2, 17–9.

Sasser, W. E. Jr, Olsen, R. P. and Wyckoff, D. D. (1978) *Management of Service Operations: Text and Cases.* Boston, MA: Allyn & Bacon.

Sonnenberg, F. K. (1989) 'Service quality: forethought, not afterthought', *Journal of Business Strategy*, 10, 5, 54–7.

Stevens, P., Knutson, B. and Patton, M. (1995) 'DINESERV: a tool for measuring service quality in restaurants', *Cornell Hotel and Restaurant Administration Quarterly*, 36, 2, 56–60.

Takeuchi, H. and Quelch, J. A. (1983) 'Quality is more than making a good product', *Harvard Business Review*, July-August, 61, 139–45.

Wheatley, J. J., Chiu, J. S. Y. and Goldman, A. (1981) 'Physical quality, price, and perceptions of product quality: implications for retailers', *Journal of Retailing*, 57, 2, 100–16.

Wuest, B. S. (2001) 'Service quality concepts and dimension pertinent to tourism, hospitality, and leisure services' in Kandampully, J., Mok, C. and Sparks, B. (eds) *Service Quality Management in Hospitality, Tourism, and Leisure.* New York: Haworth Hospitality Press, 51–66.

Wuest, B., Emenheiser, D. and Tas, R. (1996) 'What do mature travelers perceive as important hotel/motel customer services?', *Hospitality Research Journal*, 20, 2, 77–93.

Zeithaml, V. A., Berry, L. L. and Parasuraman, A. (1996) 'The behavioral consequences of service quality', *Journal of Marketing*, 60, 4, 31–46.

Zhang, J. J., Smith, D. W., Pease, D. G. and Lam, E. T. C. (1998) 'Dimensions of spectator satisfaction toward support programs of professional hockey games', *International Sports Journal*, 2, 2, 1–17.

CHAPTER 8

Service Productivity and Best Practice in the UK Leisure Industry

Jetske van Westering, Jessica Hwang and Peter Jones

INTRODUCTION

High productivity is generally regarded as an advantage by nations, companies and employees; it can lead to an increase in national tax income, company profits and employee wages. Unfortunately, productivity in the UK overall falls significantly below that of its overseas competitors, namely, for example, the USA, France or Germany (Best Practice Forum 2002). These countries have productivity levels twice as high as the UK and, of equal significance, they are also recorded as achieving higher levels of customer satisfaction.

Productivity in the service sector is generally lower than in production industries. This is because the sector is typically labour intensive, is often difficult to mechanise or automate and tasks are usually executed on an individual basis. The recent combined Department of Trade and Industry (DTI) and UK trade associations' 'Profit through Productivity' initiative (Best Practice Forum 2002) has generated a £4 million + investment. The sum is totally directed at helping businesses to improve their productivity, to provide better value and to raise their ability to compete, thus equipping these businesses with the potential to match world-class standards. This investment is just what the sports and leisure sector needs: in recent research into sport and leisure provision by local authorities the majority (55%) of provision was judged as fair, 39% as good and 6% as excellent (Audit Commission 2002). Fifty per cent were judged as likely to improve, however, another 50% will find it hard to improve, with the majority of these 'giving only fair service with uncertain prospects for improvement' (Audit Commission 2002). Considering the increasing competition from private sector facilities this situation is rather disconcerting.

This chapter investigates productivity improvement and Best Practice in service industries and considers critical success factors for the industry as mentioned by Best Practice operators in leisure and sport.

PRODUCTIVITY

Productivity is a concept that most people recognise but would find hard to define (Heap 1992). For the purpose of this chapter productivity can be defined as the ratio of inputs to outputs as exemplified in the following simple equation:

$$\text{Productivity} = \frac{\text{Outputs}}{\text{Inputs}}$$

In this ratio inputs refer to the resources used to make a product or to provide a service; outputs are seen as the products or services produced or the wealth generated. This ratio can be applied to measure the productivity of the operational subsystems as well as to the business as a whole. Sasse and Harwood-Richardson (1996) identify three main categories of measurements: financial, physical and a combination of financial and physical. Financial ratios widely used are, for instance, profit against sales revenue and sales revenue against labour costs. The physical ratio mostly used is the number of visitors against staff but other ratios can include floor space, number of complaints or electricity consumption per guest or cost of equipment against hours used. Combined measurements are, for instance, number of staff or man hours used versus sales revenue. Measuring productivity in these ways provides management with a way of checking on operational effectiveness, especially when measured against set targets. Heap (1992) suggests that both financial and non-financial data can be combined into a productivity index, based on the perceived value that has been added to the product. This index makes it possible to set performance targets and allows managers and employees to assess their own performance on a regular basis. Heap goes on to suggest a 'top-line productivity measurement programme' consisting of the following steps:

1. *Productivity and performance review*: an overview of all measurements made, as well as the way in which their results are used.

2. *Training*: this step will ascertain that everyone in the organisation can apply and understand productivity and its measurement.

3. *Defining productivity measures*: assessing which measures are most significant for the organisation.

4. *Devising a revenue productivity index*: this is the overall output/input ratio for a certain year.

5. *Devising a capital productivity index*: this is the output/net capital worth ratio, often called base value.

6. *Combining financial and non-financial measures into a 'top-line productivity index'*: which is then referenced to the base value. This can then be used as an overall measure of the effectiveness with which the organisational goals are met.

7. *Targeting*: new targets can then be formulated.

Heap warns, however, that measuring productivity should not be limited to factors that are easily measured; those factors that contribute most to organisational effectiveness should be given priority.

At this stage it is may be helpful to make a clear distinction between productivity, profitability, efficiency and effectiveness; these are related but separate concepts. Productivity, as indicated earlier, is the ratio between output and input; profitability is the financial ratio between output and input. Efficiency describes the degree to which an activity generates a given quantity of outputs with a minimum consumption of inputs or, phrased differently, generates the largest possible outputs from a given quantity of inputs; while effectiveness indicates the ability to attain a goal or a purpose. Effectiveness relates the output to the goals set for the operation whereas efficiency relates the output to the resources used (input). Put simply, *efficiency is about doing things right and effectiveness is about doing the right things.*

PRODUCTIVITY IMPROVEMENT

Broadly speaking, there are two ways in which productivity can be improved. Johns and Wheeler (1991) have termed these as *expansive* (increasing output) and *contractive* (reducing input). The following permutations can be made:

1. '*work smarter*': hold inputs the same while increasing output
2. '*manage growth*': increase inputs while increasing output proportionally more
3. '*cost reduction*': hold output the same while decreasing inputs
4. '*paring down*': decrease output while decreasing inputs proportionally more
5. '*innovate*': decrease input while increasing output.

Points 1 and 3 are special cases of 2 and 4, since it is unlikely that changing either input or output will leave the other unaffected. While recognising that productivity can be improved during the lifetime of a business, it is important to emphasise that productivity is highly defined during the design stage of a building. Johns (1993) argues that if productivity is not considered in the design stage, subsequent efforts to improve productivity can be no more than remedial action.

Traditionally, organisations measured their performance in some way through financial outcomes; inputs and outputs were expressed in terms of costs and revenues; productivity was the measure of the ratio between the cost of providing the service or product and the revenue gained. In traditional management thinking, decreasing costs meant laying off staff while increasing output meant working staff (and assets) harder. Current management strategies no longer focus on laying off staff, although by definition (since the ratio of input to output is improved) employees are expected to achieve greater levels of output. There are various ways of achieving improved productivity.

Process reengineering

At the heart of process reengineering is the notion that waste is eliminated from the system. The concept of waste was first expounded by Taiichi Ohno, one-time Chief Engineer for Toyota. He set Japan en route to achieving global dominance in several industry sectors (including motorcycles and electronic goods) by identifying: doing too much, waiting, transporting too much, inflexible capacity or lack of process flexibility, unnecessary stocks, unnecessary motions and defects as the seven key types of waste – waste that needed to be reduced or eliminated in order to improve on productivity.

Such improvements can be assessed by 'blueprinting' or flow-process charting the production or service. This requires identifying each stage in the process and seeking out opportunities to reduce waste: to eliminate stages, simplify or automate stages, or do two or more things at once. It is crucial that employees working in the specific area are involved in this reengineering process.

Investment in technology

The most significant technology affecting productivity in all industries, including leisure, is information and communications technology (ICT). In a major study of leisure in the new millennium the Henley Centre (1999) argued forcibly that 'the leisure industries should embrace the internet'. They contend that it is a low-cost means of distribution that can reach an ever expanding market: it is seen both to provide important information and facilitate sales of services with a short shelf life. At a time when contemporary consumers increasingly seek spontaneity in their lifestyles, ICT could play a crucial role in enabling customers to access leisure provision at any time. New video phones will also make it possible for users to log onto web-cams of venues in order to make choices about where to go and what to do. Developing a multi-channel strategy that is able to accommodate the dynamics of customer behaviour and differences in customer loyalty level in an e-business environment is a major challenge.

Information systems integration is also a crucial issue. As a result of inherited working methodologies many operators are faced with non-integrated systems for activities such as club membership, reservations and access, food and beverage sales and inventory management. Integrated IT systems could enable employees to exchange and share knowledge and would help employees to benefit mutually from previous knowledge of a client. Managers will need to identify the knowledge resources available, determine the knowledge required, construct knowledge infrastructures for information capture and application and develop a learning organisation. In simple terms, this means identifying the type of customer information to be collected, training and developing employee skills in data gathering at every customer contact point and creating a culture of information sharing and dissemination across departments and properties. A good programme would quickly collate such data and enable predictions of consumer behaviour to be made.

Empowerment

According to Conger and Kanungo (1988) empowerment describes working arrangements which engage the empowered at an emotional level. Others describe empowerment as 'the sharing of information, rewards, knowledge and power with front-line employees' (Bowen and Lawler 1992). Hales and Klidas (1998), however, state that a definition of empowerment beyond the most rudimentary is hard to find. They argue that: 'The empowerment concept is fraught with evasions, ambiguities and disagreements over what the concept means; why, to whom and where it should be applied; and what should necessarily accompany its application.' The core problem stems from the fact that empowerment carries elements of both autonomy and control: an empowered employee is asked to make independent decisions that could affect for example the profitability or the reputation of the company. The underlying issue here is to what degree employees can or should be empowered; whether empowerment transfers real power or whether it merely transfers responsibility for work decisions. Lashley's research (1995) shows that the concept of empowerment can be used effectively to remove a layer of management and he argues that there are different managerial perceptions of empowerment, resulting in empowerment being introduced in different service organisations in different ways (Lashley 1995). Empowerment, then, is a human resource strategy that can lead to increased employee satisfaction (see following section) through work that offers greater skill variety, task identity and significance and autonomy, which, in turn, can lead to higher customer satisfaction levels.

Measuring employee satisfaction

In service industries the interaction between customers and staff is crucial to service quality; motivated, satisfied employees will give high-quality service to customers. Financial rewards alone do not give sufficient impetus to ensure employee satisfaction and loyalty. Recognition (for instance through awards), a sense of belonging (through company social schemes) and stimulation (through job enrichment, e.g. empowerment or self-directed team working) are all equally important. Employee satisfaction can best be monitored with the help of an independent third party through regular (e.g. bi-annual) surveys in which the confidentiality of answers is guaranteed. Sources of satisfaction and dissatisfaction can be identified and used to formulate strategies to improve satisfaction levels. Other indicators of employee satisfaction such as staff turnover, number of staff having left returning to the company and internal promotions should also be taken into account when assessing employee satisfaction.

Multi-skilling the workforce

Multi-skilling is not the same as multitasking, where employees are deployed across a range of activities in which they are not necessarily trained. Multi-skilling is the selection and training of staff so that they are able to work in more than one job position within the operation. The main benefits of multi-skilling are improved team working, more efficiently scheduled staff, especially during relatively quiet periods of operation and increased staff retention, especially among part-time employees. In addition to these, organisations that have adopted multi-skilling have reported further benefits. These include improved work processes (as multi-skilled employees approach their second role with experience of the organisation having also formulated objective insights towards their new department) and lower induction training costs, as multi-skilled staff need only be inducted into the organisation once.

There are, however, some potential pitfalls to multi-skilling, for example staff's reluctance to put themselves forward to work in other departments and management resistance due to the perception that staff scheduling will become more complex. These issues can be ameliorated by establishing a clear structure outlining to both management and employees how multi-skilling works in the organisation:

which is the 'home' department and how time spent in a different department is to be paid.

Labour scheduling

Allied to multi-skilling is the notion of more effective deployment of the labour force through scheduling. Many leisure providers have traditionally used unsophisticated approaches to this, despite the fact that labour is a major element of cost. On the supply side, multi-skilling enables staff to be used more flexibly. On the demand side, the effective use of ICT can greatly enhance the forecasting capability of an operation, enabling demand and supply to be matched as closely as possible. Scheduling may also entail changing employees' terms and conditions of service. For instance, in industries in the USA and some in the UK, employees work flexi-hours; that is to say, the length of their shift is agreed on their workday. Likewise staff may be scheduled to start or finish work, not only on the hour, but also the half-hour and quarter-hour. Recent research by MacVickar and Ogden (2001) into working practices in Scottish leisure facilities shows that managers of local authority operated leisure facilities currently use a broad range of flexible work practices including numerical, functional, locational and lifestyle, although not all to the same extent. They also found that some leisure sector employers, in order to get rid of expensive overtime costs, have introduced annual hours contracts for their core staff which enables the employer to schedule core staff working hours more efficiently.

As stated earlier, the traditional way in which organisations measured productivity was mainly through financial performance. This way of productivity measurement, based on cost accounting information, however, fails to measure other benefits. It also offers little to support organisations in other aspects such as quality, because the information does not map process performance and improvements as seen by the customer. In their efforts to make savings managers neglected the quality of products and services. Indeed, productivity and quality were often seen as a trade-off: one was achieved at the expense of the other. This way of thinking was gradually abandoned during the 1990s as world-class manufacturers and increasingly world-class service providers, such as Marriott, started to demonstrate that productivity and quality could be improved simultaneously. The introduction of the Balanced Scorecard approach by Kaplan and Norton (1996) and the development of the European Foundation Quality Management (EFQM) Excellence model (see, for example, www.dti.gov.uk) provided the academic theory behind these successes.

Improving productivity while at the same time improving quality could incur any of the following four cost categories:

1. *prevention costs*: setting up standards (procedures, training etc.)
2. *assurance costs*: maintaining standards (inspection, audits etc.)
3. *internal failure costs*: putting things right *before* they reach the customer
4. *external failure costs*: lost customers and putting things right *after* they reach the customer.

The emphasis in a productivity/quality improvement scenario is placed on reducing one or more of these costs. In the traditional context, where productivity and quality are seen as a trade-off, the emphasis is on inspection and putting things right, which typically results in both types of failure costs. However, as only directly measurable costs are taken into account, failure costs are ignored and external failure costs, such as lost customers, bad word of mouth and high staff turnover, are not quantified. In the modern context, the emphasis is on prevention. More emphasis is placed on procedures, training and quality systems in the expectation that failure costs will be minimal. Companies striving for total quality will create value for all customers – both external and internal – while improving productivity, competitive effectiveness and operational efficiency.

BEST PRACTICE

Best Practice companies aim continuously to improve their competitive effectiveness (delivering more value to the customer) and operational efficiency (produce that value at a lower cost). Dubé *et al.* (1999) suggest that 'best practices are exemplary or successfully demonstrated ideas or activities that are viewed to be highly valuable or effective in that organisation as top-notch standards for guiding benchmarking'. They caution that '*best*' should generally be interpreted as '*best for you*', as otherwise the term '*best*' could suggest that there is a single effective way to do something which would cause a too rigid interpretation of the concept of '*Best Practice*'.

The first step companies have to take in becoming a 'Best Practice Champion' is to benchmark their organisation against competitors, as well as the best performers in the industry. This benchmarking analysis will highlight major opportunities, threats, strengths and weakness. Cook (1995) explained that benchmarking is 'the process of identifying, understanding and adapting outstanding practices from within the same organisation or from other businesses to help improve performance and process efficiency'. Through such efforts, the firm can discover how to improve its activities and it can project future performance levels to be achieved. Codling (1998) stresses that benchmarking provides organisations with a focus on the external environment and an emphasis on increasing process efficiency. In benchmarking, it is important to focus on the individual processes or practices in the company. Bogan and English (1994) identify the following stages in the benchmarking procedure:

- *Process benchmarking* is used to compare operations, work practices and business processes to identify the most effective operating practices from many companies that perform similar work functions.

- *Performance benchmarking* is used to compare product and/or service offerings with their competitive positions.

- *Strategic benchmarking* is used to compare organisational structure, management practices and business strategies across industries seeking to identify the winning strategies that have enabled high-performing companies to be successful in their marketplace.

Benchmarking is not just copying from other companies; it is selecting and adapting those processes or strategies that are suitable and will help the company to become a Best Practice Champion.

PROFIT THROUGH PRODUCTIVITY – THE PROGRAMME

Identifying and sharing best practice was singled out as a key to success in achieving the aims of the UK government competitiveness White Paper in 1999. *Our Competitive Future* enumerated plans to develop a number of sector-specific initiatives based on earlier experience in the automotive industry. Subsequently, the British Hospitality Association (the principal trade association for the tourism, hospitality and leisure sector) took the initiative in creating the Best Practice Forum: a strategic alliance in which six leading trade associations, including Business in Sport and Leisure, are represented. With support from both the Department of Trade and Industry and the Department of Culture, Media and Sport, the Forum is investing £4 million over five years. The investment is to help businesses, particularly small and medium sized, to raise their level of competitiveness to world-class standards by improving productivity and providing better value. 'Profit through Productivity' offers a national programme of business and enterprise support for the whole of the tourism, hospitality and leisure industry. The programme incorporates three actions: the first is research, meant to identify the critical success factors that determine the success or failure of businesses. The second action aims to disseminate the outcome of research to the sector. At this stage businesses will be asked to benchmark themselves against others in the industry. Subsequently, a range of business development plans are made available: a choice of tailor made programmes can be chosen from a series of multi-media self-help kits containing videos, CD-ROMs and workbooks, to in-company development programmes and master class seminars. The final action seeks to identify those businesses that have done most to raise levels of productivity and performance, while an annual accreditation study, 'Closing the Gap', will indicate the extent to which productivity gains are being made across the industry.

Research

For the research part of Profit through Productivity the best performing companies in hospitality and leisure had to be found. Patton (1990) argues that often more can be learned from intensively studying extreme or unusual cases than can be learned from statistical depictions of what the average case is like. The most appropriate way of sampling for the Profit through Productivity research would therefore appear to be *extreme case sampling*, which meant locating information-rich key informants or critical cases. Extreme case sampling begins with *snowball sampling*: asking a broad group of knowledgeable people or institutions (for instance, tourist boards, national associations or government departments such as the DTI) to identify well-run companies. Other sources may include winners of particular specialised schemes (for example the UK's England for Excellence Award, Leisure Property Forum Award, Charter Mark, UNISYS Award for Service Excellence, Investors In People and Vision 100). Nominations for cases to study snowballed from there and then converged into a small number of core cases that were mentioned by several respondents from various sides.

For the initial part of the study three leisure centres were selected to partake. One leisure centre, the Spectrum in Guildford, is a borough-funded destination leisure centre, with a variety of commercial and social activities; customers can spend a whole day playing different sports or participating in a variety of activities and using the extensive catering facilities. The centre is profit making; profits are reinvested in the company. The other two companies are ex-borough leisure centres; both have been transferred into not-for-profit companies. Heartsmere Leisure has only just become a not-for-profit trust, managing several North London leisure facilities under lease agreements with the help of a borough grant. The third company, Greenwich Leisure, is funded similarly. It was set up in 1993 with seven centres and now manages 26 leisure centres of different types and sizes, from large regional centres with multiple function rooms and catering facilities as well as pools and other sports facilities to simple dry sports halls. It is currently the biggest leisure centre operator in London and profits have increased sixfold since start-up.

Managers in these three recommended companies were asked to identify the factors that made these companies so successful. The following issues were mentioned as particularly important in the success of these companies.

A vision and a business strategy

All managers identified having a vision as vital: 'We already got core people … who had a very clear vision about where we needed to go.' A clear business strategy was seen as equally crucial: 'We've always been very clear about where we were moving to and what our priorities are. We started off by having an annual business planning process … now, we're in a position where we know that we are developing a five year corporate plan.' Also, all mentioned that in the rapidly changing world of the leisure industry it is important that the vision and the business strategy incorporate the ability of the company to change: 'We are constantly having to reassess our services that we have on offer.'

Partnerships and networks

Although partnerships and networks are not emphasised as critical success factors, analysis of the interviews showed the importance given to being a member of a professional organisation and to networking. For example, one interviewee is Chairman of the National Training Organisation for Sport and Recreation, on the National Council, member of the board and National President of one of the institutes for sport and recreation management and he actively encourages his staff to do the same. Another interviewee mentions that she is sitting on a forum for the National Training Organisation for Sport and Recreation and has assisted with the Work Development Plan for Leisure and Recreation. Similarly, others mention being involved with South-East Leisure Contractors, playing a role in the marketing forum or the general manager's forum. Interviewees appear to see these roles and memberships as natural extensions of their work

Leadership

As one (general) manager put it: 'We are no longer managers, we're leaders and there is a big difference. Leadership is about people being able to see that there is a future.' He also states that: 'I (as General Manager) have to create an ambience, an atmosphere, a situation where people feel motivated to come to work.' Another manager asserted: 'Every team needs a captain ... the person who is going to drive the innovation and the business development and help to bring about continuous improvement. It's very much a team effort but sometimes the team needs a leader and we have one.'

Motivated staff

All managers put real emphasis on the role of staff and the importance of having satisfied and motivated staff: 'I think that the most critical thing about our organisation is the staffing; the staff are definitely our most valuable asset.' In this centre staff are invited to stand for the board of directors: all board members are elected from the staff. Which means that: 'every year we hold training sessions for all the new directors because they may be a receptionist who has never come across budgets before and they may be asked – they've got legal responsibilities of a director – to look at these figures and interpret them.' All decisions in this organisation are taken by the board of directors: 'The board in theory can throw anything out.' Training is seen to be of crucial importance in all three companies: 'We endeavour to make sure that everyone receives the training they want.' Often the managers have come up through the system themselves with the help of several training courses: 'They (i.e. the company) paid for my education.' An operations manager, who is seen as highly successful in developing staff, is convinced that: 'All the training, support that is given to staff and the involvement of various systems that are in place – things like staff reward and recognition systems – we involve staff in questionnaires, training, team briefings, all that makes the staff feel part of the organisation which enables them to want to be part of the successful service.' In another centre:

> We've started taking our own training and employment programme. We take unqualified kids on, pay them full-time equivalent. Train them intensively for five weeks and give them a full-time contract if they pass all their qualifications. I've also tried to open up the progression routes because a lot of them are very ambitiously keen to move on. So I've opened up the progression routes and come up with kind of training middle-management schemes so that they can start filtering through the organisation.

Finally, one general manager sums it up: 'If I don't offer my staff a very good service I can hardly expect them to offer a good service to my customers.'

Giving quality to customers

This is seen as the pinnacle of being successful: 'we deliver high-class leisure services' or in another centre 'we want to provide five star service for a three star price.' Managers see as one of their strengths the commitment 'to understand the customer', 'we all care about the products and the customer'. Quality is seen as independent of the premises: 'When the centre first opened, when it was glossy and smart, we relied an awful lot on the product, but now we're in the second stage the people (staff) are more important.' This is expressed similarly by another general manager: 'What we have found over the years, people are forgiving in terms of standards of facilities, of the building, if it's old. What people are not so forgiving about, and quite rightly so, is attitudes of staff. Irrespective of what services they're offering and what facility, they should be offering that customer the best personal service.' Because demands are rapidly changing systems and standards need updating in order to deliver quality:

> Inevitably people have their own ideas. I adapt the systems in place to individual's needs and that is just part of the business evolving. Although I am based at Head Office . . . I try to spend a lot of time talking to people and seeing what it's like at the sharp end as it were – people who have got the customers there demanding things from them, I don't want to produce a system and impose that on people.

Communication

Communication with other employees and customers is seen as vital:

> We think we have the ability to consult and communicate with our customers. They tell us how we are performing and we actively, physically respond to those comments through action plans, or across the whole of the operation to ultimately improve because that's what we're about.

Communicating with customers is enjoyed: 'I think the most interesting part of my job is the fact that I have the ability to talk to and communicate with so many different people as customers.' Equally important is communication with employees: 'You can't communicate enough with your staff.' Communication on a daily basis, face to face, is not often mentioned, but obviously a way of life. Opportunities to communicate are exploited:

> Everything from a staff newsletter that goes out with the payslip to update on business development right the way through to site meetings, department meetings. The managing director has what he calls breakfast meetings occasionally in which people are invited to have a chat with him about where the business is going.

CONCLUSIONS

'Profit through Productivity' aims to help businesses in service industries to find their Best Practice and their way in increasing productivity. One of the challenges to the programme is found in benchmarking; the use and usefulness of benchmarking is contested owing to problems of comparability and transferability, as situations and circumstances differ between companies. In addition, as reported by Ogden and Wilson (2001), the UK public leisure and recreation sector has been inhibited from inter-organisational collaboration due to the competitive pressures created by the policy of compulsory competitive tendering. A similar challenge is posed by the lack of meaningful comparative data – the industry needs to develop more precise and objective measurements to link a given practice to specific outcomes such as profitability and employee or customer satisfaction. Systematically and rigorously documenting outcomes and consequences of practices for analysis would require much more effort than collecting the data (Dubé et al. 1999).

The subject of productivity, once the domain of accountants, has been rediscovered as an area full of delicate and intricate linkages. Issues that previously were seen to be in the domain of other subject areas (e.g. human resources) appear to be more tightly interwoven than was ever recognised – the Best Practice research shows how these issues converge in the subject of productivity. Traditional ways of improving productivity through reducing staff numbers have been replaced by modern management thinking. Alternative methods of improving productivity as listed in this chapter have already proved to be successful in the service industry. A major problem is that when improving productivity there is no one prescribed way that will guarantee to lead to success, as each company has its own specific characteristics and parameters. It appears, however, that as a first and crucial step top management must support and be personally involved in engendering the practice from being just a 'good idea' to actual implementation.

Questions

1. Productivity in the service sector is much lower than in production industries. Research and identify which factors inhibit service industries attaining the same productivity figures as manufacturing industries and include in your answer whether in sports and leisure facilities these factors are more or less of influence.

2. Can both expansive and contractive approaches be used to improve the productivity of a leisure centre?

3. Explain why benchmarking is important in a productivity improvement programme.

References and further reading

Audit Commission (2002) *Acknowledge, Learning from Audit, Inspection and Research – Sport and Recreation*. London: The Audit Commission for Local Authorities and the National Health Service in England and Wales.

Best Practice Forum *www.bestpracticeforum.org* (accessed 25 June 2002)

Bogan, C. and English, M. J. (1994) *Benchmarking for Best Practices: Winning through Innovative Adaptation*. New York, McGraw-Hill.

Bowen, D. E. and Lawler, E. E. (1992) 'The enpowerment of workers: what, why, how and when', *Sloane Management Review*, 33, 3.

Codling, S. (1998) *Benchmarking*. Aldershot: Gower.

Conger, J. A. and Kanungo, R. N. (1988) 'The empowerment process: integrating theory and practice', *Academy of Management Review*, 13, 3, 471–82.

Cook, S. (1995) *Practical Benchmarking: A Manager's Guide to Creating a Competitive Advantage*. London: Kogan Page.

Cox, J. R. W., Mann, L. and Samson, D. (1997) 'Benchmarking as a mixed metaphor: disentangling assumptions of competition and collaboration', *Journal of Management Studies*, 34, 2, 285–314.

Drew, S. (1997) 'From knowledge to action: the impact of benchmarking on organisational performance', *Long Range Planning*, 30, 3, 427–41.

DTI website (1995) 'From quality to excellence'. *http://www.dti.gov.uk*

Dubé, L., Enz, C. A., Renaghan, L. M. and Siguaw, J. (1999) 'Best practice in the US lodging industry', *Cornell Hotel and Restaurant Administration Quarterly*, 40, 4, 14–27.

Dubé, L., Enz, C. A., Renaghan, L. M. and Siguaw, J. (2000) 'Managing for excellence', *Cornell Hotel and Restaurant Administration Quarterly*, 41, 4, 30–9.

Hales, C. and Klidas, A. (1998) 'Empowerment in five-star hotels: choice, voice or rhetoric?', *International Journal of Contemporary Hospitality Management*, 10, 3, 88–95.

Heap, J. P. (1992) *Productivity Management: A Fresh Approach*. London and New York: Cassell.

The Henley Centre (2000) *Leisure in the New Millennium*. Report presented at the Joint Industry Congress, Henley.

Johns, N. (1993) 'Productivity management through design and operation: a case study', *International Journal of Contemporary Hospitality Management*, 5, 2, 20–4.

Johns, N. and Wheeler, K. (1991) 'Productivity and performance measurement and monitoring' in Teare, R. and Boer, A. (eds) *Strategic Hospitality Management*. London and New York: Cassell.

Kaplan, R. S. and Norton, D. P. (1996) 'Using the balanced scorecard as a strategic management system', *Harvard Business Review*, 74, 1, 75–85.

Lashley, C. (1995) 'Empowerment through delayering: a pilot study at McDonald's restaurants', *International Journal of Contenporary Hospitality Management*, 7, 2/3, 29–35.

MacVickar, A. and Ogden, S. M. (2001) 'Flexible working in sport and recreation: current practices in Scottish public, not-for-profit and private leisure facilities', *Managing Leisure*, 6, 125–40.

Ogden, S. M. and Wilson, P. (2001) 'Beyond data benchmarking: the challenge of managing a benchmarking network in the UK public leisure sector', *Managing Leisure*, 6, 95–108.

Patton, M. Q. (1990) *Qualitative Evaluation and Research Methods* (2nd edn). Newbury Park, CA: Sage.

Sasse, M. and Harwood-Richardson, S. (1996) 'Influencing hotel productivity' in Johns, N. (ed.) *Productivity Management in Hospitality and Tourism*. London and New York: Cassell.

PART 3

INVENTORY MANAGEMENT

CHAPTER 9

Economics of Sport and Leisure

David Edgar

INTRODUCTION

This chapter aims to introduce the student to the economics of sport and leisure through a pricing decision framework of demand, supply and price, highlighting the concepts of inventory management and its relationship to revenue management.

While economic theory tends to be universal in nature it is essential to understand the context within which the theory is adopted. Before examining the elements of the pricing framework it is therefore useful to place the theory within the context of the sport and leisure industry. This context falls within the category of service industries.

Service industries differ in characteristics from primary or manufacturing industries in terms of a number of key areas:

- Services have a high degree of intangibility but not necessarily exclusively intangible.

- There is a high degree of customer and culture specificity and intimacy.

- Services themselves are unstorable, their experience or consequences may, however, be longer lasting.

- Consumption and production are generally simultaneous and inseparable.

Obviously, given the vast array of public and private sector operations, the different services and markets will display characteristics in differing degrees and as such each characteristic should perhaps be viewed as an element of a continuum (Bitran and Lojo 1993; Van Dierdonck 1992) ranging from low perishability to high perishability, low simultaneity to high simultaneity, low intangibility to high intangibility and low customer intimacy to high customer intimacy. In addition, while the leisure industry is relatively well developed and understood, the sports industry is less explored in terms of economic theory (Szymanski 2001). Hence, while the chapter provides the generic tools for understanding the economics of the business, there are specific examples of concepts relating to the sports and leisure industry.

As such the pricing decisions of managers will vary depending upon the continuum mix of each product (defined as a good, service or combination of goods and services offered to the market) or market. This chapter provides the tools for understanding the nature of demand, supply and pricing within organisations based on economic principle. The underlying theory should be considered in the context of a range of operations and not accepted as being consistent for all operations or markets within the sport and leisure industry.

THE PRICING DECISION FRAMEWORK

In economic theory, price is the main factor used to explain the links between supply and demand for a product (Wolfe 1993). Therefore pricing, founded on the relationship between supply, demand, competition and the environmental forces in the sport and leisure industry, has major implications on how organisations react to change and what resulting performance they achieve (Crawford-Welch 1991; Lewis and Chambers 1989; Porter 1980; Siegfried and Zimbalist 2000). Adopting this principle means that a price decision framework provides an excellent vehicle for explaining the dynamics of the economics of the sport and leisure industry and the implications for inventory management.

Pricing decision framework

The price at which sport and leisure products are offered for sale affects the demand for those products and, therefore, revenue and profit. From pricing theory (Kuncher and Hilleke 1993) the profit-maximising price of a product depends on market reactions and marginal costs, i.e. both the market and the company's internal cost structure are determinants of a product's price. This leads to the framework adopted for this section. The framework, shown in Figure 9.1, was constructed by Kuncher and Hilleke (1993) and represents the key elements of pricing and therefore forms an excellent means of examining the economics of sport and leisure.

From Figure 9.1 there are two key elements to price, the market side or demand, and the company side or supply.

The market side represents the consumer's ability and willingness to buy the product based on the perceived value of the purchase at the purchase price and the resulting opportunity cost (i.e. the next best or alternative usage of the resource). Such willingness and ability to buy leads to the volume of achieved sales.

The company side represents the logistics of providing the product, including the costs of production and gross profit requirements.

In order fully to understand the nature of pricing decisions it is necessary to focus on the market side (demand) and company side (supply) in more detail before determining pricing and yield techniques.

Demand: the market side

The market side revolves around the relative perceived value of a product and the consumer's willingness and, indeed, ability to buy that product. The perceived value will lead to the level of consumer price threshold, i.e. how much the consumer values the product and therefore how much they are willing to pay, subject to the law of diminishing marginal utility, or the value placed on each additional unit consumed.

Such value is obviously related to the nature of the product and alternative

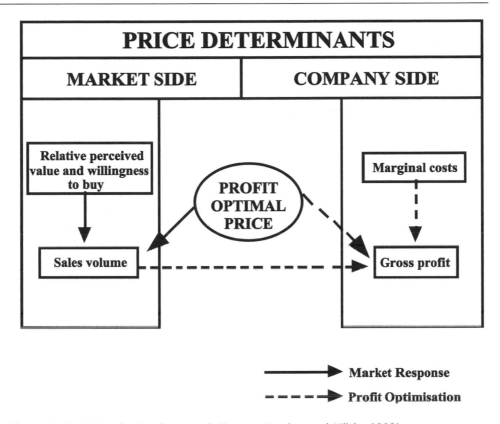

Figure 9.1 *Pricing decision framework (Source: Kuncher and Hilleke 1993)*

sources available. In the sport and leisure industry this relationship is somewhat complex. Many sporting events and sports activities are founded on a 'tribal' dimension of support and hype. Such support and hype raise the perceived value of the 'product' and create additional rents. These rents increase as timescales shorten (i.e. last minute availability) and hype increases (e.g. children must have an X-box!). Such a relationship can be managed by managing the scarcity of the product (not producing enough computer games consoles before Christmas or limiting the capacity of a stadium before a large concert or sporting event), creating priority for customer loyalty (i.e. season tickets and supporters' clubs) and using 'urgency' as a tool to raise perceived value – these are lessons ticket touts learned some time ago. However, rather than focus on a debate as to which theories of demand and definitions of product are most pertinent, this section determines the grounding theory of demand allowing later sections to explore the elasticity of demand, representing different types of product. This will allow you to apply the theory to different contexts and, it is to be hoped, understand how you can use tactics to stimulate the changes you require. (Examples are provided.)

The starting point is sales volume. Sales volume represents the amount consumed at various price levels and when combined with the value (price) indicates the turnover generated. This relationship reflects the principles of the demand curve D1 indicated in Figure 9.2.

From Figure 9.2 total turnover is calculated by multiplying Q_1 and P_1, or Q_2 and P_2. The revenue can be increased in two ways, either lower price and raise volume

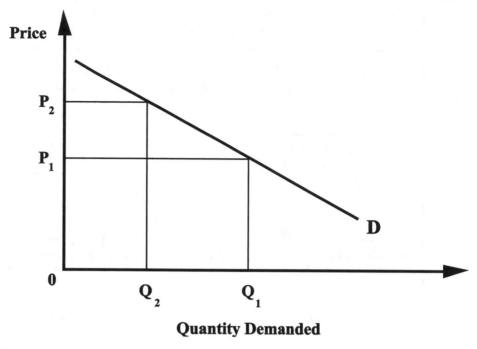

Figure 9.2 *The demand curve*

or raise price and accept lower volumes. These are called *movements along* the demand curve. As demand is an independent variable, these movements can only result from an increase or reduction in price. Such characteristics are the basics of yield management and are examined in more detail later. What should be noted here is that the price volume relationship can vary considerably between and even within markets, making the pricing decision difficult, yet critical. Such variations are usually based on the 'experience' and are reliant on time differences (which act as fences) or perceived popularity of the 'product' or experience (i.e. person branding).

In addition to such movements *along* the demand curve, the curve can also *shift*. When the curve shifts to the right it represents an increase in demand, while a shift to the left represents a decrease in demand.

The cases of such shifts stem from changes in the business environment. Examples are as follows:

Environmental change	*Increase demand* (*shift to the right*)	*Decrease demand* (*shift to the left*)
Marketing activity (e.g. adverts for the World Cup)	Successful advertising	Negative promotion
Change in fashion (e.g. membership of health clubs)	Fashionable	Unfashionable
Income (more or less disposable income)	Increase	Decrease

Price change of complementary products (e.g. price of DVD players and the impact on sales of DVDs)	Decrease	Increase
Price change of substitute products (e.g. new sports)	Increase	Decrease

Hence, a shift in the demand curve to the right can result in a greater revenue generation without a reduction in price (Figure 9.2, D2) or a potential to raise price and maintain volume, perhaps raising profitability.

While these principles assume a single demand curve it would be unwise to think that organisations have only one product or market. There is a wide range of markets serviced by operators in the industry each with a different 'perceived value' for the product on offer and as such each with a different willingness or ability to pay. This willingness and ability to pay is termed 'elasticity of demand'.

Demand: the elasticity mix

Most sports and leisure businesses serve a wide variety of client groups, although some are clearly niche players. It is feasible that operations could have different mixes of consumer, even those operating under the same company or brand name. By the same token, it is important to acknowledge that the same consumer can fall into different target market categories. Different occasions find the same consumer having different expectations and needs (Buttle 1986) and as such causes the demand curve to change in different ways. Such a concept is termed *elasticity of demand*. Elasticity of demand has three commonly adopted measures: *Price* elasticity; *Income* elasticity; and *Cross*-elasticity, representing the relationship between the elasticity measure on quantity demanded.

Price elasticity represents the relationship between a change in price and a change in quantity demanded. Income elasticity represents the relationship between a change in consumer income and quantity demanded and cross elasticity represents the relationship between the change in the price of product X and the quantity of product Y demanded.

The calculations for each form of elasticity are seen as:

$$\text{Price elasticity} = \frac{\text{Percentage change in quantity demanded}}{\text{Percentage change in price}}$$

$$\text{Income elasticity} = \frac{\text{Percentage change in quantity demanded}}{\text{Percentage change in income}}$$

$$\text{Cross elasticity} = \frac{\text{Percentage change in quantity demanded of X}}{\text{Percentage change in price of product Y}}$$

The most relevant elasticity measure for the purposes of inventory and revenue management is price elasticity of demand.

The formula provides a result of <1, >1 or =1. A result of <1 indicates a market that is highly elastic, i.e. a change in price will have little effect on quantity demanded, the lower the result, the less price sensitive the market. A result of >1 indicates an elastic market meaning a more price sensitive market, while a result of

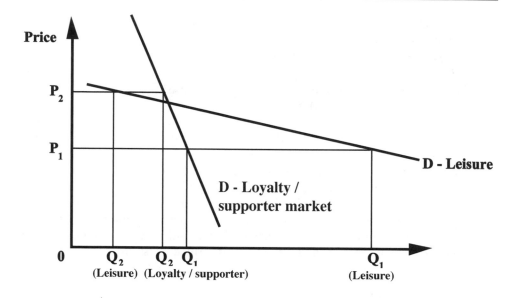

Figure 9.3 *Price elasticity of demand*

=1 indicates unitary elasticity i.e. a direct relationship between the change in price and the quantity demanded.

The elastic and inelastic markets are shown in Figure 9.3.

The loyalty/supporter market is depicted as price inelastic, i.e. a percentage rise in price is greater than the percentage fall in quantity demanded. The general leisure market demand is more elastic in nature, showing the percentage change in price is less than the percentage change in quantity demanded. Hence, if price is raised or lowered, demand levels alter considerably (Hanks, Cross and Noland 1992) merely reflecting the consumer's ability to switch to other products (competition), their perceived value for money (i.e. the balance between the product on offer and the opportunity cost) and their actual available income.

If one considers an operation which has a mixture of such elastic and inelastic markets the pricing decision becomes critical. The target is to ensure price-insensitive consumers, i.e. highly inelastic, pay full tariff and do not trade down, and that a price is reached where fewer price sensitive markets are attracted. Combine this with the nature of environments and the problems of seasonal markets and it becomes highly evident that an understanding of the nature and economics of sport and leisure units is essential in adopting a service operations approach to the business.

While the demand/price relationship is useful in determining the revenue-generating potential of an organisation it is of little use in determining actual profitability of the organisation unless it is combined with elements of supply.

Supply: the company side

Supply reflects the company perspective of the economics of the market. This perspective is more operational in nature and focuses on the nature of cost, initially marginal cost, and principles of supply management.

Marginal costs are the incremental cost per unit added to production or sales. Hence, the marginal cost is the cost of selling one extra ticket, seat or membership and is essentially the difference in variable cost between each incremental sale. This cost relationship leads to gross profit; the greater the margin between marginal cost and revenue, once fixed costs are covered, the greater the gross profit. This has been exploited in a wide range of sport and leisure operations, including low-cost airlines (e.g. easyJet, go, Ryanair) cinemas and a host of sporting events – indeed an extreme case includes football in Brazil where women and children gain free access to football if accompanied by fee-paying 'males'. The nature of unit costs warrants more detailed analysis and is therefore examined in the next section of this chapter, however, before determining in more detail the nature of costs, the supply curve is introduced and the basics of price equilibrium determined, representing the foundation of market forces.

As the demand curve indicated the quantity demanded of a product at a specific price, the supply curve indicates the quantity of a product supplied at each price (Figure 9.4).

Supply represents an inverse relationship to demand in that as price increases suppliers are willing to supply more, this represents a *movement along* the supply curve.

The supply curve also *shifts* to the left and right, as a result of elements affecting operational issues or as a deliberate action by organisations to influence levels of demand or price. If the curve shifts to the left supply is decreasing, if it shifts to the right then supply is increasing.

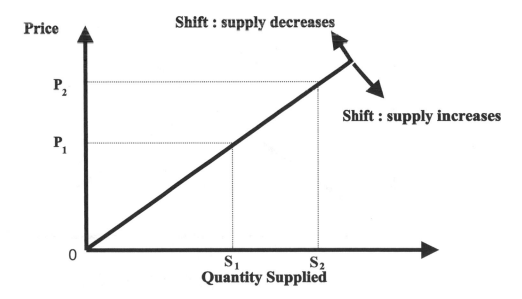

Figure 9.4 *Supply curve*

Most common issues causing shifts in supply are as follows:

Operational issues	Increase supply (shift to the right)	Decrease supply (shift to the left)
Change in government funding	Provide subsidies/lower tax	Raise tax/cut subsidies
Change in costs of production	Lower costs	Higher costs
Seasonality (e.g. skiing, World Cup, Open Golf)	In season	Out of season
Change in working practices (e.g. seating capacity)	Good techniques/more seats	Poor techniques/less seats
Change in technology (e.g. web ticketing, web viewing)	New technology	Obsolete technology

When supply is reduced, the product becomes scarce and commands a higher price. When supply increases the product becomes more available making it difficult to command higher prices.

The nature of most sport and leisure supply relative to inventory and revenue management implies fixed supply in the short term, the key issue therefore relates to the combination of supply and demand.

Figure 9.5 shows demand and supply for the same product on the same diagram.

Point B is the price equilibrium of demand, i.e. all that is produced is consumed at the price charged. If the organisation prices the product above BP there will be excess capacity requiring a price reduction (i.e. a movement along the demand

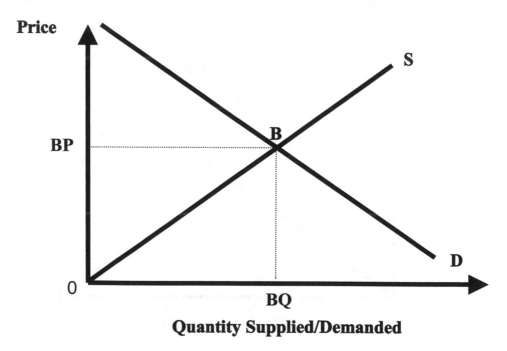

Figure 9.5 *Price equilibrium*

curve) or increase in perceived value to attract the market (i.e. a shift of the demand curve to the right). Alternatively, a reduction in supply, i.e. a shift to the left, may make the product more scarce, thus shifting the equilibrium and allowing a higher equilibrium price.

It is clearly evident that the pricing technique used will have major implications on how well the operation can adapt to changing environmental and economic conditions. Tribe (1995) highlights that such pricing is a function of more than just demand and supply. He highlights that the nature of competition and the nature of organisation ownership (in terms of private and public/voluntary sectors) play a key role. While one could argue that competition is embedded in the nature of the shift in demand and supply there is clearly more of an intangible relationship. It raises questions of operations and explains why operations offering similar (or the same products) sell at different prices, e.g. leisure centres, transport carriers, sales/special offers in pubs and clubs. These principles lead to three perspectives on pricing:

1. Organisations can be price *takers*, which indicates a high degree of competition with products that are very similar in nature and knowledge about the market is good. The implication here is that organisations will accept market prices as driven by demand, e.g. city centre pubs or a bookmaker at the races.

2. If an organisation is a price *shaper*, the market is likely to reflect monopolistic competition or oligopoly with a clearly differentiated product and fewer sources of supply, perhaps segregated by location and limited customer mobility, e.g. airlines where prices are separated by differentiation in terms of levels of service and additional products/services offered such as priority check-in, lounges, wider seats etc.

3. The third form of pricing is the price *maker*. This market reflects a monopoly and could be either national in nature or local. An example could be a highland village with one shop or one pub, this in effect allows for monopoly conditions and enables the supply to set prices at a level they wish – although they can be regulated in some countries by bodies such as the Monopoly and Mergers Commission (MMC).

The foregoing three perspectives on pricing tend to reflect the private sector approach to pricing. There are many sport and leisure operations that are publicly owned or operated as voluntary concerns. Pricing in this sector differs depending on the purpose of the organisation. The organisation could take three perspectives:

● *profit maximisation*, which reflects the previous discussions relating to the private sector

● *breakeven pricing*, which seeks to provide the best value product at cost price

● *social cost or benefit pricing*, where the operation will try to operate as efficiently as possible and will offer a price that is subsidised by some 'body', e.g. a museum.

Hence, sport and leisure operations can adopt a range of pricing approaches based on their market nature (demand and supply), competition and form of ownership. In this respect it is better to consider each operation on a case-by-case basis and to use an understanding of the former generic issues already established.

131

Hence, to appreciate fully the economic dynamic and pricing in sport and leisure it is useful to examine the dynamics of cost and then focus on the principles of marginal cost and contribution.

Supply: the cost dynamics of sport and leisure

The nature of costs is of key importance to the approach to pricing and therefore to performance. In order to determine the nature of such costs it is necessary to establish the types of costs that exist, i.e. the cost dynamics. As the industry is multi-segmented and multifaceted in nature, it is useful to focus on sectors of the principle of the dynamics of costs, keeping with the inventory and revenue management theme.

Cost dynamics

It is common practice to divide costs into categories of fixed, semi-fixed and variable costs, although some authors dispute the terminology of such categories (Davies 1990).

Each cost category displays distinct characteristics over the short and longer term.

Fixed costs can be seen as those costs that over the short term remain constant and are characterised by elements of the operation not affected by changes in the volume of supporters/guests or sales. Fixed costs include such items as rent, rates and loan interest repayments and are a large cost to most sport and leisure operations. Alternative forms of ownership can reduce the fixed cost burden, e.g. leasing; franchising; and management contracts. With the rise of the web and development of virtual spaces it is unclear as to what the future holds. The basic principle remains the same – alternative forms of ownership can restructure the organisation's cost base and thus allow for quicker cash flow or more flexibility and growth.

Semi-fixed costs are costs that remain constant for a period of time and then change either in incremental steps or gradually over time. Examples here may be permanent staffing levels or the purchase of new machinery.

Variable costs are the costs that fluctuate with the degree of production or sales and are most evident in the area of raw materials and seasonal staffing. However, variable costs will not necessarily increase and decrease directly in proportion to output (Wijeyesinghe 1993). This provides a number of profit-making opportunities in relation to margin and contribution. (This is discussed later.)

Figure 9.6 shows the cost dynamics in diagram form. Commonly, the costs are split simply into fixed costs (FC) and variable costs (VC). Adding fixed, semi-fixed (SFC) and variable costs provides an indication of the total cost, which, when combined with sales, allows a breakeven chart to be produced.

The breakeven chart illustrates that profit is made above the intersection of sales and total costs, representing the margin of safety. A reduction in sales revenue or increase in operating costs would move this point to the right, reducing the profitability of the organisation and reducing the margin of safety. Hence, for an organisation to be profitable it should seek to exploit and expand the margin of safety. However, one should consider that such calculations often represent one point in time and while providing useful information on a holistic level they should not be treated in isolation, i.e. basic profit or loss does not provide sufficient detail

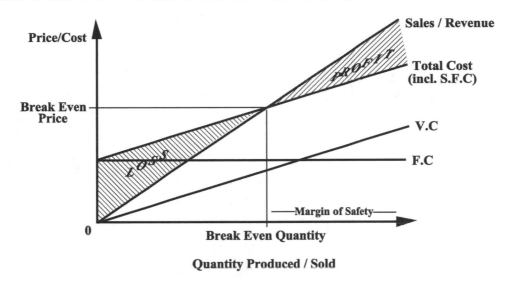

Figure 9.6 *Cost dynamics – breakeven*

of individual units of sale. Hence, it is necessary to examine the elements of operational costs.

Elements of cost

Kotas and Davis (1976) provide a simplistic breakdown of the relationship of costs relative to sales and profitability. While this is a dated reference and relative to hotels at that, it is a useful framework for understanding the cost structure of an operation. Hence it can be used for hotels or for sport and leisure operations. Figure 9.7 shows this breakdown.

From Figure 9.7, the relationship between costs, sales and profitability is clearly evident, although different operators will obviously have variations in the size of each cost. Sales can be seen to represent all costs plus profit or similarly profit can be seen as sales less costs. While this relationship is acceptable when adopting a holistic approach to the cost-profit relationship, it neglects to account for the complex package that makes up the sales structure of many sport and leisure businesses. The result is that, when related to costs, margins will vary throughout the operation and thus the contribution that each department achieves will vary, e.g. in a leisure centre the swimming pool revenues may be subsidised by the cafeteria, gym or 'room hire'.

Based on the foregoing, probably the two most important cost elements in understanding the nature of the pricing decisions are the concepts of marginal costing and contribution. These, in effect, expose the nature of costs and revenue structures, by accounting for the high fixed cost base and the importance of covering variable costs relative to seasonality and demand elasticity. Based on these key areas it is possible to determine the optimal price.

Gaining the optimal price: margins and contributions

To gain the optimum price, organisations must understand the dynamics of supply and nature of their markets – demand. Such an understanding allows more

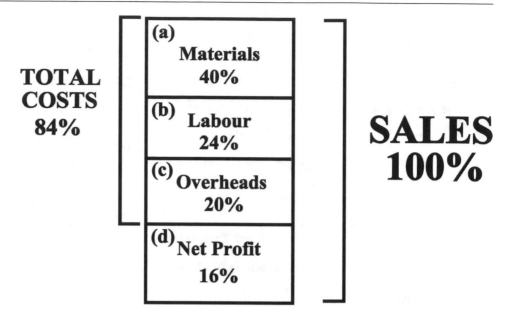

Figure 9.7 *Cost relationships (Source: Kotas and Davis 1976)*

informed and rational decision making. The contention thus far is that profit is the primary goal of any organisation. However, clearly this is not always the case (refer to previous section on public ownership and pricing). What is undisputable is that organisations must manage their cash flow and thus their tariff or cost structure to remain viable and survive.

The level of profit obtained can be expressed in a number of forms, the most simple of which, and indeed the foundation of all forms, is based on the equation:

$$\text{Profit} = \text{Total revenue} - \text{Total costs}$$

Where total revenue is composed of the price of a product multiplied by the quantity of the product sold and the total cost is represented by all costs associated with the operation.

It therefore becomes evident that to increase profit, revenue could be increased, either by increasing price, quantity sold, or both. However, the impact of price changes on profitability depends, among other things, on price elasticity (Orkin 1990), income elasticity and the possibility of substituting the product. It will also depend on supply variables such as the relative competitive position of the company (Ardel and Woods 1991; Norrbin 1993).

Alternatively, to raise profits, costs can be reduced either in terms of fixed costs such as alternative forms of ownership, in terms of semi-fixed, e.g. reducing full-time staffing levels or the variable cost, e.g. cheaper food or smaller portions. The danger when reducing costs is a reduction in quality, as the market side established the price and therefore the revenue generated is based on the consumer's perceived value and willingness to pay. Based on this premise, the most attractive way to raise profit would be to increase revenue while operating at maximum efficiency. This is the foundation of revenue and inventory management.

Pricing within this context takes two key forms: pricing based on marginal cost and pricing based on contribution.

Marginal costing

Much has been written from a technical perspective about the advantages and benefits of marginal costing and marginal income (Bonnisseau and Cornet 1990; Kelly and Gopalan 1992; Naish 1990; Vohra 1992). This section seeks to simplify the concept in relation to the sport and leisure industry.

Marginal costing can be defined as 'the increase or reduction in total cost, at a given volume of output, resulting from an increase or reduction of one unit of output' (Boardman 1978), while marginal revenue can be seen as the additional revenue obtained from producing one extra unit of output, the marginal income being the profit or difference between the marginal revenue and marginal cost.

The theory is that, for a short period, additional sales can be added to the normal sales volume profitably even at prices too low to cover a proportionate share of fixed overhead (Boardman 1978). This is because the operations overheads have been met by previous sales, so as long as the remaining units sold cover the variable cost of offering those units then additional profit is being made. This is perhaps more clearly shown through the use of an example.

If a leisure centre sells on average 8,000 memberships in a year and the total costs amount to £800,000 (£300,000 fixed costs and £500,000 variable costs) then the total cost per membership is £100. If the average achieved membership rate is £400 then a net profit of £300 per membership is made. This may be regarded the normal business of the leisure centre and every sale is expected to bear its cost burden. Once the normal business has been met, then any additional membership sales contribute to profit, as long as the price charged is greater than £62.50 (£500,000/8,000), allowing membership fees to be cut by up to 80% and hoping to attract additional spend in the supplementary areas. Marginal costing and marginal income can thus be very useful tools for the unit manager and form the basis of many pricing strategies, ranging from packaging, to 'sales' and special offers.

Contribution

The difference between the selling price per unit of additional sales and the marginal cost of those sales is the contribution per unit to fixed expenses, and profit, generally referred to simply as the 'contribution'. If the selling price is greater than the marginal cost, identified earlier, then there will be a contribution to profit from additional sales; however, if the marginal cost is greater than the selling price the extra business will result in a loss (Boardman 1978; Hughes 1989).

In a period when losses are being made due to high fixed expenses, a positive contribution may reduce the loss without actually resulting in a profit. This can be essential for survival and is well worth striving for during slack periods of demand.

While marginal income techniques and contribution may appear similar, they represent two inverted approaches. Marginal income ensures that the fixed and variable costs have been covered by the existing volume of output before allowing additional units of output, essentially representing additional variable cost only, to be sold cheaper as long as the variable cost is covered, thus making a profit. The contribution concept attempts to at least cover variable costs and go some way to contribute to fixed costs and, hopefully, profit. Obviously, the most desirable method for most sports and leisure operations is the marginal income approach, this is where revenue and inventory management can be of benefit.

SUMMARY

The management of revenue and the organisation inventory represents an intricate and complex relationship between demand, supply and marginal cost. It is based on the premise of ensuring maximum profitable revenue generation from markets of varying price elasticity evolved from different attitudes and capabilities to pay.

While the economic underpinning of such a concept is universal, it should be taken within the industrial context in order to be fully understood. As such, a range of management methods can be employed based on these economic foundations. This chapter has attempted to provide the reader with the core tools for understanding how to examine an organisation's cost structure and the nature of demand and supply. Ultimately, this allows an understanding of approaches to pricing and optimisation of revenue and/or profit.

An understanding of the economics of pricing and its relation to yield management provides the manager with an excellent tool to implement capacity management strategies.

Questions

1. With reference to a sport or leisure organisation, explain what would cause the demand curve to shift to the left. What could an organisation do to attempt to minimise or counteract this move?

2. The annual operating costs of a football club are £4 million in fixed costs and £8.6 million in variable costs. These figures are based on an average annual attendance of 80% ground capacity. The football club has a maximum seating capacity of 40,000 people and currently has 15,000 season ticket holders. Season tickets cost £500 per annum per person and are non-refundable. The normal football season runs from 1 September to 30 June and is composed of 30 home games. Using marginal costing, what is the breakeven price for non-season ticket holders? What would you advise the club to do to improve profitability?

3. Indicate which of the following statements are true and which are false:

   (i) An increase in the price of a good leads to a decrease in quantity supplied.

   (ii) Essential goods are price elastic in nature.

   (iii) A supply curve shifting to the right indicates less supplied at the same price.

   (iv) Price equilibrium is the minimum possible price suppliers will supply at.

References and further reading

Ardel, A. and Woods, R. H. (1991) 'Inflation and hotels: the cost of following a faulty routine', *The Cornell Hotel and Restaurant Administration Quarterly*, 31, 4, 66–75.

Berge, M. E. and Hopperstad, C. A. (1993) 'Demand driven dispatch: a method for dynamic aircraft capacity assignments, models and algorithms', *Operations Research*, 41, 1, 153–68.

Berry, W. L. (1991) 'Factory focus: segmenting markets from an operator's perspective', *Journal of Operations Management*, 10, 3, 363–87.

Bitran, G. R. and Lojo, M. (1993) 'A framework for analyzing service operations', *European Management Journal*, 11, 3, 271–82.

Boardman, R. D. (1978) 'Hotel and Catering – Costing and Budgets' (3rd edn). London: Heinemann.

Bonnisseau, J. and Cornet, B. (1990) 'Existence of marginal cost pricing equilibria: the nonsmooth case', *International Economic Review*, 31, 3, 685–708.

Brotherton, B. and Mooney, S. (1992) 'Yield management', *International Journal of Hospitality Management*, 11, 1, 23–32.

Buttle, F. (1986) Hotel and Food Service Marketing: A Managerial Approach. London: Cassell.

Crawford-Welch, S. (1991) 'Strategic hospitality management – theory and practice for the 1990s' in Teare, R. and Boer, A., *Strategic Hospitality Management: Theory and Practice for the 1990s*, London: Cassell, 182.

Davies, B. (1990) 'The economics of short breaks', *International Journal of Hospitality Management*, 9, 2, 103–6.

Dunn, K. D. and Brooks, D. E. (1990) 'Profit analysis: beyond yield management', *Cornell Hotel and Restaurant Administration Quarterly*, 31, 3, 80–90.

Guiltinan, J. (1987) 'The price bundling of services', *Journal of Marketing*, April, 51, 74–85.

Hanks, R. D., Cross, R. G. and Noland, R. P. (1992) 'Discounting in the hotel industry: a new approach', *The Cornell Hotel and Restaurant Administration Quarterly*, February, 15–23.

Hughes, H. L. (1989) Economics for hotel and catering students. London: Stanley Thomas.

Kelly, T. and Gopalan, R. (1992) '*Managing for profit*', *LIMRAs' Market Facts*, 11, 6, 47–50.

Kimes, S. E. and Chase, R. B. (1998) 'Strategic levers of yield management', *Journal of Service Research*, 1, 2, 156–66.

Kotas, R. and Davis, B. (1976) *Food cost control*. London: International Textbook Company Ltd.

Kuncher, E. and Hilleke, K. (1993) 'Value pricing through conjoint measurement: a practical approach', *European Management Journal*, 11, 3, 283–90.

Lewis, R. C. and Chambers, R. E. (1989) *Marketing Leadership in Hospitality: Foundations and Practices*. New York: Von Nostrand Reinhold.

Naish, H. F. (1990) 'The near optimality of mark-up pricing', *Economic Inquiry*, 28, 3, 555.

Norrbin, S. C. (1993) 'The relationship between price and marginal cost in US industry: a contradiction', *Journal of Political Economy*, 101, 6, 1149–64.

Orkin, E. B. (1988) 'Boosting your bottom line with yield management', *The Cornell and Hotel Restaurant Administration Quarterly*, 28, 4, 52–6.

Orkin, E. B. (1990) 'Strategies for managing transient rates', *The Cornell Hotel and Restaurant Administration Quarterly*, February, 34–9.

Quain, W. J. (1992) 'Analyzing sales mix profitability', *The Cornell Hotel and Restaurant Administration Quarterly*, April, 57–62.

Siegfried, J. and Zimbalist, A. (2000) 'The economics of sports facilities and their communities', *The Journal of Economic Perspectives*, 14, 3, 95–115.

Szymanski, S. (2001) 'Economics of sport: introduction', *The Economics Journal*, 111, 469.

Tribe, J. (1997) *Corporate Strategy for Tourism*, Thomson Business Press: London.

Van Dierdonck, R. (1992) 'Success strategies in a service economy', *European Management Journal*, 10, 3, 365–73.

Vohra, R. (1992) 'Marginal cost pricing under bounded marginal returns', *Econometrica*, 60, 4, 859–76.

Wijeyesinghe, B. (1993) 'Breaking even', *Hospitality*, February, 16–7.

Williams, I. (1987) 'Dark science brings boost to airline profits', *Sunday Times*, 27 November, 94.

Wolfe, A. (1993) 'How to profit from premium priced brands', *Marketing Business*, June, 28–32.

CHAPTER 10

Supply and Demand

Gerald Barlow

Supply and demand reflects itself operationally in sports and leisure organisations through its management of, and strategies for, its capacity. When a service organisation finds it has a lack of demand, it is unable to store or stock its excess of supply, as it would in other sectors such as manufacturing or agriculture. For example, a theatre unable to sell its seats for a specific night's performance cannot put the excess unsold seats into stock, to await the following day when demand might be greater and enable them to use the extra held in stock. Therefore, it has to find appropriate approaches to permit it to manage this situation. Similarly, if the next day, the demand for the theatre exceeds its ability to meet it, the initial result is likely to be a queue of waiting customers and, depending on how the organisation manages this process, it may be followed by dissatisfied or even lost customers. Service organisations, however, need to develop strategies to help manage these capacity-based problems.

The challenges that arise through a variation in supply and demand can initially be broken down into three areas: long-term, medium-term and short-term planning.

The more specific problem that faces sports and leisure operations is that, unlike many other sectors, they cannot easily change their capacity. For example, a company making baked beans, which finds that demand is increasing beyond normal ability to meet it, can in the short term, by changing its operations, increase available output capacity; it might introduce overtime, add a new working shift or possibly outsource some production. None of these opportunities would, however, exist for a football club finding its spectator demand has started to increase to a level where it exceeds its capacity to seat them. The only opportunity will be through a long-term strategy of creating more available seating, probably by building a new stand or even developing a new ground. These types of problem lead to the need for sports and leisure organisations to develop good long-term forecasting and demand patterns. Thus, most leisure and sports organisations need to take into account many influences outside the obvious trends and patterns.

Capacity is the word commonly associated with balancing demand and supply in the whole service sector; it is therefore important to understand what is meant by capacity. The *Concise Oxford Dictionary* definition reads 'a: the power of containing, receiving, experiencing or producing; b: the maximum amount that can be contained or produced etc.' There are many organisations within the field of operations management that use this last definition for their approach to capacity management. For example, a football club might say that their capacity is 22,500, meaning the number of seats available at any one game; or a property company might select a new site and build a multiplex cinema on the site, providing 12 screens seating a total of 2,200 customers. This approach does not reflect all the aspects of capacity: the football ground may seat 22,500 people today, but they need to apply to the local council and have support from the health and safety inspectorate, fire department and police to get a licence for this number. If they disagree, then the capacity may well be reduced and, as regulations change, so will/ may their capacity. The cinema does not reflect the number of showings a day and neither does it reflect the availability of aspects such as parking which might well affect their effective capacity. Similarly, neither reflects the time aspect of capacity: the football ground's capacity is for football games of which there are very few a year, often under 30. However, the ground might be used every weekday for purposes such as a conference training venue, as a market or have a busy restaurant and banqueting suite, so here the element of time needs to be incorporated into the overall picture.

LONG-TERM CAPACITY PLANNING

Given time to plan, and possibly a history of data on past events, the long-term elements of capacity planning should include:

- *Local infrastructure.* The local infrastructure is required to support long-term plans that marry demand and support services. The ability to be flexible in the medium term and to incorporate the necessary transportation network required to support the service.

- *Workers' education and skill.* It is essential that the area/region can support this service and the appropriate support services with the necessary staff at the right level of skill and education.

- *Political and economic stability.* The stability of the region will have an effect on the ability to attract visitors and investment from outside the region or country.

- *Labour costs.* The labour costs can vary dramatically within one country; this is an important factor to be considered when developing any long-term strategy involving capacity issues and investment.

- *Facility costs.* New development might be affected by the availability of government support for the development, which might affect the actual location of the facility and eventually the actual size. Consider the issues related to the site selection, nature size etc. of the New Wembley Complex or the English national football stadium.

All these aspects have to be considered alongside the detailed planning of future demand, facility requirements, layout, equipment access etc.

MEDIUM-TERM PLANNING

Having selected and established a long-term capacity, operations managers must decide how to manage the capacity to their best advantage in the medium term.

The first stage of this is forecasting demand over the medium-term period, possibly four to 24 months ahead. The job here is to try to match the supply of resources to the demand or to try to match the demand, in order that the resources available need as little adjustment as possible. Approaches for managing the demand in the medium term range from the very sophisticated as seen in some marketing techniques to quite simple almost primitive methods.

Examples of this can be seen in the way tourist or leisure attractions will plan their staffing in advance, planning the number of staff available at times throughout the day and then often moving the staff around the location or the jobs to meet the varying levels of demand. This form of medium-term planning allows for a reasonably good rotation programme and for the staff to be able to plan ahead. However, it can all be thrown into disarray by external short-term unplanned events, the weather for example, problems with the road system and so on.

The type of issues that can cause changes in demand include:

- seasonality in demand
- daily/weekly fluctuation in demand
- trends and fashions
- special events and occasions.

All of these can have a direct effect on the operations over the medium term and do need to be taken into consideration when developing a medium-term capacity plan (see Figure 10.1 and Table 10.1).

It is important for a service organisation to establish appropriate ways of measuring their capacity. The main problem is the complexity of the operation and the range of areas the customer might become involved in. It is a straightforward issue for a manufacturing company, for example, the factory making baked beans may have a capacity governed by its machines of, say, 2,000 cans per hour. The only factor to then take into account is the number of hours a day the machine will run, e.g. a seven-hour shift will produce 14,000 cans and if they run two shifts a day then they have a maximum capacity of 28,000 cans a day and so on; while the

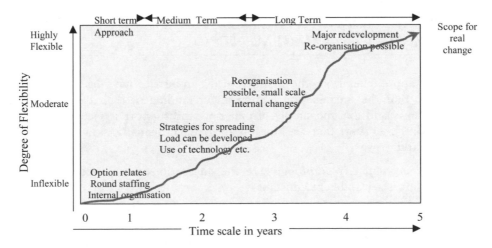

Figure 10.1 *Options available in managing existing capacity of a service organisation*

141

Table 10.1 *Options available to help capacity planning for leisure and sports operations*

Short term	Medium term	Long term
Man power planning • multiskilling • part-time staff • split shifts • overtime Using the customer as co-worker Customer participation	Use of technology • automation of services • entry systems • communication systems Adding additional capacity, temporary facilities Sharing capacity/equipment Better long-term planning forecasting techniques	Develop more permanent capacity New venue/facilities Better forecasting technology Improve/develop new service delivery and processes

number of staff needed to operate the machine will only change with the number of shifts worked. In the case of a leisure park, capacity will be governed by the number established by the licence to trade, which could be 2,000 maximum a day. But, it isn't that simple: if all 2,000 were to arrive within the first hour, the capacity will be limited to the number of people who can enter the park per minute. This will be restricted by the number of entry points and staff able to work these entry points and so it can continue, to areas like the rides and the other outlets, toilets and so on. It will even then be extended to take into account the weather. A sudden sharp rainstorm will put increased pressure on undercover areas or indoor attractions and the catering areas. This is still a basic approach, because the leisure park's rate of service will also be governed by the customers: how easily they can be processed at entry, how prepared they are at entry, money etc., how happy they are with their initial perception. A poor initial perception may cause delays, due to complaints, uncertainty etc. so, overall, the elements of service capacity can be influenced by both internal issues and elements and external, uncontrollable elements.

TRADITIONAL APPROACHES TO SUPPLY/DEMAND CAPACITY MANAGEMENT

The approaches from the manufacturing industries have been developed on the basis that the organisation has an understanding of their demand and capacity elements and that the supply of materials and support services is effectively managed. Three ways that are suitable to manage fluctuations which might occur in demand are:

1. *level capacity planning*: here the fluctuations are ignored and the capacity levels set and kept constant

2. *chase demand planning*: here the organisation adjusts its capacity to reflect the changes in demand

3. *demand management*: here the organisation seeks to change the demand in order to fit the available capacity.

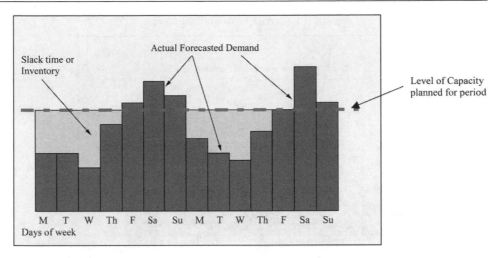

Figure 10.2 *A level capacity plan and its effect over a set period*

Level capacity planning

In the situation of level capacity planning, the capacity is set at a uniform level throughout the period of time, irrespective of any changes in demand. This type of planning is more suited to operations where the excesses between capacity and demand can be stored as inventory, as demonstrated in Figure 10.2.

In these types of situation many organisations plan ahead for all the requirements to meet their set capacity, the number of staff required, appropriate materials etc. and then any excess output is put into stock to await demand. Clearly, such plans do not suit areas where the product or service is 'perishable', such as most areas within leisure and sports operations. However, there are some areas of the sports sector where inexperienced operators tend to run a form of level capacity operations. They plan well ahead and arrange the number of staff needed for each area and then, on the day, they operate in this fixed way. For example, a football club will forecast expected demand for a match and arrange their staffing well in advance. When the day of the game arrives, if the weather is atrocious and the number of supporters is very low, they will have too many staff in all areas, the arrival booths, in the catering and bars, in the security and stewards and so on. This is not too bad a situation except for the unnecessary extra costs. However, if the opposite occurs and the forecast exceeds expectations, due to a variety of unexpected issues, recent publicity for the opposition, unexpected success and so on and the number of arrivals far exceeds the ability to deal with them, this will result in queues at the arrival booths, queues at the catering and shops and even queues to get out, resulting in unhappy supporters on both sides. There is also the potential for lost customers.

Chase demand

This is the opposite of level capacity. Here the capacity is planned to be flexible and to adjust in order to meet demand. This is clearly much more complex and difficult to manage. It may involve different staffing levels, working hours, the use of technology and even the opening and closing of areas of capacity like seating areas,

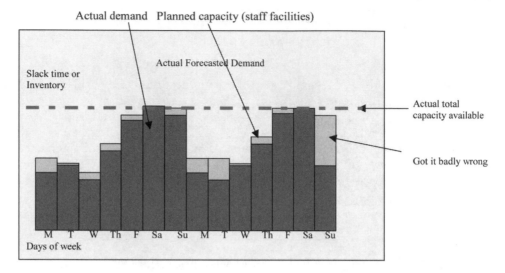

Figure 10.3 *A chase capacity plan*

rooms and special facilities. These decisions might not, however, be arranged simply around forecasting and planning in advance but around much later custo-mer-influenced decisions, like the weather, personal preferences, impulses and recent events etc. so management need to be more reactive and flexible. The whole effect might involve having available part-time labour, full-time flexible labour, staff prepared to work extra hours or the use of external contract labour. This approach can often have an effect on management's ability to control and manage quality (see Figure 10.3).

A mixed capacity plan

An alternative that comes out of the first two options is to choose a mixed capacity plan. Here capacity is managed so that it has the ability to open and close to suit the expected demand and then the available capacity is managed with a chase demand approach. This may be on a daily scale or on a period or time of year scale. For example, a leisure centre may be a mixed facility centre offering inside and outside facilities, swimming pools, gym/health centre, sports hall, running track, playing surfaces and so on. The centre may open different facilities at differing times, the swimming pool at 6.00 am until 9.00 pm, the gym/health centre from 7.00 am until 11.00 pm and the running track in daylight hours only, from March until November, with other inside facilities at specific times and days. All of these may also differ opening times during the days of the week. So the gym/health centre is open Monday to Friday from 7.00 am until 11.00 pm but on Saturday from 9.00 am until 8.00 pm and Sunday from 9.00 am until 6.00 pm therefore aiming to match forecasted and past known demands times.

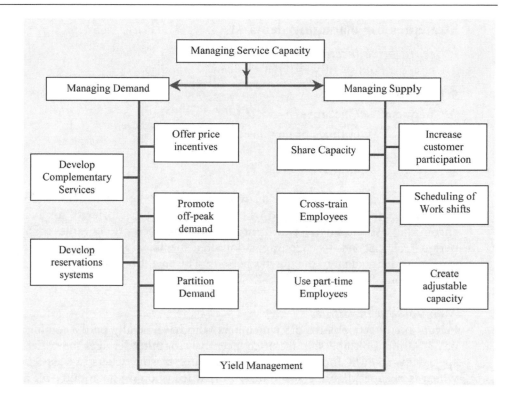

Figure 10.4 *Strategies for matching supply of and demand for services (source: Fitzsimmons and Fitzsimmons 1994)*

SHORT-TERM PLANNING

Demand management

Within service organisations, and especially areas like sports and leisure, demand is inherently variable. It is the nature of the customer-based market that demand will vary continuously and the job of operations is to manage this process.

The simplest and most important requirement for a leisure- or sports-based service is to know who the customers are and to understand their basic needs and requirements. James and Mona Fitzsimmons (1994) developed a model for managing demand. This model covers the aspects related to managing capacity very effectively and is shown in Figure 10.4.

Although variation in demand is in some ways necessary, excessive variations should not be seen as acceptable or inevitable. Leisure and sporting organisations should develop tactics to allow them to smooth the demand and where this is not possible, learn how to manage it to the best possible benefit for the customer and then the organisations. The strategies for smoothing the demand can be seen in Figure 10.4. This model separates the management of capacity into two sections, management of demand and the management of supply.

Strategies for managing demand

Offering price incentives

There are a number of ways that this can be approached:

- membership incentives
- frequent user incentives
- specific day or times of day incentives
- peak-load premiums
- off-peak incentives.

All these techniques have one or two aims, either to spread demand more evenly or appropriately over the period when the service is being offered, for example to encourage customers of a leisure centre to come at quieter times rather than at peak periods. Or, second, to encourage additional members, by offering incentives for joining and attending in the quieter periods. This might be joining the entire service or a section of the service.

Membership incentives

Private membership clubs offer members who have usually paid a joining fee and pay an annual membership fee price incentives for other services they offer and for special events. UK football league teams offer season tickets at a special price, which is cheaper than the accumulated event fee (should you attend over a certain number or all of the games); they may also offer the season ticket holder first choice for any special events, such as cup tickets etc.

Frequent user incentives

These are commonly of two types: a discounted or preference rate or a subsequent rebate or discount. This type of incentive can often be found in leisure centres and gyms, where frequent users get offered a discounted user rate on the basis of their heavy usage. This is often tied to a guarantee payment system such as direct debit. The second type of frequent user incentive is one where the user is offered price incentive, reward or future discount on the price of future usage or even a cash rebate discount to be used elsewhere within the centre. For example: a leisure centre offering a monthly rate for frequent users decided that in the run-up to a quiet period, like Christmas, where it may lose a number of monthly members, to offer an additional discount for those members using the facilities over a certain number of days during the last two months of the year, the bonus being available during the new year (often also a much quieter period). For example, any member using the facility more than 29 times in the last six-week period of the year will receive a 35% discount on their next month's (January's) membership fee. This encourages people to attend and additionally encourages the continuation of the monthly membership in the quiet months of December and January.

Specific day or time of day incentives

This approach is now becoming more widespread as organisations realise the need to bring customer into the facilities to use the services at times which are normally not popular. This may be time of day, a certain day of the week or period of the year. A good example of this can be found in a number of French ski resorts, currently actively promoting the resorts for alternative use during quiet times of the year (non-snow). Similar usage is being found in sports centres, for example, there are a number of football clubs that are trying to develop special events and visitor tours for out-of-season periods.

Peak-load premiums

Here the intention is to charge a premium price for the use of facilities/services at peak periods, where demand exceeds the ability to cope. The basic premise is to raise the price so that those people who feel the need/desire to use the services at these peak periods will be prepared to pay a premium. Health clubs in busy city environments are good examples of this strategy. This can seem to be inappropriate and when it is seen as excessive, the alternative is to offer the opposite incentive: a reduction to those people who can come during the quiet period to encourage some not to visit during peak times and to attend during quiet times. This strategy is also covered by the next approach.

Off-peak incentives

As stated earlier the aim here is to reduce the problem of over-demand at popular or peak times and to offer incentives, often financial, for people/members to attend at quieter period/times. This approach is seen in many walks of life, from the 'happy hour' in hotels and pubs, to public transportation with its ticket price/time differentiation policies, both bus and train services offer 'saver' and 'supersaver' rates for passengers travelling at off-peak times.

The other strategies for managing demand are a little more complex and need a better understanding of the systems and operations.

Partitioning demand

Demand for services seldom comes from a uniform or consistent source, for example demand for the use of a swimming pool in a leisure centre will differ by the hour and by the day. Serious training swimmers seek early morning training facilities; and demand then ranges through school visits during the day and term time to mother and toddlers at specific daytime sessions and so on. Demand can often be arranged or grouped into predictable sections, of planned arrivals, along with random arrivals. This may mean partitioning the capacity to facilitate the differing types of usage. For example, to stay with the swimming pool example: it is possible to separate sections of the swimming areas into different usage, one pool can be for mothers and toddlers, while a main pool can be subsectioned for general swimming, and a number of separate lanes for serious training and speed swimming. The aim is to satisfy all sectors of demand, while maximising the usage of capacity.

Complementary services

The idea here is that the main service develops a secondary service that complements the first. A good example of this can be found in most airports, where the main service is the transportation of people and goods from one place to another, but because of the need of the travelling public to arrive early and wait, the airports have developed a series of complementary services, from bars and restaurants, to newsagents, bookshops and duty-free shopping villages. Similarly, sports and leisure operators need to understand the varying nature of demands in their customers and develop complementary services. These can either be operated in-house or outsourced to other operators. Few professional football clubs will not have catering outlets within their grounds and most have supporters' shops selling sports memorabilia. Similarly, sports centres can today be found with restaurants, bars and shops supporting their main activities.

Developing a reservation system

Taking reservations pre-sells the potential service and helps forecast future business. As reservations are made it is possible to deflect other time slots and to pre-plan business. A reservation system also benefits the total customer base as it reduces waiting time and queues. Problems can still arise when customers arrive late for a pre-booked event or fail to honour their reservation (DNA: 'did not arrive'). But overall the benefits from a pre-booking system by far outweigh those of a non-reserved system. For example, imagine a leisure centre with six squash courts, offering to sell the courts for periods of 45 minutes. If there were no booking or reservation system the risk of queues at certain times of the day would be very high, as would the chance of dissatisfied customers. With the reservation system, the customers are able to see that it is fair and the operators can identify peaks and troughs in bookings and encourage customers to book when quiet or develop a strategy to encourage a smooth demand.

Strategies for managing supply

Fitzsimmons and Fitzsimmons (2001) suggest the following approach to be considered in combinations or separately:

- increasing customer participation
- sharing capacity
- creating adjustable capacity
- better use of labour element by:
    - cross-training employees
    - scheduling the work shifts
    - using part-time employees.

Increasing customer participation

This strategy can be seen best with hotel breakfast service, where service was traditionally provided by the waitress directly at the table, where she took the order, had the items prepared and then served it. Today, most hotels from the simple B&B through the differing star categories to the most expensive, tend to serve breakfast via a buffet. The self-service customer participation has replaced much of the service staff job. What remains has become a job of serving drinks and toast, clearing away and topping up the buffet. Similarly, the fast food industry has perfected customer participation to a point where, in many fast food outlets, the customer orders the foods, waits for it, delivers it to the table and then clears it away. The service staff simply take the order, prepare the tray of items, collect the payment and then clean the service and table areas. Through this process the customer expect a faster service and a less expensive meal. In many ways the server still provides the customer with benefits, but these are now more subtle. Sports and leisure operations can learn from the fast food operators, the aim is to encourage the customer to become a co-worker. Through this mechanism, the capacity to serve becomes more related to the demand for the service, rather than fixed to the ability of the server to serve.

There are some drawbacks to this approach: for instance the self-service customers may fail fully to understand their role which can lead to problems. Hygiene issues may arise in food service areas, and as a result the quality of the labour is no longer fully under the manager's control

Sharing capacity

An organisation may invest large sums in equipment and facilities for example sport centres, the physical facilities and then the equipment needed to set up the various activities and operations. During periods where demand is low, it might be possible to identify opportunities to put the spare capacity to other uses.

For many years, swimming pools have been willing to share their facilities with local schools or swimming clubs at times when the demand for the swimming pool was low. Sports clubs may be able to share their facilities with other organisations when their sport is not played, for example cricket clubs which share their ground with sports like hockey or lacrosse during the non-cricket season.

Creating adjustable capacity

Through the use of layout and design it is possible to create adjustable capacity. This permits the operation to plan better their cost base, use of labour and basic resources, power etc. What can be more offputting for a customer than to be the only person in a vast space? Today, many sports grounds will only open certain areas of their grounds for specific events to match expected demand and to ensure that spectators are all kept in appropriate areas. This creates a better atmosphere for the spectators and helps provide a more efficient use of the facilities for the organisation. Similarly, it is possible for leisure operator to create adjustable capacity by managing their facilities, changing or rearranging the layout and by opening and closing areas to suit demand. This might be reflected in a leisure centre by adjusting the actual opening hours for differing areas and facilities.

Better use of labour element

Cross-training employees

Most leisure and sports organisations are made up of a mixture of operations. When one operation is busy another may be quiet. By cross-training the staff to perform tasks in several operations it will help create additional or flexible capacity and so help smooth out peaks in specific demands.

Scheduling the work shifts

Traditional working shifts have stayed unchanged for decades but it is surely time in the twenty-first century for organisations to reconsider their current working practice. In many areas of sport and leisure operations it is difficult to smooth effectively the patterns of demand. Consider the pattern of arrivals shown in Table 10.2 for a dry ski centre.

From this simple chart of visitors it can be seen that demand varies between season and therefore the staff levels will also need to be adjusted. However, if we

Table 10.2 *The number of visitors to a dry ski centre per quarter*

Year	1st quarter	2nd quarter	3rd quarter	4th quarter
1995	3,203	1,908	1,861	3,415
1996	3,343	1,986	1,921	3,514
1997	3,154	1,799	1,834	3,098
1998	3,025	1,965	1,837	3,204
1999	3,414	1,967	2,073	3,229

Table 10.3 *Monthly demand patterns for the 1st quarter of visitors at a dry ski centre*

Year	January	February	March
1995	929	1,375	899
1996	973	1,279	1,091
1997	906	1,166	1,082
1998	867	1,204	954
1999	892	1,389	1,133

Table 10.4 *Pattern of daily demand for the third week in January of visitors at a dry ski centre*

	Week 3						
Year	Monday	Tuesday	Wednesday	Thursday	Friday	Saturday	Sunday
1995	104	78	108	98	141	189	211
1996	104	91	90	90	139	220	239
1997	97	82	89	73	151	193	221
1998	89	84	83	77	125	197	212
1999	101	76	101	84	143	200	227

investigate these figures further, we get results as shown in Table 10.3. From the monthly arrival figures, it can be seen that they vary still further between the months; on average the demand is 17.5% greater in February than January and 13% greater in March than January.

If we then compare the daily arrivals for a single week in January, the quietest of the months in quarter 1, the variation can be seen to become even more complex. The centre is actually open for seven days a week with Tuesday as the quietest day and Sunday the busiest, being 170% or 1.7 times busier than Tuesday (See Figure 10.5 and Table 10.4).

Finally, Table 10.5 shows the hourly variation of arrivals: here we see that not only is the centre open seven days a week but it is open for 11 hours a day. The variation in demand here, on average, is a range of 380% or four times busier between the busiest and quietest times.

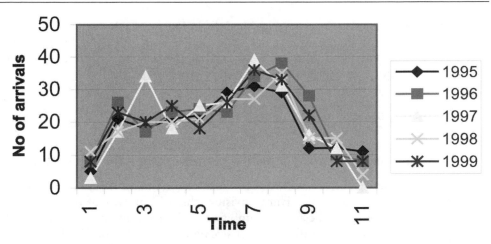

Figure 10.5 *Sunday arrivals pattern for dry ski slope*

Table 10.5 *Daily pattern of customer arrivals for the third Sunday in January at a dry ski centre*

		3rd Sunday January									
Year	Time	10–11	11–12	12–1	1–2	2–3	3–4	4–5	5–6	6–7	7–8	8–9
1995		5	21	18	21	22	29	31	29	12	12	11
1996		8	26	17	23	24	23	34	38	28	10	8
1997		3	17	34	18	25	26	39	31	16	12	0
1998		11	17	20	20	21	27	27	35	15	15	4
1999		8	23	20	25	18	26	36	33	22	8	8

All these examples show the complexity of managing staffing numbers; actual job scheduling and work scheduling become more of an issue, at times like the 10–11 slot in which very few people arrive.

The need in the modern service operation is more for daily work scheduling than the traditional weekly or monthly work schedules. It is essential that this is combined with job schedules and multi-skilling for many of the staff, to ensure effective capacity operations and management.

Using part-time employees

Leisure and sports centres experience variations in their activities on different days and at differing hours of the day, as well as seasonal variations as can be seen from the dry ski slope example of earlier. But when this is combined with a variety of uses, the centre's variations become even more complex. The operations usually employ full-time employees to cover these areas. But as the cost of labour increases for an organisation, in order to meet the demands put on it by its customers, it has become increasingly common to use part-time employees as a way of matching the demand of the customers with the organisation's financial constraints.

The planning of part-time schedules is just as demanding on management as that of the full-time daily and weekly scheduling. Today, for this to work effectively, it is necessary for the part-time employees to be trained and treated in the same way as full-time employees and acknowledged as the same as full-time employees but working more appropriate hours (probably to both parties).

OPERATIONS MANAGEMENT IN ACTION

The effects of real-life capacity planning: the Chester City FC story

In 1980 Chester City Football Club was a league club in the then Fourth Division and by 1990 it was in the Third Division; this was by way of the creation of the premier league, but Chester had ambitions. These ambitions were to see Chester open a new 6,000-seater (the smallest size permitted in the football league) stadium (Deva Stadium) for the start of the 1993–4 season, and although they were still in the Third Division, their sights were set on promotion to the Second Division and as the season progressed these ambitions grew, but so did their problems:

> Chester City have been savaged by their own fans and supporters from Preston North End FC following last Saturday's Third Division promotion clash at Deva Stadium. An estimated 300 Preston fans were locked out of the ground and despite several appeals for them to leave, dozens forced their way in 25 minutes after the kick-off. (*Chester Chronicle*, 8 April 1994)

A letter to the *Lancashire Evening Post* (2 April 1994) stated:

> What a pathetic capacity for a league football club. Chester City should be stripped of their league status.

One year later the team's form had slumped and by 2000 Chester City had been relegated from the football league to the Nationwide Conference League. During the year 2001–2 their average gates were 1,000.

They have moved from a problem in early 1994 where they had insufficient capacity to deal with demand, to a position in 2001 where they never, or hardly ever, came close to using their full capacity. This case helps to show how the issues of capacity, supply and demand are closely linked and how extremely difficult they are to get completely right in a sports or leisure environment.

CONCLUSIONS

An inherent problem for leisure and sports organisations is the variability of demand, which creates a major challenge for their managers in trying to make the best and most effective use of the fixed capacity. There are two ways these challenges can be approached: one is by trying to smooth these demands, so allowing for the best use of the fixed capacity. The second approach is by managing demand via techniques such as partitioning demand, offering price incentives and off-peak use, developing a reservations system and complementary services.

An alternative approach is to look at the supply side. Here there are a number of alternatives to help adjust capacity to match demand, for instance the use of effective work shift patterns and the involvement of part-time employee and cross-training of staff. Alternatively, it is possible to increase customer participation, to share capacity where possible or to adjust the available capacity.

These strategies are two separate ways of dealing with the same problem, one from the demand side, the other from the supply side. In some sectors, it is possible for the organisation to invest in technology to help manage this area, through the use of a reservations systems and revenue or yield management. The results these approaches are aimed at include the organisation's capacity being more effectively used, while they gain the best possible income from the capacity and the customers are offered the service they seek.

Questions

1. How can a computerised reservation system increase service capacity?
2. What possible dangers are associated with developing complementary services?
3. Select a leisure- or sports-based operation that has implemented a strategy for managing demand or supply of capacity and discuss its strategy.

References and further reading

Armistead, C. G. and Clark, G. (1994) 'The "Coping" capacity management strategy in services and the influence on quality performance', *International Journal of Service Industry Management*, 5, 2, 5–22.

Babert, V. A. and Schowalter, M. J. (1990) 'Measuring the impact of part-time workers in the service organisations', *Journal of Operations Management*, 9, 2, 209–29.

Bitan, G. R. and Maindschein, S. V. (1995) 'An application of yield management in the hotel industry considering multiple day stays', *Operations Research*, 25, 5, 84–104.

Concise Oxford Dictionary (1991) St Ives: Oxford University Press.

Dobson, S. M. and Goddard, J. A. (1992) 'The demand for standing and seating viewing accommodation in the English football league', *Applied Economics*, 24, 10, 1155–63.

Fitzsimmons, J. A. and Fitzsimmons, M. A. (1994) *Service Management For Competitive Advantage*. Singapore: McGraw-Hill.

Fitzsimmons, J. A. and Fitzsimmons, M. A. (2001) *Service Management – Operations, Strategy, and Information Technology*. Singapore: McGraw-Hill.

Goodale, J. C. and Tunc, E. (1998) 'Tour scheduling with dynamic service rates', *International Journal of Service Industry Management*, 9, 3, 227–47.

Hesket, J. L., Sasser, W. E. and Hart, C. W. L. (1990) *Service Breakthroughs: Changing the Rules of the Game*, New York: Free Press.

Ng, I. C. L., Wirtz, J. and Lee, K. S. (1999) 'The strategic role of unused service capacity', *International Journal of Service Industry Management*, 1, 1, 47–64.

Radas, S. and Shugan, S. M. (1998) 'Managing service demand: shifting and bundling', *Journal of Service Research*, 1, 1, 47–64.

www.chester-city.co.uk/
www.the-seals.co.uk/

CHAPTER 11

Leisure Revenue Management

Una McMahon-Beattie and Ian Yeoman

INTRODUCTION

Revenue management (RM) or yield management marries the issues of supply, demand and price, when the organisation is constrained by capacity. It is a management tool or technique which has gained wide acceptance in many service industries (airlines, hotels, golf, car rentals and cruising) and there is substantial evidence that it is effective in improving revenues. This chapter will explore the application of RM to the leisure experience and sets out to explain the process of RM, through a holistic model that brings benefits to managing leisure properties and events.

THE LEISURE EXPERIENCE: TIME AND PRICE

What is the leisure experience and how do we manage a unit of leisure inventory such as a trip to the gym, a round of golf or a holiday on a cruise ship? It has been said that leisure is something that is difficult to define (Grainger-Jones 1999). If we put it in the context of time, Grainger warns that there is a danger of saying that 'leisure is whatever occupies my leisure time'. However, within a business context, the leisure experience is all about managing time and price. It is about being able to match a customer's time against when a leisure property is available in order to achieve optimum revenue. In the terms of economics of leisure property, it is about addressing a pricing and capacity framework where the role of the leisure manager is to align the supply, demand and price of the leisure product or service. When a leisure manager makes informed decisions in this relationship, he/she improves profitability or generates the best type of revenue, whatever the objectives of the organisation or business.

In making these decisions the leisure manager encounters the classic debates about revenue management within service industries (Cross 1997). Why do leisure centres charge a premium price in the evening and a reduced price during the day? Why do tourists pay different prices for the same holiday experience at different times of year? This is revenue management in action. Essentially, we use revenue management because the leisure experience is different from a manufactured product. In common with the service industries (Sharples, Yeoman and Leask 1999), leisure differs in its characteristic from manufacturing industries:

- The leisure experience is a moment in time, 'a holiday', 'a round of golf' and 'a stay in a hotel'.
- Consumption and production of that unit of time is generally simultaneous and inseparable.

These leisure experiences therefore operate along a spectrum from low to high perishability, low to high simultaneity, low to high intangibility and low to high customer intimacy. Leisure organisations operate in a range of markets that comprise a vast array of elements to differing degrees. Therefore, finding the optimum price for the leisure experience at a specific time period is a challenge for the leisure manager.

The revenue management problem involves matching a probabilistic demand to a set of finite resources in such a manner, which will optimise profits (Cross 1997). In the leisure industry, RM or 'yield management' can be used to find that answer.

ORIGINS AND APPLICATIONS OF RM

The airline industry has been credited with the development and refinement of RM following the deregulation of the US airline industry in the 1970s, when airlines such as American, Delta and United used a capacity management strategy in order to compete with the success of People's Express. People's Express was a new airline that offered customers a low-priced and no-frills service from Newark Airport. American competed by offering a few seats at even lower prices than People's Express but maintaining higher fares for higher paying passengers. In this way, American attracted the low-spend passenger who would book flights well in advance from People's Express, but maintained the higher spend passengers who booked flights one or two days before departure. As a result of this policy, People's Express was eventually declared bankrupt. Today, RM is a management technique being utilised by an increasing number of service industries in order to maximise the effective use of their available capacity and ensure financial success. The application of RM can be seen in hotels (Huyton and Peters 2001), package holidays (Hoseason and Johns 1998), air transport (Ingold and Huyton 2001), rail transport (Hood 2001), cruising (Hoseason 2001) and football (Barlow 2001).

Definition of RM

In general terms, RM is the process of allocating the right type of capacity or inventory unit to the right type of customer at the right price so as to maximise yield or 'revenue' (Kimes 1989, 2001; Weatherford and Bodily 1992). In the airline industry, RM can be considered to be the revenue or yield per passenger mile, with revenue being a function of both the price the airline charges for differentiated service options (pricing) and the number of seats sold at each price (seat inventory control) (Donaghy *et al.* 1998). In hotels, RM is concerned with the market-sensitive pricing of fixed room capacity relative to a hotel's specific market segments. Indeed, Kimes (1989) states that RM in hotels consists of two functions: rooms inventory management and pricing. The goal of RM is the formulation and profitable alignment of price, product and buyer. As such, RM can be defined in the service industries as a 'revenue maximisation technique which aims to increase net revenue through the predicted allocation of available inventory capacity to pre-determined market segments at optimum price' (Donaghy *et al.* 1998). In leisure revenue, it becomes the 'ability to sell the right experience to the right leisure goer, for the right price in order to optimise revenue'. It is essential to design a revenue management decision-making framework in which decisions about revenue can be focused. This enables the leisure manager to make effective decisions that are proactive about revenue in relation to the rest of the organisational business.

Similarity of inventory units

As a general rule, RM assumes that inventory units are fairly similar. Most airline RM systems are designed to deal solely with seats, with configuration between different grades of seating. Similarly, in the car rental business, cars are considered easily interchangeable. Rates for different cars are sorted and placed within rate tiers and then rate tiers and all corresponding rates are opened and closed as necessary (Cross 1997). Within a leisure experience the unit of inventory becomes time, therefore decisions focus on time utilisation and the appropriate price to charge for that time unit.

Preconditions

Revenue management suits leisure organisations where capacity is relatively fixed, where the demand is unstable and where the market can be segmented. Combining these features with low marginal costs and the ability to sell a perishable product to leisure customers well in advance of consumption are the key characteristics of companies that can adopt RM. Developing these ideas further, Kimes (2001) has outlined a number of preconditions for the success of RM.

Relatively fixed capacity
Revenue management is suitable for services industries where capacity is constrained. Capacity cannot be inventoried to deal with fluctuations in demand, however, capacity can be measured in the terms of physical and non-physical units. Physical capacity is about bedrooms, number of theatre seats or exhibition space. In non-physical terms, capacity can also be thought of as time based. For example, tee-off times in golf, time slots for aeroplane departures and landings etc. Therefore, time becomes the unit of inventory which is also a constraint on capacity. In the long term, capacity can be changed, for example, by adding extra a new function suite in a hotel or reconfiguring the seating in a theatre or restaurant. However, this usually involves a large financial investment in terms of equipment or plant.

Predictable demand
This is about managing leisure customers who book through reservations and those who simply 'walk in'. The leisure manager will need to develop strategies to manage both types of customer. It is about predicting what advance bookings will be made at different price levels against walk-in or 'on-demand' situations (otherwise known as demand forecasting). It is about being able to manage and balance both forms of demand. In order to do this, a leisure manager needs to

compile information about percentage of reservations, walk-ins, customer time periods and service duration (Kimes 2001). Collecting information on extraneous variables which can affect demand, such as weather conditions, school holidays, local festivals or sporting events, will also assist the leisure manager to make effective forecasts.

Perishable inventory

As stated earlier, the inventory of capacity constrained firms should be thought of as a unit of time. Airlines, hotels, package holidays and cruises all have the characteristics of service, or particularly, they are selling an inventory unit of 'a piece of time'. This may be a journey from Los Angeles to London, an FA Cup Final or car hire for a day. All these industries have commonality, in that firms working within them are constrained by capacity. Since unsold capacity cannot be inventoried, it is lost forever. For example, an afternoon visit to Leeds Castle is a time slot on a given day. If the opportunity to sell that experience is lost, the revenue cannot be recovered. The perishability of the capacity-constrained service organisation adds to the complexity of finding the optimal revenue (Kimes 2001).

Appropriate cost and pricing structures

Where leisure organisations are constrained by capacity, the premier function of management is to utilise the available capacity to ensure financial success. RM is used in service industries that are capital intensive because of the nature of their high fixed costs. The marginal contribution of selling another leisure experience is so small to the marginal revenue as to render the costs inconsequential. Because of this, revenue management is often associated with revenue optimisation because of the fairly low level of variable costs. Indeed, the relatively low level of variable costs allows leisure managers some flexibility in pricing (Edgar 2001).

Time variable demand

The leisure customer varies by the time of the year, day of the week or time of the day. Managers must be able to forecast the uptake of the leisure experience. Allocations of available inventory units can be given effective pricing decisions against demand and supply issues. This flexible pricing structure against time varied demand enables organisations to make decisions against off-peak and peak periods.

Necessary ingredients

Kimes (2001) has also categorised the ingredients necessary for a RM system: 'A company must possess the ability to segment the market based on willingness to pay, information on historical demand and booking patterns, good knowledge of pricing, a well developed overbooking policy and a good information system' (Kimes 2001: 9).

Market segmentation

Within RM systems an organisation can segment its leisure users by degree of revenue. This relates to purpose, time and price sensitivity. Airlines are a good example: they can predict demand per type of passenger for a given flight (Ingold and Huyton 2001). Airlines place restrictions on purchase depending on demand

and supply, i.e. non-refundable cancellations and APEX fares. They also know for example, that business travellers are not price sensitive. As such airlines hold capacity in order to sell to this type of customer rather than selling the capacity in advance to budget travellers. In addition, business travellers are time sensitive and do not mind paying higher price only a few days before departure. By holding capacity available, airlines risk not selling the capacity but understand the missed opportunity of selling to a higher yielding passenger. Therefore, leisure organisations can segment their leisure customers by purpose, price and time. It is about balancing these dimensions.

Historical demand and booking patterns

An essential element of an effective RM system is the ability to produce accurate forecasts. As such, appropriate management systems are required. Leisure organisations must be able to predict likely demand by leisure goer or customer type in advance. This is based on extensive information and tracking systems which allow for the development of historical booking patterns per leisure customer type which assist the leisure manager to forecast into the future. These forecasting systems develop and mature over time. They act as a self-learning experience. Knowing booking patterns helps manage demand and revenue optimisation.

Pricing knowledge

This is about knowledge of situations and how to manage price in different situations. By using multiple rates to optimise revenue, the revenue manager must know when to use price discrimination and how. Typically, when demand is high, no discrimination takes places but when demand is low, concentration moves to discounting.

Overbooking

Currently, hotels (Huyton and Peters 2001) and airlines (Ingold and Huyton 2001) use overbooking for the purpose of protecting themselves against no shows and cancellations by forecasting their predictability. Kimes (2001) suggests, however, that a good way of reducing cancellations and no shows is through methods of control such as pre-payment. Within the leisure experience, decisions must also be made about the ethical, health and safety issues of overbooking (Barlow 2001), especially in fixed-capacity sports stadium. Overbooking also relates to the issue of space utilisation and its implications for a favourable experience. Boella (2001) also highlights the legality of overbooking, as selling an experience for capacity you have not got (the venue is full) breaches the Trade Descriptions Act of 1968.

Information systems and knowledge management

Successful implementation of RM depends on the quality of knowledge the organisation holds about its leisure customers. It is necessary to develop an effective process of holding knowledge about leisure customers through knowledge elicitation, retrieval, coding, storage and dissemination (Sparrow 1998). It is about manipulating and analysing 'multiple knowledge' which is a management device to integrate different types of knowledge such as hard factual information and personal recounts of experiences within RM systems. The use of artificial intelligence (AI) has enormous potential for handling the complexities of RM because of its abilities in complex problem solving, reasoning, perception, planning and analysis of extensive data. Expert systems (ES) are 'knowledge-based' software packages that reflect the expertise in the area of the application and have extensive capacity in dealing with non-numeric, qualitative data (Russell 1997).

Strategic levers of RM

Kimes and Chase (1998) have outlined the two strategic levers that managers can use to manage demand and, hence, revenue: duration management and demand-based pricing.

Duration management

Capacity-constrained firms face decisions between unpredictable duration of the experience or fixed time slot. Therefore, decisions need to be made over the control of the length of time that leisure users have of the experience. The management of duration focuses on uncertainty of arrival, reducing the uncertainty of duration or reducing the time between customers. Duration is how long leisure users use an experience in the terms of, for example, the number of bed nights or a round of golf. What RM is about is questioning the inventory unit as fixed or variable. Are you selling a fixed time slot, i.e two hours or the whole duration of the leisure experience? Managing duration control is about getting leisure visitors to honour their reservations. Leisure goers who do not arrive or arrive late have lost the organisation the opportunity to use that capacity, as the time slot has gone. Therefore, leisure organisations need to use systems to manage this scenario. Within the hospitality sector, for example, methods such as overbooking have been used, however, whatever the approach, a clear cancellation policy is needed. The issue of uncertainty of duration is about gauging business levels with capacity constraints and space utilisation for a favourable experience. It is about forecasting accurate length of usage in order to determine the number of units of inventory based on time. Reducing time between leisure customers is about the service time between units of inventory. By reducing this service time, the organisation has more time slots to sell.

Price

Organisations need to develop appropriate pricing policies. In traditional RM industries this has involved differential pricing. Leisure users may be charged different prices for the same experience depending on the leisure customer's characteristics. This variable pricing structure can be based on monthly passes, advance bookings, age, economic grouping or by demand. The aim is to achieve an optimal pricing mix depending on the purpose of the experience. This draws us into the area of price elasticity (Edgar 2001) and understanding the issues of demand and supply. What tends to happen, according to Kimes (2001), is that pricing decisions are made on supply or competition factors rather than demand characteristics. In RM, the focus switches to demand. Purpose, physical and revenue barriers can be used to manage this. Revenue barriers are about using price discrimination to justify demand and involve putting a qualification onto a leisure experience. For example, charging premium prices only for peak periods. Physical barriers on price relate, for example, to the view or position in a football stadium (Barlow 2001). Purpose barriers are about exclusions of certain types of customers, for example, women-only gym classes on a Monday night or an inclusive purpose barrier to encourage patronage to a museum (Leask and Yeoman 1999).

Purpose of experience

While RM is widely used in commercial organisations to enhance profitability, the leisure manager may have to take other organisational objectives into consideration. In line with this Leask and Yeoman (1999) have highlighted the purpose of the leisure experience. For example in heritage visitor attractions, the role of accessibility of the experience to the community is raised. There is a debate that the museum experience should be free, therefore, price can act as a barrier to accessibility. Similarly, local authorities may want leisure centres to be affordable and accessible to the local community that they serve. There needs to a balance between accessibility and the necessity of generating revenue in order to operate.

CONSTRAINTS OF LEISURE REVENUE MANAGEMENT

There exists, however, some concern over the applicability of RM to different capacity-constrained firms (Donaghy *et al.* 1998). Although leisure organisations have similarity, they are not all the same. It would be dangerous for organisations to follow directly the RM practices from different industries. Each industry must identify is own, unique characteristics and encompass the principles of revenue management that are suitable for them. Some of these boundaries are now examined.

Unique demand features

In the football industry, for example, the price of a ticket will vary according to the strength of the opposing team, a local derby and the time of day (Barlow 2001). With hotels, guests can arrive on a low rate and stay through a number of high-rate days. This obviously leads to a problem with determining the right rate to charge the customer for the unit of inventory, when using multiple units.

Multiplier effect

If an hotelier focuses on the revenue that can be generated from the accommodation function, he/she may be ignoring the revenue that could be generated in other departments of the hotel such as restaurants, conference and banqueting and leisure facilities. Alternatively, when holidaymakers book a holiday package, this may involve air tickets, car hire and accommodation. Therefore, what should the tour operator concentrate revenue-pricing decisions on? If the tour operator focuses all revenue decisions on flights, this will have an effect on car hire and accommodation (Donaghy *et al.* 1998).

Lack of distinct rate structure

An RM management approach leads to a range of prices for products and services depending on the demand and supply equation. A multiple set of pricing structures can alienate the customer and cause confusion (Edgar 2001). The customers do not understand the process and eventually look for an alternative. Simply put, the process is perceived by the customer as unfair (Kimes 1994). In order to deal with this, leisure managers should provide customers with full information on restrictions associated with discount prices or rates and give them sufficient benefits to offset any imposed rate and booking restrictions. However, if RM results in a decline of customer satisfaction or repeat business, leisure managers may decide that it is unwise to use RM.

Distribution of information

A revenue manager must know that the inventory he/she is selling is a true reflection of the available inventory. Research has concluded that when inventory is sold, that inventory must reflect the true availability of inventory available (Yeoman and Ingold 2001). Therefore, the distribution system must be able to provide accurate, up-to-date and reliable information (Donaghy *et al.* 1998).

Market segmentation

RM can only operate, if capacity-constrained firms have a diverse customer base. The principles of RM cannot function, if the organisation only has one type of customer (Orkin 1990).

RM, TRUST AND THE LEISURE CUSTOMER

Variable pricing is an inevitable consequence of RM. Airlines for example, charge multiple prices for what is essentially the same flight. It is also apparent that segmented customers have different levels of price sensitivity. These different degrees of price sensitivity are based on an infinite range of utilities which include perceptions of value, time of purchase, elasticity and trust. Indeed one of the key determinants of understanding the perceptions of variable pricing is trust (McMahon-Beattie, Yeoman and Palmer 2002). It has been stated that there is a clear relationship between RM and customer satisfaction (Kimes 1994). If RM results in a serious decline in customer satisfaction and repeat business, the use of RM may be unwise. The biggest influence on this conclusion is if leisure customers perceive a lack of trust and fairness from the leisure provider (Kahneman, Knetsch and Thaler 1986). Kimes states that trust will be higher if customer have a full and clear understanding of the choices and restrictions that may be placed on purchase. McMahon-Beattie, Yeoman and Palmer (2002) also suggest that customers should be made aware of ways in which they could save money, e.g. by shifting their booking or reservation to a quieter period.

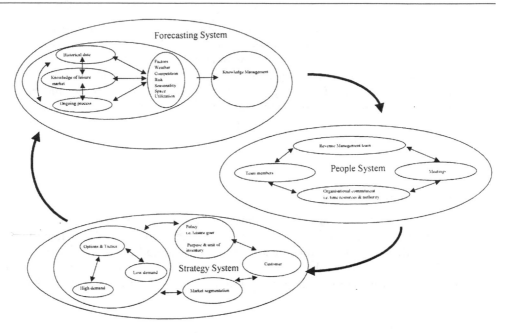

Figure 11.1 *Leisure revenue management: a systems model*

TOWARDS A MODEL OF LEISURE REVENUE MANAGEMENT

Based on the work of Yeoman and Watson (1997), a systems model of revenue management activity is presented in Figure 11.1. This systems-based model presents three activities of management: forecasting, people and strategy.

Forecasting

The ability to forecast accurately is an enshrined principle of RM (Raeside and Windle 2001). This means knowing your leisure goers, their habits, their likes and their movements and, fundamentally, producing a model of your users. Cross (1997) states that RM is about the ability to make forecasting decisions on knowledge, not feelings. Forecasting is an essential element of revenue management in order to predict consumer behaviour. The better the forecast the better the business decisions, therefore the better the profits. Accurate and reliable forecasts provide a rational view of the market. The more accurate the forecast, the less chance of being wrong. Forecasting means combining knowledge of the factors of weather, risk, booking patterns, no shows, cancellations, supply factors, market assessment and historical data to name but a few. Combining these factors to make accurate forecasts relies on information technology, since humans cannot digest such huge and growing amounts of information about all these variables. Information technology presents the information in order for the revenue manager to make a prediction that is better, more accurate and probable. The science element of RM is drawn from operational research (Cross 1997), in order to manage all the variables to improve forecasting and achieve revenue optimisation. Operational research is the engine behind RM. It is what makes the difference. Operational research approaches to RM allow the manager to concentrate on making decisions, rather than processing data. The RM forecasting subsystem is an ongoing process, as information is constantly entering and leaving the subsystem for evaluation. As Robert Cross (1997) states, RM is about forecasting, reforecasting, reforecasting and . . .

Strategy

RM is a decision-making process (Yeoman and Ingold 2001). The design of that decision-making process is a cornerstone of effective and efficient revenue management systems. A firm needs a revenue management strategy in order to guide revenue management decisions. Strategy needs to be developed based on a range of scenarios and options, so that a leisure organisation can maximise revenue in different market segments. An evaluation of the leisure behaviour is required, through the customer's variables and approach to price (Cross 1997). From the forecasting subsystem, the information that is provided needs to be evaluated through a range of options and tactics. Scenarios need to be measured for their effect on optimisation. What are the options for high-demand scenarios? What are the options for low-demand scenarios? Once the scenarios have been evaluated, what tactics are available? These options and tactics are developed from using a range of computer simulation packages that will quantify the benefits of different scenarios. Simulation is about optimisation and minimisation. Simulation is all about revenue, costs and displacements (Raeside and Windle 2001). It is about modelling risk without taking the risk and modelling all possibilities.

People

The process of managing revenue is basically a human activity. Forecasting and strategy subsystems may produce information and options. But it is the revenue manager who takes the decision and is accountable for those decisions. The subsystem of people requires an organisation to make commitment in the terms of resources and authority over the typology of RM. This requires the organisation to evaluate the principles of RM through defining, documenting and addressing the issues of RM operations. This means a commitment from the director of leisure to the leisure operative in understanding the principles of RM. RM is a buzzword not just with superficial meaning, but with depth and breadth. To manage the RM process a team is required. RM is about commitment, focus and boundaries within the organisation. It is a team effort. Within these variables, RM is about creating an environment where accurate decisions are taken. One person must coordinate RM. This must be somebody who is respected, commands leadership, is a team player, articulate and a believer in the benefits of RM. This is a person who is not necessarily a technical expert, but who is, rather, a champion of a cause. This person will lead a revenue management team, which is made up of players who are part of the RM equation. The RM team must have responsibility, accountability and authority to manage revenue within the organisation. A RM team is responsible for the implementation of policy, decisions and tactics. A RM team will integrate with all aspects of the organisation. This RM team will be responsible for the evaluation of this RM systems model.

The model of RM in Figure 11.1 allows the reader to study RM in a holistic manner. The subsystems of forecasting, strategy and people present the inter-relationships and dimensions of RM. No one subsystem is more important than another. Each subsystem within the model has mutual interflows, such that the outflows from some are the inflows to others. One subsystem's residue becomes another subsystem's energy source. This explains the interdependent nature of the model. For RM to work, all subsystems have to be in place. No one subsystem can survive without the other, therefore an organisation should take a preferred holistic approach to RM.

CONTRIBUTION OF REVENUE MANAGEMENT TO THE LEISURE INDUSTRY

The leisure industry has an opportunity to take on board the contribution that RM can make to managing profitability in the leisure industry. It is a management tool that allows leisure managers to focus on the variables of price against a unit of inventory. RM is a holistic approach to leisure organisations constrained by capacity, whether physical or non-physical. It is a process that involves making accurate decisions in a holistic manner, involving the subsystems of people, forecasting and strategy. It provides a foundation for the leisure manager to manage the purpose of leisure against needs of leisure customers and the capacity constraints of the leisure organisation. Overall, RM allows the leisure manager to maximise the efficient use of their resources and ensure financial success.

SUMMARY

This chapter has used Kimes's (2001) ingredients and preconditions to discuss RM. An alternative platform draws on Robert Cross's (1997) core concepts of RM. These core concepts are as follows:

- Focus on price rather than costs when balancing supply and demand.
- Replace cost-based pricing with market-based pricing.
- Sell to segmented micro-markets, not to mass markets.
- Save your products for your most valuable customers.
- Make decisions based on knowledge, not supposition.
- Exploit each product's value cycle.
- Continually re-evaluate your revenue opportunities.

Questions

1. Pick a leisure organisation with which you are familiar and discuss how it exhibits Kimes's (2001) preconditions and ingredients.
2. What pricing and duration control management strategies are currently

being used by your chosen organisation? Can you suggest any additional strategies?

3. Discuss Cross's (1997) core concepts of RM in relation to your chosen leisure organisation.

References

Barlow, G. (2001) 'Capacity management in the football industry', in Ingold, A., McMahon-Beattie, U. and Yeoman, I. (eds) *Yield Management: Strategies for the Service Industries*. London: Continuum.

Boella, M. (2001) 'Legal aspects', in Ingold, A., McMahon-Beattie, U. and Yeoman, I. (eds) *Yield Management: Strategies for the Service Industries*. London: Continuum.

Cross, R. (1997) *Revenue Management*. London: Orion Publications.

Donaghy, K., McMahon-Beattie, U., Yeoman, I. and Ingold, A. (1998) 'The realism of yield management', *Progress in Tourism and Hospitality Research*, 4, 3, 187–96.

Edgar, D. (2001) 'Economic theory of pricing for the hospitality and tourism industry', in Ingold, A., McMahon-Beattie, U. and Yeoman, I. (eds) *Yield Management: Strategies for the Service Industries*. London: Continuum.

Grainger-Jones, B. (1999) *Managing Leisure*. London: Butterworth-Heinemann.

Hood, I. S. A. (2001) 'Merlin: model to evaluate revenue and loadings for Intercity' in Ingold, A., McMahon-Beattie, U. and Yeoman, I. (eds) *Yield Management: Strategies for the Service Industries*. London: Continuum.

Hoseason, J. (2001) 'Capacity management in the cruise industry', in Ingold, A., McMahon-Beattie, U. and Yeoman, I. (eds) *Yield Management: Strategies for the Service Industries*. London: Continuum.

Hoseason, J. and Johns, N. (1998) 'The numbers game: the role of yield management in the tour operations industry', *Progress in Tourism and Hospitality Research*, 197–206.

Huyton, J. and Peters, S (2001) 'Yield management in the hotel industry', in Ingold, A., McMahon-Beattie, U. and Yeoman, I. (eds) *Yield Management: Strategies for the Service Industries*. London: Continuum.

Ingold, A. and Huyton, J. (2001) 'Yield management and the airline industry', in Ingold, A., McMahon-Beattie, U. and Yeoman, I. (eds) *Yield Management: Strategies for the Service Industries*. London: Continuum.

Kahneman, D., Knetsch, J. and Thaler, R. (1986) 'Fairness as a constraint on profit seeking: entitlements in the market', *The American Economic Review*, 76, 728–41.

Kimes, S. (1989) 'Yield management: a tool for capacity constrained firms', *Journal of Operations Management*, 8, 4, 348–68.

Kimes, S. (1994) 'Perceived fairiness of yield management', *Cornell Hotel & Restaurant Administration Quarterly*, 1, 2, 156–66.

Kimes, S. (2001) 'A strategic approach to yield management', in Ingold, A., McMahon-Beattie, U. and Yeoman, I. (eds) *Yield Management: Strategies for the Service Industries*. London: Continuum.

Leask, A. and Yeoman, I. (1999) 'The development of core concepts of yield management', *International Journal of Heritage Studies*, 5, 2, 96–110.

McMahon-Beattie, U., Yeoman, I. and Palmer, A. (2002) 'Customer perceptions of pricing and the maintenance of trust', *Journal of Revenue and Pricing Management*, 1, 1, 25–34.

Orkin, E. (1990) *Yield Management*. Orlando, FL: Educational Institute of American Hotel and Motel Association.

Raeside, R. and Windle, R. (2001) 'Quantitative aspects of yield management', in Ingold, A., McMahon-Beattie, U. and Yeoman, I. (eds) *Yield Management: Strategies for the Service Industries*. London: Continuum.

Russell, K. (1997) 'Expert systems', in Yeoman, I. and Ingold, A. (eds) *Yield Management: Strategies for the Service Industries*. London: Cassell.

Sharples, E., Yeoman, I. and Leask, A. (1999) 'Operations management', in Leask, A. and Yeoman, I. (eds) *Heritage Visitor Attractions: An Operations Management Perspective*. London: Continuum.

Sparrow, J. (1998) *Knowledge in Organisations*. London: Sage.

Yeoman, I. and Ingold, A. (2001) 'Decision making', in Ingold, A., McMahon-Beattie, U. and Yeoman, I. (eds) *Yield Management: Strategies for the Service Industries*. London: Continuum.

Yeoman. I. and Watson, S. (1997) 'Yield management: a human activity system', *International Journal of Contemporary Hospitality Management*, 9, 2, 80–3.

Weatherford, L. R. and Bodily, S. E. (1992) 'A taxonomy and research overview of perishable asset management: yield management, overbooking, pricing', *Operations Research*, 10, 5, 831–44.

CHAPTER 12

Ticket Operations in a Professional Sports Team Setting

James Reese

TICKET OPERATIONS DEFINED

Many fans are under the impression that the ticket process ends once a season is completed. This is far from the truth. The process of ticket operations is year-round. Although out of the public eye in the off-season, many customer service-oriented processes take place in preparation for the upcoming season. These pre-parations make the sport entertainment experience more pleasurable for season ticket holders and fans. The definition of ticket operations is twofold. The first aspect of ticket operations is defined as the process by which tickets are distributed. The second aspect of the definition that is equally important is the high level of customer service that must accompany the distribution process in order to meet the needs of the season ticket holders and fans. Due to the high demand for tickets to some sporting events, the customer service aspect of ticket operations sometimes falls short of an acceptable level. This 'if you don't buy them someone else will' attitude can be damaging to the development of a long-term relationship with customers. If sport organisations are to be successful in building long-term fan support, both aspects of ticket operations must be addressed. For the remainder of the chapter, the discipline of ticket operations in a professional sports team setting will be dissected and analysed by the different types of responsibility owed to season ticket holders and fans.

ESTABLISHING PRICES

The establishment of ticket prices for sporting events is still an imprecise science (Howard and Crompton 1995: 139; Reese and Mittelstaedt 2001). A recent study of (the US) National Football League (NFL) ticket pricing strategies indicated that the primary factors influencing ticket prices were, in order of importance: team performance, revenue needs of the sport organisation, public relations issues, tol-eration of the market regarding price increases, fan identification (level of emo-tional attachment of the fan to the sport organisation) and, finally, the average league ticket price (Reese and Mittelstaedt 2001). Since each city and sport orga-nisation has a unique mix of all these factors, it is very difficult to establish a formula that could be applied to every situation.

STAFFING

Ticket office employees must be extremely versatile and have the ability to handle multiple tasks at once while maintaining a high level of productivity. This is so due to the seasonal nature of ticket operations. It is not cost effective to hire a large full time staff due to a certain level of downtime associated with the off-season. Therefore, most ticket offices are staffed with a few very versatile full-time employees supplemented by seasonal part-time staff. One major drawback of this staffing method is that it is difficult to find qualified employees available to work seasonal hours. Interns are routinely used by sport organisations to fill this void. Local universities with sport management programmes are an excellent source for these types of intern. The utilisation of seasonal part-time staff and interns allows sport organisations to manage labour costs as efficiently as possible.

HANDLING OF TICKETS

Single-game ticket distribution can be contracted to an outside ticket distribution company or handled in-house by the staff of the sport organisation. Season tickets may be received by the organisation and then distributed to season ticket holders. In contrast, a new option from ticket-printing companies is to have tickets sent to season tickets holders directly from the printer. Remaining single-game tickets if handled in-house would then be sent to the sport organisation to be put on sale to the general public.

When single-game and season ticket seat locations arrive from printing companies to be handled in-house by a sport organisation, they are usually in the form of a perforated sheet rather than as individual tickets. Ticket sheets should be counted by hand when they arrive from the printer to verify that each stadium seat location was printed correctly and accounted for. Then all season ticket sheets are grouped into individual season ticket accounts, counted again for accuracy and inserted into envelopes to be mailed to season ticket holders. If the sport organisation will be handling the remaining single-game tickets in-house, the remaining single-game ticket sheets should be separated into individual game tickets, grouped by game or event and stored in a secure location. Assess to all tickets should be limited to as few staff members as possible to avoid shrinkage and/or ticket errors.

JOB RESPONSIBILITIES IN TICKET OPERATIONS

Season ticket holders

Season ticket holders are the lifeblood of any organisation. They are the repeat customers who pay a significant amount of money to receive tickets for an entire season. Their financial support is crucial to the success of the organisation for several reasons. First, season ticket holder revenue is guaranteed. Regardless of what the weather is the day of the game, injuries to key players, win/loss record, illness of the season ticket holders, car trouble or lost tickets, the sport organisation has received payment for the tickets to the game regardless if someone attends the game or not. Second, since payment for season tickets, club seats or luxury suites is typically received in full several months before the start of the season, the sport organisation has financial capital to negotiate player contracts and secure free agents for the upcoming season. The availability of financial capital is key in acquiring free agent players due to the impact of signing bonuses. Since signing bonuses are paid upfront at the beginning of the contract, having liquid assets available enables sport organisations to outbid competitors for the services of the best available players in the free agent market.

Season ticket holders normally have a certain level of emotional attachment to the sport franchise. The emotional component of the sport relationship is what makes it unique from many other consumer products in the world. This can be both positive and negative in regard to its effects on a sport organisation. Research has long confirmed that there is a positive correlation with the revenue and emotional attachment of fans to sport organisations (Danielson 1997; Wann and Branscombe 1990, 1993; Zillmann and Paulus 1993). Other research indicates that associating with sports teams can affect the self-image of fans (Cialdini *et al.* 1976; Kahle, Kambara and Rose 1996; Murrell and Dietz 1992; Snyder, Lassegard and Ford 1986; Wann and Branscombe 1990, 1993, Zillmann and Paulus 1993). This usually occurs in areas where fan identification, or level of emotional attachment, is considered to be strong (Wann and Branscombe 1990, 1993). However, the fan identification of season ticket holders, in addition to the amount of money paid annually in the form of season tickets, can sometimes lead season ticket holders or fans to believe that they are entitled to more than is specified in the season ticket brochure or by the sport organisation. This can sometimes create an unattainable expectation of service from the sport organisation. Sport organisations must balance a high level of customer service with what is considered reasonable and affordable requests from the target market of fans.

Transfers

Transfers apply to season ticket account holders who wish to transfer the name on their season ticket account to another party. Some sport organisations limit the recipients of season ticket transfers to immediate family members who typically include only parents and siblings. Grandparents may also be included under unique circumstances. Season ticket transfers are sometimes limited to avoid creating a 'black market' bidding war for scarce season tickets. This may be created in areas where fan identification is high and season ticket availability is scarce. This type of environment is created when sport organisations either completely sell out or when they cap the amount of season ticket accounts. This is sometimes done to provide single-game tickets for those fans who may not be able to afford the cost associated with season tickets. When demand for season tickets outweighs the supply, a secondary market is created. In an effort to capitalise on the secondary market, some season ticket holders may be willing to transfer their season ticket accounts to another party if they receive a payment from the outside party. The payment that takes place between the transferor and the transferee is rarely disclosed to the sport organisation for fear of penalty because the policies and procedures of most sport organisations clearly state that no money may change hands during the season ticket transfer process.

Priority numbers

In most cases, new season ticket holders are assigned a *priority number*. A priority number is a numerical representation of the duration of a season ticket account. The date on which an account is opened is sometimes used to establish priority. Typically, the lower the priority number, the longer the season ticket account has been active. Since low priority numbers represent the fans who have been associated with the sport organisation the longest, they may receive special benefits not available to season ticket account holders with higher priority numbers. For example, benefits available to season ticket holders with low priority numbers may include: preferential parking accommodations; priority opportunities for seat relocations; a higher probability of receiving championship tickets (if applicable); priority consideration in relocation to new facilities; and exclusive opportunities to interact with players, coaches and staff.

Depending on the administrative policies of the sport organisation, managing the impact of priority numbers can be a challenging process. Organisations that allow transfers have more difficulty managing season ticket accounts, especially if the organisation utilises an open transfer process. An open transfer process allows season ticket holders to transfer the account to anyone without limitation. A limited transfer process restricts season ticket holders to transferring ticket accounts to immediate family members. The process becomes even more complicated if the organisation allows groups of seats to be divided and transferred to multiple new account holders. Significant complications have been experienced by sport organisations when an open transfer process has been utilized. This is especially true in an environment where there is a strong demand for tickets. Examples of complications include: current season ticket holders charging a fee, ranging from hundreds to thousands of dollars, to potential transferees in order to execute the transaction; and ticket scalpers who actively solicit transfers in order to build a base of season tickets to resell for maximum price on the open market.

Scalpers

Ticket scalping is defined as selling a ticket for a price in excess of the established price printed on the ticket. Dealing with scalpers, or independent ticket agents as they like to refer to themselves, is always a challenging process. Each state and city may have differing laws and interpretations on how to handle incidents of ticket scalping. Since attempting to control ticket scalping is labour intensive and provides no financial gain, few sport organisations will make a serious commitment to addressing the problem. Local police and postal inspectors are sometimes utilised to provide a presence and to attempt to prosecute the most serious offenders.

Ticket scalpers acquire tickets for resale by becoming season tickets holders and by purchasing tickets from other season tickets holders or fans who offer to sell tickets. Scalpers will typically offer to buy the ticket at a lower price than the value printed on the ticket (wholesale). This is done so the scalper can resell the ticket and generate a profit. This approach is usually successful since people looking to sell tickets are motivated to find a buyer before the game or event takes place before else the ticket becomes financially worthless. Have you ever seen people standing on corners near stadia or arenas with signs that read, 'I need tickets'? The majority of these people are ticket scalpers. It is sometimes comical to watch scalpers working in the same area. If you look closely, you can sometimes witness one scalper holding a sign looking for tickets while another stands a few feet away holding a handful of tickets in the air for sale! As a fan, it is important to understand that sport organisations have no obligation to honour any ticket not purchased from an authorised agent. Authorised agents typically include the sport organisation or a ticket distribution company such as TicketMaster. If for some reason the ticket purchased from a scalper turns out to be counterfeit or stolen, standard policy is to remove the fan from the stadium without a refund. Some sport organisations will offer to allow fans to remain in the stadium if they purchase a legitimate ticket. A service such as this would be based on the demand for tickets and subsequent ticket availability.

Holdbacks

Holdbacks are stadium seats held for the use of the organisation. Typical uses include complimentary seats for team owners, players, coaches, administrators, staff, dignitaries, sponsors, visiting teams, media and miscellaneous ticket problems such as duplicate or counterfeit tickets. The allocations for each of these different areas vary by sport and team.

All ticket managers hold back a certain number of tickets for emergency situations. Depending on the size of the stadium or arena, it could be as many as 100 seats or as few as 20 seats per game. The held back seats usually incorporate a variety of seat locations including all price points at all levels of the stadium. The variety of seats locations allow ticket office staff to handle ticket problems for fans and season ticket holders regardless of where they occur in the stadium with confidence that they will have a similar ticket location to resolve the situation.

Most sport organisations provide at least two *complimentary tickets* per game to players, coaches, administrators and full-time staff members. Any tickets over and above two per game requested by these individuals usually need to be purchased at face value. Based on expected ticket demand, a different limit for each game can be placed on tickets per individual to ensure that the total demand for tickets from the owner, players, coaches, administrators and staff does not exceed the holdback allocation. The complimentary seat locations assigned to players in the stadium are usually done according to seniority within the respective league. For example, a player with 14 years' experience would receive better seats than a player with 13 years' experience etc. For situations where players have the same amount of league experience, the determining factor can be the seniority on each respective team. Sport organisations also provide a limited number of complimentary tickets to the community for each game. For community organisations to receive complimentary tickets they must normally submit a written request and description of why the tickets are needed and what they will be used for. To provide a check-in balance between the ticket office and the organisation, an administrator outside the ticket office may be responsible for approving all requests for complimentary tickets.

Individual game tickets

At the conclusion of the season ticket renewal process and after the decision is made regarding the amount of holdback tickets, all remaining tickets are put on sale to the public as *individual game tickets*. Individual game tickets are also referred to as single-game tickets in some areas. Individual game tickets can either be handled in-house by the sport organisations or they can be subcontracted out to an external ticket distribution organisation such as TicketMaster. Although an extensive base of season ticket holders is desirable for sport organisations, too many season ticket holders can actually be detrimental to the long-term success of the organisation. In order to ensure that fans at all economic levels have access to tickets, many sport organisations will place a limit on the number of season ticket accounts that can be established per year. In addition, some organisations will place a limit on the actual number of seats that may be used for season ticket accounts. These limits are placed for several reasons. First, the policy is designed to restrict the corporate involvement in the ticket-purchasing process. Although a corporate presence is necessary to ensure the sale of club seats and luxury suites, too much of a corporate presence can reduce the access of families and fans to tickets. Guaranteeing at least a minimum number of individual game tickets ensures that families and non-corporate fans will have an opportunity to attend games. Second, this policy ensures that new generations of fans have an opportunity to be exposed to the core product first hand. This helps to build long-term fan identification and provide live product exposure to new generations of future fans. A perpetual shortage of tickets could result in fans becoming frustrated and relegated to media consumers. Media consumers are fans who provide support by following the sport organisation through media and print outlets such as television, radio and newspapers, but never actually attend sporting events. This is contrary to the level of fan involvement that teams desire (Mullin, Hardy and Sutton 2000: 36).

Will call

Will call is an area of the stadium where tickets that have been paid in full can be picked up or left for other parties. Will call sounds like such a simple process, however, it is much more complicated than it appears. When tickets are left at will call, corresponding will call envelopes should be filled out completely. Will call envelopes include information regarding the name of the individual for which the tickets are intended, the name of the person leaving the tickets, the game the tickets are for, and the number of tickets included in the envelope. There are a number of common problems that routinely occur at will call.

Incorrect or incomplete will call envelopes are a common cause of problems on game day. When envelopes are filled out completely and correctly will call operates relatively smoothly. However, spelling errors or poor handwriting sometimes causes envelopes to be placed incorrect alphabetically. Subsequently, when John Gant comes to the will call window, the person who filed the envelope may have misread the last name 'Gant' for 'Cant' and filed the envelope in the wrong location causing a delay when Mr Gant arrives at the will call window. Therefore, a standard will call policy if a envelope cannot be found is to double check the spelling of the name and to check the alphabetical index to determine if the tickets were filed incorrectly prior to turning the customer away from the window disappointed.

Another common problem at will call is fans who fail to bring photo identification with them when they come to pick up tickets. The only way to ensure that the correct person is picking up the tickets is to require them to present photo identification. Unfortunately, many people forget to bring photo identification with them to the stadium or arena and have to be turned away when they cannot prove their identity. It is important for ticket offices to communicate policies and procedures regarding will call and photo identification in all literature and season ticket holder mailings on the organisational web page, as well as posting the policies in and around the ticket office.

The last common will call problem is a miscommunication among fans regarding which name will be on the envelope. Many times a group of fans will come to the will call window expecting tickets to be waiting under the name of one of the group members. Sometimes those tickets are actually at will call but under the name of one of the other group members. This miscommunication can sometimes delay the group of fans from getting into the game and can sometimes cause the group to miss the game altogether. A properly trained will call staff should ask the right questions in order to attempt to avoid all these problematic situations.

Duplicate tickets

Season ticket holders who determine their season or individual game tickets to be lost, stolen or destroyed may have them replaced for a nominal service charge; this process is called *duplicate tickets*. The nominal service charge is a standard charge per ticket and is used to offset the fixed and variable costs of providing the service for season ticket holders (i.e. computer equipment, supplies, labour etc.). A designated service area for season ticket holders is usually reserved at the ticket office of a sport organisation to handle duplicate ticket problems.

In order for duplicate tickets to be issued for *lost or misplaced tickets*, the duplicates must usually be repurchased at face value in full. Unused tickets that are found after the completion of the sporting event can then be returned to the sport organisation for a full refund of the face value amount. The reason the service is handled in this manner is to discourage season ticket holders from taking advantage of the duplicate ticket process in order to gain access to additional tickets for high-profile or sold-out games. Fans can take advantage of the duplicate ticket process to gain access to tickets to sold-out or high-profile events and then utilise the tickets on a standing room-only basis. Under these circumstances, you could literally have 80,000 fans gaining access to a stadium that seats only 76,000. This could cause a major traffic flow problem, not to mention the associated risk management and legal implications.

Stolen tickets may be handled in a different manner provided that they are accompanied with a police report. Since it is against the law in the USA to file a false police report, most sport organisations will replace stolen tickets without charging a fee to season tickets holders as long as they submit a police report, even if they are at fault or partially responsible for the theft due to negligence. However, if it is determined that the season ticket holder filed a false police report in order to receive a duplicate set of season tickets, most sport organisations will cooperate with local police authorities to prosecute the season ticket holders for fraud, in addition to possibly cancelling their season ticket accounts.

The last category of tickets included under the umbrella of duplicate tickets is *destroyed tickets*. Destroyed tickets may be the most difficult situation to handle since in some cases no evidence of the original tickets remains for verification. For example, let's hypothetically assume a season ticket holder accidentally washes and dries a set of four tickets to an upcoming game in his jeans' pocket. The season ticket holder brings the only remaining fragments of the four season tickets to the ticket office of the sport organisation, a bagful of dryer lint with the tiny ticket fragments. If you are the ticket representative who helps the season ticket holder, how do you handle the situation? Bear in mind that you do not know for sure that there were actually four individual game tickets in the jeans in the first place. As time consuming as it may be, the job of the ticket representative will be to reconstruct the ticket fragments in an attempt to determine exactly how many different tickets can be identified. If all four tickets can be identified, ticket office personnel can be sure that the original tickets will not show up at the stadium and the original tickets can be replaced without recharging the season ticket holder for the face value of the tickets. However, if only two of the four tickets from the wash could be identified, ticket office staff would have to use judgement to decide whether to charge the season ticket holder face value for the remaining two unidentified tickets. Factors that should be considered when making these types of decision include priority number (i.e. tenure of the season ticket account), payment history, stadium incident reports etc.

These judgement decisions are what make the discipline of ticket operations a difficult profession. On the one hand, you have valued customers to whom you are trying to provide a high level of service. Charging them a second time for two additional tickets, assuming that there really were four in the wash, could damage customer relations and goodwill with that season ticket holder due to the high cost associated with tickets to sporting events. Although the season ticket holder may understand why they had to be recharged for the duplicate tickets, they may be offended that the ticket office staff questioned their integrity. On the other hand, the ticket office staff has the responsibility to protect the financial resources of the sport organisation and implement policies and procedures that are consistent and fair to all season ticket holders and fans. In order to be successful, a delicate balance of customer service and accountability to the organisation must be reached.

Seat improvements

Each year, after the season ticket renewal process, many sport organisations allow season ticket holders to go through a process that enable season ticket holders to upgrade their seats. This *seat improvement process* is a great service to the season ticket holders of a sport organisation. However, it is an imprecise, time-consuming process with numerous flaws.

Season ticket holders are usually mailed a seat improvement card with their season ticket invoice. Those season ticket holders desiring a seat improvement are instructed to return the completed card with their payment indicating the location of their first and second choices of desired seat improvement locations. The seat improvement cards are placed in order based on priority number. The priority number determines who has access to the best seats for seat improvements when accounts are cancelled and seats are turned back into the organisation. Some seats from cancelled season ticket accounts are kept in the holdback account for the use of the organisation and some are released to the general public for the seat improvement process. The location of the seats and the needs of the organisation determine the ultimate destination of the cancelled seats. The standard in the sport industry is to view lower level sideline seats at the centre of the field or court as the benchmark for the ideal seat location. Although this is considered the ideal seat location in the industry, some fans prefer alternate locations.

Next, the manifest of available seats is reviewed and compared to the seat improvement request cards returned by season ticket holders. Beginning with the lowest priority number, season ticket holders who requested a seat improvement receive either a phone call or postcard with a seat improvement location or a postcard indicating that no seat improvement was available in the areas identified on the seat improvement request card. Season ticket holders who receive an opportunity to upgrade have a limited time to reply in order to take advantage of the upgrade, otherwise the seats are offered to someone else on the priority list. This is done in order to get through the seat improvement process in a timely manner. The following US football situation provides an example of why the process is flawed.

Mrs Lynn has a priority number of 1,000. She is offered an improved seat location and has five days to reply to the offer. She currently has a pair of aisle seats in the lower level of the stadium on the 35-yard line, ten rows off the field and is offered seats at the 40-yard line in row 25 in the centre of the section. At the same time, in order to make progress on the list of thousands who are requesting a seat improvement, Mr Goetz, who has a priority number of 1,050, is also offered a seat improvement. Mr Goetz currently sits in the lower level on the 30-yard line, 27 rows from the field and is offered a seat on the 35-yard line at the same row level. Mr Goetz also has five days to reply to the offer. After two days, Mrs Lynn declines the seat improvement offer, indicating a desire to remain in aisle seats and not wishing to move from row 10 to row 25. Since the organisation has not heard back from Mr Goetz, and since he has three days remaining until his deadline, the organisation offers the seats originally presented to Mrs Lynn to the next person on the seat improvement list, Mr Holman. Mr Holman has a priority number of 1,200 and currently sits in the lower level at the 25-yard line, 20 rows off the field. As with the other offers, Mr Holman has five days in which to accept the offer. After two days, Mr Holman accepts the offer of the seats at the 40-yard line originally offered to Mrs Lynn. On the last day of his offer, Mr Goetz calls and accepts the seat improvement offer. Table 12.1 illustrates a summary of how the seat improvement process served the three season ticket holders in the example.

As you can see from the results, due to the flaw in the seat improvement process, Mr Holman, who has a higher priority number than Mr Goetz, was able to secure a better seat improvement. The problem with this system is that while the organisation is waiting to hear from one season ticket holder, they need to offer tickets to the next person on the list. It would be impossible to offer seat locations one at a time in order of priority number, allow time for a decision to be made and still complete the seat improvement process in a reasonable amount of time in order to facilitate the printing and mailing of season ticket invoices. Even with the overlapping system, the seat improvement process may still take several months to complete, depending on the base of season ticket holders and the number of season ticket holders who request an upgrade. In the future, the use of technology should present a more efficient solution for the seat improvement process.

Table 12.1 *Seat improvement process summary*

	Mrs Lynn	Mr Goetz	Mr Holman
Priority number	1,000	1,050	1,100
Current location	35-yard line, row 10	30-yard line, row 27	25-yard line, row 20
New location	Same	35-yard line, row 27	40-yard line, row 25

Stadium incident reports

When a fan has a negative experience at the stadium, sport organisations typically have the disgruntled fan complete a *stadium incident report*. These reports serve several functions. First, they are used to document stadium incidents that can be used by law enforcement officers in court to prosecute violations of the law. Violations of the law such as assault and/or battery, indecent exposure, public urination, drug violations, public intoxication and ticket scalping are all examples of situations that could occur at a stadium or arena that could require the use of a stadium incident report.

Second, stadium incident reports allow the ticket office to file permanent documentation regarding incidents that have occurred in regard to individuals using the seats of a season ticket holder. Season ticket holders are responsible for the behaviour of those who utilise their tickets to attend games, whether it is themselves or others. A sport organisation reserves the right to cancel a season ticket account for behaviour that is considered unacceptable. Stadium incident reports provide documentation to justify such a decision should it become necessary. When a stadium incident report is generated that applies to a season ticket holder account, ticket offices generally send a letter informing the season ticket holder of the disturbance and informing them of the consequences if the behaviour is not immediately corrected.

Visitor's allocation for away games

Most sport organisations receive an allocation of tickets from the host team when they are travelling to away games. All tickets made available by ticket offices in visiting stadia need to be purchased by the visiting team. Sometimes visiting teams do not use the entire number of tickets allocated to them for a particular game. When this occurs, several things can happen in order to provide outstanding customer service to season ticket holders and fans. First, the organisation may need to address ticket needs for administrators. Once that is accomplished, the organisation has the opportunity to make the returned tickets available to season ticket holders who wish to travel to support the team at away games. This can be done by priority number or on a first-come, first-served basis. If tickets are still remaining after they are made available to season tickets holders, they can be made available to the general public. However, visiting teams sometimes choose to return the remaining tickets to the home team so they do not end up in the hands of ticket scalpers.

Seat licences

Seat licences have been disguised under many creative names over the years including personal seat licences or permanent seat licences (PSLs), and most recently stadium-building licences (SBLs). Regardless of what they are called, the intent for using them is the same: to generate revenue for either the city or the sport organisation. Usually the purpose of generating the revenue is to offset the cost of constructing a new facility. Seat licences require season ticket holders to pay an upfront fee for the right to purchase season tickets in a specific location for a specified number of years. Some seat licences are permanent and are considered to be property similar to real estate; others are only for a limited number of years and grant the users a limited amount of rights regarding the use of the seats. The fans in some areas, due to the way they have been implemented, have not received seat licences favourably. For example, the Oakland Raiders of the National Football League (NFL) implemented a PSL at a cost of up to $4,000 upfront for the right to purchase the normal season tickets; it expired in only ten years (Murphy and Silver 1995). Fans in other NFL cities such as Charlotte have paid similar prices for seat licences that do not expire. Fans in Charlotte purchased permanent seat licences ranging from $600–$5,400 (Carolina Panthers 1998). Inconsistencies such as these can make it difficult to sell short-term PSLs in the future unless they are structured differently.

In the autumn of 2001 the Philadelphia Eagles of the NFL announced the use of seat licences to construct a new stadium for the Eagles in downtown Philadelphia. In order to satisfy the fans that the seat licences would not be used to take advantage of the fans in any way, the licences were named stadium-building licences (SBLs). The SBLs are permanent seat licences and can be sold by the season ticket holders at any time after the season ticket holder pays the one-time SBL fee. In addition, all revenue generated from the SBL programme will go to offset construction costs associated with the new stadium and no portion of the revenue will be provided to the Philadelphia Eagles organisation (George, 2001). Under a system such as this, season ticket holders in a stadium not currently utilising a seat licence system (such as the case in Philadelphia with Veterans' Stadium) would be more likely to approve a new stadium referendum with a public vote.

Publications/printing

A ticket office issues many pieces of literature and publications each year. In addition to millions of dollars in tickets, this includes season ticket invoices, fan guides, season ticket holder policies and procedures, brochures regarding items allowed in the stadium or arena and team schedules, to name but a few. Mistakes made on any of these items can have damaging financial consequences. It is imperative that proofs of all tickets, publications and literature that will be distributed to the public be dispersed to staff to be checked and doubled-checked for accuracy. Even with this safeguard in place some mistakes will probably still slip through the system. The goal of the organisation is to minimise the impact of these mistakes.

TICKET MANAGEMENT SYSTEMS AND SOFTWARE

Utilising professional ticket management systems and software packages can allow ticket offices to incorporate technology to provide fans with a superior level of customer service. Some of the advanced features offered by these systems include: the ability to sell unused tickets to other season ticket holders online; the option of paying for season ticket invoices online; and the opportunity to wholly manage season ticket accounts online. This includes customising tickets, monitoring debits and credits, paying for post-season tickets etc. In addition, these systems are able to generate financial reports that can be used to provide documentation to professional sports leagues regarding ticket sales and profit/loss. Some leagues, such as the NFL, share ticket revenue with visiting teams as part of the league revenue-sharing agreement (Reese and Nagel 2001). This type of revenue sharing makes documentation even more important and necessary.

CONCLUSION

The discipline of ticket operations can be an extremely rewarding profession and career path. Due to the sales component associated with ticketing, ticket operations may be one of the easiest ways to break into the sport industry. Ticket operations personnel must be friendly, customer service oriented, have the ability to handle multiple tasks at once and have the ability to communicate and sell effectively.

Activity

You are a ticket representative working the duplicate ticket window for a sport organisation and Mr Brown, a fan, comes to the window with his wife and two children, asking for duplicate tickets because his four season tickets to today's game have been lost. You ask him for his account number and photo identification. You discover that the name on the season ticket account is Smith, which is different from that of the person presenting the photo identification. When you investigate further you find out that Mr Brown has been buying the tickets from the season ticket account holder of record for a few years. Due to his financial commitment and use of the seats for the past few years, Mr Brown considers himself to be a season ticket holder, even though his name is not officially on the account. Mr Brown decided to buy the tickets from Mr Smith to avoid the established process of going on the waiting list for season tickets through the organisation. This option was less desirable to Mr Brown since the seats provided by the organisation to fans on the waiting list are historically less desirable seats in the upper level of the stadium.

The sport organisation's policy is to provide duplicate tickets only to the season ticket holder whose name is on the record. What is your course of action if you are the ticket representative?

References

Carolina Panthers (1998) *Carolina Panthers 1998 Media Guide*. Charlotte, NC: Electric City Printing.

Cialdini, R. B., Borden, R. J., Thorne, A., Walker, M. R., Freeman, S. and Sloan, L. R. (1976) 'Basking in reflected glory: three (football) field studies'. *Journal of Personality and Social Psychology*, 34, 3, 366–75.

Danielson, M. N. (1997) *Home Team: Professional Sports and the American Metropolis*. Princeton, NJ: Princeton University Press.

George, J. (2001) 'Eagles stadium hunts $50M from seat fees', *Sports Business Journal*, 4, 13, 42.

Howard, D. R. and Crompton, J. L. (1995) *Financing Sport*. Morgantown, WV: Fitness Information Technology, Inc.

Kahle, L. R., Kambara, K. M. and Rose, G. M. (1996) 'A functional model of fan attendance motivations for college football', *Sport Marketing Quarterly*, 5, 4, 51–60.

Mullin, B. J., Hardy, S. and Sutton, W. A. (2000). *Sport Marketing* (2nd edn). Champaign, IL: Human Kinetics.

Murphy, A. and Silver, M. (1995) 'Just move, baby: Al Davis left LA to return his Raiders to Oakland and, he hopes, to glory', *Sports Illustrated*, 83, 1, 26–30.

Murrell, A. J. and Dietz, B. (1992) 'Fan support of sport teams: the effect of a common group identity', *Journal of Sport & Exercise Psychology*, 14, 28–39.

Reese, J. T. and Mittelstaedt, R. D. (2001) 'An exploratory study of the criteria used to establish NFL ticket prices', *Sport Marketing Quarterly*, 10, 4, 223–30.

Reese, J. T. and Nagel, M. S. (2001) 'The relationship between revenues and winning in the National Football League', *International Journal of Sport Management*, 2, 2, 125–33.

Snyder, C. R., Lassegard, M. and Ford, C. E. (1986) 'Distancing after group success and failure: basking in reflected glory and cutting off reflected failure', *Journal of Personality and Social Psychology*, 51, 2, 382–8.

Wann, D. L. and Branscombe, N. R. (1990) 'Die-hard and fair-weather fans: effects of identification on BIRGing and CORFing tendencies', *Journal of Sport and Social Issues*, 14, 2, 103–17.

Wann, D. L. and Branscombe, N. R. (1993) 'Sports fans: measuring degree of identification with their team', *International Journal of Sport Psychology*, 24, 1–17.

Zillmann, D. and Paulus, P. B. (1993) 'Spectators: reactions to sports events and effects on athletic performance' in Singer, R. N. (ed.), *Handbook of Research on Sport Psychology*. New York: Macmillan, 600–19.

PART 4

OPERATIONS STRATEGY

CHAPTER 13

Sports Events: A New Planning Process

Guy Masterman

INTRODUCTION

The importance of sports events in terms of their impacts and benefits, particularly major international events, is well documented and also well covered in the media. In the main, it is the economic benefits that receive the most attention, due mainly to the fact that they are more easily quantified (Jones 2001; UK Sport 1999a). However, it is the other less quantifiable benefits, those that are regeneration, legacy, cultural, social, environment and tourism in nature, which may be of more significant value over the long term.

In 2001 a lack of planning led to the loss of the 2005 World Athletic Championships for the UK. The government promised a London venue in its bid with Picketts Lock, intended as a long-term legacy for the sport. On discovering that the costs would be too high the government tried to offer an alternative location away from London, which resulted in the IAAF deciding to put the event out to bid again. While it is commendable that an uneconomic project was aborted, a potentially beneficial event and its stadium legacy might have been better planned for. Alan Pascoe, who runs Fast Track, the organisation responsible for UK athletics' commercial activities, estimates the loss for athletics to be £15–20 million but recognises that it is not just about the financial loss. A world championships could have helped the development of the sport as well as create a legacy of a national stadium for future athletics events (Hubbard 2002).

Much of the theory that underpins the teaching of event management in higher education is centred on how important the event planning process is for event organisers. The theory that is offered, however, appears to be more appropriate for the short- and medium-term benefits that events can bring rather than for the long-term value that major international events can be strategically planned for. An evaluation of the theories of Allen *et al.* (2002), Bowdin *et al.* (2001), Getz (1997), Shone (2001), Torkildson (1999) and Watt (1998) shows that they propose that event planning is a staged process. Others such as Catherwood and Van Kirk (1992), Goldblatt (1997) and Graham *et al.* (1995) propose a less formal approach to event planning.

These theories and models generally accept that event organisations should strategically plan for the long term including there being a responsibility for the ongoing and long-term management of the financial and physical legacies of major events. *Getz (1997)* maintains that long-term gains and losses should be assessed at the feasibility stage of the planning process. Allen *et al.* (2002) and Bowdin *et al.* (2001) follow a similar approach. Hall (1992) stresses the importance of long-term planning with the acceptance that it is the long-term legacies of an event that have the most consequence. Several of the theories also consider wind-up or shutdown (Allen *et al.* 2002; Catherwood and Van Kirk 1992; Getz 1997; Shone 2001). The last recognises that some thought should be given to intended legacies in the formation of objectives at the beginning of the planning process.

What the models do not cover are where the development of strategies for successful long-term legacies should sit in the event-planning process. There is a need for the inclusion of specific long-term strategies when planning major international sports events; strategies that will extend beyond the end of the event itself. Second, it is accepted that current event-planning theory and models adequately cater for the execution of events, although not specifically for major sports events. What is required, therefore, is a more comprehensive sports event-planning process, a process that can accommodate sports events of all scales and intentions and provide benefits in the short, medium and long term.

BENEFITS

It is first important to identify what short-, medium- and long-term benefits and impacts major sports events can bring. Spilling (2000) lists the main potential long-term impacts of events as falling into four categories: enhanced international awareness, increased economic activity, enhanced facilities and infrastructure and increased social and cultural opportunities. Getz (1997) makes the distinction between various economic impacts, including those of tourism, whereby the event acts as a marketing mechanism for the event host as a destination. UK Sport (1999b) identifies three main impacts: winning performances and the social effect that has, the development of sports and economic benefits. Allen *et al.* (2002) splits the impacts into four spheres: social and cultural, physical and environmental, political and tourism and economic. There is general agreement here then on what the main impacts are, with the only differences being in the way they are grouped or categorised; a brief discussion now follows on each.

Land regeneration

Cities that have made bids for the right to stage major sports events in recent years have included plans to build new facilities. In many cases, these plans have had to look to the regeneration of land and buildings due to the scarcity and cost of utilising prime inner-city development sites. In the cases of Sydney and Manchester this has necessitated the development of land beyond inner city boundaries; the Homebush Bay area in Sydney Harbour, for the 2000 summer Olympics, and Sports City, in Eastlands, East Manchester, for the 2002 Commonwealth Games. This not only allowed for the development of disused and defunct land but also the opportunity to create a central site and focus for each event. The municipal justification in each case was that the regenerated land would have remained defunct had it not been for the opportunities given by the requirement to have new state-of-the-art sports facilities for these events. Further examples are the development of

Fremantle for the 1987 America's Cup and throughout the 1990s Melbourne Docklands for Olympics and Commonwealth Games bids (Hall 1992, 2001).

Facilities and services

The buildings that are newly erected and redeveloped to house major sports events are generally seen as long-term legacies. To justify the investment in them, the appropriate city authorities look to their usage beyond the end of the event. They look for two types of usage:

1. sports, leisure and recreational use by the local community
2. the further staging of other events.

Again using Sydney and Manchester as examples, there are two contrasting cases to consider. The Olympic Stadium in Sydney, intended as a facility for other major events, has been in operation for under three years and has not attracted sufficient revenue and events and as a result is financially threatened (Holloway 2001). However, the City of Manchester Stadium is already contracted to become the new home of Manchester City FC in 2003/04 (Manchester 2002 Ltd 2001). There were clear strategic objectives set by Manchester and they were a part of the planning process long before the 2002 Commonwealth Games took place. Critically, they included a contracted handover of the stadium in an attempt to ensure its long-term usage.

The 1992 Barcelona summer Olympics were a part of a wider long-term strategy for modernisation. The strategy known as 'Barcelona 2000', was implemented in the mid–1980s and included six new sports stadia, an Olympic village on the waterfront, a new airport and communication towers (Roche 2000). In what it titles its 'sustainable strategy,' Manchester 2002 Ltd (2002) declared that the new sporting facilities for the 2002 Commonwealth Games were to provide an important legacy for future improved health, jobs and the regeneration of derelict urban land.

Other cases include the Millennium Stadium in Cardiff, built to stage the 1999 Rugby World Cup, researched and planned with its long-term usage in mind. In particular, it was designed to house different events, not just sports; the location is very accessible to central Cardiff; and there was a need for a national venue. The acquiring of FA and league cup football finals must be an extra bonus for a legacy Jones (2001) claims will not be underutilised. However, according to Cardiff City Council (2000) the urgency of the task in building the stadium meant that there was little time to consider future usage at the planning stage and that bookings were acquired after the event via post-event marketing. The planning of the Stade de France for the 1998 FIFA World Cup consisted of a complicated process in order to justify the build in Paris, where there are already many other stadia. Dauncey (1999) describes this process and highlights the moving in of a top flight football club as one of several solutions to a long-term usage problem. At one point thought was even given to creating a brand new club for that purpose, when there was no agreement on which existing club should go in. The thoughts as to future usage were retrospective to the already done deal to build the stadium, but there were at least strategic considerations taking place as part of the planning for the World Cup as a whole for the long-term usage of the facility.

Other legacies include transport infrastructure. In building facilities in disused and outer-city areas there arises the need to provide adequate transportation if only for the event itself. High on the scrutiny of any Olympic bid are the provisions made for people flow (IOC 2002a). For example, intended for the Athens 2004 summer Olympics are 120 kilometres of new roads, an expanded metro system, a new traffic management centre and a new international airport (Athens 2004 2002a). However, if the facilities are going to be a legacy of any success at all then the planning for the provision of transportation infrastructure goes hand in hand with the facility plans. Clearly, this requires further investment, $80 million in Sydney's case (Holloway 2001), and its future use becomes reliant on the long-term success of the facility it serves. Hence the all-round importance of long-term strategic planning for future usage.

Another legacy is the event management expertise that is gained in staging an event. If the facilities are to stage further events, then such expertise not only serves as an attractive asset in future event bids but also gives the city itself an internal understanding of what it is capable of, which of course will enable it to improve its performance. A dedicated municipal department, now known as the Sheffield Event Unit, was set up in Sheffield in 1990 to make full use of the facilities built for the 1991 World Student Games. It has now staged over 300 events with 88 receiving national or international television coverage (Watt 1998). The impact study for Euro 96 and its affects on Leeds, albeit commissioned by Leeds City Council Leisure Services, concluded that Leeds gained world-class recognition in its co-hosting of a major football tournament (The Tourism Works 1996).

Social regeneration

The regeneration of land, the building of new facilities and the planning of events provide employment opportunities prior to the event. The implementation of the event also provides short-term event jobs but as it can be seen in Sheffield, major sports events can also lead to the employment of personnel in the long term. If the facilities are going to be legacies they require staffing with teams that will plan their economic futures either to provide local community services or to attract further events which, in themselves, provide further employment opportunities. The very origination of Sheffield's plans to bid for the World Student Games were focused on a solution to the downturn in its economy with the local iron, steel and coal industries in steep decline in the late 1980s. Unemployment was as high as 20% in some areas of the city and an event-led strategy offered a way forward (Gratton and Taylor 2000; Watt 1998) and still provides employment today. Hall (1992) maintains that events can improve the cultural identity of a host city, develop community involvement and integration and instigate local economic benefits. Similarly, Hughes (1993) maintains that Manchester's unsuccessful bid for the 2000 summer Olympics was intended as providing solutions to its inner-city problems with the likes of short- and long-term employment and future benefits from the use of the facilities built as a result of staging an event.

Cultural development

Major sports events can offer wider programmes that are seen to be culturally and socially beneficial. The Spirit of Friendship Festival, part of the overall 2002

Commonwealth Games programme, was planned by Manchester to offer more than just sport to its local community. They saw the opportunity to provide food, drink and music events that would be entertainment for incoming event tourists as well as participating teams and businessmen (Manchester City Council 2000). The long-term benefit of this will be difficult to measure but the importance of the effect it has on attracting future tourists to a city that tries hard to be an attraction should not be overlooked. The IOC recognises the importance and requires cultural events to be an 'essential element of the celebration of the Olympic Games' and a required provision by any bidding host city (IOC 2002b). The winter Olympics hosted by Salt Lake City in 2002 staged 60 performances, ten major exhibitions and 50 community projects in its Olympic Arts Festival (Salt Lake City 2002).

Political development

The improved profile of government at national and international level as a result of staging a successful major international sports event is considered of value. The extent to which profile and prestige can be taken, though, is clearly difficult to assess, but economic development as a result of the enhanced profile is perhaps more quantifiable. Increased inward investment is a possible impact (Allen *et al.* 2002). Individuals can gain, too, as Hall (1992) suggests that both politicians and governments can benefit at both collective and individual levels.

Sports development

Another area of benefit that is difficult to measure is the level of development a sport can achieve as a result of being showcased by a major event. National and international governing bodies are aware of the importance of exposure via the likes of the Olympics and, of course, the profile television brings to any potential participants in their sports. UK Sport (1999b) states that hosting events can lead to the winning of more medals and a greater stage for sports. According to Hall (1992) this benefit is one a sporting organisation might be more interested in than the event host. The IOC (2002a) is an example of a body that is concerned with the broader goals of competitive sport including the provision of facilities that become legacies for sports by stimulating performance and participation. The important point, however, is not who benefits or benefits most, but that the planning for the event would be incomplete *without* such provision.

Environmental development

In an age of concern about our environment, major sports events can play a key role in incorporating operational policies that can be not only efficiency conscious for the event itself but also lay down legacies for the host city for the future. Sydney has played what may well turn out to be an important role in this area and Athens 2004 plans to 'leave behind a cleaner, healthier environment, improved environmental awareness and performance, and a lasting legacy for generations to come,' (Athens 2004 2002b) with programmes that include new planting, building with environmentally friendly materials and improved waste management.

Economic development

The economic impact of major sports events is of critical importance when it comes to justifying the investments made. The impact, if negative, can be a lasting and costly legacy for local taxpayers but, if positive, can bring important revenue to bolster municipal budgets. In some cases, achieving revenue from the operation of a major sports event that exceeds the initial investment is not as important as the long-term economic benefits that will come from tourism and future usage of the facilities. The 2002 Salt Lake City Olympics is reported to have produced a relatively small surplus of $40 million but there are significant expectations for the future return on the original investment (Mackay 2002).

Another area that is difficult to assess is how much new business can be attributed to the staging of a major sports event. That does not, however, detract from the inclusion of business development objectives in event planning. Take, for instance, Manchester's plans for its staging of the 2002 Commonwealth Games. Increased export opportunities, enhanced inward investment and the use of local organisations as preferred suppliers are all stated business objectives in the KPMG report on the potential impacts of the Games (Manchester City Council 1999).

Tourism

Event tourism is one of the current key phrases of the events sector. Events are seen as catalysts for driving tourism but not just for the event itself. Major sports events can develop high profiles for host cities, particularly if they are televised, and are claimed to be good for attracting future tourists long after the event has been staged. Many of the objectives and criteria set out by Sheffield's Event Unit in deciding on the staging of an event are linked to how much media attention it can gain and improve its tourism profile (Watt 1998). Tourists are also attracted to future staged events and can therefore potentially improve the local economy that way.

The Sydney 2000 Olympics bid documentation claimed that there would be event tourism but also national tourism growth right up to 2004 (Brown 1999). However, while some authors agree that tourism is a long-term benefit of events, including Getz (1997) who states that every destination should formulate an event tourism plan and Keller (1999) who maintains that major events are important for the national economy, Hughes (1993) doubts whether event tourism is that sustainable.

A NEW APPROACH TO THE EVENT PLANNING PROCESS

It is essential that any long-term attributable benefits inherent in the planning process should be comprehensively covered by strategies that ensure that long-term success. First, including a cost-benefit forecast at a feasibility stage of the event-planning process would enable organisers not only to forecast the extent of the benefits of their events and budget accordingly, but, through that forecast, gain support for the event at an early and appropriate stage. Second, implementation strategies for the use of new facilities and/or regeneration projects need to be built in to ensure their long-term futures. Third, assessing the impact of such an event requires not only an evaluation of short- and medium-term economic and cultural benefits, for instance, but also a long-term evaluation, possibly even ten years on or more, of the sustainability and durability, in other words, the success of the regeneration and the legacies that were created as a result of staging the event. Fourth, in order for objectives to be met there is a case for the inclusion of mechanisms in the process that will allow continuous alignment with short-, medium- and long-term plans.

The decision to bid to stage a major international sports event will depend on more than just its own potential budgeted economic benefits. The wider benefits that can be gained by incorporating regeneration projects and new facility provision can lead to critically important local community support as well as political and financial assistance to ensure the bid goes ahead. An event that necessitates the development and utilisation of land that would otherwise not be used can then leave physical legacies for future social, cultural and economic benefit and for some these can help justify the initial event staging costs. Indeed, without such support the bid may not even get off the ground. Hughes (1993) maintains that Manchester's bid for the 2000 summer Olympics was intended as providing solutions to its inner-city problems. Some of the objectives for the event can be met in the short term but evaluating the value of regeneration and new facilities, especially if they are to help solve social problems, have to be implemented over the long term. Therefore the 'fast track planning' talked of and criticised by Hall (2001) where government reaction to short timeframes in hosting events results in the pushing through of proposals without due economic, social or environmental evaluation procedures is indeed clearly inadequate. Long-term strategies to ensure that these benefits are achieved over time are a required part of the event's planning. Jones (2001) suggests that a balanced economic analysis of whether to host an event is overshadowed somewhat by the political objectives of event organisers and local and national politicians. The contrasting examples of Sydney's and Manchester's stadia discussed earlier suggest that within the planning process there is a need for strategies that ensure the long-term success of any facilities that are built and intended as, and importantly, financed as, legacies.

The regeneration and legacies are not always of the built environment, of course. Social regeneration involves the creation of employment but while the initial job years created in order to develop disused land and build new facilities can be measured in the short term, any jobs created to run such facilities should be viewed in the long term. We can look at Sheffield's Don Valley Stadium, Arena and Pond's Forge Aquatics Centre, which were built to stage the 1991 World Student Games, and note that employment *has* been sustained over the long term. As discussed earlier, the events-based strategy adopted by Sheffield was as a result of considerable unemployment and recession in the city and so employment objectives were high on the list. In the short term they will have been met in the building of the facilities, but the long-term employment value can only be seen in the manning of the facilities and the running of its events over the last ten years or so since the original Games.

Environmental policies laid down as a consequence of the staging of events can also be legacies. Whether at a local or international level, an environmental policy could lead to wider benefits, as Sydney may go on to show. Its policies were planned to benefit the whole of society with conservation programmes over the long term (Bowdin *et al.* 2001; Hall 2001). The key factor here was that the Sydney bid for the 2000 summer Olympics was focused on these policies and while many of them were intended for the games themselves, they remain intrinsic to the operation of the venues in the long term, (Allen *et al.* 2002). The ultimate success of the management blueprints for the future of which Allen *et al.* (2002) talk can only be evaluated when they have been running over the long term. It is therefore argued here that strategies for their long-term management were required in the event's planning process to ensure they would be successful.

The economic benefits are often the focus of most events, whether large or small. The impacts of direct, indirect and induced income are always of great interest to organisers, the local community and the media. If they are considered strategically and early enough in the planning process they may lead to more success and greater support for an event. A feasibility report that forecasts economic impact can help justify an event as the KPMG (Manchester City Council 1999) report for Manchester City Council for the 2002 Commonwealth Games was no doubt intended. On being shown that the 2002 Commonwealth Games could achieve 6,432 ten-year equivalent jobs and 0.5m visitors the council could assess the benefits against the proposed costs and, at the same time, lobby for support at local and government level. What is interesting is that the report was commissioned after the Games bid had been won in November 1995; the city had been invited to bid in 1993. It is argued here that the decision to bid should be preceded by such reports and that they form the basis for later evaluation. If they include such long-term benefits, they should form the focus for the necessary long-term strategy making which should form part of the event-planning process. Indeed, the report indicated that there would be a £110 million increase in gross value added for Manchester as a result of staging the Games, from 1998 to 2009. This would indicate that a measurement of some kind is required seven years down the line.

The costs involved in staging the 1991 World Student Games in Sheffield required a return on investment that could only be achieved over the city's long-term event-led strategy. The Games made an operating loss of £10 million and proved to be a political burden and a threat to the long-term strategy for some time. However, the events staged in and since the facilities were built for the event have generated £30 million (Gratton and Taylor 2000). The issue is wider in Sheffield's case, however, in that the initial investment of £150 million in the facilities has materialised into a debt that the city has struggled with and now mortgaged. The result is a negative legacy of repayments of £25 million per year over 24 years (Wallace 2001). This goes to show that there is a need for a long-term view for events that include long-term benefits and for such events to be strategically planned so that these benefits are successfully achieved over the long term.

The inclusion of long-term strategies, at the implementation planning stage of the process, is necessary in order to ensure the success of long-term benefits. By determining and contracting the handover of City of Manchester Stadium as part of its planning of the 2002 Commonwealth Games, Manchester was implementing strategies for the long-term usage of an important facility. Sheffield too showed signs of early implementation strategies for its facilities with the formation of its Event Unit and the determination of criteria for the future bidding of events. While Sheffield did not secure specific bookings for its facilities prior to the World Student Games it was pursuing several contracts (Foley 1991) and it can now be seen that it has nevertheless vindicated its approach with a great deal of operational success.

Watt (1998) claims that for every £1 invested in bringing over 300 events to the city the return is £37.50.

The evaluation techniques used to assess the importance of major international sports events and how much of a success they have been in relation to their originally stated objectives is an area of contention, in particular with regards to the assessment of economic impact, as organisers have a number of different ways of measuring the economic impact that is attributable to an event. For instance, there are a number of multiplier calculations that can be used to process data to assess the direct, indirect and induced income that can be attributed to an event and produce a figure (Hall 2001; UK Sport 1999b). The problem does not only lie in there being a lack of one standard of measurement that all organisers can adhere to, thus enabling true comparisons from event to event. It also lies in there being an opportunity to select an evaluation process that allows for the event to be flatteringly shown in its best light.

An event that is even evaluated in the medium term, say within two years, may be seen as a success, when over the longer term the same measurement criteria may show that it is not. It can be seen how critical the timing of evaluation is when the very justification of the decision to stage the event in the first place is at stake. Despite the staging of 300 plus events in Sheffield's purpose-built facilities (Watt 1998) and considering the employment that has been created as a result, the cold economic reality is that the residents of the city are still paying for their investment. Similarly, the Sydney Olympic Stadium might have been seen as a medium-term success by now had there been strategies put in place to ensure its future usage and financial success.

The evaluation of an event needs to be able to consider the immediate short-term impacts, of course, but, in addition, it should be capable of assessing medium- and long-term impact as well. This does not just apply to economic impacts but also social and cultural costs and benefits too, not least of all the sports showcase itself and whether any objectives set for increased awareness and sustainable sports development have been achieved.

Finally, it is important that the planning process has built-in alignment mechanisms that ensure that objectives are met throughout the planning process. This can be achieved with the identification of performance indicators. In setting objectives that include the long-term success of facilities and a resultant economic gain from the staging of an event, the planning process automatically gains performance benchmarks. These objectives *can* be measured, but only in the long term. To ensure an alignment with the objectives it should be possible to set performance indicators at appropriate stages of the process and adjust iteratively. For example, by setting deadlines and cut-off points for the achievement of certain levels of income, achieving prescribed levels of media coverage or the signing of appropriate contracts, the process has its own integrated performance indicators. By incorporating mechanisms and operational systems throughout the implementation planning stage, thus allowing for further thinking on why a project is failing in its objectives, it can be ultimately ensured that the event achieves what it is supposed to achieve.

A NEW PLANNING PROCESS MODEL

Prior to the Los Angeles Olympics, major international sports events were considered loss-making millstones and a civic duty to avoid; the Los Angeles Olympics in 1984 made a £215 million surplus, while Munich (1972) and Montreal (1976) made losses of £178 million and £692 million respectively (Gratton *et al.* 2001; UK Sport 1999c). Since then highly competitive bidding processes have evolved for all the world's major sporting epics leading to a second tier of major international sports events now also being competitively sought after, world championships, international fixtures and the like. UK Sport, for example, was involved with bids for over 35 events in more than a dozen sports in 1999/2000 (DCMS 2000). Following the staging of several major events in the UK the response is somewhat mixed with, on the one hand, a drive to win a bid for the Olympics still strong but, on the other, the sufferance of an economic backlash from the staging of major events (Chaudhary 2001). It may therefore be of value to consider an event-planning process that considers not only the short-term benefits but can also strategise to achieve success over the longer term.

The process model in Figure 13.1 is an attempt to incorporate a comprehensive approach to the task of sports event planning. This process should be of practical use whatever the scale of the sports event. It should be possible to move to the next stage entirely and successfully achieving all that is necessary in the previous stage. However, the planning process, when elongated over a long-term period, seven years in the case of an Olympic Games, needs to be able to adapt to ever changing requirements and so a staged process that can be iterative is key, provided that all immovable factors are identified at the outset. These are unique to each event and could include deadlines and cut-off points. What *are* immovable are the event objectives, as alignment with them occurs throughout the process and evaluation is against objectives at the end of the process. The following boxes describe how the model should progress.

OBJECTIVES

☐ Why?
☐ What is the event to achieve in the short, medium and long term?
  ➢ Who is to benefit?
  ➢ How are they to benefit: are there political, social, cultural, environmental, economic objectives?
  ➢ Consider any briefs as set by clients or bid requirements if applicable

---

CONCEPT

☐ What?
☐ Design an outline for what the event is and what it looks like
  ➢ Perform a situational analysis to determine where strengths, weaknesses, opportunities and threats lie
  ➢ Perform a competitor analysis to identify areas for competitive advantage
  ➢ Consider scale, operational format, timing, locations, facilities, audiences
☐ Identify the strategic partners required – such as local and national Government

---

agencies, national and international sports governing bodies, event owners and promoters, charities, participants and for the handover of facilities

☐ Identify the decision makers involved in allowing the event to go ahead – internally within the organisation and externally, including the process involved, e.g. bidding procedures, grant and other funding application processes

☐ Identify all stakeholders in the event

☐ Identify the organisers to be involved in running the event

☐ Align the design so that it can fulfil the objectives set in the short, medium and long term

---

FEASIBILITY

☐ How and when?

☐ Test the design

  ➢ Identify who is responsible for the delivery of the short-, medium- and long-term objectives

  ➢ Identify resources required: human resources, facilities, equipment, marketing, services

  ➢ Consider these requirements over the short, medium and long term: bidding, event implementation, handover of the facilities, long-term usage of the facilities

  ➢ Determine the nature and timing of the partnerships to be involved including those that are required at this stage of the process prior to the proceed decision, e.g. bidding finance if applicable, any finance required to underwrite the event, any handover agreements or operational strategies required for the long-term success of facilities

  ➢ Budget according to these requirements

  ➢ Perform a costs versus benefits forecast for the short-, medium- and long-term objectives

  ➢ Determine the critical path involved over the short, medium and long term: whereby a chronological plan of all critical decisions is mapped out

☐ Ensure that there is alignment with the short-, medium- and long-term objectives

---

PROCEED DECISION

☐ Present to all internal decision makers and decide

  ➢ Not to proceed

    ■ Return to the concept and reshape so that a proceed decision can be made

    ■ Or shelve the project

  ➢ Proceed to

    ■ The short-, medium- and long-term implementation stage or if appropriate via a bid

    ■ Bid procedure

      ● Prepare the bid

      ● Market the bid

      ● Present the bid

      ● Accept the award to stage the event and proceed to the implementation stage or if not awarded the event, shelve the project

---

SHORT-, MEDIUM- AND LONG-TERM IMPLEMENTATION PLANNING

☐ Determine operational strategies
  ➤ Financial
  ➤ Human resources
  ➤ Partnerships, suppliers and services
  ➤ Facilities and equipment
  ➤ Sales and marketing
☐ Develop and enhance the critical path and performance indicators to incorporate all the fine detail involved in executing the event in the short term and realising the benefits planned for the medium and long term
☐ Ensure alignment with short-, medium- and long-term objectives

---

IMPLEMENT EVENT

☐ Implement the operational strategies
☐ Execute the event

HANDOVER

☐ Prepare for and execute the handover of facilities to the identified organisations for continued operation
☐ Handover of the responsibility for the successful delivery of medium-and long-term objectives including evaluation of such

---

EVALUATION

☐ Evaluation against the short-, medium- and long-term objectives set involves
  ➤ Short-term evaluation of the costs, benefits, impacts and measurement against objectives set for the event: to be performed immediately after the event
  ➤ Medium-term evaluation of the costs, benefits and impacts after a predetermined time period in accordance with the objectives set
  ➤ Long-term evaluation of the costs, benefits and impacts after a longer period and in particular of the legacies, in accordance with the objectives set for them
☐ The use of performance indicators and the applying of continuous alignment with the objectives set, throughout the planning process and during the event, will help to ensure that evaluation provides positive results

---

FEEDBACK

☐ Feedback should be made after each short-, medium- and long-term evaluation
☐ Feed both positive and negative evaluation into new or repeat projects

---

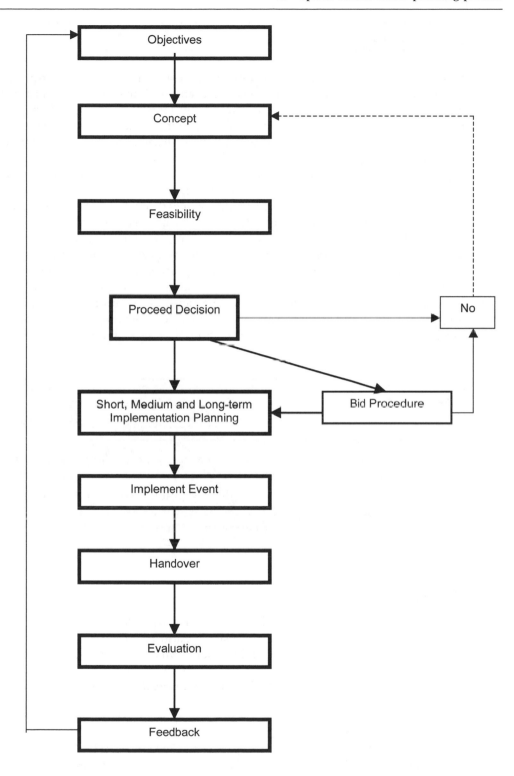

Figure 13.1 *The sports event planning process*

SUMMARY

Current theories and models are predominantly concerned with an event-planning process that caters for the execution of the event itself and its short-term benefits and not the benefits that can be achieved over the longer term. This is despite clear evidence that, in practice, events, particularly major international sports events, are created with objectives involving regeneration and legacies set to achieve long-term cultural, social, political, environmental, tourism and economic impact. Some high-profile events have failed to achieve their long-term and even medium-term objectives, thus raising the question as to whether the planning that is being undertaken in the industry is comprehensive and early enough. There is therefore a case for a planning process that is at least applicable for sports events, of all scales, and one that considers the bigger picture. Current theoretical models may be used successfully by event organisers at an operational level, but for a strategic view, particularly for major international events, a process that considers longer term costs versus benefits at the feasibility stage, the implementation of strategies for long-term operational plans of facilities in particular, evaluation that considers the long-term impact and the inclusion of performance indicators that can ensure an alignment with short-, medium- and long-term objectives will be a more practical model for the industry.

Questions

1. Describe the main ways in which the hosting of major international sports events can benefit the host city in the long term.

2. Provide one example of a host city that has strategically planned for the long-term success of a newly built facility. How did the city achieve this?

3. What would you consider to be the key strategic considerations that are required in order to ensure that the long-term legacies of a major international sports event are of benefit to the host city?

References

Allen, J., O'Toole, W., McDonell, I. and Harris, R. (2002) *Festival and Special Event Management* (2nd edn). Queensland, Australia: John Wiley & Sons.

Athens 2004 (2002a) 'Legacy'. Available at *www.athens.olympics.org* (accessed 24 April 2002).

Athens 2004 (2000b) 'Environment' Available at *www.athens.olympics.org* (accessed 24 April 2002).

Bowdin, G., McDonnel, I., Allen, J. and O'Toole, W. (2001) *Events Management*. Oxford: Butterworth-Heinemann.

Brown, G. (1999) 'Anticipating the impact of the Sydney 2000 Olympic Games' in Andersson, T. (ed.) *The Impact of Mega Events*. Ostersund, Sweden: ETOUR, 133–40.

Cardiff City Council (2000) *The Economic Impact of the Millennium Stadium and the Rugby World Cup: Summary Report*. Edinburgh: Segal Quince Widesteed and System 30.

Catherwood, D. and van Kirk, R. (1992) *The Complete Guide to Special Event Management: Business Insights, Financial Strategies from Ernst & Young, Advisors to the Olympics, the Emmy awards and the PGA Tour*. New York: John Wiley & Sons.

Chaudhary, V. (2001) 'Mayor Ken backs London 2012 bid', *The Guardian*, 16 May, 32.

DCMS (2000) 'Culture, media and sport, 3rd report: the priority of events'. Available at *www.publications.parliament.uk* (accessed 30 April 2002).

Dauncey, H. (1999) 'Building the finals: facilities and infrastructure' in Dauncey, H. and Hare, G. (eds) *France and the 1998 World Cup; the national impact of a World sporting event*. London: Frank Cass, 98–120.

Foley, P. (1991) *The Impact of Major Events: A Case Study of the World Student Games and Sheffield*. Sheffield: University of Sheffield Press.

Getz, D. (1997) *Event Management and Tourism*. New York: Cognizant.

Goldblatt, J. (1997) *Special Events: Best Practices in Modern Event Management*. New York: John Wiley & Sons.

Graham, S., Neirotti, L. and Goldbatt, J. (1995) *The Ultimate Guide to Sport Event Management and Marketing*. Chicago: Irwin.

Gratton, C. and Taylor, P. (2000) *The Economics of Sport and Recreation*. London: E & FN Spon.

Gratton, C. and Henry, I. (2001) 'The role of major sports events in the economic regeneration of cities: lessons from six world or European championships', in Gratton, C. and Henry, I. (eds) *Sport in the City: The Role of Sport in Economic and Social Regeneration*. London: Routledge, Chapter 3.

Hall, C. M. (1992) *Hallmark Tourist Events – Impacts, Management and Planning*. London: Bellhaven Press.

Hall, C. M. (2001) 'Imaging, tourism and sports event fever', in Gratton, C. and Henry, I. (eds) *Sport in the city: the role of sport in economic and social regeneration*. London: Routledge, Chapter 11.

Holloway, G. (2001) 'After the party, Sydney's Olympic blues.' Available at *www.europe.cnn.com.2001* (accessed 13 March 2002).

Hubbard, A. (2002) 'The interview: Alan Pascoe: a sport stabbed in the back, a nation and its youngsters badly let down.' *The Independent on Sunday*, 6 January.

Hughes, H. L. (1993) 'Olympic tourism and urban regeneration' in *Festival Management and Event Tourism*, vol. 1. New York: Cognizant, 157–62.

IOC (2002a) 'Host city election procedure'. Available at *www.olympic.org/uk/organisation/missions/cities* (accessed 13 March 2002).

IOC (2002b) 'Birth of the Olympic Movement.' Available at *www.olympic.org/uk/organisation/movement* (accessed 29 February 2002).

Jones, C. (2001) 'Mega-events and host region impacts: determining the true worth of the 1999 Rugby World Cup', *International Journal of Tourism Research*, 3, 241–51.

Keller, P. (1999) 'Marketing a candidature to host the Olympic Games: the case of Sion in the Swiss canton of Valais (Wallis), candidate for the winter Olympics in the year 2006', in Andersson, T. (ed) *The Impact of Mega Events*. Ostersund, Sweden: ETOUR, 141–56.

Mackay, D. (2002) 'Tainted games hailed a success,' *The Guardian*, 26 February, 26.

Manchester City Council (1999) *2002 Commonwealth Games: Background Information and Overview*. Report prepared by KPMG, 16 June.

Manchester City Council (2000) *Spirit of Friendship Festival Executive Summary*. Manchester: Manchester 2002 Ltd.

Manchester 2002 Ltd (2001) *Our Games*, Issue 4. Manchester: Manchester 2002 Ltd.

Manchester 2002 Ltd (2002) 'The Games: sustainability – strategy'. Available at *www.commonwealthgames2002.com* (accessed 24 April 2002).

Roche, M. (2000) *Mega-events and Modernity: Olympics and Expos in the Growth of Global Culture*. London: Routledge.

Salt Lake City (2002) 'Olympic arts festival.' Available at *www.saltlake2002.com* (accessed 24 April 2002).

Shone, A. with Parry, B. (2001) *Successful Event Management: A Practical Handbook*. London: Continuum.

Spilling, O. (2000) 'Beyond intermezzo? On the long-term industrial impacts of mega-events – the case of Lillehammer 1994' in Mossberg, L. (ed). *Evaluation of Events: Scandinavian Experiences*. New York: Cognizant, Chapter 8.

The Tourism Works (1996) *Economic impact of the European championships 1996 on the city of Leeds*. An image volume value study for Leeds City Council Leisure Services.

Torkildsen, G. (1999) *Leisure and Recreation Management* (4th edn). London: E & FN Spon.

UK Sport (1999a) *Major Events: A Blueprint for Success: Measuring Events*. London: UK Sport.

UK Sport (1999b) *Major Events: A Blueprint for Success: A UK Strategy*. London: UK Sport.

UK Sport (1999c) *Major Events: A Blueprint for Success: The Economics – A Guide*. London: UK Sport.

Wallace, S. (2001) 'Behind the headlines', *The Telegraph*, 15 June.

Watt, D. (1998) *Event Management in Leisure and Tourism*. Harlow: Addison Wesley Longman.

CHAPTER 14

Strategic Planning

Manuel Recio Menéndez and Javier Martínez del Río

INTRODUCTION

Companies of all sizes are beginning to realise the importance of planning and for long-term objectives to be consistent with short-term action. Such coherence is more difficult to achieve every day as surroundings become more and more competitive, global and changing. Strategic thought and action are thus transformed into necessary activities for those businesses that want to survive in this new environment.

Regardless of the pertinent sector, size or experience of an organisation, in order for the planning and design of new products to be successful, management must understand the process, must become involved in its performance and be committed to the final plan that comes out of the process of analysis, reflection and decision making. In this chapter we shall attempt to clarify what is understood by strategic planning, what the different phases that comprise it are and how it must be developed in a given company.

Concept development influences the competitiveness of a company in a definitive manner and is the main way a sustainable competitive advantage can be achieved, since the decisions made in this phase will affect the entire organisation. Thus, if a restaurant specialises in fast food, its establishment, its equipment, its staff and its marketing activities will be completely different from those of a restaurant that specialises in fine quality and excellent service. Specifically, the design of the product (or service):

- must take into account consumer needs
- must take into account the cost, quality and time a service is to be delivered
- must take advantage of existing organisation synergies and background
- decisively influences the rest of the areas of the company (quality of raw materials, equipment necessary, financing requirements, qualifications of personnel etc.).

WHAT IS STRATEGIC PLANNING?

Planning determines what a company wants to achieve, how to do it and where it is in the road towards its goal(s). The plan is a means of reaching the company's objectives, although the purpose of the strategic planning process is not to produce a document called the strategic plan, but to be able to achieve specific results by taking certain actions decided on and based on an analysis of reliable data.

The term 'strategic' refers to the long term, while the term 'operations', or 'tactics', refers to the short term. What is considered short and long term is going to depend on many factors. In general, when we speak of a strategic plan, operations are designed for a time horizon that is at least three years away from the moment at which the plan is put into practice and short term refers to the actions that are undertaken the following year.

Strategic planning is the process by which a company studies the opportunities that arise in a changing market, defines the objectives to be reached and assigns the resources necessary to achieve them. The objective of strategic planning is the modelling and restructuring of company products and areas of business in such a way that they produce satisfactory profit and growth. Therefore, it should not be considered an annual activity, but a permanently current process throughout the life of the company.

The top football clubs in Europe, such as Manchester United, Bayern München or Real Madrid have created masterful cycles of success thanks to strategic planning. The income from television rights is used to acquire one or two top-level players who improve the club's image and make their success in the game more likely. Successful teams receive more income from ticketing, merchandising, licensing, television rights and sponsorships. However, these teams do not forget long-term planning and invest lots of time and money working with young kids, which supplies them with players like Raul, Beckham or Scholes at a much lower cost.

THE STRATEGIC BUSINESS UNIT

According to Aaker (1987), a strategic business unit (SBU) is an organisational unit that has (or should have) a defined company strategy and a manager with responsibility for sales and profit performance. For example, in a restaurant chain, each restaurant is an SBU.

These organisational units, formed according to strategic action criteria, do not necessarily have to coincide with the divisions or departments into which companies are normally structured. The strategic unit is built around the different businesses that make up the organisation's activity. Sometimes there is only one business and, therefore, only one strategic business unit would have to be analysed.

The ideal situation is for the SBU to have its own operations, among which are production, logistics, distribution, sales, administration, human resources etc., although they may share some of these functions and resources with other units.

Each SBU must be assigned a clear strategic objective and associated action to be taken for reaching it. The company management usually considers each SBU a different business and therefore a different centre of profit in and of itself.

In professional sport, players' salaries have risen greatly and it is generally accepted that ticket prices alone cannot cover the payrolls. Many teams are looking for additional sources of money in the long term through strategic planning. In the USA, baseball attendance averages around 50 million fans per season while attendance for the NBA, NHL and NFL averages between 10 million and 20 million; despite the higher attendance, MLB revenues are lower than NBA and NFL.

Evaluation of the strategic business unit

Once the company has been divided into the different SBUs that comprise it, we are in a position to evaluate it as if it were an investment portfolio. The company must decide which of them it wishes to build, maintain, harvest or divest. In order to make these decisions, the company has to use evaluation methods, the two most common being the Boston Consulting Group matrix and the General Electric matrix.

Some European football clubs own a part of their players' image rights. So companies trying to have a player appearance in an ad have to pay its team. Both Spanish top clubs, Real Madrid and FC Barcelona, realised that this would be a suitable source of money in about 1999 and started to invest money buying image rights from every new player they signed. They have chosen a couple of key members of the staff to contact companies potentially interested in having such a player in an advertising spot and negotiate this possibility with them. Those teams planned to acquire more than 3 million euros in the 2003–2004 season in this way.

Boston Consulting Group Matrix

The Boston Consulting Group matrix is presented in Figure 14.1. The various SBUs that make up the company are represented in a business portfolio as circles with a radius proportional to the volume of their sales.

The relative market share is measured on the horizontal axis and is calculated with regard to the most important competitor. It distinguishes between high or low market share, with a dividing value of 1. Below this, the figure indicates the SBU market share with regard to the leader in that market: 0.5 means that the SBU represented has a market share that is half that of the leader; 5 means that the unit is the leader in its market and its market share is five times greater than its next closest follower. The scale on which the values are represented on this axis is

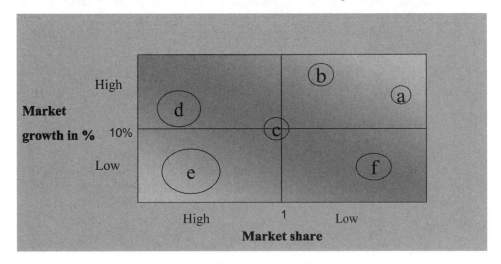

Figure 14.1 *Boston Consulting Group matrix*

logarithmical, so that equal distances represent the same percentage of increase in share.

Market growth rate is represented on the vertical axis, divided into high and low growth. In the majority of the sectors to which this matrix is applied, the midpoint is 10%.

The matrix is thus divided into four cells:

1. *Question marks.* As the name implies, feasibility is uncertain. These are businesses that are just starting out, with high-growth but with scant market penetration. Such business units require large investments and represent the company's future.

2. *Stars.* These SBU are the leaders in a high-growth market. If the competitive dynamics that generate high-growth rates continue, an infusion of investment funds may be necessary to maintain the dominant position (negative cash flow), but if competition diminishes, they may generate cash. These businesses, in general, are profitable and in the mid-term should become cows.

3. *Cows.* These units are major sources of revenue for the company since they dominate the market and production costs are lessened thanks to economies of scale. The cash they generate must be used to strengthen stars and those question marks considered feasible.

4. *Dogs.* Dog SBUs are usually associated with a negative cash flow. They are slow-growing businesses in which the company has a small share.

Finally, the Boston Consulting Group matrix has certain weaknesses that it would be advisable to know about, for example:

- It takes only two factors, market growth and relative market share, into account, thus losing track of many other factors that are usually involved in a company's decisions.

- The strategic advice that derives from the matrix seems to be oriented more towards large corporations than the small and medium-sized companies. In trying to overcome this weakness, it is usually justified by saying that the small and medium-sized companies address more specialised markets (segments or niches) and the analysis would then have to be adapted to the relative market share in that area.

- From simple observation of the matrix it is impossible for us to know where the SBU is coming from or where it is going to.

- There is no consideration of possible synergies that could exist between two or more SBUs.

The General Electric Matrix

In an attempt to overcome some of the limitations pointed out in the Boston Consulting Group matrix, the General Electric Company used a model from the McKinsey Consulting firm to create the analytical matrix that appears in Figure 14.2.

Competitive position is plotted on the horizontal axis instead of the relative market share and, on the vertical axis, industry attractiveness instead of growth rate. These two new axes include multiple factors and not just single data, such as appear on the previous matrix. The factors on these axes will have to be particu-

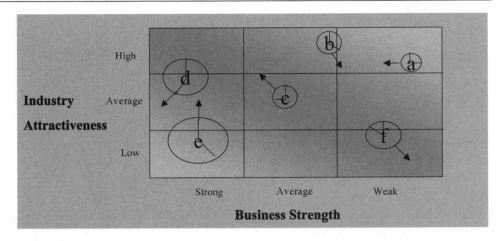

Figure 14.2 *General Electric portfolio*

larised in each case. It is the task of the person who is doing the planning to select the factors that are a measure of these two aspects. As an example, consider Table 14.1 (Aaker, 1987).

Some factors specific to the sports industry are: attendance, team performance, team attractiveness, team quality, customer closeness, sponsors' interest, local tradition, stadium capacity etc.

The analytical space in the matrix is divided into three different cells for each axis, delimiting whether the competitive position is strong, average or weak and whether market attractiveness is high, medium or low. The circles, instead of representing company sales, show sector sales and pie slices inside the circle show the company's share of the market. Observe that arrows in the figure indicate what direction the SBU is headed in according to the analyst.

From all this, you can see that this method has a potential for analysis because of the large amount of data than can be handled in the decision making process, while

Table 14.1 *Competitive position versus market attractiveness*

Competitive position (evaluation of capacity to compete)	Market attractiveness
• Company size	• Market size
• Company growth	• Growth rate
• Share by segment	• Customer satisfaction
• Customer loyalty	• Competition: quality, types, effectiveness
• Profit margin	• Commitment
• Distribution	• Prices
• Technological ability	• Profitability
• Patents	• Technology
• Marketing	• Government regulations
• Flexibility	• Sensitivity to economic trends
• Organisation	

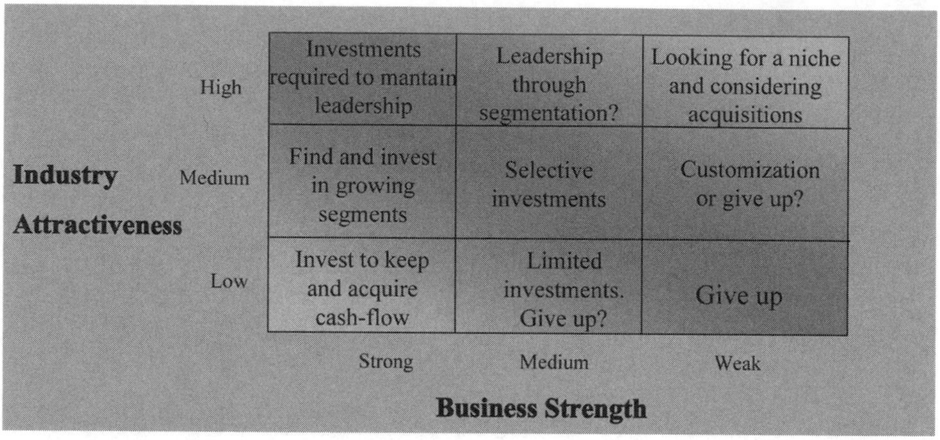

Figure 14.3 *Strategies according to the General Electric matrix*

remaining quite flexible, since it allows the diversity of factors considered on the axes to vary depending on the nature of the SBU being analysed (see Figure 14.3).

Market attractiveness configures three different cells: at the top left, those SBUs that require strong investment; on the secondary diagonal of the matrix, medium investment, and at the bottom right, low or even negative investment.

In a more in-depth analysis of each specific situation, the following alternative strategies might be found (Aaker 1987):

- *Invest to maintain the position.* Try to keep the position from eroding by investing enough to compensate for the efforts of the competition.
- *Invest to penetrate.* Aggressively try to improve the position, even sacrificing profit.
- *Invest to rebuild.* Try to recover the position lost due to a strategy to materialise gains that, for some reason, is no longer appropriate.
- *Selective investment.* Try to gain a stronger position in certain segments while allowing the position of others to weaken.
- *Withdrawal.* Sell or liquidate the business.

To complete the description of this strategic analysis technique, some of the most important disadvantages of using it are:

- It is complicated, due to the amount of detail and knowledge required that may not be available to many company managers/directors.
- Its strict application requires a large amount of information, otherwise it becomes a merely descriptive exercise.
- Unless evaluation is decisive, there is a risk that all of them will be located in the middle of the matrix, with the implicit difficulty for decision making.
- Evaluation may be heavily subjective.

THE STRATEGIC PLANNING PROCESS

The strategic planning process presented here is divided into two phases: the diagnostic phase and the planning phase. The objective of the diagnostic phase is to determine markets, target populations and segments the company wishes to address.

In the first place, to achieve this, the company mission has to be defined. Then, the opportunities and threats that may be derived from the environment and that are not controllable by the company must be identified so that an introspective process can begin, whereby the former can be taken advantage of and the latter avoided, based on an analysis of company strengths and weaknesses. Comparison of this data (SWOT analysis) will enable selection of markets, target populations and the segments to be entered.

The second phase a strategic action design process is divided into is called planning. The operations plan and control method will emerge in the stages that comprise it.

The company mission

The first step to be taken in the strategic planning process is the definition of the company mission. This concept is the basis on which the rest of the decision-making process will be developed, in the planning process, in analysis, execution and control.

The company mission is understood to be whatever the owners or interest groups expect finally to achieve from it, as well as the image they intend it to project in the environment the company moves in and belongs to and the philosophical principles that are behind its actions. Thus, in the sports and leisure industry, the company mission might be to entertain for a while or give a dinner. The company mission is defined to:

- assure the consistency and clarity of the ends pursued throughout the life of the organisation
- offer a point of reference for all planning decisions that may be taken later
- obtain the commitment of all those who make up the company through a clear communication of principles that must be observed in their actions
- obtain the support and commitment of important persons outside the organisation to the achievement of these objectives

The different aspects of the mission are understood to be long-range goals, so they are only going to change after a long period of time has elapsed. Any distinctive characteristics of the company must be included in this definition, converting them in capital that can be taken advantage of. The NBA could go into the fast food business, but it would not take advantage of its distinctive abilities which are the organisation and exploitation of a professional sports league.

There are still differences in the way North American and European sport teams fix the company mission. While in Europe most teams, until the 1970s or 1980s, traditionally sought to maximise team sport quality having neither benefits nor loss in the long term, American professional sport have always been a profit-seeking business. These differences are still in the mentality of the fans and the press and affects how owners act in the present. For example, Spanish league team Barcelona does not display advertising on its football (soccer) jerseys, in spite of having received very good offers to do so but they show it on the basketball and handball jerseys. Soccer managers think supporters would not like to see anything on the t-shirts other than the traditional red and blue colours and give more importance to this than to the money the club could raise.

Analysis of the external environment

The analysis of the external environment consists of an in-depth examination of the various factors that could have a major impact on the evolution of the company's activities. The analysis needs to be limited to the events that are really important from the point of view of the company's commercial interests, from which three dimensions that delimit the environment are distinguished:

1. A physical dimension, either spatial or geographic, in which the company can be influential and influenced.

2. A relational dimension, that includes market data (such as size, degree of penetration, segments, analyses of consumers and their purchasing behaviour, studies of the competition, legal restrictions and market regulations) and those elements that make up the company's macroenvironment (such as technology, demography, culture, economy and government). The objective pursued in this section determines the attractiveness of the industry for our business and identifies the key factors for success:

   - *Analysis of the competition.* Identification of the competitors and the intensity of their competition.

   - *Consumer analysis.* Customer analysis is usually carried out at three different levels, since it is of interest to find out the different segments that comprise the market, the motivations it responds to and whether any of its requirements are not being adequately satisfied or whether it can be improved.

   - *Scenario analysis.* The complex environment commercial decisions must confront makes it necessary to consider several probable alternatives in which these parameters can be oriented. Some authors advise not using more than three due to the enormous complexity in which the process is situated.

3. A time dimension that allows us to project the preceding two dimensions into the future.

The consumers of sports products services usually have two characteristics which distinguish them from other consumers. On the one hand, they see themselves as experts and, on the other, they feel an extraordinary emotional link (Mullin 2000).

When looking for the information required, both customers and dealers are valuable sources of information and those companies on the stock market have certain obligations concerning statements. Other secondary sources of information are government authorities, market research firms, investment analysts, specialised publications and the testimonies of the competition through their publicity, annual reports etc.

Major League Baseball's San Diego Padres, which has had sizeable gains in attendance in recent years, attribute much of its success to the establishment of the Compadre Club, a programme designed to identify, profile, track and reward registered members with team merchandise and prizes (Irwin, Zurick and Sutton 1999). The internet has become a new revenue source because of its ability to target a special segment (a team's fans) and enforce a relationship. The internet is a convenient way for a team to sell tickets and merchandising to its fans. It also provides a way to keep them informed about news, rumours, interviews etc. relating to the team. Those aftermarketing activities create a stronger commitment between the supporters and their teams.

Analysis of the internal environment

First, the different factors to be considered have to be determined and then the method to be used to evaluate them with must be studied.

The products the company works with have to be evaluated. A series of parameters has to be established which considers the consumer at the moment he is selecting his purchase for comparison with the competition:

- The first factor to be studied is the range of products and services, the weight the different families of products have and the degree to which the ranges are complementary or replaceable (e.g. in Spain and Greece the same club frequently participates in several different sports, with different plans and strategies).

- Questions concerning atmosphere and decoration where a service is to be given, the quality of product components or services offered (a restaurant, for example, would have to study the decoration and atmosphere, study how long and detailed the menu should be and the quality of prime materials).

- Product brand names and the control we have over them in the markets selected in the first phase of planning. For example, NBA's Grizzlies moved up from Vancouver to Memphis in summer of the 2001, where there are no grizzly bears. The franchise thought the name did not fit the city that much and conducted several focus groups to find a more appropriate name for the team, such as 'Memphis Blues'. The focus groups revealed people really liked Memphis Grizzlies' name and preferred it to any other tested, hence, the Memphis team will remain grizzly.

- The sales price of each of the products and brands worked; the perception of quality the consumer has of the company, the quality segment we are working or intend to work and quality improvement.

- The phase of the lifecycle the products, families and ranges are at.

Another aspect to be considered are all those tools related to the company's marketing communications activities and, specifically, advertising, promotion, salesforce and public relations. A decision must be made with regard to which of them should be used, at what cost and to what degree of efficiency. For a more precise evaluation, the analysis must be both individual as well as of the complete set of actions that comprises what is called the communications mix.

Human resource aspects to be evaluated are the adaptation of the company organisation chart, the training and characteristics (age, personality etc.) of personnel, willingness to accept functional and spatial mobility, evolution of the professional curriculum and aspirations with regard to their progress within the organisation, the work atmosphere etc.

Finally, the company's economic–financial and legal situation must be considered. The cost and margin structure must be studied by product and its contribution to the total gross margin, the financial structure of the company and the degree of embededness.

SWOT analysis

SWOT is an acronym for strengths, weaknesses, opportunities and threats. As mentioned earlier, these are precisely the variables that correspond to the purpose of the two previous stages of the strategy planning process. It is an exercise in synthesis, an attempt at matching the pieces of the strategic puzzle, so that once it is put together, the most important decisions in the diagnostic phase can be made: the selection of the markets, the target populations and the segments that the company's commercial actions are going to address.

In the analysis of the market environment we obtained a series of data on the consumer and the competition. Our chain of values will also be compared with the chain of values of the competition based on the information obtained. From all this, opportunities and threats may be identified. These are evaluated by the company based on the attractiveness and the likelihood of success of the first and the importance and probability of the latter. The main consequences obtained from the internal analysis will identify our weak points.

Selection of markets, target population and segments

This is the last stage of the diagnostic phase and the objective of all the analyses that we have carried out up to now. Once the company has accurate knowledge of the most relevant factors concerning the markets that it was tentatively thinking about working, it is in a position to select those that offer the best expectations and is capable of undertaking.

At this point, it is important to be realistic and consider the markets to be worked. More detail will be necessary and, if possible, the target population must be defined and whether all the consumers that make up the market are to be included, the segments to be reached and their most relevant characteristics.

A game hall located in a shopping centre might opt to focus on a young population from 18 to 30 years of age and average and high purchasing power (for their age) with higher prices and the latest high-tech games for their ages or they might focus on a younger segment (from 6 to 16), eliminating the excessively violent games and automobile racing (it is hard for children this age to drive such simulators), offering cheaper games and special birthday promotions.

PLANNING

Definition of objectives

In this stage we now move on to the actual planning phase of the strategic marketing planning process. The objective to be pursued here is the short-term specification of what up to now has been proposed as the organisation's commitment to try to reach certain consumers in selected markets profitably.

The first step, as mentioned earlier, is to set the objectives. This is necessary in order to be able to graduate the effort to be made and know how they will be achieved.

This task must be approached from the quality as well as the quantitative point of view. Quality objectives are usually set in terms of presence or maintenance in markets, attainment of a certain image, a place in the general distribution, recognition by the consumers or establishment of certain brands. Objectives may thus be seen as:

Being recognized in the quality market in our sector

However, the objectives must be established quantitatively, since it is the only way really to find out the magnitude of the commitments to be fulfilled. Quantitative objectives are usually set in terms of volumes, price or market share.

In the sports industry, objectives used to be in terms such as attendance, TV audience, season tickets, season tickets renewals, merchandise income, ticket prices etc. and also in terms of team achievements such as European competition qualification, winning a championship, staying in the category next year etc. Special care must be taken when establishing criteria for the sports business. One-dimensional measures such as the number of wins and losses or attendance at games may cause problems in evaluating the performance of sports businesses since a good trend in sports does not always imply strong attendance at the games or increased profits. To measure the success of these businesses, a synthetic index must be created that includes the game results, profit, customer satisfaction, team quality, management of human resources or others that would depend on the type of sport (e.g. technology in automobile events).

Furthermore, a timeframe must be defined for the objectives, they must be possible and they must be hierarchical in such a way that they establish the priority objectives for the organisation.

Laying the strategy

Strategy may be defined as the line of action to be followed by the company in attempting to achieve the objectives set. Several conditions limit the way the company can go about this. Porter (1980) distinguishes three possibilities:

1. *Specialise in cost*, originating from some competitive cost advantage of the company which enables it to lower prices further than competitors. This alternative is almost always associated with the effects derived from the experience curve, although there may be other reasons such as cheaper labour.

2. *Differentiation*, in which the idea would be to differentiate the product or service from the competition, so it is impossible or difficult to imitate. Companies

209

that apply this strategy try to get customers to trust the product and, most of the time, be willing to pay more for it. This is the classic strategy of the sports sector and the tourist industry.

3. *Focus*, which is what companies that only work one part of the market do, whether the strategy is cost or differentiation. By working only one part of the market we refer to applying this strategy only to a specific line of products, a segment of consumers or a certain geographic area.

When the company has selected the strategy it wishes to apply for each product market, it must narrow that decision down for the marketing mix variables, which will be detailed later in the following stage.

Timetable

For greater recognition of a certain picture (qualitative objective) yielding 10% of the market share (quantitative objective), a company might decide to launch a communications campaign targeting both the final consumer and dealers. An advertising agency must be selected to do this, since the company does not have a large enough staff neither is it qualified to do it alone; briefings will have to be held in which the purpose is given and media and dates, coordination with other activities, both in marketing and operations etc. will have to be settled.

But the development of a programme of action must also assign responsibilities. From the design point of view, it is necessary to decide who is responsible for carrying out the action, differentiating functional and operative responsibility. The first would designate the person whose obligation it is to see that a certain action is carried out, while the second assigns a person to actually do it.

Another point to be considered in this section is when each of the actions is to be carried out. This timetable coordinates not only all marketing operations, but also the marketing department with the rest of the company. Finally, the schedule should include their cost and development of each over time, so their efficiency, effectiveness and efficacy can be controlled.

Execution

The execution of the plan is the main objective of strategy planning. In the execution of the strategy there are three critical points to be considered:

1. Leadership of the process must be identified in specific persons. By leadership we mean not only the need of everyone that has been assigned some responsibility to recognise it and do it, but there must also be some kind of 'motor' in the organisation that aims at achieving the strategic objectives.

2. A flow of information must be established that enables us to know at all times how our plan is going. This information will help improve coordination, as well as take appropriate corrective action if necessary. Such a flow of information must comply with the budget as well as with any milestones set.

3. Execution must be flexible. The commercial reality is sometimes unpredictable, in spite of the fact that we devote great effort and resources to trying to anticipate it. If the scenario should change substantially, the company would

have to correct its plan as rapidly as possible, cancelling those activities that make no sense under the changed circumstances.

Control

The control stage is the last strategic planning process and from the analyses that are carried out during it, feedback can be provided to the whole system we have been building up. In this stage, the degree to which the objectives marked by the organisation and how the different tools we have used for it have contributed are measured.

The most common type of control is the annual control, in which the progress of product sales in the different markets and market share are analysed. If sales and market share were reached, then the marketing effort made to reach them should be examined. Normally, this is done by a percentage analysis of total marketing costs over sales, both compared to the most direct market competition as detected in the first phase of the planning process and the evolution of the percentage within the company.

Finally, among the tools that can be used to control the annual plan are the financial analysis and customer satisfaction. The first places marketing in the framework of the profit they are deriving, both in terms of market and competition and other company activities.

The analysis of customer satisfaction is basic, since it makes up the fundamental principle by which our activity is governed and also helps anticipate tendencies that may affect the company's financial results.

STRATEGIC PLANNING IN SPORT AND LEISURE AND ITS OPERATIONAL LINKAGES

Strategic planning is particularly important in sport and leisure because many of the most important variables of those businesses cannot be changed in the short term. For example, the size of the city where the team is settled, the characteristics of the sport facilities, the support of the team among the public or even the sport quality cannot be easily changed from one year to another.

For many years NBA's LA Clippers has been too frequently settled in the regular season standings last place. In spite of playing in a big market and in a city with very good weather, which makes it much easier to sign free agents, they have had only one winning season since 1978 and on many occasions the Clippers had good young players who went to other teams because of the lack of money and the team's losing streak. In 1999 they changed from the LA Sports Arena (13,657 seats and no luxury suites) to share one of the USA's most luxurious arenas, the Staples Center (19,964 seats), with their city rivals LA Lakers. The team has improved every year since then and they (that also benefited from the NBA new bargaining agreement) came out of the red in 2000. Now the franchise is highly profitable ($16.4 million by 2002) and has doubled its value from $103 million in 1999 to $205 million at the end of the 2001–2 season (*Forbes* 2003).

The goal of the operational subsystem is to produce the goods and services to satisfy consumers' needs as detected by the marketing subsystem. Such a goal is common to every sport and leisure company.

Strategic planning is the first step in the operational management process. This process starts establishing long-term goals under which an operational subsystem must be designed and investment decisions must be carried out, taking into account many heterogeneous criteria. These criteria must be identified and assessed during the strategic planning process. Hence, through strategic planning the company develops a framework where long-term goals, methods to reach this goal and means needed are established.

Operations management must translate the strategic plan into concrete actions in the short run:

- providing objectives in the short term
- planning quantities of products and services to be produced/delivered and the moment in time this will be done
- programming which components must be produced by the company or bought to a provider and fixing right dates to accomplish it
- always taking into account possible capacity problems, in order to develop realistic programs and plans
- developing the right stock management and control policy.

When those plans and programmes have been carried out, they must be executed and controlling activities must be developed in order to detect and correct possible deviations from the foreseen dates, qualities and quantities.

Thus, strategic priorities must be specified for every SBU in the organisation and must be stated in an understandable way for every worker. For example, the person in charge of a restaurant inside a sport arena or leisure facility should not be the only one to be told to raise the service quality. This person and his/her personnel should be told what must be done to achieve that goal. It is not enough to tell a worker to be efficient or flexible or to increase productivity by 10%. It is necessary to explain to him/her which activities must be carried out and train this person in those activities in order to achieve an increase in efficiency, flexibility and productivity.

Questions

1. What is a strategic business unit? Why should we assess them? How can we do it?
2. How must company goals be stated? What are the specific problems sport companies have to face while fixing objectives?
3. Which internal factors should be specially considered in strategic planning?

References and further reading

Aaker, D. A. (1987) *Strategic Marketing Management*. Barcelona: ESADE.

Abell, D. (1980) *Defining the Business: The Starting Point of Strategic Planning*. Englewood Cliffs, NJ: Prentice Hall.

Forbes magazine (2003) 'NBA teams valuations', 17 February 2003. www.forbes. com

Harris, L. C. and Jenkins, H. (2001) 'Planning the future of rugby union: a study of the planning activities of UK rugby clubs', *Marketing Intelligence and Planning*, 19, 2, 112–24.

Irwin R. L., Zwick, D. and Sutton W. (1999) 'Assessing organizational attributes contributing to marketing excellence in American professional sport franchises', *European Journal of Marketing*, 33, 3/4, 314–27.

Levitt, T. (1960) 'Marketing myopia', *Harvard Business Review*, July–August.

Lineman, R. E. and Klein, H. E. (1979) 'The use of multiple scenarios by US industrial companies', *Long Range Planning*, 12, 1, 83–90.

Mullin, B. (2000) 'Characteristics of sports marketing'. In Appenzeller, H. and Lewis, G. (eds) *Successful Sport Management*. Durham, North Carolina: Carolina Academic Press.

Parks, J. B. (1998) *Contemporary Sports Management*. London: Human Kinetics.

Porter, M. E. (1980) *Competitive Strategy*. New York: Free Press.

CHAPTER 15

Risk Management

Bryn Parry

INTRODUCTION

Risk management (RM) is like playing chess. It's fairly easy to grasp the basic 'rules' but can be difficult to master, hence it gains an unfair reputation for being difficult to apply – especially if mathematics are used.

So, in this chapter, focus on the key 'rules' and have the practicalities of a sports or leisure venue in your mind as we work through critical issues. Leave the complexities of the finer details for when you have mastered how to integrate RM into day-to-day sport and leisure operations management (SLOM).

SCOPE AND SCALE

While RM is an expanding discipline, most sports- and leisure-related texts still seem to focus on health and safety issues (Frosdick and Walley 1997; HSE 1999, 2000), or total quality management (TQM) (Slack *et al*. 1998: 760–91); though Tarlow (2002) offers a good overview for events management and Laybourn (2004) looks at RM from a decision-making perspectives. This chapter will look to those sectors that have made a significant contribution to *RM* and apply the lessons learned from them to the practicalities that you will face in implementing SLOM.

To help keep on track, a simple model will be used to help us work through the key issues, in manageable stages (see Figure 15.1). For simplicity, the model used has been adapted from a variety of RM-related models (CFM 1994; Slack *et al*. 1998: 765), but presented in a format that relates RM directly to those aspects of SLOM with which you should be familiar – many of which are explored in other chapters of this book.

RISK MYTHS AND METAPHORS

Perhaps the biggest block to effective *RM* is the simplistic picture that we have each built of the world that we think we know. This helps us to manage our daily lives but will lead us astray when it comes to dealing with the reality of *RM*.

Lagadec (1982) reminds us that:

> The disaster must not be seen like the meteorite that falls out of the sky on an innocent world: the disaster, most often, is anticipated, and on multiple occasions.

Figure 15.1 *An approach to managing risk*

How often have you seen a major disaster (even the 1993 and 2001 terrorist attacks on the World Trade Center towers) described as unprecedented or unforeseeable; then, sometimes within days, precursors and ignored warnings begin to emerge?

Looking at some of the myths of RM should help us to rid ourselves of some of our preconceptions and look at RM afresh, before we turn to the specifics of OM. After considering the following four myths, we should be much more likely to be able to anticipate potential risks than our competitors.

Lightning never strikes twice

In 1945 the Allied forces drop atomic bombs on Hiroshima (killing some 80,000 immediately) and Nagasaki (killing some 50,000 immediately), in Japan. One man is credited with surviving the Hiroshima bomb, returning to his native Nagasaki, just in time for the second atomic bomb, which he also survived.

Within a few months in 1980–81 three major hotel fires (at the MGM Grand, Las Vegas, where some 85 people die; at the Stouffer Hotel, New York, where some 36 die; and at the Las Vegas Hilton, where some eight people die) occur in USA, prompting changes in legislation; a business man is credited with being a guest at both the MGM Grand and Stouffer.

Disasters arrive without warning

In 1987 the *Herald of Free Enterprise* (roll-on roll-off) ferry capsizes off Zeebrugge, Belgium, after sailing (it is alleged) with her bow doors open; resulting in some 200 deaths and major changes to safety legislation. The disaster was not, however, without warning:

- It is alleged that there were several previous instances on which that company's ferries sailed with their bow doors open; indeed, after an earlier such incident, a captain is said to have asked for warning lights to be installed (to confirm that the doors are shut).

- In 1982 a 'wall of water' is credited with hitting the engine room of the *European Gateway* ferry; within three minutes, the roll-on roll-off ferry keels over and, within ten minutes, it rolls over; shallow water helps to keep the death toll at six.

- In 1994 the *Estonia* ferry sinks – probably, when the bow 'visor' (or its seals) failed – with the loss of some 852 lives.

- In 1953 the *Princess Victoria* (roll-on roll-off) ferry sinks in the Irish Sea, after a storm stoves in her stern doors; only 43 of the 182 passengers survive; the same ferry had survived a similar incident in 1951.

The publicity surrounding disasters reflects their impact

In the same year (1987) that 200 lives are lost aboard the *Herald of Free Enterprise*, the *Dona Paz* ferry sinks off Manila, Philippines – following a collision with the *Vector*, an oil tanker – resulting in a fireball and the loss of some 4,325 lives; although well below the death toll associated with the sinking of the *Wilhelm Gustloff*, it is the largest loss of life from a single maritime incident in peacetime and some three times the number lost aboard *RMS Titanic*, yet it rarely registers on lists of key events.

When the *RMS Titanic* sank in 1912, with the loss of some 60% of her almost 2,400 passengers, the tragedy prompted changes in safety legislation but demand for passenger liners remained strong. In 1937, meanwhile, over 60% of the passengers aboard the *Hindenburg* airship escaped, when it exploded in flames (since hydrogen burns upward); the harrowing film and emotional live radio broadcast of the event are credited, however, with stalling the development of rigid airships.

You can't plan for the unexpected

NASA and its network of suppliers famously used all their ingenuity to return the astronauts aboard the stricken *Apollo 13* spacecraft safely. One employee argued that although the things done during the rescue had never been done (or thought of) before, each specific step derived from something that had been simulated, planned or done previously.

You should now be beginning to appreciate why 'risks' can seem tricky to evaluate. Indeed, over time, the term risk has evolved from something that merely denoted an 'unexpected outcome' to today's implication of 'undesirable outcomes' and their probability (Ansell and Wharton 1992: 4). Many words have suffered such negative drift (think of 'Machiavellian' or 'meticulous'), but with 'risk' it can colour how we approach the topic; thereby affecting how we attempt to manage perceived risks. Some argue that the very language used can influence the chances of success in RM (Marks 2002).

DEFINITIONS AND INTERPRETATIONS

Adam, Beck and van Loon (2000: 2), who take a sociological approach to risk and its definition, argue that we must consider five issues when investigating risk:

1. the necessary involvement of a sense of 'construction' in the configuration of risk perception

2. the inevitability of the contested nature of these constructions as 'relations of risk definition'

3. the need to transgress the disciplinary boundaries of knowledge and instead focus on the 'unbounded' nature of knowledge practices which might include those of science, the media, politics and commerce

4. the appeal to transform 'the language of risk' from the ethos of calculation (and binary logic) to the ethos of mediation

5. the imperative of positioning technologically induced 'risks' in relation to the future, for which we cannot but take some semblance of responsibility.

Gigerenzer (2002: 25) while, essentially, addressing these same critical issues offers a more user-friendly approach:

- *ignorance of risk*, where a person is not aware of the risks

- *miscommunication of risk*, where a person knows the risks but cannot communicate them in an understandable way

- *clouded thinking*, where a person knows the risks but not how to draw conclusions from them.

Since we need to relate these to the sports and leisure sectors, take a moment to think about each set of statements. Together, they are telling us that in the complex inter-connected world in which we live, many of the risks that must be dealt with are no longer easily isolated or immediately identifiable. Indeed, some risks – such as long-term health risks – can be very difficult for the average person to comprehend.

This chapter, therefore, does not focus your energies on simply calculating the risks, but on how you can manage the interplay between conceptions of risk and the means by which appropriate responses are chosen. This should help you to explore the ways in which particular risks are perceived, defined, mediated, legitimated and/or ignored (Adam, Beck and van Loon 2000: 6).

Gigerenzer (2002: 26–8) goes on to offer the following framework for addressing uncertainties and risks:

- *degrees of belief*: essentially, a subjective probability, as when most drivers consider themselves 'above average'

- *propensity for risks*: the traits that determine the risk of an event, as is the case with a die (where there is a one in six chance of rolling a specific number)

- *frequency of risk*: Gigerenzer reminds us that if we do not compare the relative frequency of a risk to the appropriate reference class we will get a 'false reading'. For instance, mile for mile, air travel is seen as safer than car travel but, as most plane accidents occur on take-off and landing and most car accidents occur close to home it is the accidents per trip that gives the truer comparison (Weir 1999: 67–77).

Let us return to the disasters that befell the *RMS Titanic* and the *Hindenburg*, discussed earlier. In the first, 60% of passengers died and in the second 60% survived; yet, the world seemed to perceive the risks differently from the evidence of the survival rate. What might cause this? Which of the issues listed earlier are at play? How might this affect how we manage risks in the sports and leisure sectors?

In the 1970s Kahneman and Tversky advanced the notion of loss aversion (Mandel 1996: 152), whereby perceived losses, below a benchmark expectation, are actually more painful than the foregone gains. For instance, a sports or leisure venue close to bankruptcy may focus more on avoiding this than it does on raising profits, while a premiership football club may focus more on avoiding relegation than it does on playing well. Although this appears to contradict the widely used notion of 'opportunity costs', this phenomenon can be observed in the commercial world – as BBC (2003) demonstrates – and must be incorporated into any approach to RM that we adopt.

Integrating all of these components should now give you a competitive advantage in addressing SLOM, but we still need a more simplistic working definition. Tweeds (1996: 11) argues that: 'A risk management strategy can be considered as a framework for managing risk to ensure that time, cost and quality targets are met.' This might encompass a range of risk types (Dowd 1998: 3–4):

- *business risks*: e.g. those specific to the sports and leisure sectors
- *market risks*: e.g. movements in share prices
- *credit risks*: e.g. money owed may not arrive
- *liquidity risks*: e.g. assets potentially sold at a loss
- *operational risks*: e.g. failure of internal systems
- *legal risks*: e.g. third-party contracts that may not be enforceable.

While, for SLOM you may focus on only a few of these, you must never forget that each of these is a constant threat to your organisation. For a club like Manchester United, success or failure in a single Champions League fixture is now measured in millions of pounds, determining both the year's profit performance and the share price (O'Connor 2002).

RISK CONTEXT

Any effective evaluation of risks in the SLOM sector needs to address the entire system in which your organisation operates (Forrester 1995; Johns and Jones 1999a and b, 2000). Senge (1990: 40) is among many who point out that, much more than we think, systems usually cause their own crises. He uses the Sloan School of Management's 'beer game' to illustrate that decision makers who don't address all the critical 'players' in a system will fuel increasing turbulence throughout the system; while those looking at the full system accommodate changes much more easily (Senge 1990: 27–54). Beinhocker (1997) argues that we should really be evaluating risk at the sector level and not at the organisational

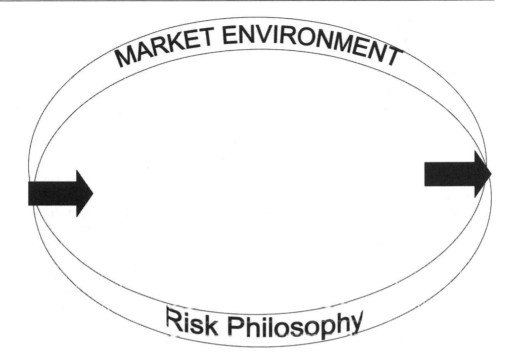

Figure 15.2 *RM model – external hemispheres*

level, as most texts would have you believe; since, while individual companies may come and go, the sector itself normally survives.

Given this, the model that we are using begins with the interplay between the market environment trends (political, economic, social, technological, environmental, legal, etc.) and the risk philosophy of the specific organisation(s) in question (see Figure 15.2).

To demonstrate this, let's look at the lead up to the collapse of ITV Digital and its impact on football league teams (Mann 2002). Media commentators seemed to have taken heed of Senge (1990: 50) and looked at how much cash was leaking from the full system; within months of the deal they were questioning how long it would be before disaster struck, well before the advertising and sponsorship markets began to soften. So far, so logical. The world of football, meanwhile, seemed indifferent to ITV Digital's reputed losses of £1 million a day. Not only were teams budgeting for the cash to arrive each year, but many were borrowing against this 'guaranteed' income to fund current spending and fuel unsustainable increases in players' wages (BBC 2002).

Before we move on, stop for a moment and think about what this incident tells us about the interplay of market environment issues and the risk philosophy of the various individuals and firms. Relate your points to the risk types of Dowd (1998: 3–4) and the frameworks of Adam, Beck and van Loon (2000: 2) and Gigerenzer (2002: 25–6) which we examined earlier. The actions of the football companies seem to illustrate what Mandel (1996: 152) means by loss aversion: the teams knew that their wage rises were unsupportable but saw promotion/relegation as far more pressing and were seduced by the £20 million extra in revenues that promotion to the Premiership brings (BBC 2003).

The ITV Digital debacle also reminds us that risks rarely occur alone, but tend to involve a 'risk cascade' of interrelated events; something we will return to later.

Virilio (1983: 32) goes further and argues that as we seek to 'improve' a system and minimise the associated risks we usually do the very opposite:

> Every technology produces, provokes, programs a specific accident ... The invention of the boat was the invention of shipwrecks. The invention of the steam engine and the locomotive was the invention of derailments ... if we wish to continue with technology ... we must think about both the substance and the accident.

This is paralleled in extreme sports, where safety innovations can tempt more of us to strive to go higher, faster, deeper; actually heightening the levels of risk. Hence, our model includes feedback to help us track how the longer term impacts of a risk event can influence future perceptions of market environment issues and the company's risk philosophy.

Before even beginning to evaluate the levels of risk, therefore, we must ensure that the risk philosophy of our organisation is not at odds with its market environment. You might think about different sports and leisure markets that you've come across and look for examples of where one organisation is comfortable in a 'high-risk' environment, whereas another seems to be very concerned about a much 'safer' environment.

Douglas and Wildavsky (1983) take a wider view than Dowd (1998: 3–4) and suggest that we look at three broad groups of risks:

1. socio-political risks
2. economic risks
3. natural risks.

The sports and leisure sectors have a tendency to ignore 1 and 3, focusing purely on economic risks. You would do well to rethink this approach. Any sports or leisure outlet that has suffered from the fallout of a terrorist outrage or sudden unemployment in its locality knows the error of this thinking. Similarly, those venues affected by flooding, turbulent weather or the recent foot and mouth outbreak are much more likely to consider natural risks – *now*.

Corporate risk philosophy

We have seen that risk is not a tangible thing, rather, it is a way of thinking (Douglas 1992: 46; Laybourn 2004). The mental models that ease our decision making (Prahalad and Bettis 1986) can also impose a dominant logic that determines the success of a system's perception (Bettis and Prahalad 1995). This helps to explain the phenomena of '*groupthink*' (Janis 1971) and '*risky-shift*' (Mullins 2002: 510), which can cause groups of individuals to adopt some highly inappropriate risk strategies.

Evaluating the host and sector corporate risk philosophy is an important early step. Frameworks, such as an organisation's Ashridge Mission Model (Segal-Horn 2000: 284–95) should provide the necessary breadth and depth of analysis, from which appropriate SLOM decisions can be made.

Douglas (1992: 47) believes that analysing risk requires communities – and, hence, organisations – to be typified according to the support that their members offer to authority, commitment, boundaries and structure. She goes on to observe that: 'Public perception of risk is treated as if it were the aggregated response of millions of private individuals.' Arguably, therefore, we should aggregate the corporate culture (Deal and Kennedy 1988; Johnson and Scholes, 2002: 540–3) from the beliefs and values of relevant strategic business units and employee groups.

Take motor racing's worst tragedy, the 1955 crash at Le Mans, when a car was vaulted into the crowd and killed some 84 spectators. At a time when many people had seen close friends killed, during the Second World War and when motor racing fatalities were expected, few would have questioned the decision to continue with the race. Mercedes, however, withdrew from racing for almost three decades and Switzerland banned circuit racing. How did the culture of the different groups influence those decisions? What would be the outcome today? Are there parallels with the tragedy at Roskilde?

Adam, Beck and van Loon (2000: 218) recognise that technicians can argue that there is 'no risk' while insurers decline cover as the risks 'are too high'. The probability of a terrorist attack on a sports venue has not changed, mathematically, since 11 September 2001 and yet many organisations experienced prohibitive insurance premiums – rises of 400% were seen (Hart 2002). This is exacerbated because the mismatch in the definitions of terrorism in the Reinsurance (Acts of Terrorism) Act 1993 (used by Pool Re, the government-backed reinsurer of last resort, to deal with terrorism insurance excesses being raised after the Baltic Exchange bombing) and the Terrorism Act 2000 (on which most commercial insurance exclusions are based) was leading to a significant lack of cover anyway (Riley 2002).

MANAGING THE RISK PYRAMID

Having identified the primacy of systems (Forrester 1995; Johns and Jones, 1999a and b, 2000; Senge 1990: 40) and their tendency to undermine and/or cancel established safety systems (Beck 1996: 31) we can move on and investigate this in more detail (Bignell and Fortune 1984). The risk pyramid has been chosen as it mirrors the different levels of activity that you are likely to be familiar with from TQM (Slack *et al.* 1998: 760–91) and, so, you will be better able to decide which SLOM techniques are appropriate at each level (see Figure 15.3).

We have seen how the dynamics of the business environment and company risk philosophy will determine how an organisation interprets risk (Bettis and Prahalad 1995). Douglas and Wildavsky (1983) argue that there is no increased level of risk in today's society, only a heightened *perception* of risk. This may be partly due to a reluctance to accept risk and partly due to the perception that wealth (which used to be perceived as a general protection from the misfortunes of the poor) no longer insulates one from today's intangible and global risks (Adam, Beck and van Loon 2000: 36).

The demise of the *Challenger* space shuttle (Feynman 1993; Vaughan 1996) best exemplifies the key issues raised by the risk pyramid. Shopfloor workers seemed surprised that management was tolerating such 'obviously' flawed operating parameters for the critical O-rings; while the management had rationalised a whole set of criteria which seemed to indicate their reliability. This is no different from the 1993 Lyme Bay canoe tragedy (AALA 2000), where the written concerns from activity centre staff were found to have been ignored, prompting a rare imprisonment for corporate manslaughter (BBC 2000). NASA's loss of a second shuttle should serve as a stark warning to the sports and leisure sectors that you have never *learned* RM – you are always learning.

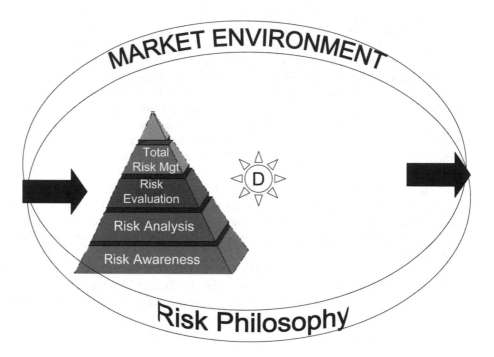

Figure 15.3 *Managing the risk pyramid*

Risk awareness

We've already seen some of the ways in which organisations can fail to spot risks and the penalties. Handy (1990) uses the analogy of frogs. Apparently, a frog will jump out of hot water but happily allow itself to be cooked in slowly boiling water; because the sensors in its skin are designed to spot sudden changes in the environment, but not slow changes. Many of our organisations are the same. They can be in front of a critical set of risks and still not 'see' them (Mezias and Starbuck 2003).

The simplest and most dramatic improvement to SLOM that you can make is likely, therefore, to be a heightened awareness of risk issues. You have already made a start by considering the issues raised earlier, but the greatest block is likely to be convincing your superiors that the relatively small-scale risks identified deserve the time and effort associated with their potential outcomes.

The much misquoted Heinrich's Ratio (Davies and Teasdale 1994: 6–7; Heinrich 1959) demonstrates that, left unchecked, 'unsafe acts' will eventually escalate into major incidents (see Figure 15.4). You must use appropriate SLOM techniques that your senior management and operational staff understand to get over to them how seemingly low-risk 'unsafe acts' can trigger a risk cascade and result in a major incident. For instance, Ishikawa diagrams (Slack *et al.* 1998: 703–707) can help to highlight how a collection of factors might combine to trigger a tragedy.

Although this should improve your level of foresight compared to your competitors, we have seen how the perception of risk at NASA and Lyme Bay became distorted (Toft and Reynolds 1997: 55). So, you will need to focus on what your senior management and operational staff consider critical.

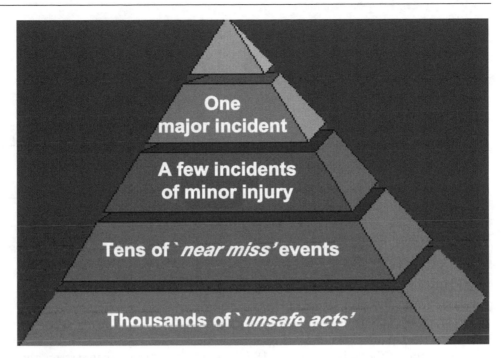

Figure 15.4 *Heinrich's Ratio (amended from Davies and Teasdale 1994: 6–7)*

Risk analysis

One of the challenges that you will face in persuading senior management and operational staff of the importance of specific risks is that: 'The essence of risk is not that it *is* happening, but that it *might* be happening' (Adam, Beck and van Loon 2000: 2). Hence, risk analysis must focus on applying the propensities and frequencies Gigerenzer (2002: 26) dealt with and which we looked at earlier.

Since the potential risks will form a 'risk cascade', we need to analyse all risks accordingly. Figure 15.5 is a widely used matrix for formulating appropriate responses to potential risk situations. All too often, though, the two components of the risk matrix (level of probability and level of severity) are compacted, to give an artificial and (ultimately) meaningless numerical value (Shone and Parry 2001).

Adam, Beek and van Loon (2000: 13) recognise the tensions associated with this desire to convert the information-rich data into an oversimplified, but easy to comprehend, numerical value:

> The established institutionalization of 'risk' in terms of 'insurance' (coupling risk with money and the future) has collapsed. .. Hence, as the need for more complex and more precise calculations rises with the increased complexity of risk, so does the impossibility to establish such calculations.

Thus, your analysis should keep to the framework in Figure 15.5. Take a moment to see how many of the risks that you face in SLOM can be positioned on this framework – which are the most difficult to position? Why? To retain a credible spacing on Figure 15.5 you'll need to adopt this approach, taken by the 'Richter Scale', so each whole number represents a ten-fold likelihood of severity.

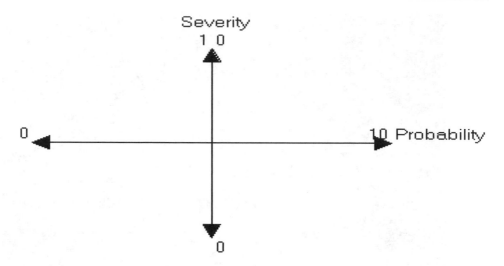

Figure 15.5 *Strategic risk*

Risk evaluation

The 'impossibility' of achieving accurate calculations should not cause us to stop attempting them. Peters *et al.* (1974) have demonstrated that systems that give a broadly accurate forecast are eminently more desirable than those that give a precisely accurate forecast, but with a highly dispersed range of 'wrong readings'. Learning from failures and exploring potential impacts can be much more rewarding to our approach to RM than a 'correct' calculation that delays our exposure to a risk.

Travel Inn knows that it offers a competitive service but recognises that it will, inevitably, fail in some areas. So, having planned as best it can, the chain offers a money-back guarantee if guests are not totally satisfied. The annual £1 million in rebates equates to 0.5% of revenue but provides an improved base for evaluating risks (*Caterer and Hotelkeeper* 2002); since it learns of individual issues and can prevent their escalating (Davies and Teasdale 1994: 6–7; Heinrich 1959), while avoiding 'hidden costs' and 'false economies'. How difficult would it be to integrate a similar scheme within SLOM?

As with most aspects of SLOM, the key to success is to use a range of techniques, rather than relying on a single method. Dowd (1998: 15) observes that 'quantitative methods need to be used very carefully ... the [first trap to avoid is] using these approaches mechanically ... [the second is to] avoid getting caught out when using dynamic hedges ...' – which only work against small changes in risk factors and need constant revision.

Too often, SLOM seems to echo other sectors and adopts approaches that rely on historical data/interpretations compounded by subjective techniques and assumptions (Ansell and Wharton 1992: 79–81) – the 'degrees of belief' that Gigerenzer (2002: 26) warned us about earlier. We should be trying to make the 'unpredictable predictable', while accepting that: 'Risk statements are neither purely factual claims nor exclusively value claims' (Adam, and van Loon 2000: 215–16).

Total risk management

At the top level of the risk pyramid, we are ready to explore an holistic approach to total risk management.

Adam, Beck and van Loon (2000: 219) argue for the benefits of an open culture, with a high degree of trust, pointing out that: 'the impacts of risks grow precisely because nobody knows or wants to know about them ... the less risks are publicly recognized, the more risks are produced'. This is a prime example of what Senge (1990) meant by systems creating their own crises and mirrors what we saw with the ITV Digital debacle.

Effective SLOM should, therefore, strive for the kind of 'no-blame' culture that Travel Inn seeks, where each member of staff takes personal responsibility for dealing with potential risks in an open environment. Indeed Travel Inn argues that not only did quality rise, due to its initiative, but that staff retention increased by 25% (*Caterer and Hotelkeeper* 2002).

The first three levels of the risk pyramid should go a long way towards improving your success with managing risks. This last level is, though, critical and you cannot achieve it without 'thinking the unthinkable', expecting the unexpected – and doing so in a no-blame culture that puts RM to the fore.

Hence, you should not be saying that you've done everything expected to protect your organisation; you should be asking, given everything put in place, how could it be disrupted? How could you tweak the potential risk cascades to cause the most damage? After all, if you are undertaking the effective SLOM suggested in other chapters, your organisation will have all the information to hand.

Commercial imperatives can tend to create pressure to investigate 'mistakes' quickly, with a very focused approach, and to seek a single cause (Toft and Reynolds 1997: 34). The reality of the SLOM environment is, however, far more complex with causes and effects often widely dispersed.

So, never say 'if'; always say 'when' and use an appropriate version of the Heinrich Ratio to see which minor incidents are warning you of a future tragedy.

POTENTIAL RESPONSES

We now turn to the issue of appropriate responses. Their evaluation (represented in our model by the central wheel) is necessarily influenced by the market environment and the risk philosophy of our company, but the outcomes tend to be fairly obvious – if not always palatable.

To illustrate the appropriateness of the typical risk outcomes, we have added them to the strategic risk framework from Figure 15.5 (see Figure 15.6).

Retain	Revenue account	Budget for these small amounts whilst investing in training and equipment
	Self-fund	Hope that these don't occur and pay for replacements when they do (if you can still afford it)
Transfer	Insure	Pay an insurance premium to guard against the risk
	Contract out	Outsource an activity to a more experienced company

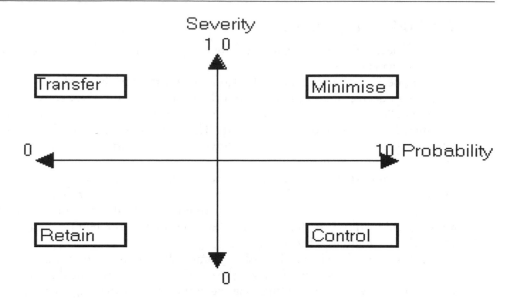

Figure 15.6 *Strategic RM responses*

The retain options illustrate how the effective management of the issues addressed in this chapter will have a profound impact on profitability and cash flow.

Considering the transfer options, we have already looked at how the conservative approach of insurance companies can impose prohibitive restrictions and premiums; while the loss-aversion culture of companies (Mandel 1996: 152) can result in inappropriate insurance cover. Jarvis (1995), meanwhile, illustrated how outsourcing can be a risky option in itself – setting in train a series of steps that reduce the host company's asset values. Indeed, poorly specified outsourcing contracts can create their own problems (Mandel 1996: 133–4).

Choice of responses

We've already recognised that, even after all that we have discussed, your choice of response is still likely to be subjective. We're only scratching the surface in this chapter, but the following points should give you food for thought and help you to apply RM to SLOM more successfully:

- Langer (1980) argues that people 'attribute desirable outcomes to internal factors but tend to blame external factors for failures'.

- Fischoff (1980) argues that 'people consistently exaggerate what could have been anticipated in foresight'.

- Kogan and Wallach (1964) argue that, when skill is involved, people tend to be moderately risky; when pure chance is involved, however, they tend to become much more extreme – either risk taking or risk averse

- Gumerlock (1994) argues that risk will always find a way to express itself – learn to accept this.

- Weir (1999) argues that airlines would achieve much more if they switched their focus from making aircraft crashes rare to making them survivable.

For your organisation, consider how this collection of advice should influence your choice of strategic RM responses.

Now that you're beginning to appreciate that *RM* is all about doing your best to prevent disaster while accepting that you'll be left picking up the pieces after something else went wrong, you can begin to think about the recovery process – represented by the feedback arrow in our model.

Turner (1978) offers a disaster sequence model that SLOM would do well to work through regularly, as opposed to waiting until disaster strikes:

1. *notionally normal starting points*: system's beliefs, values and codes
2. *incubation period*: unnoticed set of events, at odds with accepted beliefs on hazards and norms for their avoidance
3. *precipitating event*: transforms our perceptions of stage 2
4. *onset*: immediate consequences of collapse of cultural precautions become apparent
5. *rescue and salvage*: first stage adjustment: post-collapse recognition and ad hoc adjustments enabling rescue and salvage
6. *full cultural readjustment*: inquiry/assessment: beliefs and precautionary norms adjusted to fit new understanding of system.

After all:

> Once a system contains the possibility of its own failure, it becomes a matter of time and luck as to whether failure actually occurs ... Most system failures originate in a prior failure to anticipate that failure will occur. They originate in failures of the perception of risk. (Ansell and Wharton 1992: 44)

CONCLUSIONS AND RECOMMENDATIONS

The fundamental themes offered by Toft and Reynolds (1997: 115) serve as a useful framework for SLOM practitioners to establish suitable guidelines:

- large-scale accidents/disasters are generally failures of socio-technical systems
- typically, disasters are low-frequency events within any single industry or field
- each industry or profession needs to look outside its own immediate scope, and examine disasters occurring elsewhere – in order to maximise the chances of finding repeated patterns and of learning isomorphically
- the goal of the isomorphic learning process is 'active foresight' regarding safety – both elements are equally important: generation of foresight and active implementation of risk reduction procedures/systems
- an organisation's safety culture determines the extent to which foresight is generated and the level of implementation.

In order to gain a competitive advantage, you should resist the temptation to establish operational guidelines until you have worked through the issues and concepts mentioned earlier. The result should be an improved understanding and appreciation of the critical success factors – relevant to the sports and leisure sectors.

Questions

1. Given the seriousness of the risks highlighted in this chapter, should you focus on the 'big risks' and leave simple issues to your staff?

2. Are you able to fit the full range of risks likely to face your organisation to the framework in Figure 15.5?

3. If *Marriott* and *Travel Inn* hotel staff have considerable leeway in solving customer problems, why don't we see this more often in the sports and leisure sectors?

References

AALA (2000) '*From Lyme Bay to licensing – past, present and future – the development of current regulation of outdoor adventure activities*'. Available at http://www.aala.org/lymebay01.html (accessed September 2002).

Adam, B., Beck, U. and van Loon, J. (eds) (2000) '*The Risk Society and Beyond*'. London: Sage.

Ansell, J. and Wharton, F. (eds.) (1992) *Risk Analysis Assessment and Management*. Chichester: John Wiley & Sons.

BBC (2000) '*Calling companies to account*'. Available at http://news.bbc.co.uk/1/hi/uk/743306.stm (accessed September 2003).

BBC (2002) '*The business of football*'. Available at http://news.bbc.co.uk/1/hi/business/1898854.stm (accessed September 2003).

BBC (2003) 'Football "Facing up to reality" '. Available at http://www.bbc.co.uk/1/hi/business/3109835.htm.

Beck, U. (1996) 'Risk society' in Adam, B., Beck, U. and van Loon, J. (eds) (2000) *The Risk Society and Beyond*. London: Sage.

Beinhocker, E. (1997) 'Strategy at the edge of chaos', *McKinsey Quarterly*, 1, 24–39.

Bettis, R. A. and Prahalad, C. K. (1995) 'The dominant logic: retrospective and extension', *Strategic Management Journal*, 14.

Bignell, V. and Fortune, J. (1984) *Understanding System Failures*. Manchester: Manchester University Press.

Caterer & Hotelkeeper (2002) 'Complaints at Travel Inn up by 17%', 10 January.

Centre for Facilities Management (1994) *Introduction to Risk Management*. Glasgow: CFM.

Davies, N. V. and Teasdale, P. (1994) *The Costs to the British Economy of Work Accidents and Work-related Ill Health*. Sheffield: HSE Books.

Deal, T. and Kennedy, A. (1988) *Corporate Cultures: The Rites and Rituals of Corporate Life*. London: Penguin.

Douglas, M. (1992) '*Risk and blame: essays in cultural theory*' in Adam, B., Beck, U. and van Loon, J. (eds) (2000) *The Risk Society and Beyond*. London: Sage, 38.

Douglas, M. and Wildavsky, A. (1983) 'Risk and culture' in Adam, B., Beck, U. and van Loon, J. (eds) (2000) *The Risk Society and Beyond*. London: Sage, 48.

Dowd, K. (1998) *Beyond Value At Risk: The New Science of Risk Management*. Chichester: John Wiley & Sons.

Feynman, P. (1993) *What Do You Care What Other People Think?* London: HarperCollins.

Fischoff, B. (1980) 'For those condemned to study the past: reflections on historical judgements' in Toft, B. and Reynolds, S. (1997) *Learning From Disaster: A Management Approach* (2nd edn). Leicester: Perpetuity Press, 68.

Forrester, J. (1995) 'The beginning of systems dynamics', McKinsey Quarterly, 4, 4–16. Available at http://mckinseyquarterly.com (accessed October 2002).

Frosdick, S. and Walley, L. (eds) (1997) *Sport and Safety Management*. Oxford: Butterworth-Heinemann.

Gigerenzer, G. (2002) *Reckoning with Risk*. London: Allen Lane & the Penguin Press.

Gumerlock, R. (1994) in Dowd, K. (1998) *Beyond Value At Risk: The New Science of Risk Management*. Chichester: John Wiley & Sons, 15.

HSE (1999) *The Event Safety Guide*. London: Health and Safety Executive.

HSE (2000) *Managing Crowds Safely* (2nd edn). London: Health and Safety Executive.

Handy, C. (1990) *The Age of Unreason*. London: Arrow.

Hart, S. (2002) 'Gambling on the threat of terrorism', *Sunday Telegraph*, 8 September.

Heinrich, H. W. (1959) *Industrial Accident Prevention: A Safety Management Approach* (4th edn). New York: McGraw-Hill.

Janis, I. L. (1971) 'Groupthink', *Psychology Today*, November, 43–76.

Jarvis, P. (1995) 'Contracting out facilities and services affects fixed asset valuations', *Public Eye*, October-December 14, 2–3.

Johns, N. and Jones P. (1999a) 'Systems: mind over matter'. *Hospitality Review*, 1, 3.

Johns, N. and Jones P. (1999b) 'Systems and management: the principles of performance', *Hospitality Review*, 1, 4.

Johns, N. and Jones P. (2000) 'Systems and management: understanding the real world', *Hospitality Review*, 2, 1.

Johnson, G. and Scholes, K. (2002) *Exploring Corporate Strategy: Text and Cases* (6th edn). Harlow: FT/Prentice Hall.

Kogan, N. and Wallach, M. A. (1964) *Risk Taking: A Study in Cognition and Personality*. New York: Holt, Rinehart and Winston.

Lagadec, P. (1982) 'Major technical risk: an assessment of industrial disasters', in Toft, B. and Reynolds, S. (1997) *Learning From Disaster: A Management Approach* (2nd edn). Leicester: Perpetuity Press, 54.

Langer, E. (1980) 'The psychology of chance' in Toft, B. and Reynolds, S. (1997) *Learning From Disaster: A Management Approach* (2nd edn.). Leicester: Perpetuity Press, 66.

Laybourn, P. (2004) 'Risk and decision-making in events management' in Yeoman, I., Robertson, M., Ali-Knights, J., Drummond, S. and McMahon-Beattie, U. (eds) *Festival and Events Management*. Oxford: Elsevier Butterworth-Heinemann.

Mandel, M. (1996) *The High-risk Society: Peril and Promise in the New Economy*. New York: Random House.

Mann, C. (2002) 'Football falls flat as TV cash dries up', *The Business*, 11/12 August, 1 and 6.

Marks, P. (2002) 'Texts that trigger meltdown', *New Scientist*, 7 September, 12.

Mezias, J. and Starbuck, W. (2003) 'Studying the accuracy of managers' perceptions: A research odyssey', *British Journal of Management*, 14(1) 3–17.

Mullins, L. (2002) *Management and Organisational Behaviour* (6th edn). Harlow: FT/Prentice Hall.

O'Connor, A. (2002) 'Television spies a view to a kill'. *The Times*, August 26.

Peters, J. T., Hammond, K. R. and Summers, D. A. (1974) '*A note on intuitive vs. analytic thinking*' in Mintzberg, H. (1994) *The Rise and Fall of Strategic Planning*. Hemel Hempstead: Prentice Hall, 327.

Prahalad, C. K. and Bettis, R. A. (1986) 'The dominant logic: a new linkage between diversity and performance'. *Strategic Management Journal*, 7, 485–501.

Riley, A. (2002) 'Hidden peril of the lone terrorist', *The Times*, 10 September, law supplement, 5.

Segal-Horn, S. (2000) *Strategy Reader*. Oxford: Blackwell/Open University Press.

Senge, P. (1990) *The Fifth Discipline: The Art and Practice of the Learning Organization*. London: Century Business.

Shone, A. and Parry, B. (2001) *Successful Event Management*. London: Continuum.

Slack, N., Chambers, S., Harland, C., Harrison, A. and Johnston, R. (1998) *Operations Management* (2nd edn). London: Pitman.

Tarlow, P. (2002) *Event Risk Management and Safety*. Chichester: Wiley.

Toft, B. and Reynolds, S. (1997) *Learning From Disaster: A Management Approach* (2nd edn). Leicester: Perpetuity Press.

Turner, B. A. (1978) 'Man made disasters', in Toft, B. and Reynolds, S. (1997) *Learning From Disaster: A Management Approach* (2nd edn). Leicester: Perpetuity Press, 22.

Tweeds (ed.) (1996) *Laxton's Guide To Risk Analysis and Management*. Oxford: Laxton's.

Vaughan, D. (1996) *The Challenger Launch Decision: Risky Technology, Culture, and Deviance at NASA*. Chicago: University of Chicago Press.

Virilio, P. (1983) 'Pure War' New York, Semiotext(e), in Adam, B., Beck, U. and van Loon, J. (eds) (2000) *The Risk Society and Beyond*. London: Sage, 33.

Weir, A. (1999) *The Tombstone Imperative: The Truth about Air Safety*. London: Simon & Schuster.

CHAPTER 16

Legal and Ethical Issues in the Design and Delivery of Sport and Leisure Facilities

John Wolohan

While I was preparing this chapter, a 13-year-old girl, attending her first professional hockey game, died after she was hit in the head with a puck as it was deflected over the glass. All the parties involved, the National Hockey League (NHL), the team and the facility, have publicly stated that it was a freak accident and that no one was at fault. To support this claim, the league noted that this was the first fan hit by a deflected puck ever to die while attending a NHL game.

Unfortunately, this was *not* the first hockey fan to die after being hit by a deflected puck. There were, in fact, a couple of deaths reported in Canadian junior leagues. After the accident, to prevent any lawsuit over the incident, the team and facility quickly paid the girl's family a cash settlement (Farber 2002). Even though there was no lawsuit, sport and leisure facility operators should be asking themselves an important question: could anything have been done differently to make the facility safer? The answer is *yes*.

For example, in an attempt to make NHL facilities safer, the league has announced that, as of September 2002, it would standardise the height of the glass around each rink to a minimum of five feet, as well as require every facility to install safety netting behind both goals. The safety netting, which has long been used in European hockey arenas and some Canadian and American junior and college hockey rinks, will hang from the ceiling and rest on top of the glass.

Using this tragedy as a backdrop, this chapter will examine the legal and ethical issues involved in the design and delivery of sport and leisure facilities. While it may seem that all the source material in this chapter involves legal concepts developed in USA, relevant linkages to UK and European law are included when possible.

Before we begin to examine the legal and ethical issues, however, we must first develop a working definition of facility. As it is discussed in this chapter, sport and leisure can take place anywhere. Therefore, the definition of facility should not be limited merely to buildings and stadiums, but must, as one commentator stated, include natural outdoor settings including parks, lakes, trails and woods (Maloy 2001). In other words, the concept of a facility needs to be broad enough to include any area in which sport and leisure activities are performed.

Now that we have a working definition of facility, we can begin to examine the legal and ethical issues involved in the design and delivery of the sport and leisure facilities. The chapter will begin with an overview of the legal theory of negligence. In particular, since negligence is the most common tort claim sport and leisure facilities will face, the chapter will review the elements required to show a negligence claim. In addition, the chapter examines some of the defences available to facility owners. Next, the chapter examines the legal status of those using the facility, such as participants, spectators and recreation users. The chapter will also examine some of the most common problem areas. These areas include: inspection of facility; maintenance and repair; duty to warn of concealed dangers; advising users of risks; the duty to hire competent personnel; the duty to provide supervision; and the duty to provide for emergency care. Finally, the chapter looks at the issue of ethics and what sport and leisure facilities administrators can do when faced with ethical dilemmas in the workplace.

LEGAL THEORY OF NEGLIGENCE

Negligence, the most common tort in the sport and leisure industry, is an unintentional tort that focuses on an individual's conduct or actions (Gardiner *et al.* 2001). Negligence is based on the legal theory that people are required to act in a way that avoids creating an unreasonable risk to others (Schubert *et al.* 1986). Therefore, any conduct or action that falls below this standard and creates such an unreasonable risk is negligence. In determining whether the conduct was reasonable, the courts use what is known as a reasonable person test. The reasonable person test examines whether a reasonable prudent person, under the same circumstances, would have acted in the same manner.

Before any action will be considered negligence, the injured party must be able to establish four basic elements: duty of care; breach of duty; causation; and damages.

Duty of care

The first question in any negligence case is whether the defendant owed the injured party or plaintiff a duty of care. Duty of care refers to the standard of care the law has established for the protection of others (Schubert *et al.* 1986). The courts will impose a duty of care on an individual, facility or organisation if there is a special relationship, which requires that individual, facility or organisation to protect another from unreasonable risks that may cause injury. It is important to note that the law of negligence does not require that you protect every individual using a facility from every conceivable injury; it merely requires that you do not create an unreasonable risk and that you protect people from risks that are foreseeable. If the risk is not foreseeable, there is no liability.

Breach of duty

Once a duty of care has been established, the second question the court must answer is whether or not the duty of care required has been met or whether it was breached (Schubert *et al.* 1986). In order to determine whether the defendant has breached his or her duty and created an unreasonable risk of injury, the court will examine a number of factors such as the experience and age of the participants. For example, is this the first time an individual has tried an activity or are they experienced? Are there any individuals with physically disabilities; are there any children? All these factors will dictate the standard of care that is required.

In addition, facility operators should also be aware of environmental conditions. Environmental conditions include both the inside physical environment, as well as the outside weather conditions. For example, what is the layout of the facility or the condition of the field or the gymnasium? Facility operators also need to take into consideration the outside environment and the impact weather conditions will have on those playing, watching and travelling to an event.

When dealing with individuals such as coaches and medical staff, the standard of care is based on the qualifications or certification of a prudent professional in that industry, not on their professional experience. Everyone, therefore, no matter how experienced or inexperienced, must meet the same the standard of care.

Causation

Once the injured party is able to establish that the defendant breached his or her duty or standard of care and acted in a negligent manner, they still must show that the conduct complained of actually caused the injury. In other words, was the breach of duty the legal cause of the plaintiff's injury? Legal or proximate cause is established when there is a casual connection between the negligent conduct and the injury (Schubert *et al.* 1986).

In the hockey example in the introduction, if the plaintiff (the girl's family) is able to show that the facility breached its duty of care by failing to provide netting behind the goals, thus allowing the puck to go into the stands, the facility's negligence would have caused the girl's injury. It is important to note here, however, that just because someone is injured, it does not necessarily mean that the facility's conduct caused the injury.

Damages

The final element of any negligence claim is damages. The plaintiff must suffer some form of injury or damages, in order for the courts to award compensation. If there is no injury, there is no liability.

DEFENCES TO NEGLIGENCE

The most common defences to negligence are: assumption of risk, agreements to participate, waivers, immunity, facility lease agreements and the use of independent contractors.

Assumption of risk

There are two key elements to an assumption of risk defence. First, the plaintiff must have knowledge of the risks inherent in the activity. Second, the plaintiff, with knowledge and appreciation of the risks inherent in the activity, must voluntarily participate in the activity or assume the risks (Wong 1994). If the plaintiff, knowing the inherent risks or dangers involved in an activity or event, voluntarily participates anyway, the court will typically find that the sport and leisure facility operators are *not* liable for any injuries resulting from those inherent risks. In the UK, the assumption of risk defence is known as *volenti non fit injuria* (Gardiner *et al.* 2001).

It is important that sport and leisure facility operators understand that an individual can only assume those risks that are inherent to the sport or activity, not those incurred as a result of the negligence of the sport and leisure facility.

Agreements to participate

One way to strengthen the assumption of risk defence is through the use of an agreement to participate. The agreement to participate is a document that helps sport and leisure facilities inform participants of the nature of the activity, the risks involved in the activity and the behaviours expected of the participant (Cotton and Cotton 1997).

Waivers

While the use of waivers in England and Europe is unlawful (Gardiner *et al.* 2001), in the USA and Canada, a well-written and properly administered waiver, voluntarily signed by an adult, can be used to protect the sport facility from liability for ordinary negligence by the business or its employee (Cotton and Cotton 1997).

A waiver is a written contract between the facility and the participant in which the participant or user of a service agrees to relinquish the right to pursue legal action against the service provider in the event of an injury caused by the negligence of the provider.

Immunity

While not justifying the defendant's negligent conduct, in certain situations the plaintiff is prevented from suing the defendant based on the theory of immunity (Schubert *et al.* 1986). There are several forms of immunity that impact sport and leisure facility. These include the traditional ones of sovereign immunity (which prevents an injured party from filing suit against the government and its political subdivisions without their consent) and charitable immunity (which prevents an injured party from filing suit against a charitable organisation).

In addition, a number of jurisdictions have added newer ones including recreational user immunity (discussed later); and volunteer immunity (which protect volunteers of non-profit organisations from liability for negligence).

Facility lease agreements

When an injury occurs at a sport and leisure facility, the court, in order to determine the liability of the facility owner and those leasing the facility, will examine whether the injury was activity related or premise related. Generally, injuries that are activity related are the responsibility of the lessee. With premise-related injuries, liability may rest on both the entity conducting the activity and the facility owner. The facility owner is generally responsible for structural-type problems, while the lessee conducting the activity is often responsible for maintenance-type problems (Cotton 2001).

Use of independent contractors

Sport and leisure facilities can also cut down on their liability by using independent contractors to perform certain functions. While the facilities are still responsible for using reasonable care in selecting a competent independent contractor and for 'inherently dangerous activities' (e.g. fireworks displays), the benefit of using an independent contractor is that it shifts the liability for ordinary negligence from the sport and leisure facility to the independent contractor (van der Smissen 1990).

To be classified as an independent contractor, an individual must be free to conduct the task as he or she sees fit using his or her own methods, using his or her own tools and being subject to the employer's control only as to the final result of the work (Cotton 2001).

LEGAL STATUS OF FACILITY OWNERS AND USERS

The nature of the duty that a sport and leisure facility owes to those using the facility depends on the relationship between the user and the facility. These relationships can be defined in terms of the status of the visitor: invitee, licensee, trespasser and recreational user (van der Smissen 2001).

Invitee

Generally, users, participants and spectators of sports and leisure facilities are legally termed invitees. An invitee is a person whose presence will produce direct or indirect economic gain for the facility operator (Maloy 2001). An operator owes an invitee the obligation to exercise reasonable care to keep the invitee safe, to protect the user from unreasonable risk and to avoid acts that can create risks.

There are two types of invitee: business and public. Some examples of a business invitee include spectators who pay admission to watch an event or someone who has paid a membership fee to join a health club. The payment, or expected economic benefit for the operator, is the key to this legal designation (Maloy 2001). A public invitee is a person whose presence was encouraged by the facility operator. The key to this designation is the encouragement given to the general public to use the facility (Maloy 2001).

Licensee

A licensee is a person who has the permission or consent of the operator to use the facility and provides no real or expected benefit to the facility owner. A licensee enters the facility for his own purpose. The only obligation an owner owes a licensee is to warn of hazards or dangers, which the licensee may not be able to discover. The owner has no duty to inspect or discover dangers or give any warnings of obvious dangers (Maloy 2001).

Trespasser

A trespasser is a person who enters the facility without the permission of the operator. Generally, since no consent has been given to use the facility, the only obligation owed by the operator is to refrain from any intentional conduct that would cause injury to the trespasser.

Recreational user

A recreational user is a person who is on the premise specifically for recreational purposes. To claim that the user was a recreational user, the owner must not have charged a fee or been paid by the user and the user must have been directly involved in a recreational activity at the time of the injury. Generally, the facility owner owes the recreational user a duty comparable to the duty owed a trespasser. That is, they must refrain from any intentional conduct that would injure the user (van der Smissen 1990).

LEGAL DUTY OF FACILITY OWNERS AND OPERATORS

Since many sport and leisure activities are conducted in natural settings, there are three general rules regarding liability for injuries caused by natural conditions that sport and leisure professionals should be aware of. First, the traditional rule in English and American courts is that a facility operator is not obligated to remedy or correct any natural conditions on the land. Second, the facility operator can be held liable for any changes or alterations he makes to natural conditions on the land. Finally, the law regarding natural conditions is generally applicable only to rural and unimproved areas (van der Smissen 1990).

These three rules, however, do not apply to arenas or other spectator facilities. In those facilities, the legal responsibility for providing a safe facility is placed on the possessor or occupier of the property. The theory behind this rule is that the possessor or occupier of the facility is in the best position to discover and control any risks or hazards. Sport and leisure facility owners, therefore have a legal duty to:

1. inspect regularly for hazards or dangers
2. maintain the premises and correct defects
3. warn users of any hazards or dangers that are not readily apparent
4. warn users of any participatory risks of the sport or activity
5. keep users safe during their use of the facility by having a plan for reasonable supervision and security, using reasonable employee recruiting, selection, hiring and training practices and having an emergency medical plan.

Duty to inspect facility

Facility operators have a duty to inspect the facility for risks or hazards that threaten invitees. In addition to inspecting the facility, once a facility operator or his or her employees become aware of a risk or danger, they have a duty to correct or remedy the problem or to warn participants of the danger if remedial steps cannot be taken immediately.

To assist in performing this duty, facility operators should develop a schedule of when to conduct inspections. In making a schedule, inspections may be classified according to type or frequency. They may be informal or they can involve comprehensive checklists. The inspection may be a general inspection of the total facility or focus on a designated location. Inspections may be conducted daily, weekly, monthly, seasonally or annually. The critical feature of any inspection plan is to meet the facility's obligation to discover hazards (Maloy 2001).

Duty to keep the facility in safe repair

Since the facility operator has a duty to keep the facility in safe repair, a facility maintenance plan should be developed and followed. Included in any facility maintenance plan should be a schedule for the regular maintenance of all areas of the facility as well as the correction of any defects found through inspections. In addition, a facility maintenance plan helps to insure follow-up of inspections and will minimise any risks that may not have been discovered during an inspection.

Duty to warn of concealed dangers

The facility operator has a duty to warn users of concealed dangers that are not usually visible or apparent. To satisfy this duty, the warnings must be reasonably sufficient to bring the danger to the users' attention. In addition, the operator may be required to provide a barrier near the hazard or to prevent access to the hazard if the warning is not sufficient to make the risk of danger apparent to the patrons.

There are situations, however, where the risks are known or where they are so obvious that the user should reasonably be expected to discover them. In those situations, the law will usually recognise that the user is responsible for his or her protection from a known risk of injury. It is expected that a premise patron, knowing of the open and obvious risk of injury, will take reasonable precaution against injury from the known risk. An exception to the open and obvious rule, however, is called the *distraction exception*. This occurs when the facility owner has reason to believe that an individual's attention may be distracted so that they will either fail to discover the obvious risk or will forget what they have discovered or fail to protect themselves against it (Maloy 2001).

Duty to warn of participatory risks

Sport and leisure facility operators have a duty to warn individuals of any risks associated with an activity. In assessing the type of warning necessary for a particular activity, facility operators should keep the following issues in mind. First, the nature of the activity and the skills and abilities needed in order successfully and safely to participate in the activity. If the activity is difficult or potentially dangerous, direct supervision by experienced professionals is going to be required. If, by way of contrast, the activity is simple and safe, less direct supervision is required. It is the duty of individual supervising the activity to identify the inherent risks of the activity and warn the participant of these risks.

Second, it should be noted that there is a difference between participants and spectators. Unlike participants, who are usually familiar with the nature of the activity and the risks involved, spectators are not always knowledgeable of the potential dangers or risks. Therefore, facility operators have a duty to advise spectators of the dangers or risks. Facility operators can satisfy this duty through the use of signs throughout the facility warning fans of the potential dangers or risks (such as hockey pucks flying into the stands). Besides warning signs, facility operators should also make periodic public address announcements throughout the event warning spectators of the risks.

Finally, facility operators should also consider providing a reasonable number of seats protected by screens or barriers. This would allow those spectators who ask for protected or safe seats to have them (van der Smissen 1990).

Duty to provide proper emergency medical care

Generally, sport and leisure facility operators have a duty to provide timely and capable medical assistance. Additionally, facility operators have a duty to refrain from taking any actions that could aggravate the injury. This means that the operator has to be able to recognise when serious injury has occurred (Wong 1994).

It is important to understand that the duty to provide emergency care encompasses not only the rendering of care once the injury has occurred but also the preparation for emergency care prior to the activity. For example, a sport and leisure facility may do everything humanly possible to provide care to an injured participant, but unless there has been adequate planning for the emergency situation and the appropriate medical personnel were on hand to carry out the plan, the standard of care required may not have been met (Hall and Kanoy 2001).

When considering the duty to provide emergency medical care, sport and leisure facilities need also to consider medical trends. For example, due to the high incidence of cardiac arrests at sports stadia and golf courses, automated external defibrillators (AEDs) are increasingly being placed in a wide variety of sport and leisure facilities (Connaughton and Spengler 2001).

ETHICAL ISSUES IN SPORT AND LEISURE

Are ethics and the law the same? No. In business and all other areas of life people can act unethically and yet still stay within the law. Therefore, it is important that students have an understanding of the distinction between law and ethics. In order to help understand the distinction between law and ethics we must first develop a foundation for ethical analysis by learning the fundamental concerns of ethics and morality (Branvold 2001).

Ethics is defined as a systematic attempt to make sense of our moral experience to help determine what rules should govern human conduct (Branvold 2001). In other words, ethics is concerned with issues of right and wrong, good or bad in human conduct. Although the terms right and good refer to ethical standards, there are differences among them. Generally, we employ the terms right and wrong in situations where rules and laws are applicable; we use the terms good and bad when we focus our attention on the consequences of the act (Malloy, Ross and

Zakus 2000). Ethics is also concerned with the notions of duty, obligation and a set of moral principles or values. As such, ethics are manifested in behaviour and assessed through the application of ethical inquiry and critical moral reasoning (Malloy, Ross and Zakus 2000).

Morality, as the term is generally used, refers to a special set of actions and behaviours and the principles that guide them. The term moral is usually applied to an individual's action or behaviour, thereby allowing us to determine whether an individual's behaviour is right or wrong, good or bad (Malloy, Ross and Zakus 2000).

WHY THE SPORT AND LEISURE INDUSTRY IS PRONE TO ETHICAL DILEMMAS

In sport and leisure, the ethical guides that influence our behaviour, right and wrong, good and bad, have been exchanged for sportsmanship and fair play (Malloy, Ross and Zakus 2000). Unfortunately, in today's sports world, the final score is often more important than how you played the game. Therefore, some athletes are willing to act unethically if it will help them win an event, even though they know they are violating the spirit of sportsmanship and fair play. This win-at-all costs mentality has had a tremendous influence on the moral reasoning of sport and leisure participants. In fact, studies indicate that the longer an athlete competes in organised sport, the more their moral reasoning decreases (Branvold 2001).

Since most sport and leisure administrators are former athletes it should not be surprising that they run their business with the same win-at-all-costs mentality that they had as athletes. This type of mentality increases the likelihood that administrators, in an effort to make a profit, will face unwanted ethical dilemmas such as disregarding the safety of those using the facility by cutting back on staff or safety equipment or failing to provide the proper equipment or to provide a safe environment.

A CODE OF PRACTICE

Since ethical dilemmas in sport and leisure are unavoidable, it is important to have a code of practice or code of ethics by which to guide you and your employees. In developing such a code, sport and leisure administrators should define accepted/ acceptable behaviour and establish a framework for professional behaviour and responsibilities. In addition, a code of practice or code of ethics should try to promote a high standard of practice and provide a benchmark for employees to use for self-evaluation.

CONCLUSIONS

As this chapter has shown, sport and leisure administrators face numerous legal and ethical issues every day. In order to run your business successfully, therefore, it is essential that, as sport and leisure administrators, you have a solid understanding of the legal and ethical duties owed to people using the facility.

A negligence lawsuit, the most common tort claim sport and leisure facilities will face, can be financially damaging to any business. Therefore, it is essential that sport and leisure administrators understand the four elements to a negligence claim: duty, breach of duty, causation and damages and how to protect themselves from legal liability. In particular, sport and leisure administrators should be aware of the legal duties they owe to people using their facility. These duties include: inspection of facility; maintenance and repair; duty to warn of concealed dangers; advising users of risks; the duty to hire competent personnel, the duty to provide supervision; and the duty to provide for emergency care.

No matter how careful you are or what precautions you take, you need to know that accidents are going to happen and people are going to get hurt. Therefore, administrators need to protect themselves from a lawsuit by using defences such as assumption of risk, agreements to participate, waivers, immunities, facility lease agreements and the use of independent contractors.

However, if someone *is* injured at the facility, the first thing an administrator should do, after getting medical care for the injured person, is to gather as much information as possible about the accident. If it is discovered that the accident could have been prevented, the administrator should take corrective measures so that it does not happen again. If it was unavoidable, the information can help in any lawsuit that may be filed.

In addition to the legal issues, sport and leisure administrators must also be prepared to face a number of ethical issues every day. Since ethical dilemmas are unavoidable, it is essential that administrators develop a code of practice or code of ethics to guide you and your employees. In developing such a code, sport and leisure administrators need to make it clear what is and what is not acceptable behaviour.

Questions

1. What are the four elements necessary to establish a negligence claim?
2. Are facility owners legally liable for all injuries that occur in their facility?
3. What is the importance of a code of practice or code of ethics?

References and further reading

Branvold, S. (2001). 'Ethics' in Parkhouse, B. L. (ed.) *The Management of Sport: Its Foundations and Applications* (3rd edn). New York: McGraw-Hill.

Connaughton, D. P. and Spengler, J. O. (2001) 'Automated external defibrillators in sport and recreation settings: an analysis of immunity provisions in state legislation', *Journal of Legal Aspects of Sport*, 11, 51–68.

Cotton, D. J. (2001). 'Which parties are Liable?' in Cotton, D. J., Wolohan, J. T. and Wilde, T. J. (eds) *Law for Recreation and Sport Managers* (2nd edn). Dubuque, IA: Kendall/Hunt Publishing Co.

Cotton, D. J. and Cotton, M. B. (1997) *Legal Aspects of Waivers in Sport Recreation and Fitness Activities*. Canton, OH: PRC Publishing.

Farber, M. (2002) 'Put up the Net', *Sports Illustrated*, 1 April, 62–5.

Gardiner, Simon, James, M., O'Leary, J., Welch, R., Blackshow I., Bayes, S. and Caiger, A. (2001) *Sports Law* (2nd edn). London: Cavendish Publishing.

Hall, R. and Kanoy, R. (2001) 'Emergency care' in Cotton, D. J., Wolohan, J. T. and Wilde, T. J. (eds) *Law for Recreation and Sport Managers* (2nd edn). Dubuque, IA: Kendall/Hunt Publishing Co.

Keeton, W. Page, Dobbs, D. B., Keeton, R. E. and Owens, D. G. (1984) *Prosser and Keeton on the Law of Torts* (5th edn). St Paul, MN: West Publishing Co.

Malloy, D. C., Ross, S. and Zakus, D. H. (2000) Sport Ethics: Concepts and Cases in Sport and Recreation. Buffalo, NY: Thomson Educational Publishing, Inc.

Maloy, B. P. (2001) 'Safe environment' in Cotton, D. J., Wolohan, J. T. and Wilde, T. J. (eds) *Law for Recreation and Sport Managers* (2nd edn). Dubuque, IA: Kendall/Hunt Publishing Co.

Schubert, G. W., Smith, R. K. and Trentadue, J. C. (1986) *Sports Law*. St Paul, MN: West Publishing Co.

van der Smissen, B. (1990) *Legal Liability and Risk Management for Public and Private Entities*, vols 1 and 2. Cincinnati, OH: Anderson Publishing Co.

van der Smissen, B. (2001) 'Elements of negligence' in Cotton, D. J., Wolohan, J. T. and Wilde, T. J. (eds) *Law for Recreation and Sport Managers* (2nd edn). Dubuque, IA: Kendall/Hunt Publishing Co.

Wong, G. M. (1994) *Essentials of Amateur Sports Law* (2nd edn). Westport, CN: Praeger Publishers.

PART 5

MERCHANDISING AND MARKETING

CHAPTER 17

Sports and Leisure Marketing

Adrian Palmer

INTRODUCTION

Sports and leisure have for a long time been dominated by clubs and associations which exist for the benefit of members. In this situation, members were likely to have owed a strong allegiance to their club and marketing would have had little role to play. Increasingly, however, sport and leisure are becoming the domain of market forces and commercial operators. Sports clubs and associations are becoming less confident about taking their members' support for granted and must apply principles of marketing to recruit new members, retain existing ones and to secure a higher level of expenditure per customer. For many sports and leisure organisations, 'supporters' have become 'customers'. The number of commercial organisations operating in the sports and leisure field has been increasing and their success depends on their ability to market profitably their services. Many local authority facilities that were previously provided as a service to the community have now been given much clearer marketing objectives.

The aim of this chapter is to explore the concept of marketing in the context of sports and leisure facilities. After discussing some of the underlying principles of marketing, applications are considered. An important theme of this chapter is that marketing and operations are closely related – an organisation that cannot operationally deliver what its marketing promises is unlikely to survive and prosper.

WHAT DO WE MEAN BY MARKETING?

A traditional definition of marketing is provided by the Chartered Institute of Marketing, which defines marketing as:

> The management process which identifies, anticipates and supplies customer requirements efficiently and profitably.

Marketing orientation first emerged in the relatively affluent countries for goods where competition between suppliers had become the greatest. Adoption of marketing by the sports and leisure sector generally came later, largely due to the effects of significant public sector providers and the existence of voluntary clubs and associations which had a relatively assured take-up of their services.

Many people have tried to define just what is meant by marketing orientation.

Work by Narver and Slater (1990) has sought to define and measure the extent of marketing orientation and their analysis identified three important components:

- Customer orientation, meaning that an organisation has a sufficient understanding of its target buyers that allows it to create superior value for them.

- Competitor orientation, defined as an organisation's understanding of the short-term strengths and weaknesses and long-term capabilities and strategies of current and potential competitors.

- Interfunctional coordination, referring to the manner in which an organisation uses its resources in creating superior value for target customers.

Marketing orientation is used to describe both the basic philosophy of an organisation and the techniques which it uses:

- As a business philosophy, marketing puts the customer at the centre of all the organisation's considerations. Basic values such as the requirement to identify the changing needs of existing customers and the necessity constantly to search for new market opportunities are instilled in all members of a truly marketing-oriented organisation, covering all aspects of the organisation's activities. For a gym operator, the training of staff would emphasise those items – such as courtesy and reliability – which research had found to be particularly valued by existing and potential customers. The personnel manager would have a selection policy which sought to recruit staff who fulfilled the needs of customers rather than simply minimising the wage bill. The accountant would investigate the effects on customers before deciding to save money by cutting equipment levels, thereby possibly reducing customer choice. It is not sufficient for an organisation merely to appoint a marketing manager or set up a marketing department – viewed as a philosophy, marketing is an attitude of mind which pervades the whole organisation.

- Marketing orientation is associated with a range of techniques. For example, market research is a technique for finding out about customer needs and advertising is a technique to communicate the service offer to potential customers. However, these techniques lose a lot of their value if they are conducted by an organisation which has not fully embraced the philosophy of marketing. The techniques of marketing also include, among other things, pricing, the design of channels of distribution and new product development (see box).

Many sports and leisure operators claim to be marketing oriented, but in fact they pay only lip service to the concept. Consider your own visits to a sports facility and ask whether the operator fell down on any of the following all too frequent giveaways:

- Were opening hours designed to suit the interests of staff rather than customers (very common among many public sector services)?

- Did administrative procedures appear to have the aim of making life easier for the organisation rather than its customers (e.g. expecting customers to contact several sections of the organisation, rather than offering a 'one-stop' facility)?

- Were prime car parking spaces reserved for staff rather than customers?

- Was advertising aimed at the egos of managers rather than the needs and aspirations of potential customers?

Can you think of any further give-aways?

DISTINGUISHING FEATURES OF SPORTS AND LEISURE SERVICES

Services have a number of distinctive characteristics which differentiate them from goods and have implications for the manner in which they are marketed. These characteristics are often described as intangibility, inseparability, variability, perishability and the inability to own a service. These are now considered in the context of sports and leisure services.

Intangibility

A pure service cannot be assessed using any of the physical senses – it is an abstraction which cannot be directly examined before it is purchased. A prospective purchaser of most goods is able to examine the goods for physical integrity, aesthetic appearance, taste, smell etc. Many advertising claims relating to these tangible properties can be verified by inspection prior to purchase. Contrariwise, pure services have no tangible properties which can be used by consumers to verify advertising claims before the purchase is made. The intangible process characteristics which define services, such as reliability, personal care, attentiveness of staff, their friendliness etc. can only be verified once a service has been purchased and consumed. The lack of physical evidence which intangibility implies increases the level of uncertainty that a consumer faces when choosing between competing services. An important part of a services marketing programme will therefore involve reducing consumer uncertainty by such means as adding physical evidence and the development of strong brands.

Most sports and leisure services contain many tangible components and operators seek to use these to reinforce images of the service that they offer. The tangible elements of the service offer can comprise the physical environment in which a sport takes place. Within this environment, the design of buildings, their cleanliness and the appearance of staff present important tangible evidence which may be the only basis on which a buyer is able to differentiate one service provider from another.

Inseparability

The consumption of a service is said to be inseparable from its means of production. Producer and consumer must interact in order for the benefits of the service to be realised – both must normally meet at a time and a place which is mutually convenient, in order that the producer can directly pass on service benefits. In the extreme case of personal care services (e.g. physiotherapy) the customer must be present during the entire production process – a doctor cannot normally provide a service without the involvement of a patient. For services, marketing becomes a means of facilitating complex producer–consumer interaction, rather than being merely an exchange medium.

Variability

The opportunity for pre-delivery inspection and rejection which is open to the goods manufacturer is not normally possible with services – the service must normally be produced in the presence of the customer without the possibility of intervening quality control. Particular problems can occur where personnel are involved in providing services on a one-to-one basis – such as tennis coaching – where no easy method of monitoring and control is possible.

The variability of output can pose problems for brand building. The service sector's attempts to reduce variability concentrate on methods used to select, train, motivate and control personnel. In some cases, service offers have been simplified, jobs have been 'deskilled' and personnel replaced with machines in order to reduce human variability.

Perishability

Very few services face a constant pattern of demand through time. Many show considerable variation, which could be a daily variation (sports clubs' bars in the evening), weekly (weekend peaks for many family-based leisure services), seasonal (the demand for tennis courts in summer), cyclical (demand for time share properties) or an unpredictable pattern of demand.

The perishability of services results in greater attention having to be paid to the management of demand by evening out peaks and troughs in demand and in scheduling service production to follow this pattern as far as possible. Pricing and promotion are two of the tools commonly adopted to tackle this problem.

Ownership

The inability to own a service is related to the characteristics of intangibility and perishability. In purchasing goods, buyers generally acquire title to the goods in question and can subsequently do as they wish with them. By way of contrast, when a service is performed, no ownership is transferred from the seller to the buyer. The buyer is merely buying the right to a service process such as the use of a swimming pool or a physiotherapist's time.

The inability to own a service has implications for the design of distribution channels, so a wholesaler or retailer cannot take title, as is the case with goods. Instead, direct distribution methods are more common and where intermediaries are used, they generally act as a co-producer with the service provider.

DISTINCTIVE CHARACTERISTICS OF PUBLIC AND NOT-FOR-PROFIT SECTOR MARKETING

A high proportion of sports and leisure services are provided by public and not-for-profit organisations. The range of not-for-profit organisations covers local authorities, charities and various quango-type organisations that have been set up to run leisure centres and sports facilities, among others. Here, marketing managers' financial objectives and the requirement to meet customers' needs must be further constrained by wider social objectives. In this way, a swimming pool may be set an objective of providing the public with affordable access to healthy activities, as well as revenue objectives.

Many not-for-profit sector services are increasingly being given clearly defined business objectives which make it much more difficult for officers to continue doing what they like doing rather than what the public they serve wants. Marketing orientation has been most rapidly adopted by those public sector services which provide marketable goods and services, such as swimming pools. While developing a marketing framework for public sports and leisure services may sound fine in principle, new problems may be created. If consumers of services express their preferences for a provider, there is no guarantee that additional government funding will be provided to make available the additional capacity which consumers have demanded. And how able are government funding agencies to take a view of long-term capital commitments based on possibly short-term changes in consumer preferences?

It is difficult to generalise and talk about not-for-profit and public sector services as though they comprised a distinctive and homogeneous range of activities sharing similar marketing needs. There is, in fact, a range of activities from the pure public service to the pure private service and the marketing needs of 'pure' public services can differ quite markedly from those of the private sector. Some of the more important differences as they affect the sports and leisure sector are as follows:

1. The aim of most private sector organisations is to earn profits for the owners of the organisation. By contrast to these quantifiable objectives, many not-for-profit sector services operate with relatively diverse and unquantified objectives, for example a museum may have scholarly objectives in addition to a more quantifiable objective of maximising revenue.

2. The private sector is usually able to monitor the results of its marketing activity as the benefits are usually internal to the organisation. By contrast, many of the aims that not-for-profit organisations seek to achieve are external and a profit and loss statement or balance sheet cannot be produced in the way which is possible with a private sector organisation operating to narrow internal financial goals.

3. The degree of discretion given to a public sector marketing manager is usually less than that given to a counterpart in the private sector.

4. Many of the marketing mix elements which private sector organisations can tailor to meet the needs of specific groups of users are often not open to the not-for-profit marketer. For non-traded public services, price – if it is used at all – is often a reflection of centrally determined social values rather than the value placed on a service by the consumer.

5. It can be difficult in marketing non-traded public services – e.g. public open spaces used for recreation – to identify who the customer is. It could be argued that, unlike most private sector services, the recipient is very often not the customer. In the case of a recreation area, the customer could be viewed either as the people who actually use the recreation area or society as a whole, which benefits from an additional green space.

THE MARKETING MIX FOR SERVICES

The marketing mix is the set of tools available to an organisation to shape the nature of its offer to customers. Goods marketers are familiar with the 4Ps of product, price, promotion and place. More recently, a number of attempts have been made to redefine the marketing mix in a manner which is more applicable to the service sector. While many have sought to refine the marketing mix for general application, the expansions by Booms and Bitner (1981) and Christopher, Payne and Ballantyne (1991) provide useful frameworks for analysis, although they are not empirically proven theories of services marketing. In addition to the four traditional elements of the marketing mix, both frameworks add the additional elements of people and process. In addition, Booms and Bitner talk about physical evidence making up a seventh 'P' while the latter add customer service as an additional element.

The principle of the extended marketing mix (as indeed with the traditional marketing mix) is to break a service offering down into a number of component parts and to arrange them into manageable subject areas for making strategic decisions. Decisions on one element of the mix can only be made by reference to other elements of the mix in order to give a sustainable service positioning.

A brief overview of these marketing mix ingredients follows.

Product

Products are the means by which organisations seek to satisfy consumer needs. A product in this sense is anything which the organisation offers to potential customers, whether it be tangible or intangible. After initial hesitation, most marketing managers are now happy to talk about an intangible service as a product. Product mix decisions facing a sports and leisure marketer can be very different from those dealing with goods. Most fundamentally, pure services can only be defined using process descriptions rather than tangible descriptions of outcomes. Quality of service becomes a key element defining a product.

Price

Price mix decisions include strategic and tactical decisions about the average level of prices to be charged, discount structures, terms of payment and the extent to which price discrimination between different groups of customers is to take place. These are very similar to the issues facing a goods marketer. Differences do, however, occur where the intangible nature of a service can mean that price in itself can become a very significant indicator of quality. The personal and nontransferable nature of many services presents additional opportunities for price discrimination within service markets, while the fact that many services are marketed by the public sector at a subsidised or no price can complicate price setting.

Promotion

The traditional promotion mix includes various methods of communicating the benefits of a service to potential consumers. The promotion of services often needs to place particular emphasis on increasing the apparent tangibility of a service.

Place

Place decisions refer to the ease of access which potential customers have to a service. Place decisions can therefore involve physical location decisions (e.g. deciding where to locate a new gym); decisions about which intermediaries to use in making a service accessible to a consumer (e.g. which ticket agents will be used for selling tickets for a major sporting event) and non-locational decisions which are used to make services available (e.g. the use of telephone delivery systems by theatre box offices).

People

For many sports and leisure services, people are a vital element of the marketing mix. Where production can be separated from consumption – as is the case with most manufactured goods – management can usually take measures to reduce the direct effect of people on the final output as received by customers. Therefore, the buyer of a car is not concerned whether a production worker dresses untidily, uses bad language at work or turns up for work late, as long as there are quality control measures which reject the results of lax behaviour before they reach the customer. In service industries, everybody is what Gummeson (1999) calls a 'part time marketer' in that their actions have a much more direct effect on the output received by customers. For this reason, it is therefore essential that services organisations clearly specify what is expected from personnel in their interaction with customers. To achieve the specified standard, methods of recruiting, training, motivating and rewarding staff cannot be regarded as purely personnel decisions – they are important marketing mix decisions.

Process

Production processes are usually of little concern to consumers of manufactured goods, but are often of critical concern to consumers of 'high-contact' services where the consumers can be seen as a co-producer of the service. A customer of a health spa is deeply affected by the manner in which staff serve them and the amount of waiting which is involved during the production process. Issues arise as to the boundary between the producer and consumer in terms of the allocation of production functions – for example, a snack bar in a leisure centre might require a customer to collect their meal from a counter or to deposit their own rubbish. With services, a clear distinction cannot be made between marketing and operations management.

Physical evidence

The intangible nature of a service means that potential customers are unable to judge a service before it is consumed, increasing the riskiness inherent in a purchase decision. Many people considering paying an upfront membership fee for a gym may be quite concerned to verify the level of facilities that will be available to them. An important element of marketing planning is therefore to reduce this level of risk by offering tangible evidence of the nature of the service. This evidence can take a number of forms. At its simplest, a brochure can describe and give pictures of important elements of the service product – the equipment available in a gym, for example. The appearance of staff can give evidence about the nature of a service – a tidily dressed receptionist gives some evidence that the gym as a whole is run with care.

Customer service

The meaning of customer service varies from one organisation to another. Within the service sector, it can best be described as the total quality of the service as perceived by the customer. As such, responsibility for this element of the marketing mix cannot be isolated within a narrowly defined customer services department, but becomes the concern of all production personnel, both those directly employed by the organisation and those employed by suppliers. Managing the quality of the service offered to the customer becomes closely identified with policy on the related marketing mix elements of product design and personnel.

THE SERVICE ENCOUNTER

Service encounters occur where consumer and producer meet in order for the former to receive the benefits which the latter has the resources to provide. The concept has been defined broadly by Shostack (1985) as 'a period of time during which a consumer directly interacts with a service'. This definition includes all aspects of the service firm with which a consumer may interact, including its personnel and physical assets. In some cases, the entire service is produced and consumed during the course of this encounter. Such services can be described as 'high contact' services and the encounter becomes the dominant means by which consumers assess service quality. At other times, the encounter is just one element of the total production and consumption process. For such 'low contact' services, a part of the production process can be performed without the direct involvement of the consumer.

Incidents occur each time producer and consumer come together in an encounter. While many incidents will be quite trivial in terms of their consequences to the consumer, some of these incidents will be so important that they become critical to a successful encounter. Bitner, Booms and Tetreault (1990) define critical incidents as specific interactions between customers and service firm employees that are especially satisfying or especially dissatisfying. While their definition focuses on the role of personnel in creating critical incidents, they can also arise as a result of interaction with the service provider's equipment. At each critical incident, customers have an opportunity to evaluate the service provider and form an opinion of service quality. The processes involved in producing services can be quite complex, resulting in a large number of critical incidents, many of which involve non-frontline staff. The complexity of service encounters – and the resultant quality control problems – can be judged by examining how many critical incidents are present.

Identifying critical incidents

It may be easy to say that companies should pay attention to critical incidents but it is much more difficult to identify just how a customer defines a critical incident. It can be even more difficult to determine when a company has failed in a critical incident. Many companies now facilitate complaining behaviour by customers in order that they can more precisely identify failed critical incidents. The increasing use of Freefone helplines and customer comment cards is evidence of this. There is a suggestion that complaining may in itself lead to a feeling of satisfaction, simply because the complainant has managed to get the feeling off their chest. In one study of members of a fitness centre in the USA, it was found that the greater increase in satisfaction from customers who had been asked for their views came from the most dissatisfied customers (Nyer 2000). Providing the opportunity to express feelings about a service can prove beneficial to satisfaction levels but must be seen in the context of the business's willingness to correct errors or offence. Against this, it must also be noted that many companies have experienced an increase in 'bogus complaints'. With such encouragement to complain, some customers may be tempted to push their luck in the hope of getting some form of compensation for quite spurious complaints.

Defining the service process

Critical incidents can only be understood in the context of the whole service process. Services cannot be as easily reduced to objective descriptions as in the case of most tangible goods. For example, it is possible to give a fairly precise description of a food snack item, so that it allows a buyer to judge it and a manufacturer to replicate it. Such a description is much more difficult in the case of a service encounter such as a visit to a gym where a large part of the outcome can only be subjectively judged by the consumer and it is difficult to define the service process in such a way that it can be easily replicated.

This problem in defining the service encounter has given rise to a number of methodologies, which essentially 'map out' the service process. Some of the more important contributions to this debate follow.

Blueprinting

Where service production processes are complex, it is important for an organisation to gain a holistic view of how the elements of the service relate to each other. 'Blueprinting' is a graphical approach proposed by Shostack (1984) designed to overcome problems which occur where a new service is launched without adequate identification of the necessary support functions. The approach essentially attempts to draw a map of the service process.

A customer blueprint has three main elements:

- All of the principal functions required to make and distribute a service are identified, along with the responsible company unit or personnel.

- Timing and sequencing relationships among the functions are depicted graphically.

- For each function, acceptable tolerances are identified in terms of the variation from standard which can be tolerated without adversely affecting customers' perception of quality.

The essence of a blueprint is to show how customers, possessions and information are processed, an implication being that customers are inputs that can be viewed as sources of uncertainty.

A customer blueprint must clearly identify all steps in a service process, that is, all contacts or interactions with customers. These are shown in time sequential order from left to right. The blueprint is further divided into two 'zones': a zone of visibility (processes that are visible to the customer and in which the customer is likely to participate) and a zone of invisibility (processes and interactions that, although necessary to the proper servicing of a customer, may be hidden from their view).

The blueprint also identifies points of potential failure in the service production process – the critical incidents on which customers base their perception of quality. Identifying specific interaction points as potential failure points can help marketers focus their management and quality control attentions on those steps most likely to cause poor judgements of service quality.

Finally, the blueprint indicates the level of tolerance for each event in the service process and indicates action to be taken in the event of failure, such as repeating the event until a satisfactory outcome is obtained.

Blueprinting is not a new idea, with many precedents in methods of critical path analysis. What is important here is that marketing, operations management and human resource management focus on processes that deliver benefits which are effective to customers and efficient for the company. High-involvement personal services can only be sensibly understood in terms of their production processes rather than outcomes, so blueprinting assumes particular significance.

It doesn't matter how a blueprint is expressed, whether it is in form of a diagrammatic portrayal of processes or simply in words. The important point is that it should form a shared and agreed basis for action which is focused on meeting customers' needs effectively and efficiently. Of course, a blueprint cannot anticipate all contingencies for which a response will be required, for example a bomb explosion in a restaurant or the kidnapping of a staff member. Nevertheless, if the general nature of a process problem is identified, the outline of possible next steps can be developed.

Dramaturgical approaches

The concept of role playing has been used to apply the principles of social psychology to explain the interaction between service producer and service consumer (e.g. Solomon *et al.* 1985). It sees people as actors who act out roles which can be distinguished from their own personality. In the sociological literature, roles are assumed as a result of conditioning by the society and culture of which a person is a member. Individuals typically play multiple roles in life, as family members, workers, members of football teams etc., each of which comes with a set of socially conditioned role expectations. A person playing the role of worker is typically conditioned to act with reliability, loyalty and trustworthiness. An analysis of the expectations associated with each role becomes a central part of role analysis. The many roles an individual plays may result in conflicting role expectations, as where the family role of a father leads to a series of role expectations which are incompatible with his role expectations as a business manager. Each role might be associated with competing expectations about the allocation of leisure time.

The service encounter can be seen as a theatrical drama. The stage is the location where the encounter takes place and can itself affect the role behaviour of both buyer and seller. A scruffy service outlet may result in lowered expectations by the customer and, in turn, a lower level of service delivery by service personnel (see Bitner 1990). Both parties work to a script which is determined by their respective role expectations – a receptionist at a sports centre is acting out a script in the manner in which they welcome customers. The script might include precise details about what actions should be performed, when and by whom, including the words to be used in verbal communication. In reality, there may be occasions when the receptionist would like to do anything but wish their awkward customers a pleasant visit. The theatrical analogy extends to the costumes which service personnel wear. When a physiotherapist wears a white coat or a business manager of a football club a suit, they are emphasising to customers the role which they are playing, just like the actor who uses costumes to convince his audience that he is, in fact, Henry VIII.

It is not just customers who bring role expectations to the interaction process. Service producers also have their idea of the role which their customers should perform within the co-production process. In the case of sports coaching, there may be an expectation of customers' roles which includes giving clear instructions at the outset, arriving for the appointment on time and (in some countries) giving an adequate tip. Failure of customers to perform their role expectations can have a demotivating effect on frontline personnel. Staff who have been well trained to act in their role may be able to withstand abusive customers who are acting out of role – others may resort to shouting back at their customers.

Servicescapes

The concept of a 'Servicescape' was developed by Booms and Bitner to emphasise the impact of the environment in which a service process takes place. They defined a servicescape as, 'the environment in which the service is assembled and in which seller and customer interact, combined with tangible commodities that facilitate performance or communication of the service' (Booms and Bitner 1981: 36). In the service encounter the customer is in the 'factory' and is part of the process. Production and consumption of the service are simultaneous.

The design of a suitable service environment should explicitly consider the likely emotional states and expectations of target customers. Booms and Bitner distinguished between 'high-load' and 'low-load' environments, both of which can be used to suit particular emotional states and customer types. They noted that:

> A high-load signifies a high information rate; a low-load represents a low information rate. Uncertainty, novelty, and complexity are associated with high-load environments; conversely a low-load environment communicates assurance, homogeneity and simplicity. Bright colours, bright lights, loud noises, crowds, and movement are typical

elements of a high-load environment, while their opposites are characteristic of a low-load environment. People's emotional needs and reactions at a given time determine whether they will be attracted to a high- or a low-load environment. (Booms and Bitner 1981: 39)

The servicescape must encourage target customers to enter the service environment in the first place and to retain them subsequently. Booms and Bitner discuss 'approach behaviour' as involving such responses as physically moving customers toward exploring an unfamiliar environment, affiliating with others in the environment through eye contact and performing a large number of tasks within the environment. Avoidance behaviour includes an opposite set of responses. Brightly lit entrances, a prominent and open front door and front-of-house greeting staff are typical actions designed to induce approach. A door which is difficult to find or to open is more likely to achieve the opposite effect.

After entering the service production system, the servicescape must be efficient and effective for the service provider in securing customers' cooperation in the production system. Clearly explained roles for the customer, expressed in a friendly way will facilitate this process of compliance. The ambience of the environment, such as lighting, floor plan and signposting contribute to the servicescape. The physical aspects of the environment are brought to life by the actions of employees, for example staff could be on hand to help a customer who finds themselves lost in the service process. Ultimately, the servicescape should encourage customers to repeat their visit. The environment should leave no reminders of poor service (such as unpleasant queuing conditions) which will cause negative feelings about the service provider. The servicescape may include tangible cues to facilitate repeat business, for example a schedule of forthcoming special events being hosted by a football club.

Questions

1. Critically assess the role of marketing within a publicly owned sports facility. Is marketing compatible with social objectives?

2. What is the relationship between marketing and operations management? What do you understand by the term 'part-time marketer'?

3. Using a leisure facility of your choice as an example, use a blueprinting approach to identify the critical elements of the service process

References

Bitner, M. J. (1990) 'Evaluating service encounters: the effects of physical surroundings and employee responses', *Journal of Marketing*, 51, 69–82.

Bitner, M. J., Booms, B. H. and Tetreault M. S. (1990) 'The service encounter: diagnosing favorable and unfavorable incidents', *Journal of Marketing*, 54, 71–84.

Booms, B. H. and Bitner, M. J. (1981) 'Marketing strategies and organisation structures for service firms in J. Donnelly and W. R. George (eds) *Marketing of Services*. Chicago: American Marketing Association, 51–67.

Christopher, M., Payne, A. and Ballantyne, M. (1991), *Relationship Marketing*, Heinemann: London.

Gummesson, E. (1999) *Total Relationship Marketing*. London: Butterworth-Heinemann.

Narver, J. C. and Slater, S. F. (1990) 'The effect of a market orientation on business profitability', *Journal of Marketing*, 54, 20–35.

Nyer, P. U. (2000) 'An investigation into whether complaining can cause increased consumer satisfaction', *Journal of Consumer Marketing*, 17, 1, 9–19.

Shostack, G. L. (1984) 'Designing services that deliver', *Harvard Business Review*, January-February, 133–9.

Shostack, G. L. (1985) 'Planning the service encounter' in Czepiel, J. A., Solomon, M. R. and Suprenant, C. F. (eds) *The Service Encounter*. Lexington, MA: Lexington Books, 243–54.

Solomon, M. R., Surprenant, C., Czepiel, J. A. and Gutman, E. G. (1985) 'A role theory perspective on dyadic interactions: the service encounter', *Journal of Marketing*, 49, Winter, 99–111.

CHAPTER 18

E-commerce in Sport and Leisure

Mike Jordan

The most significant recent development for organisations has been the rapid emergence of the internet and the World Wide Web. Within a five-year period between 1993 and 1998, 50 million people became connected worldwide (*http:// www.nua.ie/surveys*). As a measure of the speed of growth, this can be compared to the fact that it took the telephone 70 years to achieve the same level of coverage and the growth is showing no sign of abating. It was estimated at July 2002 that there were in excess of 150 million servers connected to the internet (*www.isc.org/ ds/*). The number of actual internet users is now estimated to be in excess of 553 million (*http://www.nua.ie*).

The internet has made global communications not just possible but has also created a revolution in how communications are carried out. With one email, it is possible to contact every employee of a large organisation using the company's intranet. That same email can have attached files or documents that might previously have required faxing or posting.

At the same time, the World Wide Web (WWW) has provided a medium for every organisation to market its merchandise. So it is now possible for any firm, small or large, to be supplying a global market. Alternatively, it is possible for any consumer to search the web for information and to purchase products and services at a price and time that best suits themselves.

In the sport and leisure industry, there has been phenomenal growth in the use of the internet and the World Wide Web. Most hotels and leisure clubs have developed their own web pages to market their facilities and generate bookings online. Even the smallest B&B has the capability of a worldwide market.

In sport, football clubs can now provide their global fan base with up-to-the-minute team news, downstream live matches to a PC and offer the complete range of club merchandise whether the consumer is living in Manchester or Mongolia. In fact, all club information or items that are available locally can also be acquired from the net.

Such is the interest in sports news that over 9.3 million internet users visited sports sites in the first week of the World Cup in June 2002 (*www.nielsen-netratings.com*) with over half a million accessing the official FIFA website (*www.fifaworldcup.yahoo.com*).

In the related travel industry, online travel spending rose to US$1.3 billion for the week ending 23 June 2002, according to comScore Media Metrix (*www.comscore.com*). Budget airlines like easyJet and Ryanair have turned around a struggling industry into a highly successful one with over 90% of their market now being generated by online sales. (*www.easyjet.com* and *www.ryanair.com*).

DEVELOPMENT OF E-COMMERCE

Electronic commerce or e-commerce is defined as the process of buying and selling or exchanging products, services and information via an infrastructure of computer networks including the internet (Turban *et al.* 2002).

Wherever there is a marketplace there has always been a need for buyer and seller to communicate. Telephone and fax have provided the media for communication in traditional markets. In the electronic marketplace the medium is the internet.

Yet electronic communication is not new. For over 30 years electronic fund transfer (EFT) has allowed banks to exchange funds between different banks and clearing houses. Electronic data interchange (EDI) has likewise allowed commercial transactions between organisations to take place, linking supplier and consumer across a supply chain with various intermediaries as electronically linked elements of that supply chain. Initially electronic communications was dependent on a third party, such as IBM or Cisco providing the communication infrastructure, known as a value-added network (VAN). These value-added networks provide the necessary protocols and security measures to operationalise transactions between organisations but the arrival of the internet has introduced a new level of sophistication and availability of electronic communications. The limitations of VANs, due to cost and restricted availability, have been removed. The development of email and other applications has significantly expanded the possibilities available in electronic communications. The development of electronic commerce initially for consumers (B2C) and then shortly thereafter for businesses (B2B) was an inevitable consequence of multimedia web-based electronic markets.

The timeline for the development of e-commerce is as follows:

1970s	Electronic fund transfer (EFT) between banks
	Development of point-of-sale (POS) outlets in the retail sector
	Combination of the two in EFTPOS to link banks and retail
Early 80s	Development of email Electronic data interchange (EDI) to allow businesses to send and receive business documents
	Just-in-time (JIT) manufacturing to reduce stock levels
Late 80s	Development of groupware software for collaborative computing
	Social interaction through inter-relay-chat (IRC)
	Knowledge sharing with file transfer programs (FTP) and news groups
Early 90s	Development of internet
	Combination of email and file transfer Internet EDI as early business to business (B2B) e-commerce
Mid-90s	Introduction of WWW and web browsers
	Commercial websites for business marketing
	Multimedia additions to websites
	Business to consumer (B2C) e-commerce
2000 on	Wireless and mobile applications

TYPES OF E-COMMERCE

The type of e-commerce that operates within a business tends to be determined by the nature of the transactions taking place. Essentially, the two main types of e-commerce are business to business (B2B) and business to consumer (B2C). There are others, such as government to consumer (G2C) and the reverse consumer to government (C2G) (Chaffey 2002).

B2B is defined as the undertaking of commercial transactions between two organisations. Normally, this will take place across the internet with one organisation acting as the buyer or consumer and the other being the seller or supplier.

Intel is an example of a company that has moved into B2B e-commerce in a big way. They are the world's largest producer of integrated circuit chips. Before the summer of 1998 Intel produced customised product catalogues that they issued to existing and potential customers such as Dell. In July 1998 the catalogue was put onto the internet and customers ordered online. In the first month alone they sold $1 billion of integrated circuit (IC) chips. The net had matured as a means of selling.

B2C is defined as the undertaking of commercial transactions between an organisation and consumers. One of the best known B2C sites is Amazon (*www.amazon.co.uk*). Amazon is a completely virtual company with 100% online sales. Originally offering cut-price books, Amazon has diversified its product range to include CDs, videos and other merchandise.

Another example of B2C is in the travel industry. Air flights have become fiercely competitive with cut-price airlines generating huge sales from easy-access, low-cost flights on selected routes. EasyJet was one of the first airlines to recognise the value of internet sales and developed major marketing campaigns based on online flight bargains. The web address (*www.easyjet.com*) is emblazoned on their planes instead of the phone number. They now carry out over 80% of their business on the internet.

The Ryanair site is typical of budget airlines in that it will give special offers and by customers drilling down within the site, availability, alternatives and prices can be found (see Figure 18.1). The company saves time and money by not issuing tickets but simply asking passengers to check in with evidence of the unique booking number that they have been allocated.

Sites such as Expedia, Travelocity, Priceline and Lastminute have revolutionised the travel industry. As their share of the market increases, traditional travel agents and airlines will suffer. In May 2002 British Airways reported massive losses, due partly to the downturn in the airline industry because of threats of terrorism but also because of the fierce competition from the low-budget airlines.

The supermarket Tesco, for example, buys products from its suppliers. Tesco and its suppliers will enter a partnership and if transactions are carried out electronically across a network this is known as business to business (B2B) e-commerce. From the Tesco perspective these are transactions taking place on the *buy side* of the supply chain.

Tesco also supplies to customers via Tesco-online. This allows any consumer to log onto their website (*www.tesco-online.com*) and carry out home shopping. From the Tesco perspective this takes place on the *sell side* and is known as business to consumer (B2C) e-commerce.

Figure 18.1 *Ryanair website*

INFRASTRUCTURE FOR E-COMMERCE

On the *physical* level e-commerce is supported by a combination of local area networks (LANs), metropolitan area networks (MANs) and wide area networks (WANs) (Turban *et al.* 2002).

A LAN is a collection of computers ranging from PCs through to mainframes that are connected within a small geographic area of less than about five kilometres radius and serving a single campus, building or factory. The configuration of the LAN will be determined by the number of users, the physical layout of the location and the needs of that organisation. So, for example, an educational establishment may have a LAN made up of several departmental LANs within one campus consisting of PCs for staff, laboratories for students and servers to hold databases of files for staff, students and administration, all interconnected by fibre optic cables or high-specification twisted pair cabling.

A MAN is a collection of LANs that would cover a city and provide high-speed access between users for special applications. For example, Clydenet MAN connects all the higher education establishments in the city of Glasgow and supports applications such as videoconferencing or remote teaching carried out at speeds that have no perceptible delay to participants.

WANs have been established for over 30 years and provide links between cities and within a country, usually supplied by a telecoms company but more and more recently by cable companies. The convergence of television and computing requirements has meant that there are now many carriers such as NTL and BT

261

competing to provide multimedia communications. WANs can be used to carry digital signals for voice, video and data traffic.

This is one of the major growth areas in telecommunications where the needs of the domestic consumer for high-speed simultaneous connection to TV, telephone and internet are being provided by broadband and other expanded digital carrier provision.

On the *logical* level, users can access the internet transparently and quite unaware of the cabling, networking and protocol issues. Generally, users will access an intranet, extranet or the internet without any concern for the infrastructure unless there is a noticeable delay in response times. The users main concerns are in the features of specific applications. So the user wants to be able to use email, access the World Wide Web or use videoconferencing with the basic prerequisite knowledge of the features of these applications.

An *intranet* is an organisation's logical network. It may be a LAN located in a single building for a small business or it may extend to a whole series of interconnected LANs and WANs to serve a large multinational company. For example, IBM will have offices in many major cities worldwide. The IBM intranet allows any employee to communicate with any other. The company web page would also be posted on the intranet and every employee has access to common company information such as product information, CEO statements, internal employment opportunities and so on.

An *extranet* allows preferential customers, partner organisations or privileged users access to a company's intranet. So, for example, registered independent financial advisors can access Abbey Life Insurance intranet for details of prices, products or policies for their own customers.

The *internet* is a collection of LANs and WANs that are allowed to communicate with each other through common protocols. The two most common being transmission control protocol with internet protocol (TCP/IP) for message sending between nodes across the globe and hypertext transfer protocol (HTTP) for a unique addressing system for a web page.

BENEFITS OF E-COMMERCE

Who benefits from e-commerce? Again, that depends whether you are approaching e-commerce from the perspective of a business such as Intel or as a consumer using a site such as Tesco-online (Kalakota and Robinson 2001). The Department of Trade and Industry have sought to evaluate the reasons for companies going online and the benefits that accrue to them (DTI 2000).

Benefits to business

- *Up to date information.* For many businesses, their basic business processes will change with the introduction of e-commerce. For Intel, the production of a catalogue was a tedious and time-consuming process. By the time it went to print it is quite possible that the specifications for a number of IC chips would have changed and the catalogue would be out of date before it was published. E-commerce provides an up-to-date information source (*www.intel.com*).

- *Lower administration costs.* Intel, for example, were able to save the cost of creating, processing, distributing and retrieving paper-based information.

- *Global market.* Company details on the net are available to an international marketplace. Some of those consumers browsing on the net are potentially new customers. Therefore companies are no longer 'pushing' their products to existing and potential customers that they have identified but instead are now operating a 'pull'-type of ordering where the customers now examine the catalogue online and place orders according to their needs. That can help to customise the products and services for the customers.

- *Cash flow for businesses is much improved* when ordering online. Normally, payment is made upfront, thereby providing immediate cash to the business. The counter to that is that the customer expects the delivery of the goods to be equally as efficient and will quickly go elsewhere if it is not. This was a major problem for Toys-Я-Us during Christmas 1999, when, because of demand, many deliveries were not made until after Christmas.

- Finally, the *telecommunications costs are cheaper* for a business using the internet than leasing a value-added network (VAN) from a telecommunications company.

Generally, between the reduced costs, increased market and improved cash flow there are significant gains for a business using e-commerce.

Benefits to consumers

- Consumers can access the internet *24 hours a day* and all year round from almost any location. A busy or housebound customer can use a facility like Tesco-online to shop without leaving home (*www.tesco-online.com*).

- The consumer has *increased choice.* In the supermarket example Sainsbury (*www.sainsbury.co.uk*) or Asda will also provide online shopping (*www.asda.co.uk*).

- *Cheaper prices.* Amazon manages to undercut high street bookstores by reducing overheads in the supply chain and disintermediating the wholesalers. Interestingly, however, Amazon has only just turned the corner in profitability after over five years of trading. Sites such as Kelkoo (*www.kelkoo.com*) will compare prices for customers under a number of headings, for example CDs, books and travel.

- *Quick delivery.* Digital products such as CDs, computer games and MP3 music files can be delivered instantaneously. Sites like *www.cdnow.com* have rapidly produced a worldwide market for low-price, fast-delivery CDs and related merchandise.

- *Virtual auctions.* Sites like e-bay allow buying and selling on the net of almost every conceivable item (*www.ebay.com*).

- *Communication with other consumers.* Amazon will give examples of similar titles purchased. It is also possible to email other consumers (*www.amazon.co.uk*).

BARRIERS TO E-COMMERCE

In spite of the obvious benefits of e-commerce to organisations and customers, there are, nevertheless, significant barriers to full e-commerce adoption. In the survey of 2000, the Department of Trade and Industry has also highlighted deterrents to going online (DTI 2000). These are as follows:

- Security and privacy are issues that deter e-commerce adoption. They exist at all levels from a single consumer to major financial institutions. It is essential that the consumer knows that any transaction is secure and cannot be intercepted by a third party. The use of firewalls, private key encryption, and virus detection software can be means of reducing the risk but can never fully guarantee security.

- Many consumers will not trust an unknown and faceless vendor. Trust in the system will grow with use and with successful transactions, but there is still a need to build consumer confidence in the virtual rather than the physical vendors.

- There is a lack of touch and feel to products being purchased. Some products such as books, CDs, air flights are easier to sell on the net than others. Clothes and shoes, for example, are more difficult because customers like to see and feel what they are buying, but even then catalogue companies have managed to sustain a remote market for years.

- The telecommunications bandwidth may be insufficient. If a website contains a lot of graphics and animation then the download time may be so long as to deter customers returning to the site. Bandwidth is the term used to describe the rate of transfer that is possible. Broadband systems are one way that this problem will be alleviated in the future, however, as the internet grows so to does the volume of traffic and increased replies to search requests.

- Internet access is not evenly available across the globe and indeed even within the so-called first world countries there is a phenomenon known as the digital divide where many homes and areas are digitally disadvantaged in internet access.

- Other general barriers to e-commerce adoption are both technical, such as hardware and software incompatibilities, and social such as a lack of knowledge of the internet and related application packages.

CASE STUDIES IN THE SPORT AND LEISURE INDUSTRY

How can e-commerce be used in the sport and leisure industry? In many ways e-commerce has been so widely adopted over the last few years that it is the case that any sector or industry not using internet technologies will be seriously disadvantaged. All major hotel chains (e.g. *www.hilton.com*) have a web presence and more and more small independent hotels and B&B locations are setting up their own web page. Not to do so is to risk being excluded from a major growing channel for reservations.

Figure 18.2 *Irish Tourist Board website*

E-commerce in tourism

National tourist boards are, at the same time, developing websites as a portal to a whole range of marketing and publicity material for their own country's tourist industry. By drilling down on these sites it is possible to search, compare and then book accommodation or package deals online. The Irish Tourist Board is a classic example of a highly competitive marketing tool for the industry (*www.Ireland.travel.ie.com*). From the site a user can browse and reserve accommodation, book a tour, check out things to do, travelling and even book a game of golf (see Figure 18.2).

There are a number of key features that are necessary to provide a successful e-commerce website for tourism and leisure:

- *Visibility*. Can the site be easily found either by name or by search engine? *www.ireland.travel.ie* is not the most obvious name for the Irish Tourist Board's official site but it is immediately found by search engines.

- *Useability*. Can the site be easily navigated, does it have links to related sites for further detail and is it easy to use? It is not immediately obvious how to book on line with *www.ryanair.com* until the 'book now' button is found.

- *Is it transactional?* Can you actually purchase online? The greatest loss of customers to any business's website is the fact that a user may enter all their criteria and personal information for an enquiry only to find at the final screen that the purchase can only be made offline.

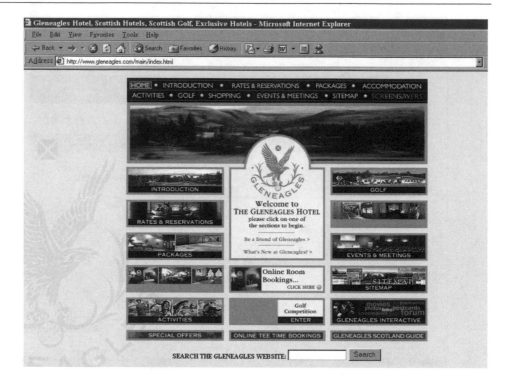

Figure 18.3 *Gleneagles Hotel website*

E-commerce in hotel management

Gleneagles Hotel in Perthshire in Scotland has a worldwide reputation as a five-star hotel with world championship golf courses as part of the hotel complex. Within the first six months of use, the interactive website for the hotel yielded £35,000 of bookings and won the Scottish Enterprise award as best large business website in 2001 (see Figure 18.3). The website is a key component of the global marketing strategy. Customer profiles are captured for market research. The hotel mail potential customers to promote special offers and use features such as callback, which allows customers to contact the hotel free of charge. Since 1999 £285,000 revenue has been generated from the website and an e-CRM (customer relationship management) strategy developed to create a more personal service (Scottish Enterprise 2000).

E-commerce in holidays

Who needs a travel agent? It is possible to customise your own holiday with minimum risk by carrying out some basic research on the web. Indeed, some office managers have suggested that holiday research is one of the largest uses of the internet in offices in the UK.

The site *www.resinfrance.com* is typical of many international sites that can capture a market that may be uncertain about arranging their own holiday because of lack of knowledge of the language or culture of the country being visited (see

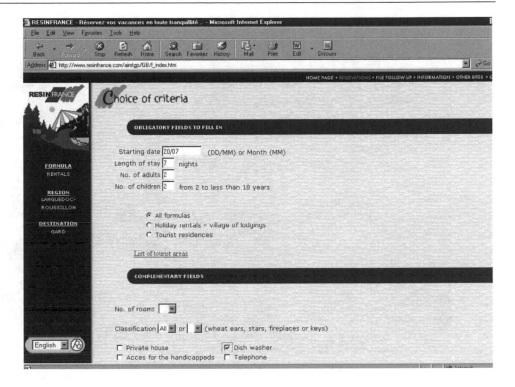

Figure 18.4 *French accommodation website*

Figure 18.4). They offer the following facilities in order to rent a holiday house anywhere in France:

- language translation (English, Spanish, German, French)
- personalised requirements such as dates, duration, location, special features, such as swimming pool, washing machine and others
- immediate retrieval of all available properties meeting the criteria requested
- online booking and no delay as there could be by post
- reduced cost, partly because of dealing directly with the owner or a local agent.

One of the effects of low budget airlines is that there are now significant numbers of travellers combining low-cost flights with online reservations and local car hire to provide a cheap and customised holiday package. The car hire firm and the airline will have links to each other's site on their web pages, for example Ryanair will promote car hire from Hertz.

E-commerce in sport

There are said to be more Manchester United fans worldwide than there are in England. Where there is a product such as football that has a very high-loyalty factor the internet can provide access to all the local facilities and products for customers worldwide. The Manchester expatriates in the USA or the Far East can purchase the same merchandise as those living next to Old Trafford through access to the club's website. Every item that is available at the club shop is available on the

Figure 18.5 *Arsenal Football Club website*

internet. There exists an online catalogue of merchandise ranging from the latest club strip, clothes, sports equipment through to club memorabilia. There may also be local distribution centres for areas of high population.

Typically, the Arsenal football club site gives stories, reports and items of news for the fans and merchandise details (see Figure 18.5).

Using multimedia it is possible to downstream videos of matches worldwide adding more value to the site. Charging for video downstreaming helps to generates valuable income for the club. The revenue from the website for many of the large European clubs can become a substantial source of income for the clubs, and it will continue to grow as more and more housholds have broadband access.

FUTURE DEVELOPMENTS

Wireless communications

As far back as 1973 radio transmission has been used to support computer communications. In the islands of Hawaii, the pioneering Ethernet LAN network system was linked by line-of-sight analogue radio signals. With current developments in wireless transmission it is now possible to support a LAN in an office or building using radio frequency signals that mean there are no wires between the PC and the server or even between the keyboard, screen and mouse and the PC itself. Wireless computing within an office has become a relatively easy option for flexible networking configurations.

Since about 1990 the development of the mobile phone based on a cell structure of transmission and reception of radio signals has generated a new phenomenon in voice communications. Typically, communication is possible from anywhere in the world at any time. These developments have evolved through several generations and are continuing to do so:

1G   Wireless technology from 1973 to 1992 based on analogue radio signals

2G   Voice and text messaging services used today based on higher speed digital signals using general protocol system for mobiles (GSM) technologies Developments into internet browsing from wireless devices using wireless application protocol (WAP) phones and higher speeds using global packet relay system (GPRS) for wider global coverage and global positioning system (GPS) for location independent connectivity

3G   Third-generation mobile computing will provide higher speed internet access using broadband technologies for rich media applications such as video clips. It is in this technology that many European telecommunication providers have risked investing £20 billion to secure the franchise

4G   A new generation of mobile communications that will support full internet access using end-to-end internet protocol (IP) networks, to be launched from 2006 onwards

Mobile commerce

Mobile commerce is one of the hottest topics in business today. The advent of wireless technology has turned internet based e-commerce into mobile or m-commerce. Analysts have predicted that the number of mobile devices such as personal digital assistants (PDA) and handsets will reach 1.3 billion by 2004 (Internet Software Consortium 2001). When these devices are connected to the internet, transactions can be conducted from anywhere at any time.

Some of the applications of m-commerce are:

- *Online banking*: Citybank has mobile services in Singapore and Hong Kong. Several Scandinavian banks allow customers to make payments from their mobile phone.

- *Micropayments*: it is possible to pay for small items via a mobile phone. For example, petrol, car parking, soft drinks, travel tickets and even taxi fares can be paid from a mobile phone where the device offering the service has a receiver to carry out the transactions. This is mostly using a technology developed by Ericsson called Bluetooth. Bluetooth provides device-to-device radio communications for distances up to 30 feet at speeds of 1Mbps.

Other services include online stock exchange trading, online gambling (very popular in Hong Kong and Japan) and online auctions.

Intelligent hotels

Using the Bluetooth technology, a typical hotel scenario of the not-too-distant future could be as follows. You, the guest, carrying a mobile device that is equipped to send and receive signals from other Bluetooth devices, enter the hotel and are

269

instantly recognised electronically. You had previously booked your reservation via your PDA and sent your personal details and preferences. The services that are now automatically sent to your PDA include:

- The hotel system responds to your PDA with your room number and your secret PIN code to enter your room.

- Arriving at your room all hotel information such as restaurant details, menus and facilities are automatically transferred to your PDA.

- The room service menu is downloaded and you may order online and have room delivery if preferred.

- Broadband access to the internet is available in your room and your own email automatically downloaded to your laptop/PDA.

- Booking a car or ordering transport to the airport, say, can be done by a click on your PDA.

- Settling the bill can be automatically done from the PDA to the hotel desk and receipt printed for your collection.

This may be the hotel of the future but it is still possible actually to speak to someone other than your computer!

CONCLUSIONS

The future of electronic commerce as predicted by the Forrester Research Institute (*www.forrester.com*) is that growth will continue dramatically. From $20 billion in 2000 transactions value will grow to between $2 to $7 trillion in 2004. Some applications such as online auctions and online stock trading are growing at a rate of 15% to 20% a month. The number of internet users is predicted to reach 750 million by 2008.

Yet there have been failures in electronic commerce. The dot com collapse of March 2000 meant that companies were not secure simply because they were operating in an internet arena. WAP phones, in spite of the hype surrounding mobile communications have not taken off as analysts predicted. Only 12 million Europeans had WAP phones by 2000 and few of these visit the WAP-enabled websites (Nairn 2001). Other mobile protocols will become available but there is no guarantee of success here, either.

But the potential for electronic commerce in sport and leisure and in the related industry of travel and tourism continues to be fulfilled. The international marketplace for the sport and leisure industry clearly generates sales for football clubs, leisure clubs, airlines, hotel chains and B&Bs and self-catering units. However, 'first-mover' advantage cannot be sustained long term for companies as others catch up and even overtake. Having a web page and selling online becomes another channel and will become the expected baseline for service to customers. In order to sustain competitive advantage companies have to offer some unique service or niche market.

In the case of football clubs, the loyalty of the global fan base may suffice. For tourism there may be local attractions that can be allied with the accommodation offerings, such as golf holidays in Scotland or vineyard trails in France.

Whatever the service or market, it is clear that e-commerce is here to stay for the sport and leisure industry and companies need to be internet enabled in the first instance and flexible and willing to adapt in the longer term.

Questions

1. Electronic commerce opens up potentially huge benefits to organisations in the sport and leisure industry yet many perceive the barriers are too difficult to overcome. Discuss, with examples, the benefits and barriers of electronic commerce for organisations and consumers.

2. Define the terms intranet and extranet. The physical networking infrastructure of the internet to support e-commerce is made up of LANs and WANs. Discuss the characteristics and operation of both of these and their interrelationships.

3. Choose one of the companies quoted in this chapter and with the help of keyword searching on the net and by visiting the web page for the company, evaluate the successes and the failures that EC has brought them. For example, search on the net on key words such as 'budget airlines' or 'travel industry' and visit *www.easyjet.com*.

References and further reading

Akaiaiwa, Y. (1999) *Introduction to Digital Mobile Communications*. London: John Wiley & Sons.

Chaffey, D. (2002) *E-Business and E-Commerce Management*. Harlow, England: Pearson Education.

DTI (2000) *Business in the Information Age*. International Benchmarking Study 2000, UK Department of Trade and Industry. Available at *www.ukonline forbusiness.gov.uk*

Kalakota, R. and Robinson, M. (2001) *e-Business 2.0*. New Jersey: Pearson Education.

Nairn, G. (2001). *Connectis 2001*. London: Financial Times Publication.

Performance & Innovation Report (1999) *E-Commerce at its best*. London: Department of Trade and Industry.

Prasad, R., Mohr, W. and Konhauser, W. (2000). *Third Generation Mobile Communications Systems*. Artech House.

Scottish Enterprise Survey (2000) *Moving in the Information Age*. Scottish Enterprise, June.

Turban, I., King, D., Lee, J., Warkentin, M. and Chung, M. (2002) *Electronic Commerce 2002 – A Managerial Perspective*. John Wiley & Sons.

Whiteley, D. (2000) *E-Commerce: Strategy, Technologies and Applications*. Maidenhead, England: McGraw-Hill.

Web sites

Department of Trade and Industry on e-commerce *www.e_trade.org.uk* (accessed 4 September 2002).

Ericsson mobile phone company *www.ericsson.com*

General Mobile commerce site *www.mobilecommerce.org* (accessed 9 July 2002).

Internet Software Consortium *www.isc.org/ds/* (accessed 9 July 2002).

Internet Surveys and Statistics *www.nua.ie* (accessed 4 September 2002).

Nokia mobile phone company *www.nokia.com*

Nokia Discussion Forum *www.forum.nokia.com*

Open Mobile Alliance *www.wapforum.org*

Organisation for Economic Cooperation and Development *www.oecd.org/subject/ electronic_commerce/documents* (accessed 4 September 2002).

Palm – Personal Digital Assistant (PDA) manufacturer *www.palm.co.uk*

Psion – Personal Digital Assistant (PDA) manufacturer *www.psion.com*

Technical definitions and acronyms explained *www.whatis.com*

Wireless LAN Alliance (1999) *Introduction to Wireless LANs www.wlana.com* (accessed 19 June 2002).

CHAPTER 19

The Role of Retailing in Sport and Leisure

Stephen Doyle

Since the emergence of localised and coordinated centres of exchange, such centres have functioned not only for the transfer of goods and services, regardless of whether money or barter was the predominant form of currency, but also as centres for socialisation. Physical retailing invariably involves some form of social interaction, the intensity and significance of which may vary according to the retail context and the individuals participating therein. There is evidence to suggest that not only was (and is) retailing an arena for social interaction, but also that it functions as a centre for recreation, either as the locus for recreation or as the factor of recreation. This chapter explores the manifestation of the interrelationship between retailing, recreation and leisure from a historical and sociological perspective.

ANCIENT ROME AND THE FORUM

It would be inaccurate and inappropriate to describe the ancient forum simply as a marketplace. However, this represented at least one element of the forum (evidence of this can be found in Bird 1999). In contemporary theories of marketing such a phenomenon would be encapsulated under the auspices of location (for additional reading on the theories of location see, e.g. McGoldrick 2002) whereby it may be argued that retailers and traders collected in close proximity to the primary congregations of customers or along routes that those customers might pass in order to arrive at the forum. The migration of retailers and traders to such locations shows that even then, as may be identified today, retailers tend towards the locations that have both high footfall and adequate levels of income to satisfactorily trade at a profit (McGoldrick 2002).

By considering the forum as an early example of the enactment of retail location theory, it is also possible to witness an early representation of the interaction among retailing, recreation and socialisation. The forum was not simply a concentrated marketplace. It represented a locus within the city walls where individuals and groups came together to socialise, to worship and to discuss. In addition they were places of recreation where performers entertained the milling crowds, where people were educated, not only through the intentional dissemination of knowledge but also through the observation of the behaviours of others. This last aspect re-emerges as a fundamental characteristic of the early department stores and reveals that this interaction of retailing with society is both complex and influential.

THE MEDIAEVAL MARKET

Throughout the course of history this interaction between retailing and recreation continues. Mediaeval markets not only included traders selling their wares, but also integrated the recreational and entertainment needs of the locals in the societies in which they congregate. These markets were, in essence, comprised of peripatetic retailers who transferred themselves and their goods to various communities on predetermined days. With their arrival came the entertainers seeking to profiteer from the traders and the customers. Once again such activity may be considered contemporaneously whereby through this mutually beneficial intermingling of retailer and entertainer the overall experience is enhanced for the customer, in effect the marketplace adds value to the shopping experience such that market days became community days. In addition, by creating this relaxed atmosphere, the customer is more likely to engage in larger spends to the benefit of the retailers, the entertainers and, by extending the concept of retailing to include hostelries (as is commensurate with current practice), then the symbiosis by which the attraction of coordinated and simultaneous attraction are enhanced through their interaction becomes clear.

DEPARTMENT STORES

In the nineteenth century a number of key factors arose that facilitated the creation of a retail format that had no direct predecessor, the department store, although certain characteristics had been established three centuries earlier by Mitsukoshi (Davies and Jones 1993). Large population migration into the cities, an increasingly affluent middle class and substantive technological developments all conjoined to establish circumstances that altered the physical limitations of retail store architecture and customer needs and expectations.

The Industrial Revolution was the underlying 'event' that resulted in the conditions appropriate to the department store's manifestation. City populations increased because of the transfer of workers from agriculture/rural to urban/industrial employment. In addition, the revolution also brought about the emergence of the middle classes as a significant economic and social force. Finally, the technology associated with the Industrial Revolution provided the means by which a new retail architecture could be formed. This architecture was typified by large open spaces over a number of floors, each linked by elevators and/or escalators for the movement, first and foremost of customers but also of merchandise throughout the stores. Large windows acted as an intermediary between the street and the shop, displaying the retailer's merchandise with the intention of informing and seducing (Henderson 1979).

In some aspects, the department store was a 'modern-day' embodiment of the mediaeval market under a single roof and a precursor of the shopping mall. Within the store not only could the (predominantly female) customer access a multiplicity of goods that would have hitherto been offered by a variety of individual retailers but she could also access a multiplicity of services that were intended to increase the social and recreational value of the retail experience (Zola 1883). It is perhaps within the format of the department stores that we first witness the attempt by a single retailer to wholly integrate and continuously manage the recreational and transactional aspects of retailing since previously these elements had been brought together by distinct entities (Hellman 2001; Schumer 1986).

For the middle-class female, the department store was akin to a mini-city. Within was contained a fascinating and fabulous array of products, advisors, cafes (Davies and Ward 2002) and with respect to Selfridges in London, a rooftop garden where the customer could partake of exercise and fresh air while in the relative safety and comfort of the store. In recreation, leisure and social terms, the department store offered a form of emancipation for females, an environment to which they could go free of husbands and chaperones. In this environment the woman was superior to the man: the woman was the primary customer, the decision maker. The department stores recognised the female customer as critical to their success and encouraged the prolonged presence of the customer through the constituent components and in-store activities. However, the department store was not simply a retailer with a recreational bent. Fundamental to its success was an educational element, whereby the female was the conduit through which middle-class values were communicated to the family and subsequently disseminated throughout society (Davies and Ward 2002). This, in turn, influenced the nature and content of middle-class recreation within the home and societal context.

The open and expansive nature of the department store added one other element central to the recreational experience of the customer – people watching. In this environment took place a form of peer review and this itself encouraged product obsolescence and replacement. The cafe and the garden, the fashion show and the atrium all allowed the customers to see and be seen. In so doing, customers competed with one another in an effort not to be outshone. Department stores encouraged conspicuous consumption within its market segment, a segment which it targeted accurately and satisfied accordingly (Kimmelman 1995; Zola 1883).

The predominance of the department store as a retail force has fluctuated since its emergence, although it remains a valid and viable retail entity. However, in examining their current strategies, it is possible to see the continuation of its original ethos of retail entertainment. The cafe still remains a staple component of the retailer's offer and in some department stores has a partially separate existence from the other store components, for example, Harvey Nichols in London has a separate and distinct access enabling the restaurant to function even when the store is closed. Similarly, the restaurant in La Rinascente, Milan, has established a reputation for offering a standard of food commensurate with the best restaurants in the city. These ventures and similar ventures in all department stores exist not only to generate profits through immediate transactions but to allow the customer to delay their departure, to refresh themselves, to enjoy the experience and in some cases to serve as a reminder of the quality of attainment.

A similarly blatant expression of the relationship between retailing and recreation is manifest in Selfridges, London. Selfridges has already established a reputation as a food retailer and is seeking to expand its food retailing space by approximately 50% (*Financial Times* 13 December 2001). More significant in terms of highlighting the link between retailing and recreation, is the company's intention to build a five star hotel on its Oxford Street site, a component of which will be a restaurant offering panoramic views across London (*Financial Times* 13 December 2001). In this example we see a clear and direct intertwining of the retailing, recreation and leisure industries. Furthermore, what this decision exhibits is a realisation that retail and recreation customers see no disparity between these sectors but instead recognise the mutuality that exists between them.

The example of the department store serves to highlight the overlap between the retail and the leisure sector whereby the boundaries as to what constitutes shopping and what constitutes recreation and leisure become blurred. Further evidence of this can be seen in the merchandise offers of stores such as Harrods and Liberty's in London, Printemps in Paris and Macy's, Bloomingdales and Saks in New York. All these stores offer not only the wide array of merchandise for local markets expected of department stores, but also a dedicated merchandise range for tourists. This reveals that these retailers view themselves as a component of the tourist offer of their respective cities rather than viewing themselves as a local retailer on which tourists may chance. In this respect, they exist as tourist destinations and as such are wholly immersed in the leisure and recreational activities not only of local customers but also of international customers.

Further evidence of the role of retailing as a tourist attraction and thereby as a component of the leisure and recreational characteristics of tourist destinations can be found in almost any destination guide book. Among the information citing local 'must sees', general history and key phrases is generally found a section on where to shop. This may be a list of the best local markets (e.g. Stanley Market, Hong Kong; Marché aux Puces, Paris) and their specialities or it may be a guide to the best shopping streets for fashion brands in the city (e.g. Via Condotti, Rome, Michigan Avenue, Chicago). Alternatively, the guide may offer an overview of the variety and location of the retailer formats, possibly including advice with respect to bargaining or sales times. Whatever the content, it is highly probable that there will be some reference to shops and shopping within tourist guides. Adding credibility to this argument are the many retailers to be found whose primary target is the tourist rather than the local customer as evidenced in primarily their merchandise offer. Once again these retailers serve to emphasise the connection between tourism and retailing and as such serve to emphasise the connection between retailing, recreation and leisure activity.

SHOPPING MALLS

Generally recognised as having their origins in the USA, shopping malls have become a common format for the grouping together of individual retailers within a controlled environment. It is perhaps worth noting that precursors to the mall can be recognised in department stores (offering a collection of disparate merchandise in one location under one roof) and in the galleries (e.g. Galleria Vittorio Emmanuelle, Milan) and arcades of Europe, the architectural forms and motifs of which are much aped in their modern day equivalents. As with the shopping mall, these galleries and arcades offered not only an opportunity to shop in relative comfort, but also served as a centre for recreation and socialisation (Hopkins 1991; Vanderbeck and Johnson Jr 2000) with cafes and restaurants comprising an integral part of the attraction (Stoffel 1988; Wakefield and Baker 1998). Such integration between retailing, socialisation and leisure can be witnessed in the Galleria Vittorio Emmanuelle which provides an offer that combines one of the city's finest restaurants (Savini) with the best bookstores (Bocca, Garzanti and Rizzoli) and premier retailing brands (Prada). In co-existence with these, there is a McDonald's, highlighting both the nature of change within the market and the continuation of the underlying principle that such venues represent a recreation and leisure experience rather than a venue in which purchase transactions occur.

The integration of recreation and leisure is even more apparent in the shopping malls of North America where, it might be argued, there exists a 'mall culture' among certain societal segments (Hopkins 1991). As with their precursors, the malls evolved into a place of congregation providing a common locus for individuals to meet and an environment that was safe, secure and protected from the elements. Over time the recreational aspects of the mall have evolved to include cinemas, hotels (package holidays to shopping malls are an option available to the American tourist), themed restaurants, bowling alleys, miniature lakes and landscaped rest areas (examples of such composite offers may be found in the Mall of America, Massachusetts and the Trafford Centre, Manchester). In effect, malls have evolved into idealised and stylised cities (Baker 1987) without the residential component, where visitors can experience edited versions of global experiences, not only through the existence of international retailers and restaurants but also through architectural, sociological, historical and mythological references.

Furthermore, the shopping mall (and possibly shopping in general) has become a centre for exercise providing both venue and destinations for mall walkers. Mall walking is an organised group of people who set themselves or are set distance goals within the shopping mall and, on the achievement of those goals, are rewarded by retailer discounts, badges of merit or prizes. In this activity, not only is the fusion of retailing and recreation manifest, but the emergence of shopping as a source of exercise, whereby the notion of the physical benefits of exercise is augmented by consumer rewards.

To endorse to the activity of mall walking, organised walking clubs may establish links with local hospitals to develop programmes geared towards improving the health of the population. Such programmes have offer benefits to the individual, to the hospital, to the general population of the nation and to the mall occupants in terms of increased and regular footfall. The Pheasant Lane Mall (Nashua, New Hampshire) has its 'Stepping Healthy' programme co-sponsored by Lowell General Hospital. The mall presents the programme as offering 'a climate controlled atmosphere which is better for your overall health and safety, especially in times of inclement weather. The programme was designed to add yet another service to our customers' (Pheasant Mall publicity material).

In this example, while the emphasis is placed on health and safety, the mall also acknowledges the influence in terms of footfall benefits. In addition, the mall presents its health programme as a means of establishing and communicating an enhanced service offer. Thus, it is stressing that this is a mall which cares about the well-being of its customers and is seeking to develop an offer that is based on more than the selling of goods, but is augmenting the individual and collective offers of its constituent retailers with additional and beneficial services.

SPORTS RETAILERS

The link between retailing, recreation and leisure also exists at a more fundamental level within the realm of sports retailing. In certain contexts the retailer exists to supply the necessary equipment and/or clothing to engage in recreational activities or clothing designed for recreational activities but adopted as casual wear (Mintel 2001), thus sportswear has left the sporting arena and entered the public arena as fashion. However, there remain customers of sportswear and equipment whose primary motive for purchase relates to the sports for which the articles were originally intended. In this respect, the retailer's function relates more to its ability to buy and break down stock, offering it to customers from an identified location, thus the role is more elemental. Nevertheless, it would be unwise to assume that, since much of this consumption activity will take place in the customer's free time (or leisure time), there will be no element of recreation incorporated in the purchase process itself (Mintel 2001).

Similarly, the rise of sports teams as brands has resulted in an increase in team-dedicated retailers (Conn 1997; Dempsey and Reilly 1998), with Dempsey and Reilly (1998) suggesting that this is a relatively recent phenomenon in the UK with only Tottenham Hotspurs having an established merchandise on offer in 1989. The purchase motive in these circumstances is less likely to be to facilitate participation in sport but to publicly demonstrate the fan's affiliation. Hence shops dedicated to, for example, Manchester United, Lazio or the Chicago Bulls, exist not necessarily to encourage direct participation in the sport, but consumption of the team's participation in the sport along with dissemination of the team brand wherever the customer publicly presents the purchased merchandise (Conn 1997; Dempsey and Reilly 1998; James 2001). In these examples the customer's participation in the sport is as a spectator rather than a player, but nevertheless, it reveals the evolution of a retail format that serves to enhance the customer's experience of the recreational activity while generating income for the organisations themselves.

The scale and financial value of such operations is highlighted by the merchandise links established between Manchester United and the New York Yankees, with each protagonist further utilising and enhancing established global brands. Lefton (1996) suggests that in the USA, the NFL sponsorship and licensing agreements represent a $250 million business, with James (2001) indicating that the value of such mutual arrangements are not only profit oriented but investment oriented: 'The tie-up's long-term benefits could see both Man U and the Yankees further distance themselves from their peers financially, giving them another advantage on game day.'

GALLERY AND MUSEUM SHOPS

The need for non-retail organisations such as sports organisations to identify and capitalise on alternative sources of income can be observed in the emergence of the gallery and museum shop (Dobrzynski 1997; Gregg 1997; Stanley 2001). While it may be argued that such shops demonstrate an educational rather than recreational role, a cursory review of the merchandise would suggest that its role is more multifaceted than education alone (Beard 1992; McKinley 1999), hence, the presence of books and CD-ROMs relating to the collection endorses the museums' and galleries' roles as social educators, but their decision to sell that education in the form of merchandise reveals the commercial need, a need which is partly addressed by retailing. However, in addition to the texts and CDs on sale, are commonly found postcards, branded pencils, branded confectionery, jigsaws etc. which serve to provide a tangible memory of the gallery/museum experience or as a gift for someone who did not participate directly in the visit (Anon 1998; Beard 1992). Some galleries have been able to establish a brand persona that is credible beyond the immediate confines of the gallery, but translating into merchandise for wholesale distribution as well as integrated shops. An example of this of this is to be found in the National Gallery, London, which has at points of ingress and egress to the gallery a gallery shop, catering to the local and tourist customer alike. In addition to this exists the National Gallery brand of greetings cards available by mail order (from the Gallery's dedicated catalogue) but also from retailers such as John Lewis as part of its wider card offer. This approach to licensed merchandise, offered both through specialist or generalist retailer is not unique to the National Gallery, but represents a means by which such institutions can generate income with which to support the organisations' activities. Thus, to experience the contents of a gallery it is no longer necessary to visit it.

SEX SHOPS

Given the subject of this chapter, it is appropriate to consider, albeit briefly, the concept of sex shops as a manifestation of the integration of retailing and leisure. The UK has witnessed a growth in the number of licensed sex shops in recent years revealing both a shift in societal and cultural attitudes and/or an increase in demand for such shops (Reuters 2002) although, it is argued, there continues to be a deficit between supply and demand (Brooks 2000). Historically, sex shops have existed either discreetly or in concentrated locations such Soho in London where they co-exist with related forms of entertainment. These locations themselves may become part of the tourist/visitor offer of cities (Wonders and Michalowski 2001), either in a observatory or participatory nature. However, the growth of this market and in particular its growth beyond its traditional, locational boundaries, suggests that there is growth in sexual variety and experimentation that should be acknowledged in leisure and recreation terms as such shops do not exist solely for the encouragement and facilitation of procreation (Reuters 2002).

Sex shops, it must be recognised, form part of a community's leisure and recreation portfolio. As with any other form of retailing they satisfy both the consumer and the social aspects of the shopping activity through their ability to supply appropriate merchandise and offer a venue whereby individuals of similar mindsets can interact.

BETTING SHOPS

Betting shops or bookmakers represent a different manifestation of the relationship between retailing, recreation and sport. The shift from sidestreet to highstreet locations indicates the significance of this retail format and the shift in societal and legal attitudes towards it (Jones, Hillier and Turner 1994). In this venue, sport provides the primary (but not the sole) motive for the customer's visit, the desire to participate in the sport through betting on a particular outcome. However, such activity is undertaken principally for a recreational and/or social purpose (Neal 1998), as once again, the shop provides both the venue for the transaction and the venue for social integration of individuals with a common interest (i.e. a specific segment).

Within this category there also exist differing levels of facility and service, reflecting the varying nature of the customer's expectations and requirements. These variations are exhibited in the aesthetics of the place; the quality of the fixtures and fittings; the cleanliness; the availability of refreshments; the location and size of the shop; the availability of augmented services such as telephone betting and accounts; the ability to process customers effectively and efficiently and the ability to pay out immediately or defer payment on successful bets. The evolution of the betting shop from a secluded retail format with generally poor amenities to an open format (in 1995 betting shops were permitted to have open shopfronts) with seating, televisions and refreshments is testament to its social and recreational significance as well as to changes in the law which facilitated the open format and food provision (William Hill press office).

SUMMARY

The purpose of this chapter was to explore the historical and contemporary manifestation of the interrelationships between retailing, recreation and leisure. In so doing, it has highlighted the role of retailing as not only a provider of merchandise but also a locus for social interaction and as a source of recreational activity in it own right. From this chapter, we can see that retailing has had an continuing role in the recreational and leisure activities of society throughout history and that while the form of this role may have altered throughout time, its principal role remains constant.

Significantly, the role of retailing within the sport and leisure context is dichotomous, existing as an independent variable in the general leisure activities of society and also as a source of income generation within specific sports and leisure situations, with key examples being team branding and museum/gallery retailing and merchandising activities. These serve to extend the experience of the fan or visitor while contributing to revenue.

However, what this chapter emphasises, is that regardless of the independent or associated nature of the retail activity, the relationship is symbiotic whereby the close proximity of leisure, sport and retail offers can have mutual benefits, not only in terms of income generation but in terms of experience as well. Hence the incorporation of sporting and leisure facilities within or near to retail facilities.

This reflects the locational draw of the combination of these elements, as well as the logistical issues associated with infrastructure and accessibility, a factor that was emphasised in antiquity, but remains equally relevant today.

Furthermore, the chapter highlights the extent to which retailing influences and is influenced by society and the environment in which society exists. Department stores present a useful example of this interplay, whereby the particular dynamics of the time contributed to the form and function of the retailer, but similarly, the manner in which the retailer influenced and modified society in the context of, for example, leisure activity, manners and the subsequent formalisation of middle-class norms. Other sector examples reveal a similar insight into society and society's concept of leisure and recreation. The increasing acceptance, legally and culturally, of sex shops and the transposition of betting shops from their previously discreet locations indicates that the activities associated with such retailer formats is becoming progressively more mainstream and that society, or at least a specific segment of society, is willing to engage more publicly with such retailers.

In addition to this, the chapter suggests that retailing is in itself a key part of a community's leisure and recreation offer, and in the case of the US malls, part of their sports/exercise offer as well. The significance of retailing to tourism and its role as a valid and valued activity of tourists as indicated in the chapter is evidenced by the ubiquitous 'where to shop' sections in many tourist guidebooks, providing information in relation to local specialities or key elevated shopping venues.

Overall from this chapter we can see the extent to which retailing has a fundamental role in the sport and leisure sectors, not only as a supplier of merchandise for participation in those sectors, but a component of the leisure concept in its own right. The symbiosis that exists between retailing, sport and leisure is one that results in enhanced experience, increased locational attraction and augmented income generation, whether the retail, sport or leisure activity exists within the for-profit or not-for-profit sectors. Thus the retail activity in the not-for-profit sector may serve to extend the experience for the individual, but critically, generate revenue that enables the continuation of the organisation (a key issue in the context of, for example, publicly funded galleries and sports facilities). Similarly, income generation can be used a means of establishing competitive advantage, as exemplified by Manchester United and the New York Yankees.

Questions

1. What are the various roles of retailing within the context of sport, leisure and recreation?

2. How are these various roles manifest?

3. What are the reciprocal benefits of locating sports and leisure facilities within or in close proximity to retail centres and who are the key beneficiaries?

References and further reading

Anon (1998) 'The art of giving', *The New Yorker*, 74, 38, 52.

Baker, R. (1987) 'Heaven in asphalt: shopping mall wonderland', *The New York Times*, 17 March.

Beard, M. (1992) 'Souvenirs of culture: deciphering (in) the museum', *Art History*, 15, 4, 505–533.

Bird, M. (1999) 'The glories that were Rome', *Time International*, 153, 1, 52.

Brooks, R. (2000) 'The R18 Story: more sex shops required', *The Sunday Times*, 5 November.

Conn, D. (1997) *The Football Business*. Edinburgh: Mainstream Publishing.

Davies, B. and Ward, P. (2002) *Managing Retail Consumption*. Chichester: John Wiley & Sons.

Davies, J. D. and Jones, P. (1993) 'Co-operation: too late or a new beginning', *European Retail Digest*, 26 June, 52.

Dempsey, P. and Reilly, K. (1998) *Big Money Beautiful Game: Winners and Losers in Financial Football: Saving Soccer from Itself*. London: Nicholas Brealey Publishing.

Dobrynski, J. (1997) 'Art to go: museum shops broaden wares at a profit', *The New York Times*, 10 December.

Fisher, E. (2002) 'United we stand ... to conquer; a British soccer team is beating the Americans at their own game ... global marketing', *Insight on the News*, 18, 19, 28–9.

Gregg, G. (1997) 'From "bathers" to beach towels', *ARTnews*, 94, 4, 120–124.

Hellman, P. (2001) 'For hungry shoppers in Paris: the restaurants of the grand magasins offer style, variety and even romantic views', *The New York Times*, 28 January.

Henderson, R. (1979) *The Grand Emporiums: The Illustrated History of the Great Department Stores*. New York: Stein and Day.

Hopkins, J. S. P. (1991) 'West Edmonton Mall as a centre for social interaction', *The Canadian Geographer*, 35, 3, 268–80.

James, J. (2001) 'United we brand: sports marketing takes a trans-Atlantic leap as the Yankees tie-up with Man U', *Time International*, 157, 7, 29.

Jones, P., Hillier, D. and Turner, D. (1994) 'Back street to side street to high street: the changing geography of betting shops', *Geography*, 79, 343, 122–9.

Kimmelman, M. (1995) 'Art in aisle 3, by lingerie, and feel free to browse: from the start, dept, stores and museums both aspired to improve public taste', *The New York Times*, 19 March.

Lefton, T. (1996) 'Union's due', *Brandweek*, 37, 32, 14–5.

McGoldrick, P. (2002) *Retail Marketing*. London: McGraw-Hill.

McKinley, J. (1999) 'See the show, buy the rat', *The New York Times*, 1 October.

Mintel (2001) *Sports Goods Marketing*.

Neal, M. (1998) 'You lucky punters!: a study of gambling in betting shops', *Sociology*, 32, 3, 581–601.

Reuters (2002), 'Sleazy Soho sex shops may give way to posh British "boutiques"', *Taipei Times*, 1 April.

Schumer, F. R. (1986) 'Those who shop also stop for lunch', *The New York Times*, 18 December.

Stanley, A. (2001) 'Modern marketing blooms in medieval Vatican Library', *The New York Times*, 8 January.

Stoffel, J. (1988) 'Where America goes for entertainment', *The New York Times*, 7 August.

Vanderbeck, R. M. and Johnson Jr, J. H. (2000) ' "That's the only place where you can hang out": urban young people and the space of the mall', *Urban Geography*, 21, 1, 5–25.

Wakefield, K. L. and Baker, J. (1998) 'Excitement at the mall: determinants and effects on shopping response', *Journal of Retailing*, 74, 4, 515–32.

Wonders, N. and Michalowski, R. (2001) 'Bodies, borders and sex tourism in a globalized world: a tale of two cities – Amsterdam and Havana', *Social Problems*, 48, 4, 545–72.

Zola, E. (1883) *The Ladies Paradise*. Berkley: University of California Press.

www.williamhillmedia.com

PART 6

CASES AND OPINIONS

CHAPTER 20

Planning for Joint Usage

Clay E. Harshaw

INTRODUCTION

This case study describes issues involved in the planning and designing of athletic and recreational facilities for a college. The unique aspect of the case is the joint use of the facilities between the college and the Young Men's Christian Association (YMCA). The process used to plan the facility was participatory planning. Participatory planning requires representatives of the various facility users to be members of the planning committee. This process allows for input from the people who will use the facility and allows for the planning of the most beneficial facility for the users.

AIMS AND OBJECTIVES

By the end of the chapter you should be able to:

1. understand the importance of participatory planning
2. identify who should be included on the planning committee
3. identify the importance of communication in the planning process.

GUILFORD COLLEGE

In 1837 the Religious Society of Friends (Quakers) founded Guilford College. The campus is located in suburban Greensboro, North Carolina, a small city with a population of 225,000. The fastest growing area of the city is the northwest corner in which Guilford College is located. The campus occupies over 300 acres, a portion of which is protected as a historical area. The college is a four-year liberal arts college of 1,300 students with most of them living on campus. As a Quaker institution, the college requires consensus for all decision making on campus. For major decisions, all college community members (faculty, staff and students) have a voice in the decisions made.

The college began constructing new facilities and renovating existing ones in the late 1990s. An ambitious $50 million capital campaign accompanied the college's building programme. During the campaign, a new technology centre with computer labs and classrooms opened. In 2001 a $14 million science centre with an observatory and planetarium opened. In addition to the new facilities, renovations to several older buildings (those built prior to 1960) were scheduled. The student centre, Founders Hall, was scheduled for expansion to serve the students better. Also in the campaign were renovations to and expansion of the athletic and recreational facilities.

Guilford College supports 12 varsity sports (five for women and seven for men). Its indoor athletic facilities measure over 64,000 square feet. The baseball, football and soccer teams use fields that are specialised for their respective sports. In an effort to increase enrolment and to comply with Title IX gender equity legislation, the college's board directed the athletic department to establish a women's softball team, men's and women's cross-country teams and men's and women's track and field teams.

For over 15 years, the college has maintained a lease agreement with the YMCA. Through this agreement, the YMCA leases the athletic and recreational facilities from Guilford College. All members of the Guilford College community use the facilities free of charge, whereas YMCA members pay annual membership fees. The YMCA programming at the Guilford College campus involves primarily youth soccer. The fields on the campus provide the YMCA with the space required for its youth soccer programme in the area. Other YMCA programmes include swimming, youth basketball and adult fitness. In the last five years, the YMCA has experienced a great deal of growth in all their programmes at the Guilford College facility. This growth prompted the administrators of the YMCA to consider expanding the programmes offered at the facility on the Guilford College campus.

In 1997 administrators from both the college and the YMCA began assessing the athletic and recreational facilities available on campus. A description of those facilities follows.

Current facilities

Alumni Gymnasium was constructed in 1940. Originally built to house the athletic programme at Guilford College, it is now the home of two academic departments (Justice and Policy Studies and Sport Studies) and most of the Athletic Department's offices (the men's basketball coaches' offices are located across the campus). The structure's style has a Georgian influence, as do most of the buildings on the campus. The building holds a historical appeal for the campus community because the men's basketball team won the 1973 National Association of Intercollegiate Athletics national championship when they played their home games in the arena. The arena floor is now used for athletic team practices, physical education classes, dance classes, campus recreation and YMCA programmes. A rehabilitation room now occupies space where bleachers once stood on one side of the arena. This 'room' is better described as a 'cage' because the walls are made of chain-link fencing. Some of the complaints from the gym's users are the poor ventilation system throughout the building, the poor lighting in the arena and the risks imposed by the various infrastructure components (conduit, piping and air exchanges) that are exposed.

Below the arena floor are the athletic locker rooms, the athletic training room and the weight training room. Most of the athletic locker rooms are shared by at least two teams. Only the men's basketball team has a locker room to itself. The athletic training room is used primarily for athletic teams for injury prevention and for limited rehabilitation purposes. It is also used for teaching the athletic training education programme courses taught by the Sport Studies Department faculty. The weight training room (625 square feet) contains free weights and machines. The college and YMCA share the weight room, which is closed only for weight lifting classes taught by the Sport Studies Department. The weight training room has a rubberised floor and an independent ventilation system. The ceiling in the room is low, approximately eight feet high at some points with a maximum height of 11 feet.

Ragan-Brown Fieldhouse was built in 1980 as an addition to Alumni Gymnasium. The structure is unique to the campus because it has a cathedral-like wooden ceiling. The building's roof forms two peaks, which led to its nickname: 'Twin Peaks'. Many Guilford College community members complain that the building's appearance is inconsistent with the other buildings on the campus.

The arena has seating for 2,500 spectators and is home to the Guilford College volleyball and basketball teams. One of the aesthetic features in the arena is the display of flags representing all the nationalities attending the college. In addition to the varsity athletic teams, the YMCA and campus recreation use the facility for various programmes. It is also used for special events such as alumni dinners, high school basketball tournaments and science fairs.

The facility houses two classrooms used by the Sport Studies Department. These rooms were often used by visiting basketball teams as a locker room and by the YMCA for its after-school programmes and summer day camps. Both classrooms seat 25 students. One of the classrooms is the lab used for teaching exercise physiology, kinesiology and biomechanics.

The construction project of Ragan-Brown Fieldhouse included a natatorium featuring a 25-metre swimming pool and a diving tank. The diving tank is no longer used except for scuba diving instruction. The swimming pool was originally built for competitions, but the college no longer has a swimming team. The pool is now utilised primarily for lap swims, aqua-aerobics and therapeutic exercise. A ramp was retro-fitted to the pool to allow disabled persons' access. The locker rooms for the YMCA members and Guilford College faculty and staff are located adjacent to the natatorium. The locker rooms feature tower showers, full lockers and half-lockers.

Four racquetball courts were added to Alumni Gymnasium in 1980 as part of the renovation to the buildings when Ragan-Brown Fieldhouse was built. At the time of construction, racquetball was at the height of its popularity in the region. Since that time, its popularity has decreased. As a result, one of the courts was converted to a fitness room with treadmills, recumbent cycles and small dumbbells. Much of the equipment in the room was moved from the weight training room in Alumni Gymnasium. The YMCA funded the conversion that included carpeting and installation of an independent ventilation system.

One of the problems with the current facilities is the lack of wheelchair accessibility. Handicapped individuals do not have access to the second floor offices of Alumni Gymnasium where the Athletic Department is located. To gain access to the lower level of Alumni Gymnasium, handicapped individuals must go outside the building to another entrance. This same situation exists in Ragan-Brown Fieldhouse. To gain access to the natatorium, a separate entrance must be used.

Armfield Athletic Center is a 3,000-seat stadium for the football (American) and men's lacrosse teams. The stadium features a natural turf playing surface and a gravel running track measuring one-quarter of a mile in length. In addition to the college's use of the track, members of the neighbouring communities frequently walk and run on it throughout the day and evening. At night, floodlamps illuminate the track. No stadium lighting is available for night competitions. The stadium is located approximately 200 metres from the locker rooms in Alumni Gymnasium. Although the stadium has a small press box, neither permanent concession booths nor restrooms exist in the stadium. Concession sales are made from either a tent or trailer next to the stadium. Restrooms for fans are located more than 100 metres from the stadium in the music auditorium.

McBane Baseball Field features a natural turf outfield and infield. A unique feature of the field is the grass first and third baselines. In May 2000 a violent windstorm damaged the outfield fence and the backstop. In addition to repairing those items, the dugouts were expanded. Spectator seating is limited to two wooden bleachers. Many spectators choose to bring lawn chairs and sit on a hillside next to the field. Groups other than the college's baseball team rarely use the field.

Eight hard surface tennis courts are located in front and along the north side of Ragan-Brown Fieldhouse. Two of the courts have a spectator seating area. The YMCA and college share the courts throughout the year. Several of the courts have cracks due to the subsurface settling after their original construction. The Guilford College tennis teams practise on the courts, but the courts are unsuitable for competition. Thus, the teams hold competitions at local high schools.

Hawthorne Fields are located across the campus approximately 400 metres from Ragan-Brown Fieldhouse and Alumni Gymnasium. These fields are the most utilised of the athletic fields on the campus. Guilford's varsity soccer and lacrosse teams practise on the fields. The women's lacrosse team and both soccer teams compete on the fields. In addition to the varsity athletic programmes, campus clubs and the YMCA use these fields. The YMCA's youth soccer programme, one of the largest in the area, holds practices and competitions on the fields during the week and on weekends.

Two softball fields are part of the Hawthorne Fields area. These fields are used for little league baseball and campus recreation. The fields have gravelled infields that are unsuitable for intercollegiate competition. These fields were originally used by the Guilford College's varsity softball team which was disbanded in the late 1980s.

Hawthorne Fields have two restrooms on the north side of the field. No concession sales are made at the fields. Spectator seating is limited to two metal bleachers for the soccer field. Like the baseball spectators, many soccer and lacrosse spectators bring their own seating.

The administrators for Guilford College and the YMCA determined that the facilities were inadequate and inappropriate for their future programming. As a result, the two parties decided jointly to develop plans to construct a new building and renovate the existing facilities.

A planning committee was named, as were two subcommittees. The members of the committees included Guilford College athletic coaches, faculty members from the Sport Studies Department, student life personnel and YMCA staff. The goal of the committees was to develop plans for a new wellness centre on campus that could be used by Guilford College students, staff, faculty, athletic teams and YMCA members. Some of committee members changed jobs during the planning process. This resulted in some instability and uncertainty in the process. As new members came on board, new ideas were introduced and plans were changed.

Eventually, the planning committee decided on a final plan of needs. The YMCA and Guilford College committee members had come to an agreement as to what features they desired in the new and renovated facilities. Some specific amenities and features requested by the committee were:

- a rockclimbing wall for campus recreation and physical activity courses
- a regulation collegiate softball field
- expanded cardiovascular fitness area for all users
- aerobics and dance space with specialised flooring
- renovated and new locker rooms for YMCA members
- expanded weight training room for athletes
- upgraded and expanded athletic training (sports medicine) room
- access for handicapped users
- classrooms with the latest teaching technology available
- concession and restroom facilities for each of the athletic fields.

Renovations and new building plans

The architects proffered their plans to the committee in the autumn of 1999. The plans included renovations to the existing facilities and a new wellness centre located in front of Ragan-Brown Fieldhouse.

Significant renovations to Alumni Gymnasium were planned. Specific renovations included improved office space for the Athletic Department and Sport Studies Department (the Justice and Policy Studies Department would move to another building on campus), an expanded athletic training room, expanded locker rooms for each sport and visiting team locker rooms. One racquetball court and the fitness court were to be renovated into the expanded athletic training room with the athletic weight training room above it. Each sport was to have its own locker room that would be larger than the previously shared rooms. In addition to the renovations to the various rooms, the entire ventilation system for Ragan-Brown Fieldhouse and Alumni Gymnasium would be upgraded.

The natatorium was to receive a facelift and expansion. A separate 6,200 square foot natatorium was to be built next to the existing one. The new pool was planned as a therapeutic exercise pool with a zero-depth entry. The primary users of the new pool would be the YMCA members.

The largest of the new buildings planned was the wellness centre. The 25,000 square foot building was to be located in front of Ragan-Brown Fieldhouse. This was partly an effort to hide the roof peaks of the fieldhouse from the campus. The placement of the building would require relocating the tennis courts to a complex behind Ragan-Brown Fieldhouse near a pond on campus. The tennis complex would have a pavilion featuring a concessions booth and restrooms in the centre of the eight tennis courts.

The wellness centre included several popular amenities that the YMCA sought. These features included a suspended running track, basketball courts, family locker rooms and child watch areas. It also included features desired by both the YMCA and the college: a large cardiovascular fitness room, a large weight training room and aerobic/dance space.

A single entrance to all three buildings was planned for security purposes. The architects described the proposed entrance as a 'knuckle' in which all facility traffic would flow. This 'knuckle' was envisioned as a three-level spiral stairway with a registration desk on the second level.

Outdoor spaces were to receive several improvements. Hawthorne Fields were to be expanded to include a new softball field for intercollegiate competition and a new soccer field. The new soccer field was to allow for more rotation in the fields' usage. Armfield Athletic Center was to have a new rubberised track constructed to meet intercollegiate competition standards and lighting for the stadium to allow for night competitions for football and men's lacrosse. No additional construction was planned for the outdoor spaces.

The plans included the proposed parking areas and vehicle entrances to the facilities. Building codes in the city of Greensboro required significantly more parking spaces (approximately 400) than currently on campus. These proposed additional parking spaces were located to the south of Alumni Gymnasium along the third baseline of McBane Field, to the east of the natatorium and to the north of the proposed wellness centre and Ragan-Brown Fieldhouse. The plans also contained a proposed new roadway that would become the main entrance to the campus. The roadway would bypass most of the campus with the intention of reducing the vehicular traffic near pedestrian areas, especially near halls of residence.

The total cost for the new facility and renovations was approximately $12 million. Guilford College was to pay $5 million of the total cost with the YMCA paying the remaining $7 million. A large portion of the total cost was to bring the existing buildings (Alumni Gymnasium and Ragan-Brown Fieldhouse) up to the current building codes.

Reactions to the architects' plans

Some committee members received the architects' plans with enthusiasm, others with disappointment. The YMCA members were enthusiastic about the plans. The plans met their desires and needs for their programmes. The Sport Studies Department faculty members were disappointed because the plans did not include additional or renovated classroom space. Additionally, the faculty were upset because the proposed athletic training room would take away another racquetball court used in the physical activity programme. The Guilford College Athletic Department staff was accepting of the plans but disappointed with the weight training facility above the athletic training room and with the absence of restroom and concession facilities for the fields. To many of the Guilford College faculty and staff, the plans for the new building looked like a YMCA facility with little, if any, instructional or athletic value.

A large number of students opposed the plans for environmental reasons. The students voiced their opposition to the plans during an open forum with the planning committee and the college president. In these students' view, the proposed roadway, softball field, soccer field and parking areas would disturb the 'green-space' of the campus. Additionally, the proposed tennis complex near the pond was viewed detrimental to the 'greenspace' and the wetland environment on campus.

The planning committee reconvened after discussions with faculty members and students were completed. The members agreed to discuss options to satisfy as many people as possible. During these committee discussions, some YMCA administrators suggested limiting the number of students who could use the new facility or limiting the times the facilities could be available to the students. The college's position on students' use was made clear. The position was that the facility was a college facility first and that the students would have priority in using the facility.

The committee could not reach consensus on the new facility. As a result, the YMCA decided to pull out of the negotiations with Guilford College officials. YMCA officials decided to purchase land and construct a new facility approximately six miles northwest of the college. The new YMCA facility will offer the same programmes as it offers at the Guilford College facility. With the new facility, the YMCA sought to attract new members in the fastest growing quadrant of the city. Guilford College's fields will continue to be used by the youth soccer programmes sponsored by the YMCA.

Guilford College officials accepted the YMCA's decision and began developing plans for a new wellness centre and renovated athletic facilities. The college's administrators established a new planning committee. The facility is expected to serve as a multipurpose building for athletics, campus recreation and instruction.

Questions

1. Assume that you have been asked to be a student representative on the planning committee. What programmes do you think should be prioritised? Why?

2. What options could you use to address the environmental concerns of the students opposing the new facility?

3. Identify the critical issue that facilitated the YMCA's decision to abandon the joint project with Guilford College and to construct its own facility.

CHAPTER 21

Almería 2005

Manuel Recio Menéndez and Javier Martínez del Río

In 2005 the Mediterranean Games will be held in Almería (Spain). This is an event similar to the Commonwealth Games, in which all the countries bathed by the Mediterranean Sea participate. On 28 April 1999 Almería was designated the seat of the 2005 Mediterranean Games by this competition's international committee, in an election which it won by absolute majority over the other candidate, the Croatian city of Rijeka. Around 5,000 athletes from 21 countries in the Mediterranean basin will participate in the Games.

THE CITY

Almería is a city with under 200,000 inhabitants located in the southeastern corner of Spain, in the region of Andalusia. The city has a Roman, Islamic and Christian past and this history reflects the spirit of the Mediterranean itself, as the refuge of ancient civilisations and a place where different cultures live side by side. For centuries the sea brought to Almería peoples from all over Europe, Africa and the Middle East. Thus Almería was always a boundary between cultures and sometimes the bridge that connected them. The heritage of this historical wealth has translated into a great diversity of traditions, holidays, cuisine and culture.

The economy of Almería is one of most quickly developing regions in Andalusia and Spain. It is based mainly on three sectors: an agricultural sector that has been able to combine the advantages of climate with the introduction of modern technologies; a strong, prosperous marble industry, and a tourist sector which takes advantage of 200 kilometres of coast and the good weather to offer over 20,000 hotel rooms. The region's economic development has attracted a large number of immigrants, making Almería a place where, today, the heirs to the cultures which dominated the city in years gone by live together.

PLANNING CRITERIA

The public offices involved in the planning of the infrastructure of the 2005 Mediterranean Games (MG) followed four general criteria:

1. To comply with the technical requirements necessary for the perfect execution of the different competitions that will be held during the event.

2. To provide the city of Almería with first-rate sports facilities to cover its long-term requirements.
3. To produce all kinds of synergies and long-term economic benefits for the city and its surroundings.
4. To do all this within a reasonable budget.

These criteria are different from those usually considered when sports facilities are built by private companies, which usually focus on maximising the income produced by sports events. Therefore the facilities lack luxury seating and such questions as the income produced by parking lots, numbers of restaurants and refreshment concessionaires and the appropriate locations for displaying advertisements in the sports facilities have not been an initial consideration.

Local authorities also put strong emphasis on the need to comply with the planned building schedule since the event is viewed as an opportunity to portray a modern and efficient image of the city, an image that could be clouded by inefficiency if delays occur.

THE PLANNING PROCESS

The planning and execution of the infrastructure necessary for the MG has the following milestones:

- *28 April 1999*: election of Almería as the organising city for the 15th Mediterranean Games in 2005.
- *27 October 1999*: the Mediterranean Games Organising Committee, in which all the governments (national, regional and local) as well as the Spanish Olympic Committee are represented, is constituted. This body prepares the Games' general plan. This plan explicitly denotes each designated facility, with building timetables, budgets, technical specifications and general organisation. This general plan was approved on 19 February 2001.
- *1 May 2002*: construction begins on the sports complex in La Vega de Acá.
- *1 December 2004*: completion of sports-related construction.
- *January/March 2005*: celebration of sports events as a test run in the facilities.
- *March 2005*: completion of the Mediterranean Village.
- *19 June to 3 July 2005*: celebration of the Mediterranean Games.

The Mediterranean Games International Committee designates a technical commission that evaluates the progress of construction of the facilities and general organisation of the games every six months starting at the beginning of 2000. In all the reviews carried out to date, the Commission has praised the effort made to comply with the deadlines set and has pointed out that more than the construction of the necessary infrastructure, the greatest difficulty in the MG is the organisation of the event itself on time.

SPORTS FACILITIES

The Mediterranean Village

The lead project of the Mediterranean Games is the construction of the Mediterranean Village, which is located 15 minutes from the city centre, surrounded by Cabo de Gata Natural Park. This village is where the athletes will live and will include the building that houses the reception and participant accreditation center (Palácio del Mar). As the President of the Mediterranean Games International Committee (MGIC), Claude Collard, says: 'The Village is going to be the heart of the 2005 Mediterranean Games in Almería.'

The construction of the Mediterranean Village is the excuse to give way to the construction of a brand new city. After celebrating the event, the area will remain as a quality leisure and tourist resort. Approximately 260 hectares will be developed, where around 5,000 homes, five luxury hotels and more than three square kilometres of gardens will be built. It will have leisure zones, an 18-hole golf course and more than a kilometre of virgin beaches. It represents a total public investment of 60 million euros and an induced investment of over 400 million euros. The project offers all kinds of tourist 'resort' features: it is a careful housing development, where 19,000 people will live, with all the latest technologies, pneumatic pickup system, optic fibre golf course, high-quality standards of housing and a rich sports and leisure offer.

It is hoped that this village will have a long-term effect on the Almería economy by attracting foreign investors, boosting the value of the Cabo de Gata Park as a tourist attraction and providing an input to the economic activity of the region in sectors such as construction, hotels and restaurants, general services etc.

Sports facilities at La Vega de Acá

All the new sports facilities are concentrated in an area called the Vega de Acá located next to the Mediterranean Village. In this area, a first-class Olympic stadium and sports arena are to be built (construction started in 2002). The third most important building for the games will be a complex of five swimming pools that will be built in the city of Almería.

The Olympic stadium will have capacity for 25,000 spectators for football (soccer) and track activities. The project will cover all the requirements of media and will have a room for officials with a complete view of the field through a large glass wall, an assembly area where press and athletes can get together, as well as a warm-up area for athletes, located under the grandstands.

The stadium also guarantees complete access all the way round in two concourses, an upper and a lower. This means that personnel and transport of equipment will be able to circulate between any two points on the same level inside the facility. With respect to the administrative area, the Mediterranean Stadium will have two floors devoted to offices, meeting rooms and exhibit halls. That is an administrative structure that will not only be useful for the Games, but also for its later use by the city.

After the MG, this stadium will be devoted to football. Spanish football clubs are reluctant to use stadia with capacity for track and field events, since this implies a

20–25 metre wide zone (the lanes) separating the fans from the players and giving rise to a colder atmosphere and a loss of spectator capacity to cheer the team on and influence the game. That is why this stadium has been designed to hold a seating deck for 5,000 above the tracks when there is a football game.

Between the pavilion and the Olympic stadium there is a warm-up field with capacity for 500 spectators, financed jointly by the different governments. Once the games are over, this facility will be very useful to the development of the city's athletes, since it will be used daily as a track.

An Olympic pavilion will also be built next to the stadium. This stadium will have a capcity for 5,000 and after the MG will house the local volleyball club's games (one of the top teams in the Spanish league) as well as concerts, congresses and a large number of other events.

Finally, several previously existing facilities will be improved to house basketball, volleyball, football, rowing, gymnastics and tennis.

FINANCING

The first source of income comes from the Mediterranean Village itself. The town council of Almería owned land where the Village as well as the sports facilities centre will be built. After open solicitation decided on the architectural project for the Olympic village, the lands were sold to private businesses that are committed to building the projects as designed by the architects and to pay a total of 33.16 million euros. In exchange, these companies will be able to sell the housing units to individuals after the Games have been held, at a preset price. By August 2002 40% of the houses had already been offered to individuals and all of them were sold very quickly. In order to assure that these companies comply with the pre-defined schedules and technical specifications, an office exclusively devoted to their control was created. The money paid by the builders was used to pay part of the cost of remodelling the existing facilities.

A second way of financing the project comes from the different public offices involved that will finance each one of the following infrastructure features:

- *Local authorities*: multiuse pavilion, where the gymnastics and fencing competitions will be held and a venue for regattas, where rowing and kayaking events will be held. They will also finance the improvements necessary in six of the already existing buildings: riding club, tennis club, indoor arena, shooting range, two football fields and venue for rowing, canoeing and kayaking.

- *The Andalusian regional authorities* will finance the MG with a total of 233 million euros of which 9 million are earmarked for construction of a sports arena with seating capacity for 5,000 spectators in the Vega de Acá. The regional government also finances small remodelling jobs in another seven already existing facilities that will be used in the MG: a swimming pool complex, an old stadium for track and field events, four indoor pavilions and a football field.

- *National authorities* finance the Olympic stadium which will be built next to the pavilion in the Vega de Acá. This stadium will be devoted to football and athletics events. Between the pavilion and the Olympic stadium there is a warm-up field with capacity for 500 people. Both facilities cost around 21 million euros, which will be contributed by the Spanish government.

A third mode of financing involved official sponsors. Three types of sponsor were defined for the 2005 MG:

- '*Official member*': companies in this classification pay a certain amount in exchange for the concession of main advertising space before and during the games.

- '*Official collaborator*': companies in this classification pay a fixed amount of 180,000 euros, in exchange for which the companies can use the logotype of the games and for the concession of advertising space before and during the games.

- '*Official supplier*': companies in this classification lend their services to the organisation for a fixed amount of 75,000 euros and pay another 75,000 euros in exchange for which the companies can use the logotype of the games and use the image of the games in their advertising campaigns.

The Organising Committee had troubles finding sponsoring companies. Perhaps the fact that Almería is a small city or that the most popular Spanish athletes will not be attending the event meant that after two years of searching only one official member was found. At the end of 2001 the Organising Committee had only agreed with one company to be an official member and with another one to be an official supplier. Thus they subcontracted the search for patrons to a specialised private company. This company made a commitment to raise at least 6 million euros (3 million by 31 December 2003) in exchange for 12% of each operation of successful patronage up to the 6 million goal and 15% after that. By September 2002 this company had been able to find some new official collaborators and some new official suppliers but no 'official members'.

The Organising Committee has foreseen other sources of income, which in this type of event, implies lower revenues: television rights, ticket sales, sale of special parallel services, special lotteries etc. However, this income is supposed to cover the expenses of the organisational activities and not improvement of the sports facilities.

Table 21.1 *Revenues from the Mediterranean Games, Almería 2005 (Source: Organising Committee 2002)*

Revenues from the MG Almería 2005		
	Amount (× 1000)	%
Income from organisation	33,879	14.46
Induced economic effects	145,334	62.03
Income generated by tourism	32,428	13.84
External effects	22,659	9.67
Total	234,300	100

ECONOMICS OF THE MEDITERRANEAN GAMES

The MG will have an effect on the city of Almería that will go beyond the mere economic figures, since they will give the city an international dimension that it did not have before and, furthermore, the city will have more appropriate facilities where sports events can be held in addition to congresses, concerts and other types of show. Moreover, it will create a tourist centre where 19,000 people will live and directly and indirectly create 7,000 permanent jobs. Thus, 57.6% of the population believes that this event will positively affect society as a whole and assigns a score of 8.5 on the Likert scale of 0 to 10, where 0 is very bad and 10 is excellent.

Table 21.1 refers only to income that will be produced before and during the MG. This amount will be surpassed by the investments made in the event, which are estimated at around 280 million euros. That implies a loss of more than 45 million euros. However, everyone hopes that the long-term economic and social effects of the event will be very positive for the city.

Questions

1. What do you think are the final objectives the city has marked for the MG? Do you think that the infrastructure has been planned according to these objectives?

2. What are the strengths and weaknesses of the project, the facilities and the site?

3. Do you think that the fact that the infrastructure has been planned and financed by the public sector will influence the long-term success of the Mediterranean Village and related sports facilities?

CHAPTER 22

Sports and Leisure Experience

James J. Riordan

INTRODUCTION

If, during a family reunion where attending members spanned three generations, the question 'why do you (did you attend) live sporting events?' was posed to a cross-section of each of the three generations, the answers of the youngest group would differ greatly from those in the 'veteran' contingent. The answers from the current, contemporary generation would create a wide and varied list of responses. The 'more experienced' bunch would probably give one simple answer. What lies between the two sets of responses is the path of change and development of new ideas with concern to the way society looks at and embraces sports and entertainment. The very fact that the phrase 'sports *and* entertainment' is still uttered as opposed to 'sports entertainment' is confusing to some. This narrowing of the abyss, the breaking down of the wall started, many will say, with the slow but consistent introduction of different media, vehicles, if you will, of how people were entertained: cable television; VCRs and videos; the construction of more stadia, arenas, performing arts centres and amphitheatres and multiplex cinemas. Suddenly, the family was not confined to watching channels 2 through 13 any more or boxed in with Lawrence Welk and Ed Sullivan. People would be afforded many new ways of spending their discretionary income. Great for the spenders. Challenging for the producer of sports and entertainment events who, at that time, depended on the support of the ticket-buying public. This chapter will discuss how a sporting event has become not only a sports entertainment event, but also a more complete leisure experience. It will look at how this true leisure experience starts when the individual is considering attending an event and how it involves nearly everyone and anyone remotely connected to the event.

CORE PRODUCT AND PRODUCT EXTENSIONS

Before proceeding into analysing the sports entertainment experience as a leisure experience, it is important to identify and define two very important terms associated with sporting events and sports organisations: *core product* and *product extension*. These two terms are discussed extensively in Hardy, Mullin and Sutton (2000). The authors essentially define the core product as the initial, primary (allegedly) reason for attending the event. The actual game of baseball would be a core product. Watching nine men on each side play for a minimum of nine innings, getting three outs per inning ... etc. The core product of the Super Bowl would be the 'four downs to make a first down, four quarter' event. Segueing into *product extensions* ... activities such as the pre- and post-game shows at the Super Bowl, give-aways of bobble-head dolls at baseball games, between innings or during time-out audience participation promotions, the concession menu and the appearance of the ticket taker who tears your ticket. All of the aforementioned are product extensions. Both of these terms will be referred to throughout the chapter.

WHY DO PEOPLE GO TO SPORTING EVENTS?

Referring back to the family reunion scenario of earlier, it was noted that responses to this question would differ greatly in both number and content. The members of the two older groups (in terms of age) would most likely, on average, limit their response to the core product. They would go to see a baseball game to see a baseball game. Except for maybe using the game as a way of having an afternoon or evening out, little else that was associated with the game would matter to them. They would not be concerned about concessions, the attitude and behaviour of service personnel, what promotions or give-aways were being done (there really was not any of these activities on a regular basis until the 1960s) etc. However, the youngest generation at the family reunion might offer more expansive reasons for going to a game. They may be somewhat concerned about the core product, but they also pay close attention to product extensions. Product extensions will be discussed in more detail later in this chapter.

With the advent of advanced technological capabilities within the media and the progressive and aggressive development of marketing, sales and promotional strategies, people today are constantly being 'reminded' about leisure activities such as sport entertainment. A 'must see' mindset takes over. Depending on certain conditions (team, league, the teams record, city) people will go to a sport enter-tainment event maybe not solely to see Shaquille O'Neal and Kobe Bryant play, but because the Staples Center is the place to be seen, since high-powered celebrities (e.g. Jack Nicholson and Goldie Hawn) are regulars there. Or maybe it is the private club at the Staples Center where individuals pay (after they get to the top of 500+ waiting list) $10,000 a year just to walk in the door. Sport marketing executives have also taken special, extraordinary events and have enveloped them with a 'Game of the Century' mentality, hiking the demand for a ticket to this event to frenzied levels: Michael Jordan's last game (part 1); Michael Jordan's return to pro basketball (part 1); Michael Jordan's last game (the sequel); Michael Jordan's return to pro basketball (the sequel). It is wondered how many people wound up with tickets to see Michael Jordan return to basketball on Halloween Night in Madison Square Garden who had not been to a pro basketball game in years or maybe never. Similarly, a story comes to mind of a well-dressed lady walking with a man toward the site of a recent Super Bowl. She was heard to enquire of the man 'Who is playing today?'

PROMOTIONS AND GIVEAWAYS: TWO MAJOR PRODUCT EXTENSIONS

While the great-grandfathers, grandfathers and some fathers of the early 2000s still hold the core product as the main reason for attending a sport entertainment event, they may still have to deal with their great grandchildren, grandchildren and children who are more apt to go more because of product extensions. And by no means is this 'decision to attend' limited to children! In the 1960s, the New York Mets baseball team had one major give-away day per year ... a replica batting helmet. The New York Yankees held the forever famous Bat Day promotion. These days were the extent of the give-away days for the New York baseball teams. Team executives still felt that people would still come to the stadium based on the team tradition and current standings. The reader needs to remember that during this period, there was much less of a choice on the leisure time and recreational menu. In the 2000s the day that there is no promotion, special event or give-away at a sports entertainment event is the exception rather than the rule. The Buffalo (NY) Bisons, the AAA minor league team of the Cleveland Indians, once coined a promotional and marketing strategy entitled 'Every Game is an Event' meaning no matter what day a person would go to see the Bisons, something besides a baseball game was taking place. From having the kids run the bases after the game, face painting, post-game concerts or fireworks, win $1 million, win a house ... the list goes on and on. Some purists will cringe at scenes showing thousands of people queuing the night before a game in order to get the priceless bobble-head that is being given away. In 2000 the Yankees were giving away a bobble-head doll of one of their players. People lined up overnight; many came in, received their bobble-head and immediately left. Many more left after a few innings. It was indeed a shame that those 'fans' missed one of the great feats in all sports, a perfect game.

SERVICE-ORIENTED PRODUCT EXTENSIONS

Unlike their ancestors before them today's sports entertainment attendee observes and critiques every aspect of an event's and/or an organisation's operation. Later in this chapter, crucial elements of the 'leisure experience as a sports entertainment event' will be presented. For now, we'll look at the different areas of a sports entertainment event or organisation that will have an effect on a person's visit to that event. In 1960 if Ted Williams hit three grand slam home runs in one game, and the Boston Red Sox won, as far as the 35,000 individuals who jammed Fenway Park that day were concerned, all was right in the world. No matter if the plumbing didn't work or there was poor access and egress for vehicles ... no matter: the Red Sox won and Teddy Ballgame had 'a day'. In 2003 Derek Jeter could hit four homers, Roger Clemens pitch a shutout for the Yankees and the guy who slipped on spilled soda and had three drunks yelling obscenities for nine innings sitting behind him and his two young sons is not going to remember any of the heroics by the two Yankee stars. He is going to remember a very frustrating and unpleasant day at Yankee Stadium. Granted, not all negative occurrences can be completely stopped or avoided. Sometimes things really do 'just happen'. More often than not, however, it is the organisation not planning or showing proper concern for the overall well-being, the complete experience that a guest is supposed to have when he/she attends the event. For year on year the mentality of many facility managers and team executives was 'throw open the doors and let 'em in'. When the game is over, 'throw open the exit gates and herd 'em out'. Starting in the late 1980s, sports organisations began making efforts to ensure a positive, enjoyable 'total experience' for their guests. Guest services departments were formed. Training and retraining of event staff were brought to the forefront. Customer service representatives were in touch with patrons before, during and, if needed, after their visit to the venue. What were once known to be separate functions of security, ushers, ticket takers and medical staff were now positioned under the single umbrella of event services. Security guards, long known for their battle-axe demeanour, were now being trained and positioned as more of a guest/public relations job, as opposed to that of a nightclub bouncer. Teams were also making decisions on whether to run various service departments themselves (event services, concessions, parking etc.) or to outsource these services to private specialised companies. In the late 1990s, teams even became involved in managing the facilities that they played in (and often times built and own). Two prime examples of this are the NHL Los Angeles Kings at Staples Center and the NBA Miami Heat at American Airlines Arena. The main reason for sport entertainment organisations doing all the aforementioned activities is control. Teams feel that they have a better chance of satisfying a guest if they are the ones who set policy and procedure and hire and train management and staff of areas such as event services and guest relations. The following scenario (see box) is common at public assembly facilities that are owned by a municipality that still maintains some operating control.

Municipal Stadium is located in a large city in the northeast USA. The stadium is owned by the city but, for the most part, operated by the primary tenant, a baseball team called the Hammerheads. The one area that was not controlled by the Hammerheads was the operation of the parking lot. The lot was the responsibility of the city. The city would put out bids from established private parking companies. The city, feeling the economic crunch of 11 September 2001, awarded the contract to the lowest bidder. The company had many contracts to operate lots and at times had trouble assigning trained, competent and cordial individuals to man the lot booths. This resulted in the company having to hire inferior individuals, many who drift from job to job due to their inability to hold a job. Complaints of rudeness toward customers, poorly groomed attendants, cash boxes being 'short' at the end of the day started to surface. The city, to get an even better deal, signed the company to a 10-year contract. The contract also stipulated that the company had full autonomy over the individuals who were hired. The city was stuck.

The city may have been stuck, but it was the Hammerheads that were feeling the heat and taking a major hit on their image. When an individual drives to an event, who is likely to be the first individual they will come in contact with? The parking attendant. This is the start of the live event portion of their leisure experience. Most individuals attending the event are not versed in the details of the parking lot operation. They are going to a Hammerheads' game, therefore the Hammerheads must be in charge of everything. If the attendant is rude, it's the Hammerheads' fault. It gives them a black eye and has afforded the guest a negative experience before they have even turned off their car. Lessons that can be learned here include giving more thought to certain provisions placed in a contract. From the Hammerheads' side, it may mean having complete control of all service-oriented operations. For the city, it may mean having a say on employees hired by a private contractor and also requiring the contractor to provide a complete guest relations training programme for all new hires. In fact, training programmes should be required for all individuals working for a team or facility who will come into contact (even the slightest) with the public. Staff positions that should have this requirement are as follows:

- switchboard operators
- advance and event day ticket sellers
- parking lot attendants
- ticket takers
- concession stand workers and in-seat vendors
- usher and security personnel
- lavatory porters and matrons
- event maintenance staff
- event medical staff
- concierge, club/suite and guest services personnel.

Training programmes should be both job specific and organisation specific. In other words, both the popcorn vendor and ticket seller should receive the same kind of guest/fan relations training. Such training would include how to greet a guest, how to present proper posture, how to handle special situations, how to be proactive as opposed to reactive, in special situations.

THE LEISURE EXPERIENCE WITHIN THE SPORTS ENTERTAINMENT EVENT

As previously mentioned, the development of a feeling or opinion by a guest/potential guest toward a sports entertainment organisation or event begins long before the actual event takes place. The consumer will begin forming opinions and feelings about the entity shortly after they are made aware that there is an event that they may want to attend. The following eight steps chronologically depict the leisure 'experience' as presented through a sports entertainment event.

1. *The potential guest becomes aware of the event.* This step may seem mundane or oversimplified, but it is an important one. This is the first interaction a potential guest will have with an organisation or event. It is the 'jumping off' point of another leisure experience for the individual.

2. *The potential guest weighs their options and takes into consideration both internal and external variables.* 'Options' can be other leisure time activities that the individual enjoys and is able to participate in. Internal variables include the time availability and financial resources of the individual that will allow them to attend/participate in the event. External variables can include

the aforementioned 'other activities' fighting for the individual's discretionary dollars; the actual discretionary dollars that are available and the availability of tickets.

3. *The potential guest becomes a 'guest'.* The individual purchases a ticket. With this purchase, the process of having the individual as a repeat buyer and customer has begun. The reason for this is that the guest has come in contact with a member of a service-oriented product extension ... the ticket seller. The ticket seller not only sells tickets to current events, they are selling tickets by their demeanour and actions to future events.

4. *The first point of contact for the guest.* If it is not the ticket seller, it might have been the switchboard operator who answered the phone when the then potential customer called to enquire about the event. If it is neither, it may well be the parking lot attendant, if the individual(s) are driving to the event. As previously mentioned, the tone and mood of the guests concerning the long-anticipated event/leisure experience may be cemented before the guest gets out of his/her car. If the guest walks or takes public transportation to the event, the first point of contact will most likely be a ticket taker or entrance gate personnel.

5. *Entering the facility.* The 'new millennium' guest will notice items and happenings on entering a facility that long-ago guests would be oblivious to. Items of concern should be: cleanliness of facility (for now the entrance area); courteousness of event staff; directions (signage) to seats; restrooms; security; guest relations; timeliness of services; and overall ambience.

6. *The event starts!* The guest will still look for excellent service, a clean environment, a safe, family-oriented setting and, of course, will express some interest in the core product (the actual event).

7. *During the event.* The guest will want all the aforementioned comforts and services, a safe and sound ambience. They will also look for alternate means of interest-holding entertainment. This could include 'dot' races on the scoreboard, in-between innings promotions, time-out promotions, popular music that encourages audience participation, trivia contests. Many organisations have a roving 'reporter' who will conduct some of the activities within the seating area during play stoppage.

8. *The end.* The individual's leisure experience does not end when the clock goes to zero or the last out is made. It actually does not end until they are safe at home or other place of lodging. Guests are not repeat guests until they buy a ticket and return. The team, organisation and facility must show concern and pamper the guests until they are off the property, either in the car or walking. Some signs of concern and pampering are ... a simple farewell greeting to guests as they are leaving (good night; thank you for coming). Event personnel should say this to as many exiting guests as possible. The external PA system should also be thanking the guests for their attendance, to arrive home safely and a statement saying that the team hopes they come back again. Roving towtrucks and wreckers should be available to assist with dead batteries and other car problems (locked in keys).

CONCLUSION

Sports are entertainment. Games people go to watch are sports entertainment events. These events, while different, have many common characteristics that other social and leisure time events have. Guests need to be serviced at all events, regardless of the type or size. Sports entertainment events no longer attract low to middle income 'jock types'. Many sports entertainment events attract a well-to-do, high-society crowd. These guests may not care as much or understand the core product as much, but they are guests and need to be treated as such. Guests need to be entertained while they are being entertained. If the team and/or facility accomplish all this, repeat business can be almost assured.

Questions

1. Discuss the difference(s) in the reason and purpose for attending a sporting event for those living in the 1950s and those living in the 2000s.

2. The chapter discusses the idea of a sporting event being the same as or close to an entertainment event. Discuss the logic that supports this theory.

3. The author writes of the leisure experience within a sports entertainment event consisting of eight chronological steps. List and briefly discuss these steps.

Reference

Hardy, S., Mullin, B. J. and Sutton, W. A. (2000) *Sport Marketing* 2nd edn. Champaign, IL: Human Kinetics.

CHAPTER 23

Service quality at Insight Leisure Management: the role of the mystery shopper

John Harris and Julian Leybourne

INTRODUCTION

The following case study provides a comprehensive overview of service quality within sport and leisure. In the early 1990s Mills (1992) questioned whether quality would be the buzzword of the decade or just another passing fad. As we continue to become more and more discerning in our conspicuous consumption of products and services it is apparent that service quality is, arguably, more important than ever before. The highly transitory and intangible nature of sport and leisure service necessitates a clear understanding of service quality on the part of all providers.

Drawing on Insight Leisure Management's extensive experience of undertaking mystery visits (customer service audits) throughout England and Wales in a range of private and public sport and leisure facilities, this case utilises real worked examples of service quality. The concept of service quality is critically assessed through focusing on the dynamics of the gym induction. Here it is apparent that many of the basic elements of service quality are ignored. At a time when the dominant ideology of best value necessitates continuous improvement on the part of all service providers, our research highlights that much still needs to be done to improve service quality within sport and leisure.

ABOUT THE COMPANY

Insight Leisure Management (ILM) was formed by Julian Leybourne in 1994, following more than 20 years of working in the leisure industry for a number of leading organisations including Roger Quinton Associates and the Oasis Leisure Centre, Swindon. Based in Monmouthshire (South Wales), Insight Leisure Management undertakes a range of consultancy services including training and development, contract/trust preparations and mystery visits. Dr John Harris has undertaken mystery visits for the company since 1997 and it is this specific part of the organisation's operation that is the focus of this case. During the course of this study, we will explore the importance of mystery visits within the current context of best value. What follows is a snapshot of the work undertaken in this area so far, highlighting some of the key aspects that have emerged over the course of more than 200 service audits during the last eight years.

WHAT ARE MYSTERY VISITS?

A mystery visit (or customer service audit) is a form of participant observation where the researcher interacts with the people being observed. Its roots lie in the field of cultural anthropology where the researcher travelled to some far-off location with the aim of uncovering details of how individuals perceived reality. He/she aimed to become part of the group being studied while at the same time remaining distanced from it in order to analyse the world around them. The strength of ethnographic investigation is its potential to capture the finer details underlying the cultural context in which the observer is located (see Hammersley and Atkinson 1995; Spradley 1980). Similarly, the implicit aim of the mystery visit is to experience the 'natural' everyday customer experience within a particular setting. Such studies are undertaken covertly to ensure that the service experienced is as 'natural' as possible. Mystery shopping is a technique that has been used in the financial services, fast food and hotel sectors. In the 1970s more than a quarter of banks, with over $300 million in deposits, used mystery shopping programmes (Leeds 1995).

At a time when people are becoming more and more discerning in their consumption of goods and service it is inevitable that the quality of service on offer assumes an added significance. As competition increases and individuals are faced with a much wider choice of goods and services expectations are bound to change. In terms of researching customer satisfaction and levels of service quality, it is noticeable that the potential of observational methods as a tool for data collection has not been fully recognised (Grove and Fisk 1992).

A NOTE ON SERVICE QUALITY

It is the customer who judges service quality. Judgements are made on individuals' perceptions, for as Roger Quinton (1993) noted 'perceptions are the real truths'. Our expectations of service influence the resulting level of satisfaction. Service quality is a combination of a network of variables and is something that has been looked at by many researchers in an attempt to identify the most significant components. Parasuraman, Zeithaml and Berry (1988: 13) describe it as 'an abstract and elusive concept' and it is also something that is frequently ignored as it is felt that it is difficult to measure. While there have been numerous studies within areas such as banking and hospitality the role of mystery visits in the leisure industry has received scant attention.

During the course of every visit ILM aim to highlight how the total service experience unfolds and develops. On any visit, the conclusions reached and opinions expressed are based on the condition of the centre at the time of the visit.

Leybourne's definition of customer care highlights the philosophy that underpins our inspections:

> An active and ongoing demonstration of how an organisation cares for the total customer experience through its staff, its services and in the environment in which this takes place.

The focus of attention is the attitude and sales orientation of staff and the degree of frontline marketing and customer care demonstrated by staff during the time of ILM's visit. This approach identifies key aspects of the service encounter that would be hard to view in any other form. Quality, within the service sector, is particularly important due to the following factors:

- *intangibility*: services cannot be seen or tested before they are bought
- *inseparability*: services are sold first, then produced and consumed at the same time
- *variability*: the quality of service depends on who provides it, when and where
- *perishability*: services can't be stored.

Centre visits encompass a detailed and independent assessment to test and record a number of quality standards with regards to the delivery of services met. Ghobadian, Speller and Jones (1994) suggest that the service sector has emerged as the dominant force in the global economy and services now eclipse goods in the generation of business and the creation of jobs. This move towards 'creating interactions' produces the possibility of new occupations and new ways of facilitating lifestyle consumption (Maguire 2001). Service quality is the critical determinant of competitiveness and profitability. The negative and potentially damaging result of poor service quality and the relative high costs of attracting new customers, rather than retaining existing ones, through high-quality services clearly highlights its importance. Local government leisure services are faced with these same pressures, since leisure is not a mandatory service and customers, therefore, have the final choice to participate.

In today's society where an ever more discerning customer expects quality service, we can view superior service quality not only as a prerequisite for success but arguably as an essential factor for survival itself (Parasuraman, Zeithaml and Berry 1988). Our experiences of undertaking more than 200 mystery visits throughout England and Wales has provided us with a plethora of service encounters (both good and bad) that have enabled us to build a comprehensive profile of service quality in the industry. The service encounter is a unique experience, specific to time, place and environment. Despite the growing literature relating to service quality within sport and leisure, which although still not comparable to the depth of information in its sister disciplines such as tourism and hospitality, it is noticeable that mystery visits are rarely mentioned. Mystery visits can have an important role to play in developing service quality as managers often provide what they feel are important service attributes and fail to address the real issues impacting on customer satisfaction. Only by understanding the needs, wants and aspirations of users can management design and implement their service offers to achieve a sustainable, competitive advantage (see Erstad 1998).

The report produced after each individual inspection includes a summary of recommendations that may be used as part of a continuous improvement strategy to support client council's best value evidence compliance. This state-of-the-art evaluation methodology of leisure service can form an essential output management tool towards achieving independent evidence of best value.

MYSTERY VISITS IN THE CONTEXT OF BEST VALUE

Following the general election of 1997 that brought Labour to power with a landslide victory, local government awaited an announcement by the New Labour government on the replacement to compulsory competitive tendering (CCT) legislation. CCT was generally considered to be disruptive to local government leisure management due to the strong focus on commercial and cost factors.

In January 1999 the following statement was issued in a keynote speech from the Houses of Parliament:

> Local people should not have to put up with failing public services and the government will not hesitate to intervene to prevent the worst excesses of inefficiency and waste. (Armstrong 1999)

The critical tone of this statement created significant debate in leisure management publications, as very little detail was available on the content and methodologies of best value (BV) at this time. In April 2000 the government introduced the duty of continual improvement of public services. Local authorities have to deliver their services to clear standards of cost and quality but provided by the most economic, efficient and effective means available. Each local authority in England and Wales must publish an annual best value performance plan (BVPP) and review all their services every five years to ensure that they are adhering to continual improvement principles.

Each service review must show that the local authority has applied the principles of continual improvement to services structured against the broad issues of challenging why and how the service is provided, comparing its performance with others and competing fairly, transparently and with rigour. The authority must show that it has embraced the principles of fair competition in deciding who should deliver the service by consulting local users and residents on their expectations about the service. Hence, local authorities are required to show that they are improving the way in which services are delivered to achieve stakeholder value.

Local authorities must review their services on the foregoing principles and it is these reviews that are inspected by the Audit Commission's Inspection Service, to ensure that services are well managed and have the potential to improve. Inspections consider the degree to which services meet the local authorities' own corporate aims and objectives, their cost effectiveness and the quality and customer focus of the service delivered. BV is likely to be one of the most important developments to affect the management of local government. The 410 local authorities in England and Wales spend £70 billion a year providing services for over 52 million people. Income is sourced in many ways, with the council tax raising just 25% in 1999 to 2000. The balance of income is made up from central government (estimated at 48%), non-domestic rates from local businesses (25%), while the remaining 2% comes from direct charges for local authority services (Local Government Association 2001).

In the context of leisure services, which is a discretionary provision, the level of income raised by direct charges is significant and made up from swimming, lettings and other sports charges at source. The volatility of this income is dependent on many factors, including market forces, personal choice and perceived quality of service. The effect of good management practice on perceived service quality and customer satisfaction is a stated core principle of best value. Kerr (2001), in a presentation to leisure industry professionals, stated that: 'Best value is good management and good management is your day job.'

Whether democratic consultation with key community stakeholders could be achieved is still uncertain. Best value is structured on two levels and is a process leading to a practical outcome. Liddle (1999) explained that best value is based on one level of continuous self-assessment and the second level on the practical outcome of a measurable improvement in service quality together with the direct relationship between quality and cost. The principle of satisfied customers is generally regarded as being at the heart of a customer-centric business philosophy and the role of service quality is widely recognised as being 'a critical determinant for the success of an organisation in today's competitive environment' (Frost and Kumar 2000). ILM's mystery visits programme is one way of measuring the quality of service being delivered. Mystery visits play an increasingly important role in determining quality and customer satisfaction. These 'reality checks' help inspectors compile evidence generators as a measure of local authorities' performance in the delivery of service.

THE VISITS

Two auditors (one male and one female) who test a wide range of services available to the customer undertake each mystery visit. These are recorded using a simple performance checklist based on the following grading: one, excellent; two, good; three, fair; four, poor; five, bad; and six, very bad. In addition, comprehensive notes are taken to support the scores given. Scores may be seen at the end of this report with overall score averages shown in graphical representation measuring site performance and compared against UK averages. UK averages have been taken from extrapolated score results of over 200 site visits undertaken during the last eight years. ILM also include graphical analysis based on percentile performances in the final report.

As part of our overall auditing of sport and leisure centres one area that has caused us particular concern is gym inductions (see Leybourne and Harris 1999). Although ILM have seen a general level of competent technical knowledge among instructors, particularly in terms of their understanding of the mechanistic functioning of the body, it is visibly evident that the 'people skills' demonstrated are particularly poor. From our experience, sessions are often rushed affairs with little time or scope for clarification or questioning on the part of the customer.

Disturbingly, ILM have been subjected to a number of group inductions on our visits where anything up to six people are inducted at the same time. Many staff fail to distinguish between the more experienced gym user and those requiring extra attention and guidance. There is seemingly little differentiation or understanding of individual needs and, as such, organisations fail to address the basic needs of the customer. In a number of these group sessions it is rare that all inductees will be afforded the opportunity to try out all of the equipment within the gym. Given that some machines are more complex to operate than others, this could mean that having been passed as 'competent' to use the facilities, many newly inducted customers will experience many exercise stations for the first time, totally unsupervised. In addition to the obvious health and safety concerns that this brings forth it is worth highlighting that far from viewing group inductions as commercially viable sessions, it should be noted that high attrition rates often stem from poorly structured induction programmes. Fitness Industry Association (FIA) (2000) research shows that in public health and fitness centres over 66% of people quit within the first six months.

The gym is a dynamic social space where dominant ideologies are visibly portrayed. They are also gendered spaces where idealised notions of the body are analysed and assessed (see Philips and Drummond 2001). Mediated images of the body beautiful have placed a greater currency on the body than at any other time in our history (see Choi 2000; Shilling 1993; Sparkes 1997). What all this means is that for many people, visiting a gym can be quite a daunting experience. ILM have been on numerous group inductions with individuals who have rarely, if ever, visited a gym before. Many are very conscious of their body shape and are unsure how to use certain gymnasium machinery. Yet our general experience is that these individuals are treated no differently from the experienced gym user. We have often wondered how many of these individuals return to the gym after such poor, rushed induction sessions. FIA (2000) research shows that only 46% of users felt that staff had helped them achieve their fitness goals.

IS THE CUSTOMER ALWAYS RIGHT?

The interaction between an organisation's staff and its customers is the key to its very survival. Throughout the course of any visit ILM try to experience as many service encounters as possible. Before the actual visit takes place the centre is contacted by telephone on three separate occasions to measure the telephone response rate, attitude and product knowledge of the staff. It is here that problems are also frequently encountered. One organisation that ILM audited developed their own glossy customer charter promising, among other things, that they would endeavour to answer the telephone within four rings. After setting a new record of 36 rings the phone was finally answered with no apology forthcoming (this is not an isolated phenomenon). In addition to the very fact that they had failed in the simple task of answering the phone, they made it even worse for themselves by their original claim and the fact that no apology was offered. It is worth noting here that our aim as mystery visitors is to experience the service encounter in exactly the same way that the 'average' customer would. However, an example such as this is probably less of a 'natural' one as most people would undoubtedly have given up and put the phone down well before we did. How many potential customers are lost in this way?

To make the customer feel special and unique, it is apparent that organisations must cater to their specific needs. Do leisure organisations really endeavour to build relationships with their clientele? Many centres have their own screening forms that you are asked to fill in before commencing the gym induction. In what could and should be a positive and worthwhile step it appears as if these forms are merely a procedural necessity rather than a valuable relationship-building tool. To test procedures and standards we usually highlight a particular complaint such as shin splints on the forms only to find, to our dismay, that the instructor will often ask us to jump on the treadmill straight away. This is not, though, the result of a poor subject knowledge, because in an examination the instructor would probably easily identify what shin splints are and what exercises should be avoided. The fault here lies all too simply in not reading the form. In an initial encounter a screening form can provide the member of staff with an effective icebreaker and useful conversation points with the customer. The initial induction is a rare opportunity to begin to understand needs, wants and aspirations. For the operator this also presents an opportunity to convert this encounter into an effective sales platform. Building relationships with customers is the key to success in buyer-seller inter-action (Dwyer, Schurr and Oh 1987). Communication and dialogue offer the opportunity to treat customers as individuals (Peppers and Rogers 1995).

CONCLUDING REMARKS

Following the expansion of the service economy (circa late 1960s) consumer industries such as health and fitness have placed an increased emphasis on frontline service (Pine and Gilmore 1998). This interaction between the customer and the service provider needs closer analysis. Maguire (2001: 398) notes how the relational skills of service providers 'continue to be undervalued, even as front-line service becomes increasingly important to the success of businesses and to the broader consumer industries'. Our in-depth analysis of leisure service provision across England and Wales would certainly support this view.

The audits undertaken have pointed towards the need for increased education and training programmes for frontline staff involved in leisure services. It is predicted that mystery visits will continue to grow with the increasing emphasis and importance now placed on service quality. The audit can form an integral part of an organisation's customer relationship management (CRM) strategy. It is an invaluable tool, used to review, refine and improve the total customer experience. ILM encourage site management to take ownership of these reports as a valuable management tool to identify good practice, reward excellence and innovation, improve unacceptable aspects of service and to adopt a healthy and competitive attitude between sites. The audits may expose training needs for individual staff, which should be accepted as a positive aspect of the report. Other aspects may identify additional resources or investment required.

Utilising mystery visitors is a cost-effective, independent and impartial assessment of service quality as seen, experienced and reported by the customer. They offer a critical evaluation of service quality, which, if addressed as a core management principle, will reap dividends at an operational and strategic level by working towards a differentiated service and thus pursuing competitive advantage.

Traditional research methods such as attitude surveys may be of value but customer satisfaction can be misleading considering that the majority of users may be satisfied with the quality of service. Recent best value inspections have revealed fairly high levels of customer satisfaction and yet many of these local authorities have been awarded low-quality ratings for poor service (Department for Transport, Local Government and the Regions 2001). This dichotomy may be explained by customer satisfaction being relative to their expectations. Customer expectation management is at the heart of a developing a customer relationship management strategy and effective marketing programme. Raising expectations through improved quality standards will have a positive effect in that the strategy is likely to yield considerably more customers, visiting more frequently, with higher spends and with reduced attrition rates.

Questions

1. Why are mystery visits an effective way of measuring service quality?

2. How can gym inductions be improved to cater for the needs of individual users?

3. What makes a good mystery visitor? Highlight the skills she/he must possess.

References

Armstrong, H. (1999) 'Second reading of the Local Government Bill'. Houses of Parliament, London. 12 January.

Choi, P. (2000) *Femininity and the Physically Active Woman*. London: Routledge.

Department for Transport, Local Government and the Regions (2001) http://www.local-regions.dtlr.gov.uk/bestvalue/indicators/usersurvey/index.htm

Dwyer, R., Schurr, P. and Oh, S. (1987) 'Developing buyer-seller relationships', *Journal of Marketing*, 51, 11–27.

Erstad, M. (1998) 'Mystery shopping programmes and human resource management', *International Journal of Contemporary Hospitality Management*, 10, 1, 34–8.

Fitness Industry Association (2000) *Why People Quit UK Health and Fitness Clubs: A Survey of Lapsed Members*. London: FIA.

Frost, F. and Kumar, M. (2000) 'INTSERVQUAL – an internal adaptation of the GAP model in a large service organisation', *Journal of Services Marketing*, 14, 5, 358–70.

Ghobadian, A., Speller, S. and Jones, M. (1994) 'Service quality: concepts and models', *International Journal of Quality and Reliability Management*, 11, 9, 43–56.

Grove, S. and Fisk, R. (1992) 'Observational data collection methods for services marketing: an overview', *Journal of the Academy of Marketing Science*, 20, 3, 217–24.

Hammersley, M. and Atkinson, P. (1995) *Ethnography: Principles in Practice* (2nd edn). London: Routledge.

Kerr, J. (2001) *Best Value*. Paper presented at the Institute of Sport and Recreation Management South Wales and West branch seminar, Cardiff.

Leeds, B. (1995) 'Mystery shopping: from novelty to necessity', *Bank Marketing*, 27, 6, 7.

Leybourne, J. and Harris, J. (1999) 'Customer care keeps your profits healthy', *Recreation*, April, 20–1.

Liddle, D. (1999) 'Best value – the impact on libraries: practical steps in demonstrating best value', *Library Management*, 20, 4, 206–14.

Local Government Association (2001) http://www.lga.gov.uk/lga/blg/index.htm

Maguire, J. S. (2001) 'Fit and flexible: the fitness industry, personal trainers and emotional service labour', *Sociology of Sport Journal*, 18, 379–402.

Mills, P. (1992) 'Quality and quality assurance' in Mills, P. (ed.) *Quality in the Leisure Industry*. Harlow: Longman.

Parasuraman, A., Zeithaml, V. and Berry, L. (1988) 'SERVQUAL: a multiple-item scale for measuring consumer perceptions of service quality', *Journal of Retailing*, 64, 1, 12–40.

Peppers, D. and Rogers, M. (1995) 'A new marketing paradigm: share of customer, not market share', *Managing Service Quality*, 5, 3, 48–51.

Philips, J. and Drummond, M. (2001) 'An investigation into the body image perception, body satisfaction and exercise expectations of male fitness leaders: implications for professional practice', *Leisure Studies*, 20, 95–105.

Pine, B. and Gilmore, J. (1998) 'Welcome to the experience economy', *Harvard Business Review*, July–August, 97–105.

Quinton, R. (1993) *Quality in Leisure*. Paper presented at the Institute of Leisure and Amenity Management regional seminar, Worthing.

Shilling, C. (1993) *The Body and Social Theory*. London: Sage.

Sparkes, A. (1997) 'Reflections on the socially constructed physical self' in Fox, K. (ed.) *The Physical Self: From Motivation to Well-being*. Champaign, IL: Human Kinetics.

Spradley, J. (1980) *Participant Observation*. New York: Holt, Reinhart and Wilson.

CHAPTER 24

Football Revenue Management

Gerald Barlow

INTRODUCTION

This is a subject that, since the events related to ITV Digital's (Carlton and Granada) demise in May 2002 over television's funding of the football leagues, has become very sensitive, with many inches of newspaper comment, television and radio coverage. But in reality, it has been a major issue for many years, see comment by Hearne (2002) and Speck (2002). It is amazing that only two football league clubs (Accrington Stanley and Aldershot Town FC) have actually gone into final bankruptcy not to be saved at the last minute or successfully found new owners during the period of receivership. However, many clubs from the highly regarded Chelsea FC to York City FC have, over the years suffered financial problems. This case sets out to identify areas where football clubs already do use or could consider using revenue/yield management techniques. This is particularly poignant in the current situation as a result of the effects of the demise of ITV Digital and the current effect on the English football league clubs.

REVENUE MANAGEMENT

Revenue management (RM) or yield management (YM) is a concept that originated in the airline industry and has migrated to other business arenas. Hotels, rental cars, cruise lines, theatres, golf courses and container shipping companies are now applying RM to maximise their revenue. RM techniques are used to forecast customer demand, optimise price and the availability of products and services. The *Wall Street Journal* called it 'the number one emerging business strategy – a practice poised to explode'.

SEALING THE LEAK

In today's dynamic communications world, it's a certainty that organisations are leaking revenue. But do they know how much? Typical industry revenue leakage is more than 5%, and some organizations are losing as much as 15% (http://www.andersen.com/website.nsf/content/IndustriesTechnologyMediaandCommunicationsResourcesRevenueMgtHome!OpenDocument).

There can be little doubt that football clubs/business are in most cases leaking revenue and need to learn how to manage their revenue better. The first issue to perhaps learn is that it is *revenue* that they need to manage, not simply income. The second is to learn that all areas of revenue can in some way be managed providing certain circumstance can be met. Kimes (1989a), Orkin (1988) and Andersen (1997) have identified eight key elements needed for revenue management to be successful:

- *Perishability of inventory*: seats at a football match are highly perishable: consider an event such as the World Cup 2002, a game like the opening game France verses Senegal, if the seats are not sold by the kick-off, they can *never* be sold. In the case of the World Cup, which is organised by one or a number of countries, many of the countries will have invested heavily in the event and get only this one chance to sell the tickets (no next season chance) and once the game has started, that opportunity has gone for ever. Therefore it is vital to maximise sales.

- *Ability to segment the market*: football clubs usually have a number of market segments, from season ticket holders, through corporate sales to the youth and family game tickets or seats. (See the examples from Birmingham City FC and Norwich City FC later in the chapter.)

- *Product sold in advance of consumption*: there are a number of areas of pre-sales from season ticket holders, through the corporate season and month seats and boxes, to the block seats some clubs sell for short periods, e.g. one month or four games for example.

- *Fluctuation in demand*: demand is clearly likely to fluctuate and is affected by many issues, from the formation of the team or the opposition, to the time of day or year, etc.

- *High fixed costs*: these are extremely high, due to the fixed costs of the ground and the facilities, particularly with so few opportunities to use and sell the product per year. For example, take a UK premiership club: it will have a maximum of 29 home league and cup games in which to maximise sales and then only if it reaches the later stages of both league and FA cups. This will be increased if they qualify for a European competition or have a series of friendly games. (Twenty league clubs provides 19 home games, FA Cup from 0 to four depending on the home or away draw, Worthington league cup, a maximum of six games.)

- *Low marginal costs*: this is the cost of selling one extra seat, which is clearly very low.

- *High marginal production costs*: this is the cost of increasing the output or of providing extra capacity, for example more seats etc. This is clearly very high in most football clubs. Some of the smaller clubs can arrange for extra temporary stands to be erected, but this is still at a relatively high cost. However, for many of the clubs the only way the capacity can be increased is by actually developing a new stand layout, i.e. knocking down and rebuilding part of or all of the stadium, or relocation as in the case of Bolton Wanderers and the Reebok stadium.

- *Limited capacity*: Clearly, this is limited and to change it will take time and probably considerable cost. A football stadium capacity is also limited by external factors and organisations such as health and safety, local authority, fire authority and the police who all play a part in the approval of stadium capacity.

Kimes (1989b) also identified five core requirements for the operation of a revenue or yield management system:

- *Booking patterns*: revenue management systems require information on the past sales for specific dates to be maintained. In the case of football clubs this should be easy, as they should be able to maintain records for not only days and dates, but also for specific opposition. (This is considerably easier for a football club than most organisations, due to the few games played at the home ground per season.)

- *Knowledge of demand patterns by market segment*: this is similar to the previous point, but needs to be broken into all the segments the organisation identifies.

- *An overbooking policy*: this is something that football clubs may only consider in the case of cup matches, where demand can often exceed supply, but even then do not actually operate this policy as it is totally impractical.

- *Knowledge of the effect of price changes*: this is an area that the clubs might have considered but which they may not often have recorded, again this may be an effect of the low number of games and opportunities to use the facilities.

- *A good information system*: if revenue management is to be effective then a football club must be able to obtain, store and analyse data and information. This should not be too complex as the number of events is limited, but it needs to be fully recorded, not simply focused on, for example the pre-sales and season tickets, but also include the number of season or hospitality tickets declined, the number of enquiries, not just those that produced sales so that the true demand can be established.

IMPLEMENTING REVENUE MANAGEMENT

This chapter sets out to outline how a UK football club could consider implementing revenue management to allow it to maximise its income and therefore its profits.

The first stage is to identify the sources of revenue:

- ticket sales
- sponsorship
- advertising
- complementary services
- television revenue
- merchandise sales.

Let us now try to identify ways for each source to employ revenue management techniques.

Match revenue

Ticket sales are one of the main areas of revenue that permits a football club to operate in a variety of market segments and with a range of prices. It is the area of revenue and sales that has perhaps the most obvious link to the traditional yield/revenue management operations, i.e. individual sales/price interaction, where price and customer decisions are clearly involved.

Ticket sales

The sale of tickets is initially segmented into two categories, season tickets and match day tickets.

Season tickets

These are tickets sold in advance of the new season and permit the holder to attend all home league games, along with preferential treatment for home cup games (this varies between clubs). Season tickets have a restricted allocation and as such can be seen as having a fixed capacity. The ticket type can have a variety of prices depending on its location within the ground or can simply be a one-price season ticket, where only a restricted number of seats are available for season ticket sales. Throughout this chapter examples will be taken from two football league clubs of differing sizes, Birmingham City FC just promoted to the Premier League, and Norwich City FC the team that lost to Birmingham City in the 2002 First Division playoff final.

Examples of current practice

As can be seen from Table 24.1 the season tickets are broken into a number of market segments and seating position within the ground (stand) and Norwich City Football Club have, for example, started to use an age segmentation within their sales (see Table 24.2)

If the clubs were to offer a full revenue management process to this they could offer a number of price incentives related to the time of purchase, for example, offer season tickets to cover more than one season, as Gillingham Town FC did for the 2002–3 season where there is a one-, two- or three-year season ticket option available with a reduction in the overall annual price for those people buying a two- or three-year season ticket. Similarly, as the beginning of the season gets closer so the price could increase in an incremental way, until all the allocation were sold. If tickets were still available after the first game of the new season, then the tickets could still be sold, but at an appropriately reduced price.

Match day tickets

There is currently no UK football club (or at least there is no evidence of any) that only sells its tickets through season ticket sales, unlike some American football clubs. Those tickets that are not available for sale via a season ticket allocation are held back for sale to the public on a match-by-match basis and are available to both home and away fans. These tickets are often available in advance from the ground or in some cases via a club internet sales offices. Again, this type of ticket is sold on the basis of market segments, seat position (stand) and also type of game.

Table 24.1 *Season tickets data for season 2002–3*

Details	Birmingham City FC Area	Price	Norwich City FC Area	Price	Price
	Membership fee			Pre-30.06	From 01.07
			Adult, senior citizen and student	15	20
			Junior	12	
			In exile	10	
				Member	Non-member
	Olympic Gallery		*Norwich & Peterborough and Barclay Stands*		
	Adult	440	Adult	325	325
	Concession	220	Concession	190	190
BCFC non-single seats	*Family Stand Railway lower blocks 6 and 7*		16–21	220	220
	Adult	292	12–16; over 75	170	172
	Concession	146	Under 12	65	65
	Tilton Corner		*South Stand*		
	Adult	372	Adult	na	325
	Concession	185.50	Concession	na	190
	Tilton Road		16–21	na	220
	Adult	390	Under 12	na	65
	Concession	194.50	*Coca-Cola family area*		
	Kop Corner		Adult	295	295
	Adult	426	Concession	175	175
	Concession	213	16–21	220	220
	Kop		12–16	39	39
	Adult	493	Under 12	29	29
	Concession	246.50	*City Stand Wings*		
	Main Stand Flanks		Adult	na	350
	Adult	438	Concession	na	205
	Concession	219	16–21	na	245
	Main Stand Centre		Under 12	na	65
	Adult	463	*City Stand Centre*		
	Concession	231.50	Adult	na	420
	Railway Lower		Concession	na	420
	Adult	367.50	16–21	na	420
	Concession	184	*59ers & County Lounges*		
	Club Class		Adult	na	420
	Adult	544	Concession	na	420
	No Concession		16–21	na	420
	Club Class	tbc	Directors' Box	1700	1700
			Executive viewing lounge	1150	1150
			Jarrold top of terrace	920	920
	President Seating	tbc	Jarrold top of terrace no meal	595	595
			Club 101	595	595
			Car park	na	140

Table 24.2 *Match day ticket pricing structure for Norwich City FC*

Seating area	Type	Classification of ticket				
		A	*B*	*Match day saver*	*Super saver*	*Super saver special*
Norwich & Peterborough Stand, South, Barclay Stands, Wensum and Thorpe areas	Adult	20	18	14	10	6
	Concession	14	13	8	6	4
	Under 16	14	13	8	1	1
	Under 12	6	5	4	1	1
Coca-Cola family area	Adult	18	16	13	10	6
	Concession	13	11	8.50	6	4
	Under 16	5	4	3	1	1
	Under 12	3	2	1	1	1
Geoffrey Watling City Stand Wings	Adult	21	19	16	12	8
	Concession	15	14	10	6	4
	Under 16	15	14	10	1	1
	Under 12	6	5	4	1	1
Geoffrey Watling City Stand Centre Seats		22	20	18	13	9
Geoffrey Watling City Stand 59ers/County Lounges		na	20	18	13	9
		22	na	na	na	na
Geoffrey Watling City Stand Castle/Cathedral Lounges		25	22	20	15	10
		Diamond	*Platinum*	*Gold*	*Gold*	*Gold*
Jarrold top of the terrace		70	60	45	45	45
Jarrold top of the terrace no meal		50	40	25	25	25
Executive viewing lounge		80	65	50	50	50
Directors' Box		100	80	60	60	60

Birmingham City Concessions
ES40 holders receive concessionary prices in South Stand block M. only
Concessions – senior citizens (over 60s) and students in full-time education
Under 16s – supporters born on or after 1 September 1985
Under 12s – supporters born on or after 1 September 1989
No concessions in the Geoffrey Watling City Stand Lounges and Centre Seats
No concessions in Jarrold top of the terrace/EVL/Directors' Box

These can be seen as another form of revenue management the football club employs. In the case of Birmingham City games are divided into three different types, AA, A and B category games. AA games are the local derby games and top opposition, in the Nationwide First Division these included Wolverhampton Wanderers FC, West Bromwich Albion FC, Coventry City FC, and Manchester City FC during the 2001–2 season, and for the forthcoming season the teams are likely to be Manchester United FC, Arsenal FC, Aston Villa FC, West Bromwich Albion FC, and so on. The A category clubs represent top class games, such as clubs in the top quarters of the league in the previous season, those relegated from the Premier League (in the case of the First Division) or those clubs likely to bring in larger crowds; the B category being other teams, lower achieving, or less popular clubs.

This pricing structure is also followed for the early rounds of either of the cups, however, once they have got past round 4 of either cup, any home tie, against a local or top opposition side, the opportunity for an increase in price will arise. However, this policy was not one adopted by Birmingham in the past when the occasion has arisen, with such examples as the division playoffs, but now that they have achieved their initial goal of a place in the Premier League this policy may be readdressed. The 2001–2 season pricing structure for Norwich City is shown in Table 24.2. This involves a game-by-game price variation, segmented by the type of opposition in a similar way to that of Birmingham City FC.

SPONSORSHIP

Football clubs seek sponsorship in many forms. From the obvious shirt sponsorship as seen on all professional teams through a range of inventive ideas, such as:

- hospitality match day sponsorship
- match ball and programme sponsorship
- match day programme page sponsorship.

Team and shirt sponsorship is a long-term contract, operating usually for a minimum of one season, so there is little opportunity to operate a revenue or yield management process, as the price will need to be negotiated and set well in advance of the actual season. The successful club partnerships are very long term, for example the Liverpool/Carlsberg Lager link.

However, with all other types of sponsorship being based on a single event, there is the opportunity for revenue management, similar to the price mechanism operating for seating; that is to classify the games in a similar manner, with the prices varying in accordance with the anticipated demand.

ADVERTISING

There are numerous opportunities for advertising within a football club, which will include:

- ground advertising
- seat advertising
- internal and external poster advertising
- programme advertising
- website advertising
- additional shirt advertising (small usually shoulder-high ads on the shirts)
- player car advertising
- fanzine magazine advertising.

Some of these are unlikely to be suitable for a revenue management approach, those being situations where the advert is placed in non-perishable areas, such as seat advertising, where the advertisers' information is seen on a whole area of seating and is in place usually for at least a season or a set period of time. Thus the price will be negotiated on a one-off long-term basis. Others, such as website advertising and fanzine advertising, may fall into this category, but could offer opportunities for both long-term revenue generation and the short-term revenue management approach.

Of the rest, some will be long-term fixed advertising, such as the basic round-the-ground advertising, but there is the opportunity from time to time to gain additional revenue. When this occurs revenue management techniques can be used, as there is likely to be a limited capacity and limited opportunity to advertise. Such areas and opportunities will include additional shirt advertising, match day programme advertising and additional round-the-ground advertising. The most likely occasions for these opportunities to occur are in one-off games, home ties in cup competitions, against top crowd-pleasing and drawing teams or local rivals. How can this be possible? It will often rely, of course, on the attendance at the game of a television crew. If the team gets an attractive home draw in one of the cups (i.e. a top, famous team) then the sales and marketing group should immediate plan for the maximisation of that day's revenue, but not just in the gate or match day revenue, but in all the potential revenue. For example the shirts, programmes and ground advertising. Many of today's clubs will have agreements with their main shirt sponsor permitting additional sponsorship on the shirt, e.g. chest or shoulder tags. Similarly, for special games like cups and promotion playoffs, where the game is going to be televised, the club can increase their pitchside advertising by providing additional hoarding to areas not usually used, or by replacing traditional flat advertising boards with three-sided electronic rotation boards, thereby increasing the potential advertising space by a factor of three. Clearly, here is an opportunity for the use of a revenue management approach. Similar reasoning and approach can be used to areas such as one-off games ball sponsorship and the match day programme.

COMPLEMENTARY SERVICES

Within a football ground there are many opportunities for complementary services, some that only the very large and successful clubs can run, like club and ground tours, some that all clubs will run, and include areas like catering, club lotteries etc.

The range of complementary services is very broad but can include:

- concessionary merchandise sales
- football club shops either in the perimeter of the ground or in city centre shopping centres
- catering and bars
- restaurants
- renting out the ground in the off season for leisure events, e.g. pop concerts
- some large clubs now have their own pay-to-view TV channel
- conference and banqueting facilities.

Of these, only the conference and banqueting facilities could be considered suitable for yield management.

TELEVISION REVENUE

This is a very important area of revenue and a very sensitive area for all but the Premier League teams after the much publicised collapse of the sponsorship of the Nationwide League by ITV Digital. But, whichever league a club is in, this sort of advertising is a centrally negotiated, not a club negotiated deal and as such not one suited to club revenue management techniques.

MERCHANDISE SALES

This can be in a number of forms, the first being with the team shirt suppliers which provide the team kit. The revenue will normally come in the form of a commission on the sales of the kit. This can extend to a large range of items from clothing, to posters, books, crockery, linen and so on, usually providing a commission-type income.

The second is through the club's own outlets, either at the ground, via a website, mail order system or through fan shops, usually in shopping centres. It is not possible for areas like this to use revenue management as the produce generally needs to be sold at a fixed retail price, only changing for special offers etc. and then usually after being discounted.

OPERATING REVENUE MANAGEMENT

Even when the organisation is able to offer a range of market segments there are other criteria that will help an organisation considering using yield or revenue management techniques. The following are the core elements identified by Kimes (1989b) as being needed to provide the operation of a revenue management programme:

- a history of past booking patterns
- an overbooking policy

- perishability of the inventory
- knowledge of the effect of price changes
- a good information system.

BOOKING PATTERNS

Most football league clubs will have a pattern of booking for season tickets, dating back many years, which should provide a good set of basic data for use in developing a revenue management programme. This is likely to cover areas such as:

1. history of the previous season ticket sales
2. history of the season ticket holders' name and address
3. history of sales of previous seating areas.

In the case of match day sales the booking pattern is likely to be available based on the following three issues:

1. past history of the date of games and opposition
2. past history of the league position of the opposition at the time of the game and previous seasons, so enabling the AA, B, C team categories to be established for past seasons and sales
3. some possible history of recent sales trends for specific areas of the ground, stands and seating locations. This can only be from recent history, following the Taylor Report of the early 1990s, which resulted in most clubs changing their stadium capacity.

This type of data will be of significant use should the clubs decide to operate a revenue management programme.

OVERBOOKING POLICY

This is a policy widely used in both the airline and hotel industries and has received much criticism from customers and the press in the case of the airlines industry. It is, however, one that is unlikely to be available to a football club, as fans unable to use their ticket are more likely to pass them on to friends and no club could risk having fans in excess of capacity.

PERISHABILITY OF THE INVENTORY

Both the seating and the major part of the advertising capacity of a football club is highly perishable. If a fan supporting Norwich City wishes to watch the match between his team and Birmingham City at home, then he/she will have one opportunity per season to see the game. This cannot be repeated until next season and even then only if both teams retain the same division status. The same is true of

Table 24.3 *Actual total capacity currently available*

Birmingham City FC		Norwich City FC	
Main Stand	4,596	Barclay Stand	6,125
Kop Stand	5,054	City Stand	4,243
Railway Stand	7,866	Norwich & Peterborough	5,799
Tilton Stand	9,123	South Stand	3,001
Family Stand	1,837	Visitors stand	2,185
Executive	779	Disabled	115
Press area	40		
Boxes	633		
Disabled	88		
Total	**30,016**	**Total**	**21,468**
Best attendance at this ground 67,341 (1932)		Best attendance at this ground 43,984 (30 March 1963)	

much of the advertising, for example the match day sponsorship, the pitchside advertising, match ball sponsorship, programme advertising and so on.

The actual capacity itself is regulated and will also affect all the other capacity areas. Table 24.3 shows the maximum capacity available at the two sample clubs.

The reason for the vast difference between the maximum ground capacity and the best attendance figures, in the case of both clubs, is due to the changes in seating and standing capacity brought about as a result of the Taylor Report. Seating capacity is, therefore, highly perishable, as is the advertising for the day's game, be it around the ground, match day programmes, match ball or the game itself. In the case of seasonal advertising, such as team advertising as seen on shirts, permanent ground advertising as seen on stands, seats etc., then this is perishable as far as the revenue potential is concerned. Once the first game has started the number of events in a season is beginning to diminish and so is the value to the advertiser.

KNOWLEDGE OF THE EFFECT OF PRICE CHANGES

In this area, the knowledge will depend on how well the organisation has retained and made available their historic data, be it on sales generally or price and segment specific, and on advertising. In today's IT-driven world, the availability of data is almost endless, it is how well this is screened, stored and used that is important, simply having the data is of little value. The organisation needs to be able to predict levels of demand, ideally for each individual game. On the occasions that the ground reaches full capacity, they should know how much demand has been turned away, or denied, so that they can estimate the level of price elasticity for the future pricing policy within the revenue management strategy.

A GOOD INFORMATION SYSTEM

As stated earlier the information system is vital for the handling, storage and analysis of information. If revenue management is to be truly effective then the information must be constantly maintained and updated. Many operations maintain the information effectively when related to the actual business transacted, but fail to maintain information related to denied business on the occasions when demand exceeds capacity. If this information is not recorded then how do they actually know what the true level of demand for that particular event, day or service is?

IS REVENUE MANAGEMENT BEING USED WITHIN THE FOOTBALL INDUSTRY?

Football clubs clearly have differing segments of fans or customers, they also have a range of products and prices, some of which are sold in advance. The product is highly perishable, the fixed costs are high and the variable cost low, so there is little actually to stop football clubs operating revenue management techniques successfully, but there is little evidence of any of them actually operating a full revenue management system or approach. However, many operate a form of revenue management, generally speaking, the larger and more successful clubs or the ones that treat the whole process as a business. The one restriction on the successful operation of revenue management is that one of the main objectives of the business must be to maximise the business's revenue and profits. This is something that many football clubs do not appear to have as their main aim, to many it appears to simply be a sideline or maybe an obsession, a labour of love or a lifestyle business. To others such as Birmingham City, certainly since the takeover by the new board in 1993, the main aim has been the target of getting the club into the premiership. Assuming the aim is not the maximisation of the revenue then revenue management can't succeed.

Questions

1. Given the current problems faced by football clubs, particularly in the Nationwide FA League how might individual football clubs start to consider using revenue/yield management techniques and what issues should they take into account?

2. Within the Premier League, the income generated via the club's ticket sales is not of such a significant level to warrant the investment of time or money into a technique like yield management. Discuss.

3. Are football clubs being realistic in worrying about the reactions of their season ticket holders in the way that Birmingham City did, when they stop offering special prices to under 15s for mid-week evening games?

References

Arthur Andersen Consulting (1997) *Yield Management in Small and Medium-Sized Enterprises in the Tourist Industry*. Brussels: Directorate-General XXIII, European Commission.

Hearne, B. (2002) 'We could soon lose 30 clubs claims Hearne', *The Guardian*, 22 March.

Kimes, S. E. (1989a) 'The basics of yield management', *Cornell Hotel and Restaurant Administration Quarterly*, 30, 3, 14–19.

Kimes, S. E. (1989b) 'Yield management: a tool for capacity-constrained service firms', *Journal of Operations Management*, 11, 4, 348–63.

Orkin, E. B. (1988) 'Boosting your bottom line with yield management', *Cornell Hotel and Restaurant Administration Quarterly*. 28, 4, 52–6.

Speck, I. (2002) 'We could soon lose 30 clubs claims Hearne'. Available at http://www.soccernet.com (accessed 22 June).

CHAPTER 25

Revenue Management for the Movie Theatre Industry

Robert Oberwetter

INTRODUCTION

An important part of operations management for the sport and leisure service industry is revenue management. It may not be appropriate for all areas of the industry, but there are many situations where it can significantly improve revenues and profits. Current economic conditions combined with recent technological advancements make the movie theatre industry a primary candidate for revenue management applications.

Movie theatres are in the business of leasing movies from movie production companies and showing them for public exhibition in comfortable theatres with large screens, sophisticated sound systems and concession stands. In the late 1990s the movie theatre industry expanded greatly, replacing many outdated theatres with huge stadium-style multiplex theatres. During the boom economy, these companies overexpanded, creating massive debt and, with economic decline and flat ticket sales, this has resulted in overall losses for the industry.

Revenue management has the potential to revitalise this industry. Using applicable techniques, revenue management can increase revenue per movie exhibition. But to do that, movie theatres will need a tremendous amount of business intelligence information, including such things as historical attendance statistics, movie genre, type of ticket sold and time of exhibition. Further information includes ticket sales forecasting, market segmentation, understanding of local and international events that affect attendance (holidays) and the ability to use the sales history of an old movie for a new movie, with no sales history. Once this information is gathered, it can then be combined into a sophisticated computerised revenue management program to maximise revenues per movie exhibition. Maximised revenues can be used to revitalise the overstressed movie theatre industry.

WHAT IS REVENUE MANAGEMENT?

Revenue management, as it relates to service industries, is defined as the process of allocating the right type of capacity, to the right kind of customer, at the right price, in order to maximise revenue and thereby profits (American Airlines 1987). The objective is to balance capacity in relation to demand, while maximising the sales quantity and price for each unit (Oberwetter 2001). Revenue management can be summarily defined as 'the application of disciplined tactics that predict consumer behavior at the micro market level and that optimize product availability and price to maximize revenue growth' (Cross 1997a).

Product characteristics appropriate for revenue management

To determine if a product or service might be appropriate for the application of revenue management, there are six generally agreed on characteristics the product should have (Kimes 1989a and b; Kimes 1997).

The product or service must be perishable

This means the product can't be held in inventory, there is no stock-keeping unit (SKU). Generally, the product is a service, for instance, transporting people from one place to another, providing a hotel room, or providing an automobile at a certain location for use over a set period of time. All these have a time characteristic that causes the service to expire. Once the flight has left, the empty seat is worthless. The same is true for a hotel room and rental car (Kimes 1989b). Every time the opportunity to consume the product passes without a sale, there is lost revenue and that revenue can never be regained.

The capacity of the product or service is limited

There is a finite quantity of the product or service and the available quantity cannot easily be increased or decreased. Using airlines and hotels again as an example, airlines have a fixed number of seats and hotels have a fixed number of rooms; individual units cannot be added and subtracted easily as demand varies. To add more capacity for an airline means spending millions on additional airplanes. Likewise, to add more hotel capacity means spending millions on construction or acquiring new facilities. Similarly, seats and rooms cannot be easily and quickly reduced. So, supply of the product or service is effectively static.

The market can be segmented

Segmenting the market involves creating multiple sales and pricing opportunities for a product that is basically generic. By segmenting the market, the airlines make the same flight appeal to different markets depending on the return flight the outgoing flight is tied to and when the ticket is purchased. A return the same week, purchased at the last minute, will appeal to a business traveller who will pay a higher price; a return after a Saturday stayover, purchased well in advance, will appeal to a vacationer who wants to pay a lower price. Each of these combinations will be priced differently because they are for different market segments. A key factor here is that there is some service or purchase characteristic that the customer can understand as the reason for the price differential (Lieberman 1993). You cannot arbitrarily assign different prices; the product characteristics used to create different market segments must truly differentiate the product. The time of purchase is often used to segment markets.

Advanced sales of the product or service

This characteristic goes hand in hand with the ability to segment the market since time is one of the main ways to segment. In order to use time of purchase to segment a generic product, it is necessary to support advanced sales of the product. This is usually done through a reservation system.

Low variable costs for product or service

This is an important characteristic; generally it means there are high fixed costs for the product, but low variable costs. An incremental sale does not cost much in variable costs and, once fixed costs are met, an incremental sale can add greatly to the bottom line. In fact, in this situation, all revenues above variable costs go directly to profits (Oberwetter 2001). For a hotel, the fixed costs are the cost for the facility and the desk staff while the variable cost is for the room cleaning. Once enough people have booked into a hotel for an evening to cover the total fixed costs, then any additional reservations will contribute revenue, mostly to profit.

Demand varies over time

Based on the time when the product or service is consumed, the demand for it varies. For example, a flight on Tuesday generally has less demand than the same flight on Monday. It is important to know when high demand and low demand can be expected. With that information, customer demand can be shifted from high-demand times to lower demand times, thereby smoothing customer demand. This shift is done by varying price; raising it during high-demand times and lowering it during low-demand times (Kimes 1989b). Movie theatres meet these criteria and are a prime candidate for the application of revenue management.

Movie exhibitions are clearly perishable; once the movie has started, an empty seat in the theatre is worthless and the lost revenue cannot be recaptured. Since theatre seating is fixed, and it costs millions in capital to build a new theatre, the movie exhibition service capacity is limited. As with the airlines, movie theatre exhibitions can be segmented in many ways, starting with the day and time of the showing and further based on the time of purchase. For each movie exhibition there are certain fixed costs; the costs of the theatre, staff and leasing of the movie. Aside from those costs, if staffs are considered fixed costs, there really are no variable costs. The last criterion is the variability of product demand and movies certainly meet this, with exhibitions on different days and times clearly having different demand.

WHY IS THE MOVIE INDUSTRY RIPE FOR REVENUE MANAGEMENT?

Like the airline industry of the early 1980s after the passage of the Airline Deregulation Act, the movie theatre industry is depressed. Free of government restrictions, the airline industry overexpanded, took on a great deal of debt and faced fierce competition from new discount airlines. Major carriers continued to have full flights but with the wrong mix of passengers, they were still not maximising revenue. As a result some airlines experienced their first annual losses ever. Their saviour was sophisticated revenue management systems that allowed them to maximise capacity and profitability by balancing supply and demand through price and inventory management (Cross 1997b).

Although the movie theatre industry's overexpansion and revenue drain is similar to the airline industry crisis post-deregulation, the theatre industry's problems are the result of a separate set of variables. Innovation, technology, discount theatres and questionable management practices all contributed to the movie theatre industry's situation.

Stadium seating and sophisticated sound systems in newer multiplexes give the theatre customer a much more enjoyable environment in which to see a movie than previous smaller, less technologically advanced theatres. Essentially, with these advancements in technology, a new de facto standard was set for the movie theatre environment. That being the case, the movie theatre industry set out to update theatres and provide the customer with the latest and greatest theatre experience possible.

The result was rapid capital expansion in the creation of sophisticated multiplex movie theatres. As a result, the industry now has a great deal of debt and customer attendance has not grown at a rate to support it. Additionally, existing discount theatres, which show late-run movies, often for less than $2, continue to tap additional revenue. The result is that all the top movie theatre companies in the USA, Carmike Cinemas, United Artists, General Cinemas, Loews Cineplex Entertainment Corp. and Regal Cinemas, have sought bankruptcy protection.

The norm in the industry then has become large multiplexes with stadium seating; it has evolved into a capital-intensive business with a very high debt to earnings. As such, it is imperative that it maximises its revenues and increases the predictability of those revenues. The movie theatre industry can learn lessons from the airlines and implement a sophisticated revenue management programme with computerised systems to support decision making and automate dynamic pricing.

HOW CAN REVENUE MANAGEMENT BE APPLIED TO MOVIE THEATRES?

First, movie theatre companies need to accept and embrace the practice throughout their organisations. Then they must implement advanced ticket sales, as this will be critical to segmenting the market. Creating a forecast from sales history and newly developed market segments should be combined with an integrated revenue management system that enables dynamic pricing for each ticket sale.

Foster a revenue management mindset

Revenue management must be adopted through all facets of the company, from the top executives to the person selling tickets and concessions. The process starts with education of all parties and indoctrination into a revenue management mindset. Many consulting companies provide training in revenue management concepts and ideas and can help with this. Revenue management is not just a computer system: 'It is a programmed approach to increasing revenues and improving customer service by responding to current and expected demand – a process, a way of conducting business.' By using revenue management, companies will 'find that their current procedures become more systematized, improving their ability to obtain new business as well as capture revenues that previously went to competitors' (Lieberman 2002). As the programmes are implemented and used, there needs to be a mindset of continuous improvement because everything can't be in place at once.

Develop a forecasting process

A crucial part of a revenue management system is the forecast based on sales history. For movies, the challenge for the forecast will be to account for waning demand. Movies start out with high demand on opening day that fades as the days and weeks progress. How quickly the demand declines depends on the movie. So, as each new movie comes to the theatre, a forecast model, based on similar movies, needs to be applied and evaluated on a daily basis based on actual demand. A different model may have to be used as a movie goes through its lifecycle. For example, the movie *Titanic* was a blockbuster; the sales history for it and movies like *Star Wars: The Phantom Menace* would be used to develop the blockbuster forecast. A movie like *Pearl Harbor* would use the blockbuster forecast initially, but after actual demand failed to meet forecasted demand, it would be reclassified to use a more appropriate forecast model. As the movie traverses its lifecycle, it could move through multiple classifications and could be classified differently in different regions.

Create new market segments

To help shift customer demand to low-demand movies, new market segments will have to be created. Like the airlines, the day and time of the movie provide natural segments and additional ones can be created based on how far in advance a ticket is purchased. Final ticket prices will always depend on how much demand there is, but generally speaking, Friday and Saturday night tickets will be more expensive than weekday night tickets for obvious reasons. Two movies showing at the same time will have different prices, depending on the customer demand. Lastly, a ticket could be purchased days, weeks or more in advance for a discount.

New segments can also be created to stimulate additional sales. Four tickets could be sold at a reduced price as a 'double date' or for two nights in a row as a 'repeat date'. The idea is to get the customer to go to more movies than they would have otherwise and to increase customer demand for low-demand movies and exhibitions. The 'double date' tickets would pair a high-demand movie with a low-demand one. Deals for tickets and concession combinations should be introduced too. A low-demand movie combined with a free soft drink would probably still result in the purchase of a high margin popcorn and the theatre gets a sale for a low-demand movie.

Implement advance sales

Movie theatres have already started to recognise the value of providing advanced ticket sales through the telephone, box office, kiosks and via the web. Through websites like Fandango.com and movietickets.com you can buy tickets at the retail price plus a service fee for the convenience of purchasing online. Once the ticket is purchased, there are three ways in which you can physically get your ticket:

1. You can print out the ticket on your own printer.

2. You can get your ticket from the theatre box office by giving them the credit card you used to purchase it.

3. You can get the ticket from a kiosk in the theatre lobby by scanning your credit card.

Which method you use depends on the theatre and what they support. Advanced sales are important because that is how you create additional market segments and can have dynamic pricing. It is critical that all methods for advanced sales tie into the same revenue management back end.

Cancellation, no show and overbooking

As the revenue management programme gets more sophisticated, movie theatres will have more information to use for business decisions. The sales history used for forecasting can start to include segmenting information. They can start forecasting how many tickets will be cancelled (if allowed) and how many will be no shows for certain segments. With this information they can start to overbook sold-out shows to ensure all capacity is utilised and revenue is further maximised.

Any overbooking process needs to have a clear policy associated with it to maintain customer satisfaction. If an overbooking situation occurs, all people who have a ticket and want to see the movie must see it. The theaters must make it a win-win situation and get volunteers to be bumped and properly compensate them by refunding their money and giving them complementary tickets to another show of their choice.

Concessions

With a successful revenue management programme, attendance to movies will go up, which means an increase in concession sales. The concession sales will be additional revenue and profit that should be factored into the plan. Furthermore, as mentioned earlier, concessions can be used to create new segments to stimulate ticket sales and vice versa.

Frequent moviegoers' card

To encourage loyalty, movie theatres should develop a frequent moviegoer programme as part of the revenue management programme. For every purchase a customer presents their card to earn credits, like airline 'miles'. Then after a certain amount of money is spent on tickets and concessions, they can redeem their credits for free movies and concessions. The value of this is increased loyalty and marketing. The customer is more likely to go to movies at the moviegoers' card theatre because they can earn the credits, rather than going somewhere else. On the marketing side, the movie theatre is capturing a complete customer purchasing history through the use of the card. This is valuable information for developing new market segments and package combinations.

All these factors need to be coordinated and implemented using computerised systems for integration in order to open and close market segments and dynamically determine pricing in order to maximise revenues. These systems will automatically determine the ideal number of discounts that should be available and provide sales systems and personnel with up-to-the-moment information on available ticket information. Ticket prices will be carefully adjusted to match demand for each showing to maximise revenues per showing.

CONCLUSIONS

The movie theatre industry needs to find a way to forecast accurately customer demand at different prices, save tickets for late-booking high-ticket customers and allocate the leftover tickets to myriad prices, some of which would have to be purchased weeks in advance; and this has to be done for each exhibition in each location while accounting for local, regional and global external factors that can influence ticket sales both positively and negatively (Cross 1997b).

Implementing a revenue management programme that will increase revenues and profits can do this. Experts state that implementing revenue management can generally increase revenues 3 to 7% or more, with 80% of it going directly to profits (Cross 1997b), all by utilising existing assets more efficiently.

Some consumer demand will be shifted from high-demand movies and exhibitions to lower demand movies and exhibitions. This will help level demand for movies across the multiplex and reduce some of the revenue variability between movies and show times, thereby providing a more consistent revenue flow and optimising seating capacity already available but not being utilised.

More people will go to the movies than ever before. Demand for movies will increase because people can get less expensive tickets by planning ahead. The result is that people will go more often and most likely spend more overall, but for theatres there is no need to increase capacity because they will be using the seats that were previously unoccupied. The challenge, and importance of revenue management, is to sell those empty seats, increase revenue and keep the people willing to pay for higher tickets from purchasing the discount tickets.

Customer satisfaction will be increased. Customers will be able to buy tickets when they want them and, if they plan ahead, they can get tickets at a discount. Everybody wins. Furthermore, it will be easier for people who want to see a movie twice to do so. They will be willing to pay a premium for a movie the first time, but with a little planning, they can see the movie a second time at a discount.

Length of the movie run will shorten. Because people will be able to get discount tickets even in the early stages of a movie's release, many people who would wait to see the movie toward the end of the run at a discount theatre, or during the day, will see it earlier. More people will see the movie in a shorter time and the average audience size will be larger. This will shorten the run of the movie, enable a quicker payout for the movie and allow the theatre to show more movies.

Revenue management is an important piece of operations management. When it is appropriate, as in the case of movie theatres, it can revolutionise the industry.

Movies will always be a part of our culture. And as technology continues to advance and our economy continues to fluctuate, the companies that utilise the power of revenue management to provide consumers with the ultimate theatre experience, while capitalising on techniques for maximum revenue, will ultimately be the long-term winners.

Questions

1. What are the characteristics of the movie theatre industry that make it appropriate for revenue management?
2. What will be the results of implementing revenue management for movie theatres?
3. With the implementation of revenue management, what will happen to demand for movies?

References

American Airlines (1987) 'The art of managing yield', *American Airlines Annual Report*, 22–5.

Cross, B. (1997a) 'Launching the revenue rocket, how revenue management can work for your business', *Cornell Hotel and Restaurant Administration Quarterly*, April, 33.

Cross, B. (1997b) *Revenue Management, Hard-Core Tactics for Market Domination*. New York: Broadway Books.

Kimes, S. E. (1989a) 'The basics of yield management', *Cornell Hotel and Restaurant Administration Quarterly*, 30, 3, 15–9.

Kimes, S. E. (1989b) 'Yield management: a tool for capacity-constrained service firms', *Journal of Operations Management*, 8, 4, 349–50.

Kimes, S. E. (1997) 'Yield management: an overview', in Yeoman, I. and Ingold, A. (eds) *Yield Management Strategies for the Service Industries*. London: Cassell, 5–7.

Lieberman, W. H. (1993) 'Debunking the myths of yield management', *Cornell Hotel and Restaurant Administration Quarterly*, 34, 1, 34–41.

Lieberman, W. (2002) 'Yield management: system or program?'. Available at *http://www.veritecsolutions.com/doc/ym_prgrm.pdf* (accessed 1 February 2002).

Oberwetter, R. (2001) 'Building blockbuster business', *OR/MS Today*, 2001, 28, 3, 41–2.

CHAPTER 26

Strategic Direction for Sport in Higher Education

John Harris

INTRODUCTION

Contemporary sport is an area of great social, economic and political importance. The many benefits of sport have been well documented yet there is scant reference to its place in higher education (HE). The following case study aims to analyse the positionality and importance of sport in HE through drawing on relevant literature and data collected in studies at three institutions.

Through focusing on the key issues of participation, health and strategic development the study critically analyses the changes taking place. It argues that traditional modes of delivery need to be addressed as ever more discerning consumers demand improved levels of service quality. This has become increasingly salient in HE today, with the advent of fee-paying students. As student health becomes an area warranting urgent attention, there is a clear need for a strategic direction. The study also illustrates why people take part in sport and recreation and, perhaps more significantly, assesses some of the reasons behind non-participation.

CHANGING TIMES, CHANGING NEEDS

Both sport and higher education have undergone numerous changes in recent times. The new Labour government's focus on social inclusion has placed a greater pressure on all sports providers to cater for the needs, wants and aspirations of a number of divergent groups. The introduction of lottery funding has also led to major developments across the sector with some HE institutions being particularly successful in securing significant funding for sports facility development.

Higher education has itself undergone a series of changes since 1985. The introduction of periodic research assessments, external quality audits and assessment of teaching provision, growth in student enrolments and the creation of unified funding councils are just some examples of contemporary developments (Gordon 1995). The Dearing Report (1997) represented a significant landmark for all HE providers in terms of both its academic and its service provision.

Sports participation is also changing. Many higher education institutions now offer a wider variety of sport and recreational activities than ever before. The increasing attention and value now afforded to the body has placed a greater currency on it than at any other time in our history (Shilling 1993; Turner 1996). Mediated images of the body beautiful and an increased pressure for both males and females to conform to particular idealised conceptualisations make this an important area for further analysis. The process of change is also accelerating and all organisations, including academic institutions, need to adopt a proactive approach to remain ahead of their competitors for we create the future by our actions and inactions today. There is a greater demand for traditional male sports among females and activities such as women's football have developed rapidly in Britain during recent years (Lopez 1997). Developments such as this place new pressure on sport and recreation departments to satisfy the needs, wants and aspirations of the increasingly diverse and fragmented student group. Yet in much of the recent development and debate surrounding the future of HE one area that has been largely ignored is student health.

STUDENT HEALTH

Defining health remains a major challenge despite the huge progress made in treating diseases and increasing the average life expectancy in western societies. Health is a human condition with physical, social and psychological dimensions, each characterised on a continuum with positive and negative poles. In today's society the health of the nation moves ever higher up the political agenda (Department of Health 1998; Health Education Authority 1999). Each year we spend billions of pounds dealing with the effects of illnesses emanating from alcohol, tobacco, and drug abuse. The increasing inactivity of Britons, and its linked effects, also places a major burden on an already overstretched National Health Service. The obvious relationship of this to rising obesity levels and the increase in coronary heart disease (CHD) are just two examples of where physical activity levels have a role to play in maintaining and/or improving societal health (Health Education Authority 1995). Never before has there been such a strong and consistent relationship between many of the health risks facing us today and the lifestyle choices we make. Morbidity and mortality in the twenty-first century are much more likely to be the result of diseases whose aetiologies stem, at least in part, from the behaviours we regularly adopt than from infectious diseases (as was the case in the past).

Such behaviours are determined by a multitude of factors including demographics, personality, attitudes, knowledge and social support. A number of health promotion agencies have seized on this last point in an attempt to maximise the effectiveness of any campaign message. During the past few years a number of different groups have been targeted (e.g. older men and women (50+) and people with disabilities). A noticeable omission from these focused targeted campaigns are higher education students.

This is of particular concern in present times as a number of students appear to be participating in health-risking behaviours or foregoing health-enhancing behaviours (Harris and Ide 2000). Of course, alcohol has always formed an integral part of student life and the somewhat stereotypical portrayal of an individual drinking all night, watching daytime television and occasionally going to the odd lecture are firmly ingrained within many people's minds when we talk of student health. Yet there are also very real changes impacting on student health that make it a particularly pertinent time to consider the area. Few other groups appear so clearly in need of intervention strategies to work towards addressing numerous serious health issues.

The move towards mass HE has brought with it a multitude of new problems and challenges for both students and HE providers. In a stated claim to make HE available to all (an approach where the rhetoric seems far removed from the reality), the government has set a target of having 50% of people between the ages of 18 and 30 in HE by 2010. Yet within this stated aim there are a number of areas that continue to be largely ignored or conveniently glossed over. As fee-paying consumers, many young people are now faced with serious financial pressures as part of their undergraduate experience. Unscrupulous landlords have been quick to exploit this and substandard living conditions are a reality for a number of students. The need to earn money to support their studies and undertake work (part- or even close to full-time) means that much time can be spent undertaking poorly paid work in order to meet basic living costs. In addition to the widely expressed concerns as to how this may effect the learning experience of students, it is also important to note that this may also have a serious impact on their health. It is discernible that now is the least favourable time to be a student (Harris and Ide 2000). Dr Tony Butler, a student health services GP at the University of Bristol, is one of many who believe that students are under much more pressure now. He points, in particular, to the rise in mild to moderate depression and anxiety among the student group (*The Guardian* 29 January 2002).

A SETTINGS-BASED APPROACH

The settings-based approach to health promotion has gained ascendancy within the field developing from the World Health Organisation's (WHO) 'Health for All' initiative and Ottawa Charter for Health Promotion. This is reflective of a growing consensus that health is a socio-ecological product that can be developed most effectively by investing outside the healthcare sector (Dooris 2001). However, terms like 'Health for All' and 'Active for Life' often appear as little more than condescending soundbites to students juggling the many pressures of contemporary undergraduate life (Harris and Ide 2000).

HE is delineated as an environment where not only educational, but personal and social development also takes place. Dooris (2001), drawing on the experiences at one new university, rejects the view that health promotion should be about persuading people to adopt certain 'healthy' behaviours. It should, he believes, be concerned with building a foundation of 'a supportive environment to enable students to gain knowledge and understanding, to explore possibilities, experiment safely, make their own informed choices and discover and develop their potential' (Dooris 2001: 56).

Such action, however, must be located within a holistic framework where the institution is perceived, and understood, as an organisational whole. Dooris (2001) does not specifically refer to the role of sport and recreation departments within this but it is evident that they have a significant part to play. Without wishing to move too far away from the specific focus of this discussion it is noticeable that sport and recreation are rarely mentioned outside their own distinct discipline area. For far too long discussions of 'health' have taken place within (closed) subject specific settings. There is a definite need to include student health within wider policy discussion and to locate the issue within a holistic framework that recognises its quintessential multidimensionality.

'GRADUATENESS' AND EMPLOYMENT

Aligned to these changes relating to health and health promotion it would also seem that the whole concept of learning and the very notion of 'graduateness' are also undergoing a process of considerable change. The expansion of courses in areas such as sport and leisure have also brought with it new pressures for students determined to enter the industry. Given the stated oversupply of graduates (SPRITO 1996) then work experience may no longer be perceived as an optional extra but as a prerequisite for entry into the industry. The value and currency of degrees has also been questioned (Harris 1998a) and the reality for many sports graduates is that their qualification has less currency in the marketplace. SPRITO (1996) expressed concern about the number of graduates attempting to enter the industry following such diverse and varied study. Degree courses with management in their title have been identified as a particular area of concern given that many of them have little, if any, management specific experiential learning within them (Dickinson 2000; Harris 1998a).

WHY SPORT AND RECREATION ARE IMPORTANT

Regular physical activity has been shown to contribute positively to physical and psychological health. In relation to many of the aspects already listed it is easy to see why sport and recreation can have such an important role to play in contemporary student life. It is important that appropriate opportunities are readily available within the student community and there is a real onus on sport and recreation departments to develop their role as facilitators and enablers further.

Yet the new breed of students often have different demands which means that many places have had to address their traditional forms of service delivery. There is a greater expectation attached to the quality of the services and products that we buy (Harris and Leybourne 2004). As fee-paying consumers of the HE experience, today's students demand and expect quality facilities, teaching and support structures. Given the large-scale development in sports provision through lottery funding, many young people entering HE are also schooled in environments where quality sports facilities are the norm rather than the exception. They expect more of the same and it is evident that sports facilities are now ranked alongside research and teaching scores within the various good university guides. Well-equipped sports facilities can play an important role as an effective marketing tool to attract students (and staff) to an institution.

THE IMPORTANCE OF A STRATEGIC APPROACH

According to Buhler-Miko (1985: 1) master planning was the vogue in the 1960s, long-range planning in the 1970s and strategic planning in the 1980s and 90s. In the new millennium, strategic planning remains in vogue as a key management process. Strategic thought and action have become increasingly important as organisations aim to successfully adapt to the future. Many education establishments today are faced with a multitude of changes relating to factors such as ageing facilities, changing technology, increasing competition, changing demographics, rising costs and funding cuts (Kriemadis 1997). Managing change, whether it be in relation to the availability of resources, personnel or a shift in goals and direction, is key to the success of any sport and recreation department (Sutton and Migliore 1988).

Although there is a wealth of literature relating to strategy development (e.g. Mintzberg 1994; Stacey 1993), and there has been an increase in the number of texts focusing on the management of sport, leisure and recreation (e.g. Grainger-Jones 1999; Torkildsen 1999), studies focusing on the strategic development of sport are rare. What is also apparent is that in addition to their exclusion from literature concerned with the development of sport, higher education institutions are also continually marginalised (and often neglected) within discussions of sports development at the national policy level. Such an omission seems particularly strange given that somewhere in the region of 60% of British Olympians at the 2004 games are expected to be from higher education institutions (Harris 1999b). The training schedules of a number of student athletes visibly challenges stereotypical portrayals and, and in the words of one writer: 'The student myths of alcoholism, laziness and traffic cone theft are shattered' (Preece 2002). Yet, as there are some signs that HE institutions may be becoming part of the overall sporting infrastructure of the country, there should be a genuine concern that such funding and resourcing will be targeted solely at a small group of selected institutions. There is also a concern that the focus on elite performance, while highly commendable, often leads to insufficient and irregular access opportunities for the vast majority of the student population.

Luck and Ferrell (1985: 2) define strategy as 'a scheme or principal idea through which an objective would be achieved'. The development of strategies for developing sport in HE are based around three essential questions – where are we now, where do we want to go and how will we get there?

The research of Harris (1993, 1999a), at two higher education institutions, highlighted the need for a strategic approach to the development of sport and recreation. His study of one of the leading sporting colleges in the country questioned whether sports provision there was a 'golden goose' or a 'lame duck' (Harris 1993). Here it was identified that there was widespread dissatisfaction with the provision of sport and recreation opportunities at the institute. This study highlights, in particular, the challenge facing multi-site HE establishments where there is usually a dominance of particular user groups. At the time of the study there was no strategy in place for sport and recreation although there have been many changes and large-scale facility development since. A later study by the same author at a leading international university also identified an urgent need for a strategic plan for sport (Harris 1999a).

A study of women's football at a college of higher education in the south of England highlights a number of key issues pertinent to the inclusive development of sport (Harris 1998b). As a new activity, and one that did not fit with widely held conceptualisations regarding female athletes, many of the football players felt that they were treated like second-class citizens and complained that resources were only made available when the male teams did not need them. Comments such as those of one of the players, Patricia, highlights the struggles faced by those trying to develop 'non traditional' activities within many HE institutions:

> Well, basically when we started no one took us seriously .. it was OK, we set up a friendly match, but we had to use the boys kit, there was no special treatment and when we went up to the Astroturf we had to pay for it and the boys would get it for free, they would have particular times. Maybe because it was a new sport at the time and they could not fit it in, but at the time it was frustrating when you are trying to get something off the ground. (Harris 1998b: 214)

Here also, in another split-site establishment, there was much evidence of dissatisfaction relating to sporting opportunities. As equality issues move ever higher up the political agenda, it is imperative that all groups are recognised, and included, as part of any strategic development. Strategic developments at HE institutions need to ensure, for example, that their focus is not just on the top male sports teams or a select group of able-bodied athletes. There is a need to move away from working alone and hoarding resources to developing strategic alliances and providing opportunities. To take just one issue, that of the gendered nature of sport, it is clear that women's sport has developed rapidly over recent years and females now expect a wider choice of sports within any HE setting.

There is also a very fine balancing act to be managed in developing sport at this level. Harris (1999a) reflects on this and problematises the need to increase income-generating activities while also retaining the social and participation objectives. There are also issues of developing the sporting performance of leading institution teams while also ensuring that all teams are afforded development opportunities. The example of women's football referred to previously highlights an area where there is often a hierarchical system in place and resourcing may be focused predominantly (sometimes exclusively) on particular clubs. A challenge facing sport within a number of institutions lies in the 'ownership' and administration of individual teams. Anecdotal evidence collected from a number of institutions highlights the conflict between athletic unions and student unions in many places. Student sport can also be a notoriously cliquey environment where teams are selected on the basis of who you know rather than individual performance levels. The study in the south of England discovered that some of the women had decided to set up a football team, partly as a result of their frustration with the strong cliques prevalent at the hockey club (Harris 1998b). Harris (1993, 1999a) identified site-specific cliques as a constraining factor to sport participation among both staff and students at two very different institutions.

THE FUTURE

Like many other parts of the sector there is an increasing pressure on sport and recreation departments in HE effectively to brand themselves. Yet it must be noted that the structure of sport and recreation departments in the UK are varied with some being stand-alone service providers while others have much closer links to the academic department(s) responsible for delivering educational programmes in the discipline. Institutions themselves recognise the increasing importance of marketing within a more competitive environment and developing a distinctive image of value (see Bodoh and Mighall 2002; King 1995).

The sport and recreation strategy needs to be aligned closely to the mission, vision and strategic aims of the institution itself. The strategy should be a negotiating agenda built on the commitment and support of all interested parties and a means of achieving its stated aims and objectives (Harris 1999b). Such development must be based on a partnership approach at local, regional and national levels. There is a need for the sharing of resources and a move away from exclusively internal development. Existing resources and expertise from other departments should also be fully integrated into the sport and recreation development strategy. Within a service-led economy the quality of service delivery assumes an increasing importance. The findings from the three studies referred to in this case all point towards the need for a significant improvement in the levels of service quality. Respondents in the Hong Kong University study were generally satisfied with the facilities on offer but were noticeably dissatisfied with the level of service provided (Harris 1999a).

Many new developments in the area of sports-related degrees may also place a greater pressure on the service providers of sport and recreation. Dissatisfaction often surfaces when a particular course or school requires a facility for significant time periods, hereby restricting access for the majority of the student population. This may become a particular problem for the few 'chosen' institutions likely to be involved in the next phase of elite athlete development, but it is also a very real issue for institutions with limited sport and recreation provision.

Sutton and Migliore (1988), writing from a North American perspective, posit that managing change is essential to the success of all athletic departments in the future. As sport and recreation departments are so much a part of HE establishments they too must anticipate change and meet the needs of user groups together with their own mission and objectives. A strategic approach is essential to managing this change. Key stakeholders within this process are the students themselves. They occupy a unique position in that they are both customers and products. They not only consume the product, but are changed by it and then themselves become a product of the institution in the eyes of third parties.

> ## Questions
>
> 1. Why is now a particularly pertinent time to look at sport and recreation provision in higher education?
> 2. Why is student health an area warranting urgent attention?
> 3. What are the benefits of adopting a strategic approach to developing student sport?

References

Bodoh, J. and Mighall, R. (2002) 'Brand new image', *The Guardian*, 29 January.

Buhler-Miko, M. (1985) *A Trustee's Guide to Strategic Planning*. Washington DC: Higher Education Planning Institute.

Dearing, R. (1997) *Higher Education in the Learning Society: The National Committee of Inquiry into Higher Education*. London: HMSO.

Department of Health (1998) *Saving Lives: Our Healthier Nation*. London: The Stationery Office.

Dickinson, M. (2000) 'Giving undergraduates managerial experience', *Education and Training*, 42, 3, 159–70.

Dooris, M. (2001) 'The health promoting university: a critical exploration of theory and practice', *Health Education*, 101, 2, 51–60.

Gordon, G. (1995) 'Higher education 2005: pointers, possibilities, pitfalls, principles', *Quality Assurance in Education*, 3, 4, 21–9.

Grainger-Jones, B. (1999) *Managing Leisure*. Oxford: Butterworth-Heinemann.

The Guardian (2002) 'Unsung heroes', 29 January.

Harris, J. (1998a) 'The accreditation game', *On Track*, Spring, 38–9.

Harris, J. (1998b) 'Defending like women: an interpretive sociological study of female collegiate football players'. Unpublished PhD thesis, Brunel University.

Harris, J. and Ide, J. (2000) 'Graduates of health?', *Recreation*, July–August, 35–7.

Harris, J. and Leybourne, J. (2004) 'Service quality at Insight Leisure Management: the role of the mystery shopper' in Yeoman, I. and McMahon-Beattie, U. (eds) *Sport and Leisure Management: A Service Operations Approach*. London: Continuum.

Harris, W. (1993) 'Golden goose or lame duck? Sport and recreation provision at an institute of Higher Education'. Unpublished MA thesis, University of Wales.

Harris, W. (1999a) 'Sport at HKU: sport and recreation provision, patterns of their use and levels of satisfaction and importance to students, staff and the alumni at the University of Kong Kong'. Unpublished DMgt thesis, Southern Cross University/International Management Centres.

Harris, W. (1999b) 'A strategic direction for sport and recreation in further and higher education'. Paper presented at the BUCPEA Annual Conference, University of Surrey.

Health Education Authority (1995) *Promoting Physical Activity*. London: HEA.

Health Education Authority (1999) *Physical Activity and Inequalities*. London: HEA.

King, R. (1995) 'What is higher education for? Strategic dilemmas for the twenty-first century university', *Quality Assurance in Education*, 3, 4, 14–20.

Kriemadis, A. (1997) 'Strategic planning in higher education athletic departments', *International Journal of Educational Management*, 11, 6, 238–47.

Lopez, S. (1997) *Women on the Ball: A Guide to Women's Football.* London: Scarlet Press.

Luck, D. and Ferrell, O. (1985) *Marketing Strategy and Plans.* Englewood Cliffs, NJ: Prentice-Hall.

Mintzberg, H. (1994) *The Rise and Fall of Strategic Planning.* Englewood Cliffs, NJ: Prentice-Hall.

Preece, R. (2002) 'Johnson maps his route to success', *The Times*, 19 April.

Shilling, C. (1993) *The Body and Social Theory.* London: Sage.

SPRITO (1996) *Graduate Employment in the Sport and Recreation Industry: A Study of Student, Graduate and Employer Perspectives.* London: SPRITO.

Stacey, R. (1993) *Strategic Management and Organisational Dynamics.* London: Pitman.

Sutton, W. and Migliore, H. (1988) 'Strategic long-range planning for intercollegiate athletic programs', *Journal of Applied Research in Coaching and Athletics*, 3, 233–61.

Torkildsen, G. (1999) *Leisure and Recreation Management* (4th edn). London: E&FN Spon.

Turner, B. (1996) *The Body and Society* (2nd edn). London: Sage.

CHAPTER 27

Retailing Challenges within the National Museums and Galleries of Northern Ireland

Lesley-Ann Wilson

INTRODUCTION AND BACKGROUND

According to Weil (1997) the relationship between a museum and the public should be understood as a revolution in process. Their relative positions have revolved by 180°. In the nineteenth century, when regional museums where first being established, the position of the museum *vis à vis* the public was clearly a superior one:

> Museums were created and maintained by the high for the low, by the washed for the unwashed ... in order to elevate their spirits and refine common taste. The museum was established to 'do'. What was to be 'done' was the public! (Weil 1997: 257)

The role of the museum has been transformed from a position of mastery to one of service. Pivotal to this transformation over the last 30 years has been the development of museum shops. Of an estimated 2,500 museums in the UK, 80% have a shop whereas only 33% have a restaurant (MGC 1998). In terms of gross revenue generated by visitor attractions, the contribution from retailing is crucial to viability at 31% of total gross revenue (BTA 2000). Increased pressure on budgets have made retail sales a major item for many museums.

The purpose of this case study is to explore current retail challenges within the National Museums and Galleries of Northern Ireland. This institution was created through an Act of Parliament in 1998 and comprises three well-established museums of national significance: the Ulster Museum, the Ulster Folk and Transport Museum and the Ulster American Folkpark. W5, a recently opened interactive discovery centre, is the newest member of the family. While each site has its own shop the case study will focus on two of the sites.

Ulster museum

The Ulster Museum, like many museums in the UK, can trace its origins to the collection of a Natural History and Philosophical Society founded in the early part of nineteenth century. The museum has grown and evolved over time and was formally established on its current site in 1929. The collections are wide ranging and include art, history and natural sciences.

W5 interactive discovery centre

W5, Ireland's only purpose-built interactive discovery centre, opened in Spring 2001 as part of the Odyssey, Northern Ireland's landmark Millennium Project. Described as 'a world-class entertainment and leisure complex', the development plans for the 23-acre waterfront site also included a 10,000 seater arena, an IMAX theatre and multiplex cinema and an indoor 'pavilion' of theme bars, restaurants and other specialist shopping outlets.

As a subsidiary of National Museums and Galleries of Northern Ireland, W5, as its full name 'whowhatwherewhenwhy' suggests, is devoted to experiential learning through five exhibition areas. In addition to the exhibits, the centre presents live demonstrations and shows relating to science, engineering, technology and art.

THE ROLE OF THE MUSEUM SHOP

Kotler and Kotler (1998) remind us that museums have not always had shops! At some point there was a gradual recognition that visitors might be interested in purchasing souvenirs and a small space was set aside. This traditionally might have taken the form of a small kiosk or a service hatch from the keeper's room. Eventually designated shop spaces began to be created but they were generally 'drab areas, devoid of retail flair' and stocked with a limited number of items (Kotler and Kotler 1998: 279). It was only once retailing began to be viewed as a core element of the museum's business that real growth occurred. Maximisation of income was achieved by exposing as many people as possible to the shop by encouraging free admission to non-museum visitors and by creating a shop of sufficient size to stock a wide variety of items for purchase.

Recent developments at the British Museum, the National Portrait Gallery and Sainsbury Wing of the National Gallery illustrate the current wave of shop refurbishment and expansion, firmly exploiting the potential gains to be had from the synergy that comes from combining leisure and retail experiences. As Stevens (2000) indicates, changing patterns of leisure behaviour have resulted in the growth of demand for leisure shopping, eating and drinking and entertainment as essential components of a day trip.

In terms of National Museums and Galleries of Northern Ireland, the individual shops at the Ulster Museum and W5 can be regarded as 'microcosms of study' that mirror development elsewhere. At the Ulster Museum the retail experience has very much evolved from the traditional reception counter selling a limited range of items through to a designated shop space located near to the entrance. Opened in 1986 it was built by the museum's in-house design team and is currently in need of refurbishment and expansion. W5, by contrast, has a spacious contemporary shop that has been designed from the outset to be an integral part of the visitor experience and to reflect the mission of the organisation. It is also an anchor tenant within what Stevens describes as an 'urban family entertainment centre forming an essential cornerstone for city regeneration' (Stevens 2000: 68).

W5 – ESTABLISHING THE BRAND

One of the key challenges for any new visitor attraction is the creation of a memorable image or identity based on the experience offered to visitors. McLean (1996) emphasises the importance of the museum shop in further enhancing and promoting the corporate identity through the product lines available. As W5 is a member of the wider Museums and Galleries family it was essential that its identity would reflect the core values of its parent organisation but also convey its unique position within that family as a non-traditional museum.

Mike Houlihan, Chief Executive of National Museums and Galleries of Northern Ireland, was appointed at the time of the merger of the individual museums. He recognised at an early stage the importance of visually uniting each museum site under the umbrella of a clearly articulated, accessible and immediately recognisable brand. Houlihan's methodology for managing this process was inspired by the work of Collins and Porras (2000) whose research identified the successful habits of visionary organisations. The strategic planning process involved building the commitment of staff, identifying stakeholders and deciding on a core ideology in terms of mission, values and objectives. Attik, a firm of branding consultants, were then employed to develop the visual concepts and MAGNI was launched in 2000 (the acronym MAGNI is important in itself as the institution was originally named in the parliamentary Act as National Museums and Galleries of Northern Ireland).

In the early planning stages of W5 the key question explored by Sally Montgomery, Project Director, and the design team was, 'What kind of centre would W5 be?'. In discussing the core ideology, two interrelated aspects of science were discussed – its presence as a summative body of knowledge and its existence as a human process of discovery. It was felt that not only could W5 be personally transformational but that it could also encourage skills that could be transferred to virtually any aspect of life. Numerous suggestions had been made by the design team regarding the articulation of this aspiration often centring around the word 'discovery'. This became enshrined within the core ideology, mission and values:

> To fire the spirit of discovery by unlocking the scientist in everyone through innovation, imagination and integrity.

This is linked further to specific characteristics of the environment that the design team felt were important. W5 should:

- be compelling (attractive, engaging and transforming)
- be personal
- have a sense of belonging.

It was also important that the visual identity of W5 would be reinforced through combining visual elements such as colour, textures, logo, graphic and photographic style to evoke a sense of involvement and atmosphere.

Challenge 1: branding the W5 shop

It was important from the outset that the shop would reflect the organisation's core values of 'innovation, imagination and integrity'. This was to be achieved through two mechanisms:

- interior design
- product lines.

Interior design

The brief was to design a shop that would provide a friendly and accessible environment for large numbers of schoolchildren and other visitors. It was to be an exciting and stimulating space with an open and spacious atmosphere. The overall building scheme predominantly used glass, steel, wood and concrete for surfaces and features. The shop was designed with glass walls on two interfaces, between the exhibits internally, and the Pavilion shopping mall, externally, to enhance the sense of space. It was felt initially that the combination of shop fittings, lighting and stark walls would create the right ambience for the W5 shop. However, in the first year of operation the volume of visitors through the shop was disappointingly low. Research showed that 30% of visitors were purchasing items in the shop and it was felt that this could be increased. Two factors were identified as areas for improvement:

- lack of warmth in terms of the ambience – the impression was cold and unwelcoming
- visitors' perceptions of the glass wall as a barrier.

The solution to the first factor was simple – parts of the interior were painted in bright colours from the corporate palette. This not only gave more character to the space by highlighting architectural features, but created a much warmer and welcoming atmosphere.

The 'perceived' glass barrier related to physical access. In terms of visitor flow, access to the shop was initially from two directions: paying visitors coming from the exhibition areas and the general public coming in from the Pavilion shopping mall. Anticipating the mixed development of restaurants and speciality shops in the Pavilion, the shop was designed to have a presence in the public space outside W5. However, in order to prevent the public gaining free access to W5, the glass doors into the exhibition areas were usually kept closed. This resulted in a negative message being transmitted to paying visitors approaching from the other side. Early research showed that some visitors believed that the shop was, in fact, closed.

A year on from opening, almost three-quarters of the available rental space within the Pavilion had been leased. However, the majority of commercial lettings were taken up restaurateurs and two more entertainment complexes, a nightclub and a bowling outlet, are in the pipeline. Speciality shopping has not been a success and without a 'critical mass' of shoppers W5 decided to close its public access from the Pavilion. This has saved on human resources in terms of policing ticketing past the pay barrier. More importantly, it has meant that the glass doors into the shop remain permanently open, therefore drawing in more paying visitors from the exhibitions. In addition the opening between the shop and the exhibition areas have been increased so that the visibility to W5's visitors is greatly increased.

Product lines

One of the biggest challenges facing a new visitor attraction shop is selecting and developing the product lines. W5 product lines fall within three distinct areas:

- predominantly low-cost branded items which are high quality and innovative, echoing the corporate colours and the metallic detailing in the building design
- high-tech products and gadgets for corporate customers and older children which are generally unavailable elsewhere
- a wide range of toys, books, games and activity kits reflecting the themes found in the exhibition galleries.

W5 developed 30 branded product lines including pencils, notebooks, rulers and small novelty items. High-quality products were sourced with a contemporary design, that could easily be customised with the W5 logo. Ten of these products are ranked within the list of top 20 sellers and achieve a high turnover but have a low profit margin. Also featuring highly within the top 20 list are a number of unusual items which generally are not available elsewhere such as water snakes and crystal jetballs.

The provision of the shop is viewed as a service and the manager has tried to identify ways of 'adding value' to the service. School parties with some 20 or 30 pupils are booked in advance and as part of the shop service, teachers can order pre-packed souvenir bags of low-cost branded goods. This has been very effective in capturing revenue from those school parties which do not usually visit the shop. It also reduces the potential stress of time-constrained teachers and reduces considerably the possibility of 'bottlenecks' and uncontrollable numbers in the shop at one time.

Challenge 2: the role of licensing at the Ulster Museum

Product licensing and development has become a growing part of museum operations. National museums with outstanding collections have been able to capitalise on the opportunities to license wide ranges of consumer, gift and educational products. The British Museum was among one of the first in the UK to establish a separate trading company in 1973. At the time the trustees saw the introduction of non-traditional services as the means to build brand name recognition and bring the museum to non-traditional visitors. The British Museum Company manufactures a large range of products through third parties but it also owns its own casting workshop producing a variety of statues and busts and the British Museum Press is one of the largest museum-based publishers in the world (Frazier 2000: 76).

Retailers within leisure attractions have the advantage over their high street competitors in being able to forecast accurately the projected turnover, spend per head and, therefore, budget for stock. However, they are also disadvantaged because the number of visitors is limited to the size of the attraction. Livingstone-Smith (1999) comments: 'The greatest problem for many of the smaller museums and galleries in developing good products is partly a lack of imagination and expertise, but also the high minimum order quantities demanded by suppliers.' This becomes a particular problem for exhibition-related products, especially if the visitor numbers are not likely to be high.

There are generally three approaches to the development of new products:

- *commissions*: where the museum would approach a supplier to produce a product on an exclusive basis; the level of investment on the part of the museum would be high
- *joint ventures*: when both the museum and the supplier wish to invest in the development of the product and costs and returns are shared
- *licences*: where a supplier or commercial outlet wants to produce a product for its own commercial use and pays the museum a licence fee, usually for a fixed period of time.

These categories are not mutually exclusive and there can be overlaps in terms of the package negotiated in relation to investment, fees and royalties. The Ulster Museum works with a range of suppliers and craftspeople, both to source existing reproductions that are appropriate to the collections and to commission special pieces that will appeal to varied demographics and target markets. Product licensing, the most financially efficient option, has been developed primarily in two areas:

- fine art cards
- jewellery.

The Ulster Museum has an extensive collection of art and licenses the reproduction of images for gift cards to two commercial companies. The contracts have been negotiated on the basis of a one-off upfront payment made to the Ulster Museum plus royalty fees dependent on the sales volume. The Ulster Museum has the option of purchasing the cards at the normal wholesale price and, in some instances, may receive a proportion free of charge. This partnership works well as the investment and production costs of the cards are borne by the commercial companies which sell them in their outlets.

Elliott (1999) emphasises the importance of offering an enticing and attractive product range within an environment that enhances the product and provides space for customers to browse and purchase. The crafting of jewellery based on museum pieces has become increasingly popular, as customers value not only the uniqueness of the product, but the historical provenance of the object. Hupcey (1999) suggests that objects with historical or symbolic meaning to the visitor, or those for which the museum is well known, will have most appeal to the consumer.

One of the important collections in the Ulster Museum comprises a range of 'treasure' recovered from the *Girona*, a Spanish galleon that sank off the north coast of Northern Ireland in the late sixteenth century. In the 1970s an agreement was struck with a supplier to produce reproductions of the jewellery in base metal. However, Paula Talbot, marketing officer, has realised that balancing the integrity of the object with its commercial viability as a gift item in the shop is a crucial decision-making process. She comments: 'As consumers have become more discriminating there is an increasing market for high-quality exclusive items that have a higher sale value.' Recently, a one-off reproduction of one of the *Armada* pieces was licensed to a New York company for sale in their outlets. Again, the Ulster Museum benefits from royalties and can purchase the product at the lowest wholesale price.

In recent years the museum has also developed a successful licence with a local goldsmith to produce a range of Irish jewellery. This is available to the Museum shop on a sale-or-return basis at the lowest wholesale price. Not only has the Museum no outlay in terms of product development, it avoids a minimum stock purchase.

These examples perhaps reflect slow growth in product licensing at the Ulster Museum but it is crucial that wise decisions are made, particularly when financial resources are limited. Paula Talbot, marketing officer, believes that there is potential for further growth, particularly through the licensing of products in America. For regional museums operating on a tight budget, licensing provides a viable solution to generate some additional income, while at the same time providing greater public awareness and appreciation of the collections.

CONCLUSIONS

Retailing opportunities within museums are growing and diversifying, particularly with the development of mail order catalogues, online shops and licensing of new product ranges. For the museum organisation, effective retailing can add significant value to the visitor experience, promote a memorable market brand, enhance appreciation of the collections and generate additional revenue. There are many challenges involved in establishing the brand, in the development of a product range and in maximising the potential of museum collections. The retailing approach at W5 is very different from that of the Ulster Museum but both have been successful in contributing to income generation within the organisation.

Questions

1. How do museums benefit from providing a shop as part of the visitor experience?

2. Merchandising is about the planning and promoting of sales and the positioning of stock within the shop according to customer flow, product range and profit margin. If you were managing a museum shop what sort of techniques would you use to enhance displays?

3. What other methods could National Museums and Galleries of Northern Ireland consider to enhance its retailing service?

References and further reading

British Tourist Authority (BTA) (2000) *Sightseeing in the UK 2000*. London: British Tourist Authority.

Collins, J. C. and Porras, J. I. (2000) *Built to Last: Successful Habits of Visionary Companies*. London: Random House.

Elliott, F. (1999) 'Improving retail turnover', *New Heritage*, 3. Available at *http://www.heritage365.com* (accessed 27 May 2002).

Frazier, F. (2000) 'Branding beyond the new millennium', *Museum Store*, Summer.

Hupcey, M. (1999) 'Collections into products', *Heritage Retail*, 2. Available at *http://www.heritage365.com* (accessed 27 May 2002).

Kotler, N. and Kotler, P. (1998) *Museum Strategy and Marketing*. San Francisco: Jossey-Bass.

Livingstone-Smith, N. (1999) 'Towards quality retailing', *New Heritage*, 3. Available at *http://www.heritage365.com* (accessed 27 May 2002).

McLean, F. (1996) *Marketing the Museum*. London: Routledge.

Museums and Galleries Commission (MGC) (1998) 'Facts about UK museums'. Available at *http://museums.gov.uk/museums/facts/intro.html* (accessed 31 October 2000).

Nightingale, J. (1997) 'Shoppers bring in cash', *Museums Journal*, July, 17.

Stevens, T. (2000) 'The future of visitor attractions', *Travel and Tourism Analyst*, 1, 61–85.

Twelves, M. (1992) 'Retailing' in Thompson, J., Bassett, D, Duggan, Λ. J., Lewis, G. D. and Ferton, A. (eds) *Manual of Curatorship: A Guide to Museum Practice* (2nd cdn). Oxford: Butterworth-Heinemann.

Weil, S. (1997) 'The museum and the public', *Museum Management and Curatorship*, 16, 3, 257–71.

INDEX